Dr. Bob of Al

Dick B.'s Reference Titles on Alcoholics Anonymous History

Paradise Research Publications, Inc., Publisher;
Good Book Publishing Company, Distributor P.O. Box 837, Kihei, HI 96753-0837
Phone/Fax: (808) 874 4876; Email: dickb@dickb.com; URL: http://www.dickb.com

Publisher's February, 2008, List of Titles by Author Dick B.

A New Way In.
A New Way Out.
Anne Smith's Journal, 1933-1939.
By the Power of God: A Guide to Early A.A. Groups & Forming Similar Groups Today.
Cured!: Proven Help for Alcoholics and Addicts.
Dr. Bob and His Library.
God and Alcoholism: Our Growing Opportunity in the 21st Century.
Good Morning!: Quiet Time, Morning Watch, Meditation, and Early A.A.
Henrietta B. Seiberling: Ohio's Lady with a Cause.
Introduction to the Sources and Founding of Alcoholics Anonymous.
Making Known The Biblical History and Roots of Alcoholics Anonymous: A Fifteen-Year Research, Writing, Publishing and Fact Dissemination Project.
New Light on Alcoholism: God, Sam Shoemaker, and A.A.
Real Twelve Step Fellowship History
The Akron Genesis of Alcoholics Anonymous.
The Books Early AAs Read for Spiritual Growth.
The Conversion of Bill W.
The First Nationwide A.A. History Conference - Comments of Dick B.
The Golden Text of A.A.: God, the Pioneers, and Real Spirituality.
The Good Book and The Big Book: A.A.'s Roots in the Bible.
The Good Book-Big Book Guidebook.
The James Club: The Original A.A. Program's Absolute Essentials.
The Oxford Group & Alcoholics Anonymous.
That Amazing Grace (Clarence & Grace S.).
Turning Point: A History of Early A.A.'s Spiritual Roots and Successes.
Twelve Steps for You: Let Our Creator, A.A. History, and the Big Book Be Your Guide.
Utilizing Early A.A.'s Spiritual Roots for Recovery Today.
When Early AAs Were Cured and Why.

Why Early A.A. Succeeded: The Good Book in Alcoholics Anonymous Yesterday and Today (a Bible Study Primer)

Available through other distributors

Hope: The Story of Geraldine O. Delaney, 2d ed. (Alina Lodge)
Our Faith Community A.A. Legacy (Dick B., Editor and compiler). (Came to Believe Publications)
Courage to Change (with Bill Pittman). (Hazelden)
Women Pioneers of AA (Dick B., contributor). (Hazelden)

Dr. Bob of Alcoholics Anonymous

His Excellent Training in the Good Book
As a Youngster in Vermont

Dick B. and Ken B.

Foreword by Ray G.
Archivist, Dr. Bob's Home, Akron, Ohio

Paradise Research Publications, Inc.
Kihei, Maui, Hawaii

Paradise Research Publications, Inc.
PO Box 837, Kihei, HI 96753-0837

© 2008 by Anonymous
All rights reserved. Published 2008
Printed in the United States of America

Cover Design by American Creations of Maui

This Paradise Research Publications Edition is published by arrangement with Good Book Publishing Co., P.O. Box 837, Kihei, HI 96753-0837

The publication of this volume does not imply affiliation with nor approval or endorsement from Alcoholics Anonymous World Services, Inc. The views expressed herein are solely those of the authors. A.A. is a program of recovery from alcoholism—use of the Twelve Steps in connections with programs and activities which are patterned after A.A., but which address other problems, does not imply otherwise.

Note: All Bible verses quoted in this book, unless otherwise noted, are from the Authorized (or "King James") Version. The letters "KJV" are used when necessary to distinguish it from other versions.

ISBN 978-1-885803-85-6

To my son, Ken

Special thanks to:

Ray G., Archivist, Dr. Bob's Home, Newton Falls, Ohio
Bob J., Kihei, Hawaii
Steve F., Winter Park Florida
Judy Shipley, Summit, New Jersey
Diane Schulte, Oxford, Maryland
Cameron F., Canada
John O., Hereford, Arizona
Joanne Bertrand, Archivist, St. Johnsbury Academy, St. Johnsbury, Vermont
Rev. Jay Sprout, Pastor, North Congregational Church, St. Johnsbury, Vermont
Bob Swartz, Archivist at North Congregational Church, St. Johnsbury, Vermont
Nancy B., St, Johnsbury, Vermont
Jeff F., St. Johnsbury, Vermont
Bernie M., Connecticut
Rich F., San Anselmo, California
The family of the late Dennis Wayne Cassidy, A.A. Historian, Connecticut

Table of Contents

Foreword xi

Introduction xiii

1. The "Great Awakening" of 1875 in St. Johnsbury, Vermont 1

2. The Challenge and Direction of the Dr. Bob Resource Volumes 37

3. A.A.'s Dr. Bob and His St. Johnsbury, Vermont, Roots 85

4. Dr. Bob's Birthplace and Boyhood Home 113

5. North Congregational Church, St. Johnsbury 123

6. The Christian Endeavor Society and Its Legacy to Alcoholics Anonymous 143

7. The St. Johnsbury Academy 189

8. The Fairbanks Family of St. Johnsbury, Vermont 209

9. The Town of St. Johnsbury of Dr. Bob's Youth 241

10. The YMCA and St. Johnsbury, Vermont: 1875-1898 247

11. The Original, Akron A.A. Spiritual Program of Recovery 263

Conclusion 295

Bibliography 301

Index 317

Foreword

My wife and I have known, visited, and traveled with Dick B. for quite a number of years. And he has been as a guest in our Ohio home many times when he has come to Akron, Ohio, to visit, research, and speak on early A.A.'s spiritual roots and successes. We both know Dick as an AA who has not only devoted many years and many books to making the history of early A.A. more widely known, but also that Dick has had a particular interest in the wonderful contributions that Dr. Bob and his wife Anne Smith made to that recovery scene at the beginnings of A.A.

As archivist at Dr. Bob's Home in Akron, Ohio, and as one who takes the archives all over the country so that others will be blessed with an opportunity to see and learn, I have welcomed Dick's many books on Dr. Bob, Anne, Henrietta Seiberling, and the Akron roots.

But this new book uncovers, to an extraordinary degree, a virtually unknown and yet vitally important part of Dr. Bob's past—his days as a youngster in St. Johnsbury, Vermont. Dr. Bob had made a number of telling statements about his beginnings both in Vermont and in Akron. He said that he had had "excellent training" in the Good Book "as a youngster." He twice remarked that he had refreshed his memory of the Good Book in order to set forth the elements of recovery and cure. And he said many times, "We believed that the answer to our problems was in the Good Book," and he added that old timers believed that the Book of James, Jesus' Sermon on the Mount, and 1 Corinthians 13 were absolutely essential to their program.

Dick has relentlessly pursued Dr. Bob's library and reading, Anne Smith's spiritual journal, Henrietta Seiberling's papers, T. Henry and Clarace Williams' remarks, and the original Akron seven-point program as Frank Amos reported it to John D. Rockefeller, Jr. He has put a useful picture before us all. More importantly, he showed what pioneer AAs actually did as they emerged from a seemingly-hopeless, medically-incurable state to establish their relationships with God. They achieved a documented, 75%-to-93% success rate—a real model that needs to be known today.

The loose end, the one that aids materially in understanding how and why the early AAs put together such a remarkable program, was what Dr. Bob had learned as a youngster. What Dr. Bob had meant when he said he had received "excellent training" in the Good Book. And Dick and his son Ken have not only traveled to St. Johnsbury, Vermont; assembled books and records; interviewed; and corresponded; they have produced a detailed picture of the biblical influences on Dr. Bob from his parents, his North Congregational Church, his Sunday school, his Christian Endeavor Society activities, and his matriculation at St. Johnsbury Academy. Bob was surrounded by wholesome, godly, Christian training; and he brought the results to Akron to help thousands of AAs get well as he and Bill W. fashioned their early spiritual program of recovery.

I recommend this book highly to AAs and to all those who want to know why Dr. Bob so certainly and emphatically believed he was qualified to say, "Your Heavenly Father will never let you down!" Dick shows you the sources at St. Johnsbury that produced such conviction.

Ray G., Archivist, Dr. Bob's Home in Akron, Ohio

"Your Heavenly Father will never let you down!"
Alcoholics Anonymous, 4th ed., p. 181

Introduction

Dr. Bob—cofounder of Alcoholics Anonymous and the man whom Bill Wilson called "The Prince of All Twelfth Steppers"—asked:

> "Do you believe in God, young fella?"
> Clarence Snyder [the newcomer] asked, "What does that have to do with it?"
> "Everything," Dr. Bob said.
> Clarence replied, "I guess I do."
> Dr. Bob insisted, "Guess, nothing! Either you do or you don't."
> When Clarence Snyder replied, "I do,"
> Dr. Bob then said, "Now we're getting some place. All right, get out of bed and on your knees. We're going to pray."[1]

Bill Wilson—the other cofounder of Alcoholics Anonymous—brought this message to A.A.:

> "Henrietta [Henrietta Dotson, wife of A.A. Number Three Bill Dotson], the Lord has been so wonderful to me, curing me of this terrible disease, that I just want to keep talking about it and telling people."[2]

Bill Dotson—A.A. Number Three—stated this about the real A.A. message as he had heard it:

> "I thought, I think I have the answer. Bill was very, very grateful that he had been released from this terrible thing and he had given God the credit for having done it, and he's so grateful about it he wants to tell other people about it. That sentence, 'The Lord has been so wonderful to me, curing me of

---

[1] *DR. BOB and the Good Oldtimers* (NY: Alcoholics Anonymous World Services, Inc., 1980), 144.
[2] *Alcoholics Anonymous*, 4th ed. (NY: Alcoholics Anonymous World Services, Inc., 2001), 191.

this terrible disease, that I just want to keep telling people about it,' has been a sort of golden text for the A.A. program and for me."[3]

Commenting on his preparations for spiritual recovery, Dr. Bob made this statement about his religious instruction as a young person in his home town of St. Johnsbury, Vermont:

"I had refreshed my memory of the Good Book, and I had had excellent training in that as a youngster."[4]

The authors of this Dr. Bob title believe that, as Bill Wilson himself often stated, the hand of the Creator of the heavens and the earth was upon the beginnings of Alcoholics Anonymous. Whether you start with the conversion and cure of alcoholism which Bill Wilson had seen in the life of his grandfather Willie Wilson; or whether you start with the conversion and cure of alcoholism which Bill himself began to experience at the Calvary Rescue Mission altar in New York; or whether you start with Bill's conversion experience at Towns Hospital in New York; or whether you read about the William James accounts of conversion and cure that Bill studied after his experience--the hand of the Almighty, the Creator of the heavens and the earth, was the apparent causative power.[5]

But our search begins at the other, hardly recognized or discussed, root of A.A.—the excellent training in the Bible which Dr. Bob said that he had received as a youth. And whether you start with the plans and efforts of North Congregational Church, St. Johnsbury, to which Bob's parents belonged and which he attended; or whether you start with the "extended visit" of YMCA member Henry M. Moore (a layman from Boston, Massachusetts) to the home of his friend K. A. Burnell (an evangelist who lived near Aurora, Illinois) in the summer of 1871, which produced the "regular canvass of Gospel meetings" that started in the State of Massachusetts (in January 1872), was expanded into the

---

[3] *Alcoholics Anonymous*, 4th ed., 191.
[4] *The Co-Founders of Alcoholics Anonymous: Biographical sketches. Their last major talks* (NY: Alcoholics Anonymous World Services, Inc., 1972, 1975), 11-12.
[5] See Dick B., *The Conversion of Bill W.: More on the Creator's Role in Early A.A.* (Kihei, HI: Paradise Research Publications, 2006), 24-27, 58-62, 95-102, 133-35; and *Alcoholics Anonymous*, 4th ed., 13, 25, 56-57, 100.

State of New Hampshire (in November 1873), and was further expanded into the State of Vermont, resulting in the "Great Awakening" of 1875 in St. Johnsbury;[6] or whether you look at the town-wide prayers and work of five different churches (and later a sixth) in St. Johnsbury which preceded the "Great Awakening" of 1875 in St. Johnsbury;[7] or whether you look at the total change in the little New England town, its churches, and its people beginning in 1875[8]--the hand of the Almighty was the apparent causative power. These are the facts you will see set forth and amplified in this title.

This, then, is a new study. It will unearth and display the things that were happening in Dr. Bob's youth that left an indelible impression upon him which he expressed in the last line of his personal story in A.A.'s basic text—"Your Heavenly Father will never let you down!"[9]

For Dr. Bob had received instruction on God, Jesus Christ, the Bible, and prayer from his deeply religious, Christian parents. He had also learned about them from North Congregational Church, St. Johnsbury, where he, his father, and his mother were members. His father was a Sunday School Teacher at, and Deacon of, the church. His mother was also a Sunday School Teacher at, the Assistant Superintendent of the Home Department of, and the head of the intermediate and primary departments of, the church. Dr. Bob had learned from North Congregational Church prayer meetings on Wednesday evenings. He was immersed in them as a participant in the growth and vibrancy of the Christian Endeavor Society to which he belonged at his church. He had learned about them in his daily chapel, required Bible-readings, and prayers at St. Johnsbury Academy, where his father was an examiner, as well as president and chairman of the local YMCA—

---

[6] See, for example: Allen Folger, *Twenty-Five Years As an Evangelist* (Boston: James H. Earle & Company, 1905), 34-37.
[7] See, for example: *Minutes of the Eightieth Annual Meeting of the General Convention of Congregational Ministers and Churches of Vermont, Held at Bennington, June, 1875. Fifty-Seventh Annual Report of the Vermont Domestic Missionary Society, and Fifty-Fifth Annual Report of the Vermont Education Society* (Montpelier: J. & J. M. Poland, Steam Printers, 1875), 29.
[8] See, for example: Edward T. Fairbanks, *The Town of St. Johnsbury, Vt.: A Review of One Hundred Twenty-five Years to the Anniversary Pageant 1912* (St. Johnsbury, VT: The Cowles Press, 1914), 316-17.
[9] *Alcoholics Anonymous*, 4th ed., 181.

which held meetings and lectures there.[10] Where his mother was a teacher at St. Johnsbury Academy; and from her active participation in, and presidency of, the Congregational Women's Club;[11] and her activity in the Home Missionary Society.[12] The same instructional training can be said to have come from the St. Johnsbury Academy itself and from the stern rules of its Congregationalist Fairbanks family founders, trustees, and leaders as to its requirement that all trustees be members of a Congregational church; that all "scholars" (as students were called) attend daily chapel with its Bible-readings and prayers; that all scholars weekly attend church and a Bible study; and that its very curriculum and texts contain Christian and biblical materials.

And our present title is loaded with historically-accurate accounts of, and reference citations documenting the foregoing events and elements.

It is for the reader to decide: (1) how much Dr. Bob absorbed from what he himself called his "excellent training" in the Bible as a youngster; (2) where Dr. Bob received that training; and (3) what impact the very unusual Christian awakening in his home town of St. Johnsbury had on Dr. Bob during his youth.

Our account begins with the following remarks about what had happened in St. Johnsbury in 1875, shortly before Dr. Bob was born in 1879:

> REPORT OF THE STATE OF THE CHURCHES
>
> CALEDONIA CONFERENCE [Caledonia is the Vermont county in which the North Congregational Church, St. Johnsbury, is located]

---

[10] *St. Johnsbury Academy Catalogue* for 1873, p. 22.
[11] Marquis, *Who's Who in New England,* 994.
[12] Letter from Ken B. to Taylor Reed regarding Reed's article "Alcoholics Anonymous Rooted in St. Johnsbury Institutions" in *The Caledonian-Record,* online edition, October 12, 2007; and monograph of C.S. Smith, *An Historical Sketch of Home Missionary Work in Vermont, By the Congregational Churches* (Montpelier: Press of the Watchman Publishing Company, 1893)

For this county, as a whole, it is justly claimed that the past year has been one of uncommon religious prosperity. If there has been no special revival it is because there has been little of that apathy in the churches which calls for a revival. The powerful influence from on high during last year in almost every congregation, turning so many to repentance, has in a good degree continued, as an impulse to Christian work, biblical study, and growth in Christian character. The fruits of this great revival appear even more largely in the figures of the past than of the previous year, additions have been made by profession to every church in the conference—430 in the aggregate—an average of thirty to each church. The converts, as a whole, have stood the test of a year's service remarkably well, some few only in the comparison revealing the fact that they had no root in themselves. From the South church, St. Johnsbury, which has received 108 members in the past year, the report comes saying the year has been characterized by the spiritual growth and development of Christians. The weekly prayer-meetings must have averaged nearly two hundred. The Bible is much studied. Of the North church, which has received 114 members, it is said no revival is in progress, but an active, earnest religious feeling is manifest in full prayer-meetings and readiness to do any Christian work. The pastor of the church [Mr. Southgate] was dismissed in June [1875], and his successor [Rev. Henry W. Jones] installed in November [November 18, 1875] . . . ."[13]

As for the next and succeeding chapters, you will find many more reports, amplifications, and statements about the very special atmosphere in which Dr. Bob was reared as he established, and moved ahead in, his relationship with God.[14] Years later, Bob's fellow A.A. cofounder Bill Wilson underlined one portion of the remarkable faith,

---

[13] *Minutes of the Eighty-First Annual Meeting of the General Convention of Congregational Ministers and Churches of Vermont, Held at Barton, June, 1876. Fifty-Eighth Annual Report of the Vermont Domestic Missionary Society, and Fifty-Sixth Annual Report of the Vermont Education Society* (Montpelier: J. & J. M. Poland, Steam Printers, 1876), 61.

[14] See *Alcoholics Anonymous*, 4th ed., 29: "Each individual in the personal stories, describes in his own language and from his own point of view the way he established his relationship with God."

training, and personal religious work that Bob had brought with him to Alcoholics Anonymous. Bill said:

> "He prayed, not only for his own understanding, but for different groups of people who requested him to pray for them," said Bill Wilson. "I was always glad to think that I was included in those prayers," said Bill. "And I sort of depended on him to get me into heaven. Bob was far ahead of me in that sort of activity. I was always rushing around talking and organizing and 'teaching kindergarten.' I never grew up myself."[15]

We start with the context of what Dr. Bob himself actually said about the Bible and about his youth. Only then, by looking at his younger years themselves, can one gain a real understanding of Dr. Bob's very special A.A. role years later. He said:

> I was born in a small New England village of about seven thousand souls. The general moral standard was, as I recall it, far above average. . . . The town was well supplied with churches and schools in which I pursued my early educational activities.
>
> My father was a professional man of recognized ability and both my father and mother were most active in church affairs. Both father and mother were considerably above the average in intelligence.[16]

That stage setting is found at the very beginning of Dr. Bob's personal story in A.A.'s basic text. It challenges us to look for details—details about the churches and schools in which he pursued his early educational activities. Also, about the specific church in which his father, mother, and he were deeply involved. In addition, about the kind of specific training and example he received from his parents so involved. And to look for further details: About the little village where he grew up and about its morals, religious inclinations, and leadership. Also, about what Dr. Bob did and learned in his Christian Endeavor

---

[15] *DR. BOB and the Good Old Timers* (NY: Alcoholics Anonymous World Services, Inc., 1980), 315.
[16] *Alcoholics Anonymous*, 4th ed., 171-72.

society. Also, about results achieved because of his church's insistence on a vigorous home and family role in the education of a young person. In addition, about the nature and extent of emphasis by all of these on the young person's Christian training, morals, and standards, as well on that person's study of the Bible, extensive prayer life, and calling to bring others to Christ in conversions. So when we see the words "more or less forced" in the following statement by Dr. Bob, we need to turn first to, and to keep in mind the viewpoint of family, church, school, and society and its probable basis in this particular Bible verse: "Train up a child in the way he should go: and when he is old, he will not depart from it." (Prov 22:6)

Preliminarily we can say two things about this verse in Proverbs: (1) Dr. Bob's family, church, school, and disciplined religious village undoubtedly had his future, not any youthful meanderings, in mind, when they laid down his religious path. Quite possibly, they all said "jump." And in his youth, he simply asked, "How high?" (2) As happens with many alcoholics who really try later on to be cured and be restored to an honorable and useful life, and also try to remember what they were taught before they went astray, the results can be just as good for these folk as they were when Dr. Bob became "old." Let's therefore consider the following statement by him in the foregoing context:

> From childhood through high school I was more or less forced to go to church, Sunday School, and evening service, Monday night Christian Endeavor and sometimes to Wednesday evening prayer meeting.[17]

In his later and finally sober years, Dr. Bob returned to the training so heavily impressed upon him as a boy. As we noted before, he said:

> I had refreshed my memory of the Good Book, and I had had excellent training in that as a youngster.[18]

---

[17] *Alcoholics Anonymous*, 4th ed., 172..
[18] *The Co-Founders of Alcoholics Anonymous: Biographical Sketches Their Last Major Talks* (NY: Alcoholics Anonymous World Services, Inc., 1972, 1975), 11-12

Dr. Bob also made these statements:

> I'm somewhat allergic to work, but I felt that I should continue to increase my familiarity with the Good Book and also should read a good deal of standard literature, possibly of a scientific nature. So I did cultivate the habit of reading. I think I'm not exaggerating when I say I have probably averaged an hour a day for the last 15 years.[19]
>
> At that point, our stories didn't amount to anything to speak of. When we started in on Bill D., we had no Twelve Steps, either; we had no Traditions. But we were convinced that the answer to our problems was in the Good Book. To some of us older ones, the parts we found absolutely essential were the Sermon on the Mount, the thirteenth chapter of First Corinthians, and the Book of James.[20]
>
> It wasn't until 1938 that the teachings and efforts and studies that had been going on were crystallized in the form of the Twelve Steps. I didn't write the Twelve Steps. I had nothing to do with the writing of them. . . . Bill came to live at our house and stayed for about three months. There was hardly a night that we didn't sit up until two or three o'clock, talking. It would be hard for me to conceive that, during these nightly discussions around our kitchen table, nothing was said that influenced the writing of the Twelve Steps. We already had the basic ideas, though not in terse and tangible form. We got them, as I said, as a result of our study of the Good Book. We must have had them. . . . We were maintaining sobriety—therefore, we must have had them. Well, that was the way things got started in Akron. As we grew, we began to get offshoots, one in Cleveland, then another one in Akron, and all have been continuing ever since.[21]

Note all these important expressions out of the mouth of Dr. Bob: (1) "basic ideas . . . as a result of our study of the Good Book"; (2) "convinced that the answer to our problem was in the Good Book"; (3)

---

[19] *The Co-Founders*, 13.
[20] *The Co-Founders*, 13.
[21] *The Co-founders*, 14.

xx

"I should continue to increase my familiarity with the Good Book"; and (4) "I had refreshed my memory of the Good Book, and I had had excellent training in that as a youngster."

In my research of tapes at the General Services Office archives in New York, I had found this statement which Bill Wilson made in 1954 when he interviewed T. Henry and Clarace Williams on the subject of the early A.A. days:

> I had learned a great deal from you people [T. Henry and Clarace Williams], from the Smiths themselves [Dr. Bob and his wife Anne], and from Henrietta [Seiberling]. I hadn't looked in the Bible, up to this time, at all. You see, I had the [conversion] experience first and then this rushing around to help drunks and nothing happened.[22]

Once I learned the foregoing facts, largely through extensive travel, research, and interviews, I finally asked these simple questions: (1) If Bill Wilson had in fact not looked in the Bible in 1934 and early 1935, and was simply rushing around fruitlessly uttering his conversion story and trying to help drunks, what basic ideas had he learned in Akron from the Bible during the three months with the Smiths in 1935? (2) If Dr. Bob had had excellent training in the Good Book as a youngster, if he had been more or less "forced" into North Congregational Church services, Sunday School, Sunday evening service, and sometimes Wednesday prayer meetings, what had he learned then? (3) If Christian Endeavor meetings required Confession of Christ, conversion meetings, Bible study meetings, prayer meetings, Quiet Hour observances, with "love and service" as a motto, what had he learned and remembered from there? (4) If his parents were at his side in these observances and were devout church people steeped in the doctrine that the right training of the young would be fruitful, what had he learned from them? (5) If revivals, conversions, and evangelism were in the air at St. Johnsbury and bringing about conversions and church growth, what had he derived from that? (6) If St. Johnsbury Academy required daily chapel with Bible-reading and prayer, and

---

[22] From the transcript of Bill Wilson's taped interview with T. Henry and Clarace Williams on December 12, 1954, which transcript is on file in the A.A. Archives in New York. See Dick B., *The Akron Genesis of Alcoholics Anonymous,* 2d ed. (Kihei, HI: Paradise Research Publications, 1998), 64.

also required weekly church attendance and Bible study, what had he learned from that?

We turn to the history and surroundings of his youth for as many of the answers as we have thus far found; and we suggest there are mounds of evidence and repositories still to be plumbed—something that has escaped the "recovery" community historians and scholars for years and years.

"Your Heavenly Father will never let you down!"
Alcoholics Anonymous, 4th ed., p. 181

1

1875-1898:
From the "Great Awakening" of 1875 in St. Johnsbury, Vermont,
to Dr. Bob's Graduation from St. Johnsbury Academy in 1898

Something big. Something unusual. Something astonishing. In fact, something miraculous happened in the little town of A.A. cofounder Dr. Bob's youth—the "Great Awakening" of 1875 in St. Johnsbury. In this present chapter, we will discuss the major revival and its positive, godly, lasting impact on St. Johnsbury. We will also consider: (1) the preparations made by laymen of the Young Men's Christian Associations for the "Gospel canvass" of Vermont, which led to the "Great Awakening" of 1875; and (2) the prayerful preparations made by Caledonia Association members and others for that "Gospel canvass."[23] Finally, we will review here and throughout the remainder of this book, many of facts we found during our research which indicated that the dramatic, positive impact made by this great revival on St. Johnsbury may have been sustained—at least to some extent— even until the year of Dr. Bob's graduation from St. Johnsbury Academy in 1898. Along the way, we will discuss the many prayers, strong believing, and possible role of the Creator of the heavens and the earth involved in making possible the central role of God, Jesus Christ, and the Bible in St. Johnsbury between 1875 and 1898—not only at North Congregational Church, St. Johnsbury (of which Dr. Bob's parents were members and which Dr. Bob attended), but also at St. Johnsbury Academy (with which both of Dr. Bob's parents were

---

[23] "The Caledonia Association was an association of Congregational ministers of Caledonia County." From: The University of Vermont, UVM Special Collections Finding Aids, Inventory of the Caledonia Association records, ca. 1892-1910: http://cdi.uvm.edu/findingaids/viewEAD.xql?pid=caledonia.ead.xml ; accessed: 12/01/07.

involved, and at which Dr. Bob was a student from 1894 to 1898 and from which he graduated in 1898).

General Descriptions of the "Great Awakening" of 1875 in St. Johnsbury, Vermont

Various historians and eye-witnesses have described what was called the "Great Awakening" of 1875 in St. Johnsbury, expressing the events from their own viewpoints and in the following ways:

Rev. John E. Nutting wrote for the Vermont Conference of the United Church of Christ about the year 1875 and the General Convention of Congregational Ministers and Churches of Vermont:

> Caledonia Conference: The churches have been visited with one of the most remarkable and thorough religious awakenings known in modern or indeed in any time. Every church has been blest, and all but one or two have shared largely in the refreshing though upon two the dews of heaven have fallen since the first of May.
>
> St. Johnsbury has been the center of the work, not only for the churches of this Conference but also for much of the northeastern part of the state. . . . What shall be done to save souls?
>
> Meanwhile the same fire burned in the hearts of laymen and Christian women. . . .[24]

The church to which the Smith family belonged, North Congregational Church, St. Johnsbury, reported:

> The Great Awakening
>
> Foremost in time and importance in Mr. Jones' pastorate was the greatest revival this town every witnessed. It is significant

---

[24] John E. Nutting, *Becoming the United Church of Christ 1795-1995* (Burlington, VT: The Vermont Conference of the United Church of Christ, 1995), 206.

that it began, continued and ended with a consecrated group of laymen that won men and women and young people to Christ with no technique of a professional evangelist, but with the Holy Spirit working through convincing appeals of laymen for all to lead the Christian life."[25]

Town historian Claire Dunne Johnson stated:

> While the north end of Main St. was undergoing all of these residential improvements, there were also some major changes taking place just north of the business district—changes which would forever alter the skyline of St. Johnsbury.
>
> The year 1875 saw the beginning of the "Great Awakening," so-called, a tremendous surge of new religious fervor, initiated here by the Y.M.C.A. through great mass meetings at the churches and even at the scale shops. Prayer meetings and hymn-sings were attended by great numbers of people, and various religious groups in town were inspired to build their own churches.[26]

Even the Unitarian Universalist Church of St. Johnsbury commented as to its part:

> The St. Johnsbury Church participated in the "Great Awakening" of 1875. On March 28 the church was filled, "deep interest being manifest."[27]

Town historian Edward T. Fairbanks devoted several pages to describing "The Great Awakening" of 1875 (and we will quote his remarks in detail at a later point). Fairbanks remarked:

> In 1875 came the notable wave of religious uplift which none who witnessed it will ever forget.[28]

---

[25] Stone, *North Congregational Church . . . 1825-1942*, 30.
[26] Claire Dunne Johnson, *"I See by the Paper . . .": An Informal History of St. Johnsbury* (St. Johnsbury, VT: The Cowles Press, 1987), 84.
[27] "History of the Unitarian Universalist Church of Saint Johnsbury"; http://stevefinner.org/UUChurch/OurChurch/History.htm ; accessed 11/30/07.

> The religious life stood out as a manly thing to be manfully followed; the dominant note was not so much the old time solemnity, as the joy of opportunity, the cheer of the good news to every man.[29]

M. B. Critchett of Concord, New Hampshire, reported at the 1875 North American YMCA Convention:

> Memory has carried me back to a day in '73, when I was summoned by a telegram to repair at once to the city of Manchester, to meet brethren from New Hampshire, Massachusetts and New York, assembled together to consult how best to carry on the work of God in our State. Never was such enthusiasm enkindled in our minds as when we grasped the hands of those brethren and pledged ourselves to the work.
>
> In the Fall of '73, the first canvass was inaugurated. Some forty-one towns were visited, and 104 days were spent in the work. As a result, more than 500 souls were added to the Church of God. All praise to Him! The Lord is ready to work through any willing instrumentality. In first taking up this work, dear brethren, the burden will rest upon a few, because so many in the church will know little of it; but don't feel discouraged. Let a few warm-hearted men in every State consult together, and call a State Convention. Send the call to all the Evangelical Churches as well as to the Associations, and invite them to send their best men as delegates to the Convention; also, request the churches desiring visitors from the State Convention to instruct their delegates accordingly. Secure the attendance of experienced men from the various States where a canvass has been carried forward successfully, to show the Convention how the work is done; have men ready in advance to respond with pledges of time and money, and then you will find that persons all over the house will respond,

---

[28] Edward T. Fairbanks, *The Town of St. Johnsbury VT: A Review of One Hundred Twenty-five Years to the Anniversary Pageant 1912* (St. Johnsbury, VT: The Cowles Press, 1914), 316.

[29] Fairbanks, *The Town of St. Johnsbury*, 317.

and you will receive liberal pledges. In our first Convention we received pledges to the amount of $1,000; in the second, nearly $2,000, from individuals, churches and associations. The Convention elected a State Executive Committee, which organized at once, and opened correspondence with the churches to learn when and where visits should be made. In going out upon the work, the visitors go with a simple desire to honor God and strengthen His cause, and God has prepared the way for us in advance.

In nearly every one of the 41 towns and 61 visits of the second canvass some souls were brought to God; and I received a letter yesterday, stating that, in one village, 125 souls, newly converted, were rejoicing in the Saviour. We sent out large posters ahead of us, containing the topics and other details regarding the meetings; and even children noticed these, and spread their contents among their friends. Programmes [sic] were distributed in the churches two or three Sabbaths before our meetings, and many personal letters were also written, asking that they would seek God's blessing upon the Conventions, and God heard these prayers for our work. We endeavored to give at least one evening to the discussion of Association work. Hundreds of souls are rejoicing in Christ as the result of these State Conventions. **A brother from St. Johnsbury, Vermont, tells me that, since the first visit made to that place this season, 1,500 souls have been converted**. May we not rejoice here, to day, as we think of blessed results like these?"[30] (bolding added)

R. K. Remington of Fall River, Massachusetts, speaking at the 1875 North American YMCA Convention in Richmond, Virginia, on the topic of "The Work of the Executive Committees of State and Provincial Conventions," said:

I wish to speak of the importance of State work, in connection with the Y. M. C. A. of our country, as I know something of

---

[30] *Proceedings of the Twentieth Annual Convention of the Young Men's Christian Associations of the United States and British Provinces, Held at Richmond, VA., May 26-30, 1875* (New York: Published by the Executive Committee, 1875), 35 (bold face added).

the work that has been done in New England. I cannot tell how much God has blessed the labors of these brethren who have gone forth in His name. Hundreds and thousands are rejoicing in Christ, owing to these efforts. If I remember rightly, two of the brethren sitting in this place to-day [i.e., K. A. Burnell and H. M. Moore] said, at Detroit, in 1868, that by the help of God the old Bay State should be conquered for Christ. A few years after, a Committee was appointed by the Associations of Massachusetts to go out into the towns and cities of that State, and first, if possible, approach the ministry, and then the brethren and sisters, so as to awaken the churches and stimulate the laymen to greater efficiency. Some 40 or 50 towns were visited. The spirit of the Master took possession of many hearts. God seemed to honor and bless that work.

At the following Convention, the reports were so cheering, that we were stimulated to continue the work, and another Committee was appointed, and the Lord has greatly blessed it. The present season more than 150 days have been already spent in visiting 64 places, and hundreds have been added to the churches. Brethren in various denominations have entered into it as one man. Miles have been traveled over, not only in Massachusetts, but in other States, at the request of their Committees. Brethren at different times gave up their business three, five, or ten days, going out to the different parts of the State. Many Associations have been quickened; but the grandest result of the work is, that the laity of our churches have been developed to a wonderful extent.

There is hardly a church in the land that has not at least its score of members who can hold up the cross, and tell the simple story of Christ and His love. I sometimes think that the Church has never developed so largely its lay element as now through the instrumentality of our Associations. I believe that Massachusetts is alive with religious effort, and Vermont stands here today saying, Glory to God in the Highest! Souls have been saved by hundreds and thousands. How has it been brought about? Those who have gone out have given the brethren of the ministry, in the first place, the right hand of fellowship; and with the recognition of the ministry, they have stimulated the laymen, convincing many of the importance of this work.

The ministry of New England, I believe, will say very largely that the development of this work is wonderful beyond their comprehension, and that God has visited the churches as never before.[31]

Preparations, Guidance, and Streams of Efforts Preceding the Event

Let's spend a moment talking about revivals, evangelists, awakenings, and conversions. All these phrases had different meanings for different people at different times. Therefore, when some described the St. Johnsbury events of the 1870's, they used words of art which had certainly been used before. And we will devote a moment to the previous usages. But we do so with the caveat that the "Great Awakening" of 1875 in St. Johnsbury followed no prior theme. In fact it was generated by some general discontent in the community itself. It was primarily a lay effort, though very much related to several Protestant denominational concerns and efforts in St. Johnsbury. And it flourished in a community which—in contrast to a general malaise prior thereto—could boast of strong Christian leaders, a strong Congregational bent, an affinity to the YMCA and its lay and "union" and town-wide approaches, and general changes within the people of the community themselves. This distinguished it from what had been called the solemn, dead, contentious, and unfruitful growth as far as the "state of the church" (particularly that of the Vermont Congregational Churches) was concerned. St. Johnsbury was different. It was dominated by the strong and well-financed leadership of many members of the Fairbanks family. Its leaders, educational facilities, and churches were dedicated Christian agencies. And the North Congregational Church, to which the Smith family belonged, was strong on its own and much interested in helping weaker churches, uniting in salvation efforts and prayers with other churches, and open to receiving help from lay people, the YMCA efforts, and later those of the Christian Endeavor Society which was founded in 1881. As is

---

[31] *Proceedings of the Twentieth Annual Convention of the Young Men's Christian Associations of the United States and British Provinces, Held at Richmond, VA., May 26-30, 1875* (New York: Published by the Executive Committee, 1875).

our custom, we will document these latter statements in a moment, with appropriate footnote citations.

Other Revivals and Awakenings

Prior to 1875, there had been other "Awakenings" and "Revivals." But one needs to step carefully when it comes to labeling or numbering them. There were theological and denominational disagreements, divisions and diverse approaches, and usually more than one "leader" involved. In fact, for the purposes of helping AAs to deal with these terms in seeking healing and cure, it is far better simply to describe what actually happened in St. Johnsbury in 1875, the numbers of people who were converted to Christ there, and the resurgence of interest within the community and the churches in God, Jesus Christ, the Bible, Christianity, prayer, Sunday school, and conversion. Our stated purpose is to see what Dr. Bob saw, may have seen, and undoubtedly heard described in his St. Johnsbury life—as impacted by his parents, his church and Sunday school and prayer meetings, his Christian Endeavor training, and the requirements as a St. Johnsbury Academy student. Also, to get the real flavor of the St. Johnsbury difference—a community led by devout Christians, changed by a new religious fervor, and observing what the Creator had actually brought to their community as they sought to do His will. Nonetheless, because the St. Johnsbury events beginning in 1875 were frequently described as involving the "Great Awakening," it is appropriate to distinguish that date and that period from a couple of others.

The First Great Awakening (1730's)

One scholar points to what he calls "the First Great Awakening," a "colonial event of (approximately) the 1730's," which "was an intercolonial and trans-creedal occurrence which began to provide people from Massachusetts to South Carolina with some common religious symbols and rhetoric," with "Jonathan Edwards and George Whitfield. . . [as] the towering names of the era." He then points to preoccupation with colonial wars, the Revolution, nation-building, and a kind of "American Enlightenment" as leading to the demise of the movement.[32]

The Second Great Awakening (1830 to 1840)

The same scholar, along with others, refers to "a Second Great Awakening in the early 1800's," which he claimed was a "two-phased movement" that "quickened the more settled Eastern churches" and "was involved with the winning of the West and the churching of the frontier. Yale president Timothy Dwight was the leader in the former, and Charles Grandison Finney or Peter Cartwright . . . typified the latter."[33] Elmer Towns and Douglas Porter list a number of revival types and rank them. They focus on the "Second Great Awakening, 1830 to 1840," which they dubbed the "General Awakening," spurred, they say, by Finney, and followed by what they call "The Laymen's Prayer Revival, 1857-61." This, they say, involved the "Fulton Street Prayer Meeting" which began as a lay prayer meeting in New York City, and soon involved what they called the "Illinois Bank" meeting where Dwight L. Moody (who became a lay evangelist) was elected president of the Illinois Sunday School Association where an unusual group of distinguished laymen adopted their goal to bring Christ to the world.[34]

I believe the latter "Awakening" period has a bearing on St. Johnsbury's experience primarily because it marked a new enthusiasm for lay evangelism, more unity among churches, and a thrust into the community itself—rather than just a focus on this or that church or organization.

The Pre-1875 Church Slump and Conversion Slump

The "Great Awakening" of 1875 in St. Johnsbury occurred as the result of need, malaise, lack of conversions, weakened churches, lack of growth, and "dumb" self-contentment. The issue here is not what

---

[32] The remarks are those of Martin E. Marty. The title is by James F. Findlay, Jr., *Dwight L. Moody American Evangelist 1837-1899* (Chicago: The University of Chicago Press, 1969), 2-3.
[33] Findlay, *Dwight L. Moody American Evangelist*, 3.
[34] Elmer Towns and Douglas Porter, *From Pentecost to the Present: The Ten Greatest Revivals Ever* (Ann Arbor, MI: Servant Publications, 2000), 10, 17, 19, 97-136.

was happening in St. Johnsbury. For St. Johnsbury Congregational churches were generally reported as strong. But neither Vermont Congregationalists, nor their pastors, nor their churches could ignore the annual reports that were coming in. And we have gone to the actual convention minutes for a close look. You can see these reports from 1872 onward by going online.

For our purposes, the Minutes of the Seventy-seventh annual meeting of the General Convention of Vermont held at Brattleboro in 1872 contain some telling and specific examples. These are some of the doleful remarks:

> Sabbath School Report. It is a question whether the adult conversions, in most of our churches, are equal in number to the removals. If, therefore, we trust to them solely for reinforcements, we leave the church to decline.
>
> One of the first inquiries suggested by the reports as presented, is whether the difference between the whole number of scholars and the average attendance is not too great. . . . We must look then for the cause of this small average, in a great measure, outside of the scholars.
>
> Are the parents sufficiently interested? Do they take sufficient pains to prepare their children for the school, and encourage them to be regular and prompt in their attendance. Do they teach them to feel that on the Sabbath the church is the place for them. . . do they not yield to them too easily, and permit their children to remain at home on almost any excuse, imaginary as well as real? . . . Let parents show their interest in the Sabbath School by their attendance, by their instruction of their children, talking with them about the lessons. . . .
>
> Another reason for the irregularity in the attendance of scholars may be found in the teachers . . . still there are a large number who would find an excuse for absence in the absence of the teacher. . . Let parents and teachers be more faithful, and we may be sure scholars will be more regular in their attendance.

Ought there not be a larger proportion of our congregations in the Sabbath School? If Bible instruction is important, is it not so for all classes?

It is a matter of surprise that not more teachers' meetings are held.

Another question which should receive our attention is, whether the number of conversions reported is as great as we might reasonably expect. . . . We are taught to labor directly for the conversion of souls, with the expectation of success. . . . The great object of the Sabbath School teacher should be to bring his scholars to Christ, and then instruct them, so that they shall become intelligent, efficient Bible Christians.

STATE OF THE CHURCHES [In the Addison Conference, as an example:] In Addison Conference there has been no revival during the year. . . . The pulpit of the church in Bristol is vacant, and there is no Sabbath School. In Cornwall the state of religion is rather low, as might be expected in connection with an unusual neglect of prayer and conference-meeting. . . . The church in New Haven has no pastor. . . . In Ripton there has been no special interest excepting in one case of hopeful conversion. The Sabbath School is very thinly attended. The church in Salisbury is without a pastor. This Conference reports a net loss for the year of fourteen members. . . . Doubtless the Lord has rewarded us according to our faith, but is not the inquiry pressed upon us, 'Has not our faith been too weak?' Should we not accomplish much greater things if we undertook them, and shall we not in the year to come undertake them?[35]

Town, church, and Academy records are full of information about the destructive effect of the war between the states and the resultant decline in New England revivals, conversions, and evangelism. Men had been called away to serve their country. The YMCA workers were

---

[35] The foregoing remarks and more from the General Convention of Vermont for 1872 were published in Montpelier: J. & J.M. Poland's Steam Printing Establishment, 1872.

in the field with the troops.[36] They were largely unavailable for their soul-saving work in New England. Furthermore, year after year, in the minutes of the Vermont Congregational Conferences, from 1871 to 1874, there were frequent comments about the darkness, the "low state of religion," "the low state of religious feeling," and the—lack of interest in conversions, growth, Sunday School attendance, cooperation, and religious fervor.

Reports of Richard C. Morse and A. J. Howe at the 1875 North American YMCA Convention

Richard C. Morse reported at the 1875 North American YMCA Convention: (1) Vermont held a State YMCA Convention in Norwich, Vermont, on November 19-20, 1874; (2) Seven Associations were represented; (3) There were 26 delegates and 15 Corresponding Members; and (4) R. K. Remington and R. C. Morse represented the Executive Committee of the YMCA at the Vermont State Convention by.[37] Morse continued by stating:

> In the case of the New England Conventions, a special previous effort was made by communication with our Corresponding Members in that section to bring the strong Association States, Massachusetts and New Hampshire, into co-operation with neighboring States where the cause was feeble. Messrs. R. K. Remington and H. M. Moore, of Massachusetts, and M. B. Critchett and Allan Folger of New Hampshire, generously responded, and were present at the Vermont Convention last October [sic]. The State Committee, then appointed, were informed and stimulated by these brethren, and a wonderful blessing has attended their visitation

---

[36] Clarence Prouty Shedd, et. al., *History of the World's Alliance of Young Men's Christian Associations* (London: S P C K, 1955), 164-65; Sherwood Eddy. *A Century with Youth: A History of the Y.M.C.A. from 1844 to 1944* (NY: Association Press, 1944), 24-25; James L. Ellenwood. *One Hundred Years and Here We Are* (NY: Association Press, 1944); Laurence L. Doggett. *History of the Young Men's Christian Association* (NY: Association Press, 1922), 204-14, 304-17; and James F. Findlay, Jr., *Dwight L. Moody: American Evangelist 1837-1899* (Chicago: The University of Chicago Press, 1969), 100-13.

[37] *Proceedings of the Twentieth Annual Convention of the Young Men's Christian Associations of the United States and British Provinces, Held at Richmond, VA., May 26-30, 1875* (New York: Published by the Executive Committee, 1875), xvi.

in Vermont. The Chairman of the State Committee writes thus, two months ago: 'October, 1874, not a warm spot in Vermont. March, 1875, 1,000 conversions.' And since that time hundreds have been added to the number.[38]

A. J. Howe reported at the 1875 North American YMCA Convention:

> For the greater part of 1874, a heavy cloud overhung the Association horizon of Vermont. Under its shadows, and almost doubting the existence of a 'silver lining,' the State Convention assembled at Norwich on the 19th of November.
>
> The few earnest Y. M. C. A. workers present, ardently longing to perfect some plan by which Gospel truths should be carried to the many waste places in the State, were warmly supported by an unusually large clerical representation.
>
> A committee of nine members was chosen and instructed to arrange for, and carry on a State canvass, similar to those of Massachusetts and New Hampshire.
>
> Our first 'Gospel Meeting' was held the 2d of January, and up to the present date, (April 28) meetings of three and four days duration have been successfully carried on in 54 towns; showing an *unbroken service* for 115 days. The visitation is still progressing. In one of our larger towns, some hundreds of converts have confessed Jesus as their Saviour. In several others, from 60 to 100 have sought and found the pearl of price. In many small and obscure towns, comparatively considered, the number has been equally large, when but 10 or 20 have passed from death unto life.
>
> While three Associations report 'deceased,' three barely existing ones tell us they are infused with new life, and are eager to battle for the Lord. At St. Johnsbury the membership of 250 sustain three weekly meetings, where the attendance sometimes numbers 400. They have also in connection with the

---

[38] *Proceedings of the Twentieth Annual Convention of the Young Men's Christian Associations of the United States and British Provinces, Held at Richmond, VA., May 26-30, 1875* (New York: Published by the Executive Committee, 1875), xvi-xvii.

State canvass, held three days meetings in adjoining towns with glorious results. Windham, Norwich, Charlotte, South Royalton and Ludlow, report an increase of interest and activity.[39]

Out of the tragedies, deaths, and moribund enthusiasm accompanying the Civil War came something new, needed, and divinely directed.

Plans and Preparations to Call the Creator off the Bench

Many in A.A. believe that the Creator had a hand in the founding of A.A. Others scoff at the idea, point to the many aberrations in the life of Bill W., claim he was never religious, and ask why he never joined a church in later life. Some say they can't see Christianity in Dr. Bob's life either. But any and all of these commentators would be hard put to deny the need for an organization such as Alcoholics Anonymous in 1935—a time of such seeming hopelessness and medical incurability.[40] They would be hard put to ignore the imperative in A.A.'s basic text that the alcoholic "find God now."[41] They cannot ignore the many times the A.A. Big Book talks about "establishing a relationship with God" as the objective of early members—in fact among most A.A. Big Book students and "Big Book Thumpers" today.[42] Today's A.A. revisionists seem to forget the admonition in A.A.'s basic text by the eminent doctor who said there was no doubt in his mind that the two men before him were 100% hopeless without

---

[39] *Proceedings of the Twentieth Annual Convention of the Young Men's Christian Associations of the United States and British Provinces, Held at Richmond, VA., May 26-30, 1875* (New York: Published by the Executive Committee, 1875), li.
[40] See *Alcoholics Anonymous*, 4th ed., "pitiful and incomprehensible demoralization.," 30; "Neither does there appear to be any kind of treatment which will make alcoholics of our kind like other men," 30-31; "informed that it would all end with heart failure during delirium tremens, or I would develop a wet brain," 7; "once just as hopeless as Bill," 17; "has probably placed himself beyond human ad, and unless locked up, may die or go permanently insane," 24; "The doctor said: 'You have the mind of a chronic alcoholic. I have never seen one single case recover, where that state of mind existed to the extent that it does in you," 27; "One . . . staff member of a world-renowned hospital, recently made this statement to some of us: 'What you say about the general hopelessness of the average alcoholic's plight, is in my opinion, correct. As to two of you men, whose stories I have heard, there is no doubt in my mind that you were 100% hopeless, apart from divine help," 43.
[41] *Alcoholics Anonymous*, 4th ed., 59.
[42] *Alcoholics Anonymous*, 4th ed., 13, 29, 72, 100, 58, 68, 98.

divine help.[43] And they scarcely seem to mention the fact that all three of the first AAs—Wilson, Smith, and Dotson—said they were cured by the power of God.[44] They ignore the fact that Dr. Bob admonished atheists, agnostics and skeptics, and declared to them and others who were suffering that "Your Heavenly Father will never let you down!"[45] They also ignore the quote from an important speech in New York, where Bill Wilson concluded with the question: "Who invented A.A?" His answer was: "Almighty God."[46] Such, then, was the opportunity presented by the Creator to alcoholics who chose to seek, find, and follow. In fact, though most today neither know it nor believe it, the pioneer AAs chose the Bible and reliance on the Creator for their basic ideas.

There is an analogy to the St. Johnsbury situation in 1875. A few years earlier, the Vermont Congregational churches had reached a low point. The YMCA had put its community "religious work" on hold. Churches were quarreling over doctrine, and many were opposed to revivals. There was yet no Christian Endeavor Society. Still, there seemed to be an opportune time and call for all of these to get back and about their "Father's business."[47] That meant returning to prayer, returning to the Bible, and fishing for men—seeking souls to save! And here also, the hand of the Heavenly Father seemed clear when they began addressing the situation. For the miraculous began to

---

[43] *Alcoholics Anonymous*, 4th ed., 43.
[44] *Alcoholics Anonymous*, 4th ed., 191, 180.
[45] *Alcoholics Anonymous*, 4th ed., 181.
[46] Rev. Samuel M. Shoemaker, Jr., attended the New York dinner, took notes, and reported most of the talk. On the "invention" remark, Shoemaker wrote this: "Who invented A.A.?" says Bill. "It was God Almighty that invented A.A. This is the story of how we learned to be free. God grant that AA and the program of recovery and unity and service be the story that continues into the future as long as God needs it." Dick B., *New Light on Alcoholism: God, Sam Shoemaker, and A.A.*, The Pittsburgh Edition (Kihei, HI: Paradise Research Publications, 1999), 395.
[47] When chided by his mother for going to the temple and listening to, and asking questions of the doctors, Jesus replied to his parents: "How is it that ye sought me? Wist ye not [Don't you know] that I must be about my Father's business?" Luke 2:49. Dr. Bob Smith apparently called up this expression when describing his morning devotion. It consisted of a short prayer, a 20-minute study of a familiar verse from the Bible, and a quiet period of waiting for directions as to where he, that day, should find use for his talent. Pioneer Paul S.—who related the facts—said, "Having heard, he [Dr. Bob] would religiously go about his Father's business, as he put it." *DR. BOB*, 314.

happen. And it involved several different factors—the Young Men's Christian Association, some self-less lay people, the Congregational Churches, some other denominational bodies, evangelists, Gospel meetings, prayer meetings, revivals, and conversions. And it certainly involved the members of North Congregational Church, which was included in the six participating St. Johnsbury churches in all. In addition, invited lay evangelists, and other Vermont people put their shoulders to the wheel.

Detailed references will be provided. But it should be understood that there were different and carefully developed streams of action involved in the plans, preparations, and execution of the new effort to enlist God's help. The object was to do His will. This, to the participants, meant primarily bringing new people to Christ—saving souls—accomplishing conversions. The loose ends had not resulted from a lack of approaches; they resulted from dramatic changes of course. They also would be tied together by common cause, unity of effort, and persistent prayer. Though inter-laced, the ends have different origins and will be examined separately. The primary, initial moving source of activity is found in the YMCA—involving actions by Dwight L. Moody, actions by YMCA lay evangelists from Massachusetts, actions by YMCA leaders at the state and St. Johnsbury level. It definitely involved influences by Fairbanks family members, and activities by individuals in the Congregational churches, local St. Johnsbury churches, and the North Congregational Church in St. Johnsbury.

Lest we become entangled in definitions of conversion, revival, Gospel meetings, union meetings, Congregational polity, YMCA principles and practices, and prayer itself, we urge you to realize that our focus in this review is on Dr. Bob. What did Dr. Bob learn from his family? From church services? From his pastor? From his Sunday school teachers? From his own church's activities in revivals, Gospel meetings, and evangelism? From Y.M.C.A community-wide, non-denominational emphasis? From teachings, sermons, chapel exercises, texts, and lectures at St. Johnsbury Academy?

Remember that Akron A.A. was founded and focused on Bible study; prayer; devotionals; Quiet Time; God's guidance; conversion to Christ; elimination of sin; reliance on the Creator for strength, guidance, and healing; Christian fellowship; and witness. Note too that a few of these ideas are related to Bill Wilson's own conversion and beliefs about conversion; they are related to Oxford Group practices; and they are related to procedures at Gospel rescue missions, practices of the Salvation Army, and the views of Dr. William D. Silkworth.

When the "Great Awakening" in St. Johnsbury began in 1875, Christian Endeavor had not yet been founded—its founding occurring in 1881; yet the heart of the simple Akron program more closely resembles the Christian Endeavor of Dr. Bob's youth than it does the other factors mentioned in the preceding paragraph. Remember too that the cure of alcoholism was a special concern for Bob and Bill, while it took second place to Vermont's concerns about abstinence, temperance, and testimonials at revivals.

That said, let's look at the preparations that preceded and also provided the fodder for Dr. Bob's indoctrination.

The stream began with an extended meeting between Henry M. Moore and his friend, the evangelist K. A. Burnell in the summer 1871 near Aurora, Illinois. In prayer, for the extension of Christ's Kingdom, they then conceived a plan for a regular canvass of Gospel meetings in the State of Massachusetts.[48] Henry Moore returned home to Massachusetts and arranged with the Massachusetts YMCA state executive committee to commence such a canvass. It was begun in January, 1872, adopting as its motto "Massachusetts for Christ," visiting different churches in the state from which invitations might come for a series of evangelistic meetings.[49]

Nearby New Hampshire YMCA had failed, in 1872, to hold their annual state convention. By suggestion of the Massachusetts brethren, in 1873, a meeting was held in Manchester, New Hampshire, conducted similarly to meetings in Massachusetts. The Massachusetts brethren had covenanted with God not to leave New Hampshire without an agreement to wage aggressive warfare against the powers of Satan. A chairman was selected. After the regular service, a few were invited in a corner of the church with the visitors; and the

---

[48] Allen Folger, *Twenty-five Years as an Evangelist* (Boston: James H. Earle & Company, 1905), 35.
[49] Folger, *Twenty-five Years*, 35.

proposal was made that canvass work be begun in New Hampshire. It was agreed to call a state convention in Manchester in May 6th following. Earnest workers from other states were present; funds were raised to carry on the work; a committee of ten was chosen to look over the field and plan for aggressive work—the state was to be taken by storm. Following the regular state convention in Concord, a winter campaign of 100 days had been planned and was reported at that convention.[50]

In company with the YMCA activities in Massachusetts and New Hampshire, Vermont seemed to move forward with canvasses spurred by invited YMCA lay people, primarily from Massachusetts. These people were encouraged by the Vermont YMCA leaders and church people—in some cases by those wearing both hats. In fact, much of the later outreach through the YMCA Gospel meetings into surrounding areas was attributed substantially to the work of St. Johnsbury people. In keeping with YMCA practices and procedures, the Vermont work began with a YMCA canvass. "Y" people moved into communities on a non-creedal and non-denominational basis. The work was conducted largely by visiting lay people. They held Gospel meetings in various churches, the Fairbanks scales plant, public facilities, and the St. Johnsbury Academy. Their goal—reported as achieved in community after community, particularly in St. Johnsbury—was conversion—winning people to Christ.

The following analysis of the "Great Awakening" of 1875 is found in the *Minutes of the Eightieth Annual Meeting of the General Convention of Congregational Ministers and Churches of Vermont, Held at Bennington, June, 1875*:

> Agencies.
>
> Following this, on the whole, very cheering survey of the condition of the churches, it seems eminently suitable to note some of the means which the Lord has employed and blessed in the carrying on of His work. First, it is the almost universal testimony that the special work of Divine grace wherever wrought was definitely labored and prayed for. Generally,

---

[50] Folger, *Twenty-five Years*, 35-37.

preliminary work was done by the people before outside help was employed; but if not this, the people worked with a will when they were called, or when their duty and privilege were set before them. Secondly, the extent or the ability of the foreign aid introduced, but in proportion to the faith and persevering prayer of God's people, coupled with faithful and judicious personal effort. As far as special agencies of any other sort are concerned the churches enjoying revivals may be divided into three classes: First, those which have called in no outside assistance; secondly, those which have employed Evangelists; and thirdly, those that have availed themselves of the aid of the Gospel meetings or the work of the laborers of the Young Men's Christian Associations. Of the first class, the churches in St. Albans and Middlebury, with some others, seem to have wrought quite alone, yet very successfully. Others, like Vergennes and Swanton, united with churches of other denominations and doubtless gained vigor and strength simply from such association. Brattleboro and Newbury were aided by other ministers. Four or five churches, including West Brattleboro, Chester, Putney and Ludlow, have found the preaching of a professed Evangelist very helpful. On the contrary, at St. Johnsbury such an Evangelist did not reach the people.[51]

Some other man might have met with better success, but even there, I think, every one familiar with such work would say that probably no one living man, and certainly no preacher, would have so much reached the masses as did the lay workers. "In fully four fifths of the churches, where the influences of the Spirit have been most markedly manifest, the development of

---

[51] Allen Folger states: "In S----- the churches had been holding union meetings for prayer for several weeks, as if due preparation for good results had been made. There seemed to be intense interest manifested by every hearer in the words spoken and sung, but at the close not a confession was made of acceptance of salvation. The ministers expressed hearty approval of the way the meetings were conducted, notwithstanding the apparent failure, but our Lord did not suffer our faith to falter, nor did the churches give up earnest prayer. We found the following year a glad welcome, and quite a large number became inquirers; another evangelist followed in meetings, and the result was the greatest revival the town had experienced in this generation." Allen Folger, *Twenty-Five Years as an Evangelist* (Boston: James H. Earle & Company, 1905), 51. Was that town St. Johnsbury?

religious interest has been chiefly in connection with the efforts of the so-called Gospel workers. But what, it may be asked, gave to these laborers such notable success? It may be answered in the first place that, no doubt, in the absence of other available instrumentalities, the prayers of God's people were directed with reference to these helpers, and gave them, by the blessing of the Spirit in answer to prayer, very great efficiency. In many places, too, the fields were white to the harvest. Yet elsewhere such confessedly was not the case. But it was everywhere noticed that these workers were men of much prayer. They relied on God. They spent almost as much time in secret prayer as in public work. They struck the keynote of their success when in every place before each meeting, they met by themselves for prayer, for guidance and for the special presence of the Spirit. Again,--and this was perhaps the most noticeable feature of their work to the ordinary observer,--these workers gave great prominence to God's word. It was presented and enforced with great simplicity. Every child could understand. Their Bible readings were often very impressive. The Gospel plan of salvation was packed into a nutshell. They held up both sides of the picture. Men were saved or unsaved. Such plainness of speech, supported by the authority of God's word; by the evident sincerity of their own convictions; by prayer, and by the concurrent testimony of many Christians; the utterances of all being in a direct, sensible, practical, business-like way, entirely free from either cant or rhetorical art, was as effective as any human utterance could well be—and the more so, doubtless, because many of the hearers had been accustomed to quite another style of speech. At St. Johnsbury and vicinity it has been noticed that after the revival interest fairly began almost every means employed was blest to some souls. Some said it was this or that sermon of their minister that reached them; others ascribed their conversion to the prayers of friends or those of the congregations. Some were influenced by the word of this or that Gospel worker; others more by the expression of interest of some old friend in their behalf. The artless utterances of young children were winged by the Spirit to the hearts of not a few parents, and the life-long prayers of a father, or mother, or wife, or friend, were recalled to many a forgetful and wayward soul, till from very shame of its treatment of the love of others it was led to a sense of sin against God. To here and there one God spoke as directly as to Samuel or Saul of Tarsus.

SPECIAL FEATURES OF LAYMEN'S WORK.

It has been a noteworthy feature of the laymen's work that it has been wrought neither through any one man nor through any single band of men. None, judging from the results, have been able to say I or we are the Lord's special messengers. Bands quite differently constituted have had equal success. Workers from our own state have, all things considered, been as much smiled upon by heaven as those from abroad, and fresh workers have often accomplished as much as those longer in the field. Yet very much has been learned from those who have had experience of years in such work, and the charge of such a series of Gospel meetings is not wisely given to one who has not had some experience.

Another feature of these revivals is the intense, and yet sober, activity of the young converts. To this the example of Christian laymen has incited them, and for this they have seemed remarkably ready. Religious services are being conducted these summer Sabbaths in hundreds of school-houses by those who a few months ago cared nothing for a personal Saviour. The era of a dumb Christianity has its days numbered. Moreover, it has been everywhere, in connection with these meetings, held that the testimony of a woman was as good as that of a man, though women's voices have been heard generally in modest acknowledgment of a Saviour's love, rather than in bold exhortation.

A *third* feature of all this work has been the entire suppression of denominational differences, and the cordiality and harmony with which Christians of every evangelical name have worked together.

Fourthly, there has been very little of the ordinary revival machinery employed, and scarcely anything which could properly be termed excitement. No anxious seats have been used; no kneeling insisted on, nor any conspicuous gathering in front of the audience called for. There have been earnest appeals and enthusiastic singing. The latter has often been very effective, and the little volume called 'The Winnowed Hymns,' has proved admirably adapted to the requirements of such work. *Fifthly*, it is the universal testimony that the converts so far run well. The Holy Spirit has been unmistakably present in the work. Men have relied upon the Spirit, sought the Spirit, and He has come to them.

Finally, this laymen's or Gospel work has very strongly commended itself to those who have known most about it. Almost everywhere it has removed prejudice against it. Almost everywhere it has strengthened the hands of the parish ministers. The workers have not always been successful; sometimes they have made mistakes, (who does not?) but where they have not made some impression, it has generally been through lack of faith, or prayer, or hearty, united cooperation on the part of the Christians among whom they have tried to labor. This form of Christian effort is Scriptural and rational; it is simply the advance of the laymen to the proper support of the ministry, and the performing of their part in the evangelizing of the world. God has owned it by the fruits He has given to it; for in connection with it, nearly if not quite two thousand souls in this state have within the past six months been converted. We may add, by way of confirmation, that the Caledonia Conference, at its meeting at East Hardwick last week, passed a resolution most heartily endorsing this work.

There are many incidental results of the revival interest of the past year which might be mentioned were not this report already too long. Most of the churches which have not shared largely in the interest are very hopeful as to the future. They desire a blessing and expect it. May the Lord fill every longing heart!

Many churches will hereafter be better sustained financially. Public morals ought to be of a higher tone and the cause of temperance to receive a better support. It is a question worth considering whether the services of laymen may not be profitably employed in the weaker churches unable to support preaching all the year, and whether some of the churches not reporting either this or for several previous years may not by the same means be aroused at least into life enough to give some account of themselves."[52]

The "Great Awakening" of 1875 in St. Johnsbury, Vermont, As Observers Described It

Source 1 on the Great Awakening-as Dr. Bob's church described it

The Great Awakening[53]

Foremost in time and importance in Mr. Jones' pastorate [1875-1885[54]] was the greatest revival this town ever witnessed. It is significant that it began, continued and ended with a consecrated group of laymen that won men and women and young people to Christ with no technique of a professional evangelist, but with the Holy Spirit working through convincing appeals of laymen for all to lead the christian [sic] life. Early in 1875 the State Young Men's Christian Association was making a religious canvas of Vermont. On February 6 two of the committee, Messrs. Cook and Davis, came here bringing with them a couple of Massachusetts laymen, H. M. Moore of Somerville and Robert K. Remington of Fall River. They met a group at the Town Hall in the afternoon where plans were outlined for a series of gospel meetings. The following Sunday afternoon another meeting was held in the Town Hall with a meeting in the South church in the evening. When at the latter place 42 persons rose for

---

[52] *Minutes of the Eightieth Annual Meeting of the General Convention of Congregational Ministers and Churches of Vermont, Held at Bennington, June, 1875. Fifty-Seventh Annual Report of the Vermont Domestic Missionary Society, and Fifty-Fifth Report of the Vermont Education Society* (Montpelier: J. & J. M. Poland, Steam Printers, 1875), 38-41.
[53] This subheading is actually centered in the text of the work quoted from here.
[54] Rev. Henry W. Jones had begun preaching in the pulpit of North Congregational Church, St. Johnsbury, at the beginning of 1875. He was installed as the new pastor on November 18, 1875. Stone, *North Congregational Church, St. Johnsbury, Vermont: 1825-1942* (St. Johnsbury, VT: North Congregational Church, 1942), 26-27.

prayers there was no doubt that the day of Pentecost had fully come. On Monday evening at the North church 57 rose for prayers. Both on Monday and Tuesday meetings for inquirers were held in the North church vestry preceding the mass meeting in the auditorium of the church. A few weeks later two more Massachusetts laymen, E. O. Winslow [sic[55]] of Boston and Sidney E. Bridgman of Northampton, arrived. Twelve hundred people filled the South church on a weekday evening at which 140 rose for prayers. Meetings were held at the Avenue House hall and twice at the Fairbanks scale factory where much interest was manifest. On March 27 Messrs. Moore, Remington and Winslow came back here being joined by Mr. Littlefield. As no church was large enough to hold the throngs that had been coming to these services the climax in attendance and results was reached on March 28 when 1400 people crowded Academy hall and its passage ways, while 300 held an overflow meeting in old Number 10. More than 100 rose for prayers at this meeting. This was the fourth visit in two months that Messrs. Moore and Remington had made here. Noonday prayer meetings were started and sponsored by the Y. M. C. A. that continued for several years. Laymen conducted meetings in two rural schools. All the churches had much larger attendance at the Wednesday evening prayer meetings, the number at the North church rising from an average of 40 to more than 150. As a result of this great awakening 109 joined North church in 1875. At the May communion 54 joined on confession of faith which up to that time was by far the largest to join at one communion service. 'The Lord,' said Mr. Jones in his anniversary sermon, 'richly blessed the assiduous labors of those lay brethren with many conversions and much healthful rooting and growth of christian [sic] character.'[56]

Source 2 on the Great Awakening—as Town historian Edward T. Fairbanks described it:

In 1875 came the notable wave of religious uplift which none who witnessed it will ever forget.

---

[55] It was F. O. Winslow.
[56] Stone, *North Congregational Church, St. Johnsbury, Vermont: 1825-1942*, 30-31.

The Great Awakening of 1875[57]

Under auspices of the State Committee of the Y. M. C. A., meetings were held February 6, 1875, at the Town Hall Sunday afternoon, and in the evening at the South Church. H. M. Moore of Boston and R. K. Remington of Fall River, laymen, were principal speakers. It was at once apparent that deep interest was awakened, and this continued so manifestly that three weeks later, these brethren, at our request, returned, accompanied by F. O. Winslow of Boston and S. E. Bridgman of Northampton. Sunday meetings were held at the Avenue House Hall, and at the South Church, and at the latter place Monday afternoon and evening; a thousand people were in attendance. On Tuesday forenoon the wheels of the scale factory were stopped, men crowded into the machine shop were the voice of prayer and song superseded the hum of machinery. In the evening there were 1200 people at the South Church and 140 rose to say that they had begun the Christian life. The interest continued, union meetings were held thrice a week in different churches, usually conducted by laymen, almost every one present taking some brief part. Half-hour noon meetings were begun, which continued several years. On the 27th of March, Moore, Remington, Winslow and Littlefield came again, on invitation; large assemblies met at the Avenue House Hall, at North and South Churches; also next day at the Universalist Church, which was filled, 'deep interest being manifest.' In the evening of Monday, March 28, there were 1400 people crowding the Academy Hall and passage-ways and 300 more in room No. 10; more than 100 rose for prayers. During the next six weeks there was a steady, quiet continuance of the revival spirit, which received a fresh impulse by the return once more, when urgently invited, of the Massachusetts brethren. This was on Sunday, the 8th of May. Neither North nor South Churches could contain the crowds that flocked to the evening meeting, and Academy Hall was again the place of assembly. On Monday, another gospel meeting was held at the Scale factory, and in the evening some

---

[57] The words "The Great Awakening of 1875" are an actual subheading in the text quoted here.

1500 were together again at the Academy, where, as so often before, large numbers gave expression of their interest or their purpose to live a Christian life.

These and similar scenes during the year following will be forever memorable in the history of our town. The whole atmosphere of the place seemed charged with religious feeling; no one questioned the immense reality of spiritual forces that were so distinctly transforming men's lives and lifting the standards of thought and conduct in the community. The religious life stood out as a manly thing to be manfully followed; the dominant note was not so much the old time solemnity, as the joy of opportunity, the cheer of the good news to every man. Everybody was singing the bright "Winnowed Hymns," and repeating cheer-inspiring verses from the Bible. Gospel meetings, so called, with a lay brother in the chair, were a popular attraction; there was no distinction of church or creed; all, as in apostolic times, were 'continuing daily with one accord in fellowship together and in prayers, with gladness and singleness of hear, praising God and having favor with all the people.' Like the friends from Massachusetts who had left their business to bring messages to us, laymen of this town went out in bands of two to five, holding gospel meetings not only in the school districts but in near or distant towns; the influence of the religious uplift here was extended for a hundred miles around, and left its permanent mark on this community."[58]

[Again from Fairbanks:] . . . not so much the old time solemnity, as the joy of opportunity, the cheer of the good news to every man.[59]

To get a better sense of the significance of these attendance figures (e.g., 1,700 at one meeting, 1,500 at another), the population of St. Johnsbury at this time was only about 5,000 people.[60]

---

[58] Edward T. Fairbanks, *The Town of St. Johnsbury VT.: A Review of One Hundred Twenty-five Years to the Anniversary Pageant 1912* (St. Johnsbury, Vermont: The Cowles Press, 1914), 316-17.
[59] Fairbanks, *The Town of St. Johnsbury*, 317.

Source 3 on the Great Awakening--as the Minutes of the Eightieth Annual Meeting of the General Conference of Vermont Ministers and Churches described it:

> Some of us come hither to-day with the persuasion that we are living in no ordinary time, that we have but lately heard and seen what neither tongue nor pen can adequately describe, and have tasted of that which is in our souls 'as honey in our mouth for sweetness.'
>
> In taking a survey of the whole state . . . many a spot, for years all too dark, has, during the past few months, been gloriously lightened. So general, especially throughout the eastern part of the state, has been either special religious interest or the hope of it, that the churches in their reports rarely mention anything else; hence it is obvious that this general report must be chiefly devoted to an account of these—in many places—remarkable religious awakenings. Between sixty and seventy churches, or one third of the whole number reporting, send tidings of revival interest, attended with conversions numbering in each church from six or eight to nearly two hundred.
>
> Caledonia Conference: The churches of Caledonia Conference have been visited with one of the most remarkable and thorough religious awakenings known in modern or indeed any time. Every church has been blest, and all but one or two have shared largely in the refreshing, . . . St. Johnsbury has been the center, and to a great extent the radiating point, of the work, . . . also for much of the north-eastern portion of the state. . . . At the May (1874) meeting of the Caledonia Association . . . the subject of revival effort was proposed and adopted as the topic for the meetings of the autumn. . . . After the plan of the canvass of the Committee of the Young Men's Christian Association and the Vermont churches was matured . . . that God's blessing might accompany the Gospel workers . . .

---

[60] The population of the township of St. Johnsbury, Vermont, was 4,665 in 1870, and 5,800 in 1880. See: *The Encyclopaedia Britannica: A Dictionary of Arts, Sciences, and General Literature,* 9th ed.—popular reprint, Volume XXI (New York: Henry G. Allen, 1888), 176; s.v. "St. Johnsbury."

December . . . an interest, slight . . . in connection with the labors of Rev. Mr. Marsh of the Baptist church and of Rev. Mr. DeWitt, an evangelist . . . With the week of prayer the five evangelical churches of the village, *viz*: North and South Congregational, Baptist, Methodist and Free Baptist, with remarkable concord began to hold union meetings twice weekly . . . a centering of hope in the approaching Gospel meetings . . . Saturday evening, February 6, these meetings began. They were conducted by Messrs. Davis of Burlington, Cook of Ludlow, and Moore and Remington of Massachusetts, assisted by others. During the Sabbath . . . thirty or forty rose for prayers . . . A few of these were students in the Academy, and Monday morning, as members of the school, about two hundred and twenty-five in number, came together for the usual devotions, the chapel was profoundly silent; . . . the day services of Monday were largely devoted to prayer. . . . That evening ninety were present at the inquiry meeting, and fully a hundred, including many business men, requested prayers at the general meeting following. The developments of the next day and evening were hardly less impressive. New converts began to testify . . . At one of these meetings . . . Bill Robinson . . . that night . . . told how the Lord had visited him in his cell. . . . The subject of religion was the all-absorbing topic of conversation. Besides the regular Wednesday and Saturday evening prayer meetings there were two union meetings weekly and a young converts meeting in each church on Friday evening. One evening a week was always given to rest. About the middle of February Russell Sturgis Jr., President of the Young Men's Christian Association of Boston, visited St. Johnsbury and conducted meetings for two or three days. He addressed himself chiefly to Christians and incited them. . . . A few words from him to the students of the academy were very effective. . . . Twice afterwards, before May 1st, and once since, the 'Massachusetts brethren,' as they were familiarly called . . . came and held a series of two or three days' meetings. The Lord greatly blessed their labors, especially to business men. . . . The results are probably the conversion of more than five hundred souls at St. Johnsbury Plain and immediate vicinity. Of these fully one hundred and twenty were members of the academy, three fourths of whom had their homes elsewhere.

On the first Sabbath of May or earlier, nearly two hundred and fifty persons were received into the five churches which united in the work, about one hundred and forty of them coming to the North and South Congregational churches. Nearly if not quite as many more will be hereafter received to church membership. This work had not long continued at St. Johnsbury before the surrounding towns began to feel its influence. . . . Accordingly, in the latter part of February and March Gospel meetings, conducted chiefly by Mr. J. T. Quimby of Thetford, assisted by helpers from St. Johnsbury, were held in East Burke, West Concord, Danville, Lyndon, East St. Johnsbury, Lyndonville, Passumpsic and West Burke. Later, nearly every other town and village in the county has had one or more series of such meetings, conducted generally by brethren from St. Johnsbury. . . . the . . . Gospel meetings . . . The church at St. Johnsbury Center . . is revived and encouraged by interest during the spring. The pastor at St. Johnsbury East writes that probably fifty have recently endulged [sic] Christian hope in that parish and many others are interested. The church in Danville reports rather a low state of religious feeling till the Gospel meetings March 1st, . . . June 1st thirty-eight united with the church . . . There have more than one hundred conversions in the town. Barnet reports sixty hopeful conversions . . . The church at McIndoes received fifteen by profession . . . More than usual interest prevailed before the Gospel meetings. These were blest to the conversion of about fifty souls. . . . Just across the Connecticut river from McIndoes is Monroe, N. H.; a Congregational church of sixteen members was organized in August . . . under the care of Rev. J. L. Litch, the acting pastor. . . . (This church was received to the Caledonia Conference at the June meeting, . . . Lyndon and Lyndonville have both been revived and the interest continues. . . . Lamoille Conference: . . . Cambridge . . . lay work of helpers from Johnson and St. Johnsbury resulted in some conversions. . . . Johnson was visited by Gospel workers in April, . . . Orange Conference: . . . The church in Newbury has had a refreshing revival, chiefly the result of Gospel meetings. Sixty conversions are reported. The young men of the church are holding meetings in the out-districts. . . . At Strafford, the week of prayer left much tenderness of feeling, and Gospel meetings held later . . .

resulted in several conversions. . . . Orleans Conference: . . . The Gospel meetings have been greatly blessed. Barton, Glover and Newport have enjoyed revivals of marked power, resulting in from forty to sixty or more conversions in each place. . . . 'The Gospel meetings began here April 1st and continued four days. . . . Many have been born again, . . . At Greensboro, . . . the state of religion was low . . . but a change has since taken place, mainly through the influence of workers from St. Johnsbury. . . . Windham Conference: . . . the Gospel meetings . . . Windsor Conference: . . . the Gospel meetings were about the middle of March. . . . Hartford reports decided religious interest at the beginning of the year 1875, which was increased by the labors of the Gospel workers the last of January. Thirty to forty indulge hope of the new birth. At West Hartford there evidently was an increase of religious interest among the young people, for several months before the meetings held by the Young Men's Christian Association in January. . . . The Gospel meetings held by the young men called out a very general interest, when more than forty came forward as enquirers. . . . Ludlow has experienced a wide-spread awakening in connection with the Gospel meetings . . . There have been about one hundred professed conversions, . . . The annual convention of the Young Men's Christian Associations and churches in November and the Gospel meetings in the spring generally promoted the interest.' . . . Pomfret reports a successful Gospel meeting, resulting in conversions . . . The church in Royalton . . . The work was greatly accelerated by the Gospel meetings in March. . . . Sharon reports interest, dating from the Gospel meetings, . . . Windsor reports a rising tide in the church. Gospel meetings were quickening to Christians.[61]

---

[61] *Minutes of the Eightieth Annual Meeting of the General Convention of Congregational Ministers and Churches of Vermont, Held at Bennington, June, 1875. Fifty-Seventh Annual Report of the Vermont Domestic Missionary Society, and Fifty-Fifth Annual Report of the Vermont Education Society* (Montpelier: J. & J. M. Poland, Steam Printers, 1875).
http://books.google.com/books?id=ffwQAAAAIAAJ&pg=RA4-PA30&dq=johnsbury+Russell+Sturgis#PRA4-PA3,M1
"Report on the State of the Churches" [pp. 27-38]
http://books.google.com/books?id=ffwQAAAAIAAJ&pg=RA4-

Source 4 on the Great Awakening—as described by a participating Unitarian Universalist Church:

> The St. Johnsbury Church participated in the "Great Awakening" of 1875. On March 28 the church was filled, "deep interest being manifest."[62]

Source 5 on the Great Awakening--as YMCA reports described it:

Geo. E. Davis, Chairman of the Vermont Committee, speaking at the 1875 North American YMCA Convention on the topic of "Accounts of Association Work by Workers," stated:

> In Vermont we find it necessary, in leading young men to Christ, to bring them first to the House of God. We are astonished a few months ago when looking at the statistics to find how few Christian young men there were in Vermont. Last year the great question was whether we were to have a Convention at all. We decided there was not enough of life— not enough of money to have one. I visited some of the Massachusetts brethren, Messrs. Littlefield, Remington, and others. They said: 'You are to have a Convention.' And they came with loving hearts and pulled us out of the mire, and enabled us to see at Norwich one third of the population of the town attending the meetings of the Convention. A State Committee was appointed and took counsel with these experienced brethren. During the winter we held a canvass. 177 days were spent in 57 towns, besides supplementary meetings held afterward at several points. Often we had two bands of workers carrying on meetings at the same time in different parts of the State, and it was all the work of volunteers. We went to the towns by the invitation of the pastors and people; there have been conversions in all but 4 of the 57 towns. I suppose it is perfectly safe to say that from 2,300 to 3,500

PA30&dq=johnsbury+Russell+Sturgis#PRA4-PA27,M1 [= p. 27; accessed 11/19/07])

[62] "History of the Unitarian Universalist Church of Saint Johnsbury" http://stevefinner.org/UUChurch/OurChurch/History.htm.

conversions have been reported in the towns visited, and the work is still going on to day in many places. The work, especially in St. Johnsbury, has exceeded what I ever saw in my life. The five churches there came heartily into the work, and probably 1,500 souls have been converted, and among them 45 of the leading business men of the place. The great call among us is for efforts to reach young men. In towns and villages of 600 inhabitants you will find only one Church of 60 members, and 50 of these old people, with not more than one or two young men. You must not infer from this that there are but few young men in Vermont,--the truth is, we have hitherto been doing nothing to save them.[63]

The Relevance of the "Great Awakening" of 1875 in St. Johnsbury to
Dr. Bob's "Excellent Training" in the "Good Book" As a Youngster

The St. Johnsbury awakening took place in 1875. But by all accounts, it continued in progress and impact for many years thereafter.

For example, the work of Dwight L. Moody and his partner Ira Sankey in Vermont is briefly described by Sankey himself:

> In 1867, when I was twenty-seven years old, a branch of the Young Men's Christian Association was organized in Newcastle, of which I was at that time elected secretary and later president. . . In 1870, with two or three others, I was appointed a delegate to the International Convention of the Association, to be held at Indianapolis that year. For several years I had read in the religious press about Mr. Moody, and I was therefore pleased when I learned that he would be at the convention, being a delegate from the Chicago Association. . . . At the conclusion of the meeting, Mr. McMillan said to me: "Let me introduce you to Mr. Moody." . . . [Moody asked me] to come to Chicago and help me in my work." . . . We thus commenced work together in Chicago in the early part of 1871,

---

[63] *Proceedings of the Twentieth Annual Convention of the Young Men's Christian Associations of the United States and British Provinces, Held at Richmond, VA., May 26-30, 1875* (New York: Published by the Executive Committee, 1875), 90, 91.

singing and praying with the sick, speaking and singing at the daily noon prayer-meetings, and other work, until Mr. Moody's church was destroyed in the Chicago fire. . . . Speaking of the fire to a friend some time later, Mr. Moody remarked: "All I saved was my Bible, my family, and my reputation." In June, 1873, we sailed for England. . .

After our return to America, the first meeting held was at Northfield [Massachusetts], on the 9th of September, 1875. . . . Our next large meetings were held in Chicago during the fall of 1876, in a large Tabernacle erected for the occasion by John V. Farwell. It was capable of seating more than eight thousand. . . . Then, for six months we conducted meetings in Boston. On an average, three meetings a day were held, in a large temporary building. . . Here also we had the heart cooperation of many prominent ministers and laymen, among whom Dr. A.J. Gordon, Dr. Joseph Cook, Phillips Brooks, and Henry Moore may be mentioned. . . ."[64]

On November 3, 1877, *The New York Times* published this article:

> REVIVALS IN NEW-ENGLAND.
> MANCHESTER, N.H., Nov 2—The Moody and Sankey campaign in Vermont closed last night, and was very successful at every point. At Burlington they had large audiences three and four times each day. During the past month the churches have been strengthened and revived, and large numbers from all classes of citizens have been converted. . . . Mr. Merhouse [sic[65]], assisted by Mr. Sankey during the past week, has been at work in St. Johnsbury. They have had large audiences, and the work promises well."[66]

Another source sheds further light on the Moody work in Vermont:

> The first building erected on the cyclorama site was a large brick structure known as the Moody Sankey Tabernacle, which

---

[64] This material has been quoted from *Sankey's Story of His Own Life*. Christian Biography Resources. Wholesome Words. www.wholesomwords.org.
[65] This was the famous English evangelist, Henry (Harry) Moorhouse.
[66] *The New York Times*. Published: November 3, 1877.

was dedicated on January 25, 1877, and was capable of seating six thousand people. A season of daily revival meetings began that continued without interruption from the beginning of February to the end of May 1877. The meeting was attended by an overflow crowd, and special sessions had to be held at the Clarendon Street Baptist Church. Dwight L. Moody preached and Ira D. Sankey sang, supported by a vast choir under the direction of Dr. Eben Tourjee. . . . Although the revival meetings were visited by huge numbers, the enterprise did not do well financially. . . . Following their Boston sojourn, Messr. [sic] Moody and Sankey transferred their evangelizing activities to Burlington, Vermont, and the vacant Tabernacle was used for a while by the Boston YMCA for Sunday services.[67]

In fact, the continuation of the "Great Awakening" of 1875 in St. Johnsbury and other Vermont areas, was not merely confined to revivals led by YMCA lay people or by Moody's people, but was also marked by a new outreach for conversions and new buildings by the churches. Not necessarily involving revivals, but rather ministries and concerns of the churches themselves—particularly as manifested in Dr. Bob's North Congregational Church. However, many of the so-called announced and pronounced "weaknesses" among the churches, teachers, parents, and attendance records were not only addressed but overcome. The weaknesses were not necessarily in St. Johnsbury where the churches were strong; but the revival not only spurred St. Johnsbury people to unite in prayer, Gospel meetings, and conversions; it produced salutary enthusiasm and changes for the better.

The lessons for how to live a victorious Christian life seemed definitely to have been learned and applied in the Smith family itself—not only by the parents, but also in the very activities that both they and their son Bob demonstrated great participation.

Let's look in detail at the Smith family. Here we were aided by the research and report of the church archivist, Mr. Swartz, who wrote us: North Congregational Church records first listed Walter P. Smith (Dr.

---

[67] "Adventures in Cybersound: The Boston Cyclorama::
http://www.acmi.net.au/aic/CYCLORAMA_BOSTON.html ; accessed 11/22/07.

Bob's father) and Susan Smith (Dr. Bob's mother) in *Year Book* 1878. Young Bob was born in 1879. Church records show Robert H Smith (Dr. Bob) born at 20 Summer Street [his birthplace and boyhood home].[68] Bob is first listed in the *Year Book* 1880 and also as having attended Sunday School.

Stone's history of North Congregational Church, St. Johnsbury, reported: (1) In February, 1877, the church began to talk about building a new church. A building committee was then appointed with Governor Horace Fairbanks as chairman.[69] (1) "There has been an increase the past year—1878—over last year in the attendance at the morning service, Sunday School, the Sunday evening service and the Wednesday evening prayer meetings."[70] (2) "The Christian Endeavor Society which started in 1887 has continued throughout the years as the leading young people's organization."[71] (3) Then, giving 1889 as just one year's of the church's health, it reported that, for a period of eight years, "the pastor and people were 'joyfully happy and nobly useful.'"[72] (4) It went on to say that: Contributions were high. Attendance was high. (5) There were YMCA lecture courses.[73] "The church was well organized from the youngest to the oldest." (6) The Sunday School had a membership of 330 and the average attendance at the week day prayer meeting was 80. "The monthly concerts on a Sunday evening filled the church. Its program was always full of interest to young and old. Recitations by individuals and classes, vocal and instrumental music featured the program which always included a talk by the superintendent."[74] "The monthly Sunday School concerts have been well attended and are increasing in numbers and interest. They now have an average attendance of 290 and the part they are to play by their beautiful and holy sons and lisping hymns of praise, their Scripture recitations and instructive addresses and prayers, can never

---

[68] Today, Dr. Bob's birthplace and boyhood home is numbered as 297 Summer Street. The authors were told during our October 2007 visit to St. Johnsbury that at least some of the streets in St. Johnsbury (including Summer Street) had been renumbered.
[69] Stone, *The North Congregational Church*, 31.
[70] Stone, *The North Congregational Church*, 27.
[71] Stone, *The North Congregational Church*, 69-70.
[72] Stone, *The North Congregational Church*, 39.
[73] Stone, *The North Congregational Church*, 38.
[74] Stone, *The North Congregational Church*, 62.

be duly estimated in time. The library has been entirely remodeled."[75] "Through many of the years under Col. Fairbanks' leadership teachers' meetings were held each week after the Wednesday evening prayer meeting."[76]

We will have much more to say about all these items—and particularly about a similar impact through the Smith family's activity at St. Johnsbury Academy during the same bracketed period from 1875 to 1898 in which latter year Dr. Bob graduated.

---

[75] Stone, *The North Congregational Church*, 60.
[76] Stone, *The North Congregational Church*, 63.

"Your Heavenly Father will never let you down!"
Alcoholics Anonymous, 4th ed., p. 181

2
The Challenge and Direction of the Dr. Bob Resource Volumes

This title, *Dr. Bob of Alcoholics Anonymous,* is a companion to the 20 "resource binders" comprising the historical references and papers we have assembled so far about Dr. Bob, his birthplace and boyhood home, and his youth and religious training in St. Johnsbury, Vermont. The binders contain, document, and report on resources showing the many different and varied influences on his boyhood days in the historical Vermont village. The binders present an inviting body of studies about St. Johnsbury, and about Dr. Bob and his family. They suggest the value to visitors of actually traveling to St. Johnsbury and viewing the home in which Dr. Bob was born and raised, the town, and historical resources being assembled and made publicly available at North Congregational Church, St. Johnsbury. This title will give you a picture of what is in store for you as a visitor to St. Johnsbury, as well as of what you will find in the "resource binders," the boyhood home, my core library at North Congregational Church, and the many archives and resources in the town. Also, what you can learn about Dr. Bob's "excellent training" in the Bible as a youngster in St. Johnsbury. For you will find that, in those years of Bob's youth, St. Johnsbury was truly alive with religious fervor, Christian leaders, and role models. This was at the time of Dr. Bob's birth and boyhood years. All factors appeared to leave a lasting impression with A.A.'s cofounder Robert Holbrook Smith, M.D.—the cofounder whom we have chosen to call "Dr. Bob."

Our Focus:
The Creator's Role in Dr. Bob's Life and in Early A.A.

Our companion "resource binders," and the core library at North Congregational Church, contain a large body of relevant, root evidence. They cover a wide variety of subjects. Subjects directly and indirectly connected with or related to the years that Robert Holbrook Smith (A.A.'s Dr. Bob) spent from his birth at the family home in St. Johnsbury, Vermont, in 1879, to his graduation from St. Johnsbury Academy in 1898. They will also show a visitor to St. Johnsbury the excitement that lies in wait for those who want to know just what Dr. Bob learned there, where he learned it, and from which people, institutions, and agencies he learned the many principles and practices he brought with him to Akron and inculcated in the original, pioneer A.A. group and program starting in 1935.

The Facts All Center on Comments of, by, and about Dr. Bob

Though it may appear otherwise, our companion resource volumes deal primarily with two correlated bodies of facts: (1) facts about the language Dr. Bob used when speaking about the original, pioneer Akron spiritual recovery program, and (2) facts about the principles, practices, and beliefs he acquired as a youngster in St. Johnsbury. And, of course, the conclusions that can be reached by examining and comparing the following two bodies of facts.

The language Dr. Bob used in speaking about Akron A.A.: Our first group of facts has to do with the easily understood language Dr. Bob used when describing, explaining, and instructing on the program of the early A.A. Christian Fellowship of pioneer AAs in Akron. He told Akron AAs about the Creator and called Him his Heavenly Father.[77] He told them about the Bible and called it the Good Book.[78] He led them in prayer and "old fashioned prayer meetings."[79] He read, recommended, and circulated to pioneer AAs and their families books about the Bible, Jesus Christ, prayer, Quiet Time, and healing.[80] He and his wife Anne led them in Quiet Times.[81] Both Bob and his wife

---

[77] *Alcoholics Anonymous*, 4th ed. (NY: Alcoholics Anonymous World Services, Inc., 2001), 181.
[78] *The Co-Founders of Alcoholics Anonymous and The Last Talks of A.A.'s Co-founders* (NY: Alcoholics Anonymous World Services, Inc., 1972, 1975), 13-14.
[79] *DR. BOB and the Good* Oldtimers (NY: Alcoholics Anonymous World Services, Inc., 1980), 101.
[80] Dick B., *Dr. Bob and His Library*, 3rd ed. (Kihei, HI: Paradise Research Publications, Inc., 1998).
[81] Bob Smith and Sue Smith Windows, *Children of the Healer* (MN: Hazelden, 1994), 42-43.

individually studied the Bible, Christian devotionals, and Christian literature.[82] Bob led the pioneers in "surrenders" where they were required to accept Jesus Christ as their personal Lord and Saviour.[83] He called their gatherings Christian Fellowship meetings.[84] He summarized his views on A.A.'s subsequent developments by stating that A.A.'s basic ideas came from the Bible.[85] Later, he pointed out that the Steps, when simmered to their essence, amounted to "love and service"—the watchwords he had learned as a youngster in the Christian Endeavor Society in St. Johnsbury, Vermont.[86]

His "excellent training" in the "Good Book" and the many Christian influences in his youth in St. Johnsbury that appear directly connected to the Akron program he developed with Bill W. and then led in Akron with such great success. This second group of facts concerns the influences that could have produced, and very probably did produce, the language he used in formulating and discussing the Akron A.A. spiritual program of recovery: Influences emanating from the Town of St. Johnsbury itself; its famous Fairbanks family; Dr. Bob's own family; his North Congregational Church; his Sunday school; his Christian Endeavor Society; the state and local YMCA and its town-wide hot revivals, evangelism, conversions, and Gospel meetings; and his matriculation at St. Johnsbury Academy and attendance at the Academy's Daily Chapel, lectures, and school curricula. The significant dates involved in studying the second group of facts are these: The starting date is 1875 (the beginning of the "Great Awakening" in St. Johnsbury). The ending date is 1898 (the year Dr. Bob graduated from St. Johnsbury Academy).

---

[82] Dick B., *The Books Early AAs Read for Spiritual Growth,* 7th ed. (Kihei, HI: Paradise Research Publications, Inc.)

[83] Dick B., *Real Twelve Step Fellowship History: The Old School A.A. You May Not Know* (Kihei, HI: Paradise Research Publications, Inc., 2006), 9.

[84] The "Christian Fellowship" description is validated by a statement Dr. Bob's daughter Sue Smith Windows gave to me in an interview at her home in Akron. Also in two different hand-written statements by A.A. pioneer Bob Evans—one written by him to Lois Wilson on a Four Absolutes pamphlet; the other written by him on a paper addressed to Sue Smith Windows. It is also set forth in *DR. BOB and the Good Oldtimers* (See quote below).

[85] *The Co-founders,* 14.

[86] Dick B., *The James Club and the Original A.A. Program's Absolute Essentials,* 4th ed. (Kihei, HI: Paradise Research Publications, Inc., 2005), 154-55; *The Co-founders,* 9..

First, the Documented Remarks Concerning Dr. Bob Himself

Several important historical and biographical titles and pamphlets provide ample source material quoting or describing what Dr. Bob actually said and did in the earliest A.A. days as to "spiritual" matters—matters dealing with the Creator, Jesus Christ, the Bible, prayer, Christian literature, Quiet Hour, and Christian principles for living. These important items are part of the Dr. Bob Core Library at North Congregational Church in St. Johnsbury. The authoritative materials are: (1) The A.A. "Conference Approved" biography of Dr. Bob whose title is *DR. BOB and the Good Oldtimers* (NY: Alcoholics Anonymous World Services, Inc., 1980). (2) The A.A. Co-founders pamphlet containing the remarks of Dr. Bob at his last major talk to AAs in December, 1948, at Detroit, Michigan—published in A.A. "Conference Approved" literature. This pamphlet combines *The Co-Founders of Alcoholics Anonymous* and *The Last Talks of A.A.'s Co-founders* (NY: Alcoholics Anonymous World Services, Inc., 1972, 1975). (3) *RHS: Co-founder of Alcoholics Anonymous our beloved DR. BOB* (NY: AA Grapevine, Inc., 1951). (4) Several remarks from the earliest AAs and from Dr. Bob's children, as cited in the footnotes accompanying the quoted remarks. (5) Dr. Bob's personal story published in each of the four editions of A.A.'s basic text. This personal story, as well as the remarks of A.A. cofounder Bill W. and A.A. Number Three Bill Dotson, can be found in *Alcoholics Anonymous*, 4th ed. (NY: Alcoholics Anonymous World Services, Inc., 2001), 171-81, 191.

Statements of, by, or about Dr. Bob concerning the Akron A.A. fellowship he led:

- Dr. Bob asked, "Do you believe in God, young fella?" Clarence Snyder [the newcomer] asked, "What does that have to do with it?" "Everything," Dr. Bob said. Clarence replied, "I guess I do." Dr. Bob insisted, "Guess, nothing! Either you do or you don't"[87]

---

[87] *DR. BOB*, 144.

- When the Clarence Snyder reply was, "I do," Dr. Bob then said, "Now we're getting some place. All right, get out of bed and on your knees. We're going to pray."[88]

- Said the biography of A.A. pioneer Clarence Snyder, to whom the foregoing remarks were addressed: "What a sight to behold. Both men, on their knees, by the side of the hospital bed in an attitude of prayer. Doc uttered some sort of a prayer, pausing every few words so that Clarence had the time to repeat them. . . . he did remember its being something like this: 'Jesus! This is Clarence Snyder. He's a drunk. Clarence! This is Jesus. Ask Him to come into your life. Ask him to remove your drinking problem, and pray that He manage your life because you are unable to manage it yourself'."[89]

- Said the biography of Clarence Snyder, at a later point when he made his "real surrender" at the home of T. Henry Williams of Akron: "T. Henry, Doc, and a couple of other Oxford Group members went into T. Henry's bedroom. They all, including Clarence, who by now was used to this kneeling, got down on their knees in an attitude of prayer. They all placed their hands on Clarence, and then proceeded to pray. These people introduced Clarence to Jesus as his Lord and Saviour. They explained to Clarence that this was First Century Christianity. Then they prayed for a healing and removal of Clarence's sin, especially his alcoholism."[90]

- A recent biography of A.A.'s famous Dr. William D. Silkworth (who wrote the Doctor's Opinion at the beginning of A.A.'s basic text) stated this: "Several sources, including Norman Vincent Peale in his book *The Positive Power of Jesus Christ*, agree that it was Silkworth who used the term 'Great Physician' to explain the need in recovery for a relationship

---

[88] *DR. BOB*, 144.
[89] Mitchell K., *How It Worked: The Story of Clarence H. Snyder and the Early Days of Alcoholics Anonymous in Cleveland, Ohio* (NY: Washingtonville, Big Book Study Group, 1991), [ISBN 0-9664382-0-5], 58.
[90] Mitchell K., *How It Worked*, 70; Dick B., *That Amazing Grace: The Role of Clarence and Grace S. in Alcoholics Anonymous* (San Rafael, CA: Paradise Research Publications, 1996).

with Jesus Christ. If true, this reference to Jesus has all but been eliminated from the Alcoholics Anonymous History. In the formation of A.A., Wilson initially insisted on references to God and Jesus, as well as the Great Physician. As the fellowship grew, however, other members persuaded Bill that a purely Christian format would alienate many, keeping potential members away from joining the group."[91]

- Clarence Snyder related: "If someone asked him [Dr. Bob] a question about the program, his usual response was: 'What does it say in the Good Book?'"[92]

- Dr. Bob said, "When we started in on Bill D., we had no Twelve Steps, either; we had no Traditions. But we were convinced that the answer to our problems was in the Good Book."[93]

- He said, "I'm somewhat allergic to work, but I felt that I should continue to increase my familiarity with the Good Book. . . "[94]

- He also said, "To some of us older ones, the parts we found absolutely essential were the Sermon on the Mount, the thirteenth chapter of First Corinthians, and the Book of James."[95]

- He reminded his listeners, "I had refreshed my memory of the Good Book, and I had had excellent training in that as a youngster."[96]

- He also revealed, "It wasn't until 1938 that the teachings and efforts and studied that had been going on were crystallized in the form of the Twelve Steps. . . . I didn't write the Twelve

---

[91] Dale Mitchel, *Silkworth: The Little Doctor Who Loved Drunks* (Center City, MN: Hazelden, 2002), 50.
[92] *DR. BOB*, 144.
[93] *The Co-founders of Alcoholics Anonymous: Biographical sketches: Their last major talks* (NY: Alcoholics Anonymous World Services, Inc., 1972, 1975), 13.
[94] *Co-founders*, 13.
[95] *Co-founders*, 13.
[96] *Co-founders*, 11-12.

Steps. I had nothing to do with the writing of them. . . . We already had the basic ideas, though not in terse and tangible form. We got them, as I said, as a result of our study of the Good Book."[97]

- [Dr. Bob said in his last talk that the Twelve Steps:] "when simmered down. . . . resolve themselves into the words 'love' and 'service'."[98] And that phrase "love and service" was in common usage in the Christian Endeavor Society of his youth.[99]

- Dr. Bob commented, "I'm talking about the attitude of each and every one of us toward our Heavenly Father. Christ said, 'Of Myself, I am nothing—My strength cometh from My Father in heaven.' . . . . We had no humility, no sense of having received anything through the grace of our Heavenly Father."[100]

- His daughter, Sue Smith Windows, told me in a personal interview, "My dad called every meeting of the early AAs a Christian Fellowship."[101]

- [Bill Wilson recounted this story:] "We were actually afraid that all sorts of so-called undesirable people might show up—not just 'pure alcoholics,' but people with 'complications.' What about our reputation? We thought, mistakenly, that we were in a position to pick and choose. . . . For example, a fellow came to Dr. Bob and said, 'I'm an alcoholic; here is my history. But I also have this other 'complication.' Can I join A.A.?" Bob threw it out to all the other deacons, while the poor guy waited. Finally, there was some kind of hearing on it among the self-appointed elders.

---

[97] *Co-founders*, 14.
[98] *DR. BOB*, 77.
[99] Francis E. Clark, *Christian Endeavor in All Lands: A Record of Twenty-Five Years of Progress* (Boston, MA: The United Christian Endeavor Society, 1906), 326.
[100] *Co-founders*, 19.
[101] See Footnote 1.

"I remember how perfectly Bob put it to them. He reminded us that most of us were practicing Christians. The he asked, 'What would the Master have thought? Would he have kept this man away?" He had them cold! The man came in, was a prodigious worker, and was one of our most respected people."[102]

- [Dr. Bob said:] "But when we take time to find out some of the spiritual laws, and familiarize ourselves with them, and put them into practice, then we do get happiness and peace of mind. I feel extremely fortunate and thankful that our Heavenly Father has let me enjoy them."[103]

- [Dr. Bob wrote:] "From childhood through high school I was more or less forced to go to church, Sunday School and evening service. Monday night Christian Endeavor and sometimes to Wednesday evening prayer meeting."[104] [Apparently, Dr. Bob experienced a long hiatus from these disciplines during his most of his college and drinking years; but recent research shows that, when he renewed his spiritual quest on joining the Oxford Group people and others about 1933, he took the following very different position:

- (1) [Dr. Bob's son "Smitty" wrote:] "Both my dad and my mom were very spiritual people. Dad had read the Bible from cover to cover several times."[105]

- (2) Dr. Bob observed a Quiet Time three times a day, with Bible study, prayer, and seeking God's guidance. His church

---

[102] Co-founders, 30. See also the typical approach from Dr. Bob's Christian Endeavor youth—Charles M. Sheldon, *In His Steps* (NJ: Fleming H. Revell Company, Spire Books, 1963). I found a copy of this book in Dr. Bob's library. And the famous pastor and Christian Endeavor author asked over and over, "What would Jesus do?"--pp. 16, 17, 21, 28, 33, 35, 36, 49, 53, 62, 105-08, 110, 121, 123, 176, 184, 186, 188. On the liquor question, Sheldon asked at page 55: "Would the Master preach and act against the saloon if He lived today? How would He preach and act? What would Jesus do?" In short, Dr. Bob had heard this test applied before.
[103] *Co-founders*, 19-20.
[104] *Alcoholics Anonymous*, 4th ed. (NY: Alcoholics Anonymous World Services, Inc., 2001), 172.
[105] Bob Smith and Sue Smith Windows, *Children of the Healer: The Story of Dr. Bob's Kids* (MN: Hazelden, 1992), 111.

attendance resumed with far more regularity and intensity than his own and other brief statements might indicate. Thus, he belonged to and attended St. Luke's Protestant Episcopal Church in Akron; Church of Our Saviour Protestant Episcopal Church in Akron; joined with his wife Anne as a charter member of Westminster United Presbyterian Church in Akron from June 3, 1936 to April 3, 1942; and, shortly before his death, became a communicant at St. Paul's Protestant Episcopal Church located on the Firestone family's former property in Akron.[106]

- (3) Elgie R. recalled, "Doc told me that when he had an operation and wasn't sure, he would pray before he started." He said, "When I operated under those conditions, I never made a move that wasn't right. . . . Whenever he got stuck about something, he always prayed about it. . . ."[107]

- (4) Bill Wilson said, "He prayed, not only for his own understanding, but for different groups of people who requested him to pray for them. . . . I was always glad to think that I was included in those prayers. . . . Bob was far ahead of me in that sort of activity. I was always rushing around talking and organizing and 'teaching spiritual kindergarten'."[108]

- (5) A.A. historian Nan Robertson wrote: "Beginning in 1935, Dr. Bob quickly became an extraordinarily effective worker with active alcoholics. He was tough. He was inflexible. He told his prospects: 'Do you want to surrender to God. Take it or leave it.' Soon, carloads of drunks were coming to Akron from as far away as Cleveland to meet in his house. Recently, Young Bob tried to explain why his father had been so successful at 'fixing' drunks: . . . 'He knew that a drunk coming out of an alcoholic haze would be absolutely overwhelmed by anything

---

[106] Dick B., *Dr. Bob and His Library*, 3rd ed. (Kihei, HI: Paradise Research Publications, Inc., 1998), 114-16.
[107] *DR. BOB*, 314.
[108] *DR. BOB*, 315.

but a straightforward program that anyone could understand.' . . . The doctor was authoritative, and he was impressive."[109]

- (6) Bill Wilson said, "In this human laboratory, he [Dr. Bob] has proved that any alcoholic, not too mentally defective, can recover if he so desires. The possible recovery among such cases has suddenly been lifted from almost nil to at least 50 percent, which, quite aside from its social implications, is a medical result of the first magnitude. Though, as a means of our recovery, we all engage in the work, Dr. Smith has had more experience and has obtained better results than anyone else."[110]

- (7) Years later, Bill Wilson added, ". . . [Dr. Bob] had treated 5,000 drunks at St. Thomas Hospital in Akron. His spiritual example was a powerful influence, and he never charged a cent for his medical care. So Dr. Bob became the prince of all twelfth steppers. Perhaps nobody will ever do such a job again."[111]

- (8) Bill and Bob on the stage together in Los Angeles: "In 1943, Bill and Bob were on the platform together at the Shrine Auditorium in Los Angeles. 4,500 AAs and their families were present. Bill spoke about Divine Aid and the religious element in A.A. He talked of the importance of prayer and said that when he prayed, he felt released. Then came Dr. Bob's turn. The entire audience rose to its feet in respect. And, with his usual style of brevity, Dr. Bob simply stressed the importance of cultivating the habit of prayer. In closing, he urged the audience to study the Bible. And he sat down."[112]

- Dr. Bob's A.A. "Conference Approved" biography stated: "Though settled in Akron, Dr. Bob also had an abiding love for his native Vermont and made an annual trip to visit family and

---

[109] Nan Robertson, *Getting Better Inside Alcoholics Anonymous* (NY: Fawcett Crest, 1988), 48.
[110] *DR. BOB, 174.*
[111] *Co-founders,* 27.
[112] Dick B., *The Conversion of Bill W.* (Kihei, HI: Paradise Research Publications, Inc., 2006), 191-92.

friends there. While in Vermont, Doc also went to the regular meetings of the Fellowship Group in St. Johnsbury, and Ed G. recalled that Dr. Bob spoke at the group's first anniversary. Eleanor E. wrote that, while she was a college student in Vermont, she was invited by Dr. Bob's niece to attend a meeting in 1946 in Burlington [Vermont], where Dr. Bob and another man would tell some 'interesting stories' at an A.A. meeting."[113]

- Dr. Bob's daughter, "Sue also remembered the quiet time in the mornings—how they sat around reading from the Bible. Later, they also used *The Upper Room,* a Methodist publication that provided a daily inspirational message, interdenominational in its approach."[114]

- "Young Smitty was aware of the early-morning prayers and quiet time, but he didn't attend."[115]

- Bill Wilson said of his own days of living with Dr. Bob and Anne Smith, "Each morning, there was a devotion. . . After a long silence, in which they awaited inspiration and guidance, Anne would read from the Bible. 'James was our favorite. . . Reading from her chair in the corner, she would softly conclude, 'Faith without works is dead'."[116]

- Dr. Bob's daughter clearly recalled for me [Dick B.], in a personal phone conversation she had with me, that she and her brother "Smitty" were regular attenders at the Church of Our Saviour in the Akron area, that she couldn't verify her dad's membership there, but that he probably was because "We got to the Church of Our Saviour Sunday School somehow."[117]

- Henrietta Dotson, wife of A.A. Number Three, spoke of the required "surrenders." She said, "You know, at first, they made all theses new men surrender. Out at T. Henry Williams' where

---

[113] *DR. BOB,* 300.
[114] *DR. BOB,* 71.
[115] *DR. BOB,* 72.
[116] *DR. BOB,* 71.
[117] Dick B., *Dr. Bob and His Library,* 115.

they met, Dr. Bob would take them upstairs and make them say they would surrender themselves to God."[118]

- Following the theme of several hundred newspapers in A.A.'s early days, the *Cleveland Plain Dealer* reported:] "The basic point about Alcoholics Anonymous is that it is a fellowship of 'cured' alcoholics. And that both old-line medicine and modern psychiatry had agreed on the one point that no alcoholic could be cured. Repeat the astounding fact: These are cured. They have cured each other. They have done it by adopting with each other's aid, what they call a 'spiritual way of life'."[119]

- Bill Wilson specifically stated, "Henrietta [Dotson, wife of A.A. Number Three Bill Dotson], the Lord has been so wonderful to me, curing me of this terrible disease, that I just want to keep talking about it and telling people."[120]

- A.A. Number Three [Bill Dotson] specifically stated:, "That sentence, 'The Lord has been so wonderful to me, curing me of this terrible disease, that I just want to keep telling people about it,' has been a sort of a golden text for the A.A. program and for me."[121]

- Speaking of his very first meeting with Bill W., Dr. Bob said as to Bill: "But this was a man who had experienced many years of frightful drinking, who had had most all the drunkard's experiences known to man, but who had been cured by the very means I had been trying to employ, that is to say the spiritual approach."[122]

- [Dr. Bob concluded as to the A.A. program:] "It never fails, if you go about it with one half the zeal you have been in the

---

[118] *DR. BOB*, 88-89.
[119] Dick B., *When Early AAs Were Cured and Why*, 3rd ed. (Kihei, HI: Paradise Research Publications, Inc., 2006), 113.
[120] *Alcoholics Anonymous*, 4th ed., 191.
[121] *Alcoholics Anonymous*, 4th ed., 191.
[122] *Alcoholics Anonymous*, 4th ed., 191.

habit of showing when you were getting another drink Your Heavenly Father will never let you down!"[123]

The Central Purpose of This Study of Dr. Bob's Boyhood Days in Vermont

Our major purpose in this resource book effort was and is to discover and publish the sources of the foregoing and other similar, very clear, statements by and about Dr. Bob—not about his youth, but about early Akron A.A.'s pioneer fellowship, its requirements, principles, practices, Bible studies, prayer meetings, conversions, spiritual tools, and cures.

The correlative major purpose is to compare the Dr. Bob statements in and about Akron with the events of Dr. Bob's youth involving the Creator, Jesus Christ, the gift of the Holy Spirit, the Bible, conversions and salvation through Christ, prayer, Quiet Time, church, fellowship with like-minded believers, witness, love, and service.

Finally, there is need to examine the entire spectrum of what Dr. Bob described as his "excellent training" as a youngster.

For example, these points have been paramount in comparing Vermont with Akron:

> What was the "Great Awakening" that changed the whole community of St. Johnsbury, Vermont shortly before Dr. Bob was born?[124]

---

[123] *Alcoholics Anonymous*, 4th ed., 181.
[124] John E. Nutting, *Becoming the United Church of Christ in Vermont 1795-1995* (Burlington, VT: The Vermont Conference of the United Church of Christ, 1996). Rev. Nutting reports: "Caledonia Conference: The churches have been visited with one of the most remarkable and thorough religious awakenings known in modern or indeed in any time. Every church has been blessed, and all but one or two have shared largely in the refreshing, though upon two the dews of heaven have fallen since the first of May [1875]. St. Johnsbury has been the center of the work, not only for the churches of this Conference but also for much of the northeastern part of the state. . . . What shall be done to save souls?" (p. 206)

What role did the famous Fairbanks family—its three brothers, their descendents, and their platform scale business—play in the unique Christian atmosphere in St. Johnsbury?[125]

Do we yet know the details about what Dr. Bob's parents did in training Bob in the Bible and Christianity themselves and what was the nature of prayer in the Smith home?

What were the Christian education features and the family's contributions in the North St. Johnsbury Congregational Church where his father was a Deacon, superintendent of the Sunday school, and taught Sunday school for at least 30 years? Where young Bob's mother was much involved in regular church attendance, superintending two different Church School departments, its Mission work, the church choir, reporting the church's history, and participating in the many women's affairs in the church? And where Sunday school attendance was a major item in the entire family's life?

---

[125] Charles Edward Russell, *Bare Hands And Stone Walls: Some Recollections of a Side-Line Reformer* (NY: Charles Scribner's Sons, 1933). Hardly a champion of St. Johnsbury or of the Fairbanks people, reformer Russell lamented: "The place was the site of the Fairbanks scale factory; members of the Fairbanks family were the barons; in effect their word was law. Without assuming any ostensible place or reachable responsibility in the government, they ruled it absolutely. . . . It was the Fairbanks family that sustained, managed, and inspired the Academy and was responsible for the puritanical lunacies practiced there. It was also the Fairbanks family that ruled St. Johnsbury with an unassailable sway. . . . The Fairbanks barony was defended upon these grounds. . . . They were Good Men that were endowed with this abnormal sway and they used it for good ends. Of this, no doubt. They were all good men; the eulogies upon them that used to be poured forth in the religious weeklies were in a way merited. They represented, as we were told, the highest type of Christian Business Man; aptly were the Scriptures cited in their laudation, "Not slothful in business, fervent in spirit, serving the Lord: . . . They gave money for good objects, they financed the Academy, built and presented to the town the really remarkable Athenaeum, stocked it with a marvelous library, added an excellent collection of paintings. Liberally they subscribed to foreign missions; they had built one of the most beautiful churches in all New England; they were flawless in the performance of every pious duty." (pp. 15-17). For a more factual presentation, see Arthur F. Stone, *The Vermont of Today: With Its Historic Background, Attractions and People* (Vol. II; NY: Lewis Historical Publishing Company, Inc., 1929), 573, 809-12, 860-63, 872, 892-98.

Then, in the church itself, what took place in the Smith life at North Congregational Church Sunday morning worship, afternoon Sunday school, Sunday evening services, and Wednesday evening prayer meetings?

Just how much were the Smiths—any or all of them—participating in the frequent revivals, Gospel meetings, conversions, Bible studies, and community outreach?[126] What was the role of its North Congregational Church pastors and what, if any, personal relationship existed between the pastors and the Smith family members during the 1875 to 1898 period? These pastors were three in number: Henry W. Jones, Charles M. Lamson, and Albert H. Heath.[127]

What did all the principles and practices of the Christian Endeavor Society bring to St. Johnsbury and Bob's church; and precisely what did they do, teach, and require?[128]

---

[126] Claire Dunne Johnson, *I See by the Paper: An Informal History of St. Johnsbury* (St. Johnsbury, VT: The Cowles Press, 1987): "[T]here were also some major changes taking place just north of the business district—changes which would forever alter the skyline of St. Johnsbury. The year 1875 saw the beginning of the 'Great Awakening,' so-called, a tremendous surge of new religious fervor, initiated here by the Y.M.C.A. through great mass meetings at the churches and even at the scale shops. Prayer meetings and hymn-sings were attended by great numbers of people, and various religious groups in town were inspired to build their own churches." *(p. 84).*

[127] John M. Comstock, *The Congregational Churches of Vermont and Their Ministry 1762-1942: Historical and Statistical* (St. Johnsbury, VT: The Cowles Press, Inc., 1942), 117; Arthur F. Stone, *St. Johnsbury Illustrated: A Review of the Town's Business, Social, Literary, and Educational Facilities, with Glimpses of Picturesque Surroundings* (St. Johnsbury, VT: Caledonian Press--- C. M. Stone & Company, 1891), 7.

[128] For 1886, Rev. Nutting reported in *Becoming the United Church of Christ in Vermont*: "For the first time we get report of Societies of Christian Endeavor (first organized four years ago). Now twenty churches have them. . . increase in YMCA. . . . All the churches have received large accessions . . . to the Congregational about seventy-five. Enthusiasm for starting a YMCA and a Christian Endeavor." (p. 224). For 1888, "many churches report increased activity of Christian Endeavor." (p. 228). Stone, in *North Congregational Church . . . 1825-1942*, reported at pp. 69-70: "The Christian Endeavor Society which started in 1887 has continued through the years as the leading young people's organization and many an adult of today has vivid memories of the influence of the pastors, their wives and other leaders who inspired them in their formative years. In 1891 . . . there was a Junior Society of Christian Endeavor which later merged into the larger society."

What impact, if any, did the YMCA have on Dr. Bob's life—with his father's being an officer (president and chairman) of that association and with the YMCA's vigorous work with the churches and the community on revivals?[129]

How much did the YMCA Fairbanks involvement and leadership; their donation of the YMCA building; and the YMCA Gospel meetings, revivals, and personal work impact on Dr. Bob, his parents, and his church?[130]

As to St. Johnsbury Academy—where Bob's father was an examiner;[131] where his mother was a graduate, a teacher, and a very active alumna; and where Bob himself sang in, and managed the Glee Club, was a debater, was a member of the Adelphian literary society, was a class president and later Orator at his graduation, and was in fact chided for his regular and frequent church participation—what impact did these have on Dr. Bob's moral training and religious learning?[132]

---

[129] Rev. Nutting further reported in *Becoming the United Church of Christ in Vermont*: "Special reference to YMCA and Young People's Societies and Societies for Christian Endeavor and Children's Day coming to be more generally observed." (p. 226); see also his comments on the revivals helped by Gospel meetings, the work of Young Men's Christian Association, Gospel workers who were men of prayer with impressive Bible readings (p. 207).

[130] Stone, *St Johnsbury Illustrated*, 40-41; *Nutting. Becoming the United Church of Christ*: "1875 – St. Johnsbury... During the month of December there developed... an interest in connection with the labors of Rev. Marsh of the Baptist Church and of Rev. De Witt an evangelist.... With the week of prayer the five evangelical churches of the village, vis a vis,: North and South Congregational, Baptist, Methodist and Free Baptist with remarkable concord began to hold union meetings twice weekly which continued for four months. A third feature of the work of revival has been the entire suppression of denominational differences, and the cordiality and harmony with which Christians of every evangelical name have worked together." (p. 407).

[131] *St. Johnsbury Academy Catalogue* for 1873, p. 22.

[132] Richard Beck, *A Proud Tradition A Bright Future: A Sesquicentennial History of St. Johnsbury Academy* (St. Johnsbury, VT: St. Johnsbury Academy, 1992). Beck states: "Smith's unusually frequent church attendance also drew the attention of his Academy's classmates. His Class of 1898's Class Day program, containing the Class Prophecy, predicted that 'after leaving college,' he would become ''a professional fisherman,' then 'settle down' as 'Rev. Robert H. Smith, pastor of a church in Paunee, Ohio.'" (p. 49).

What about the required daily Chapel at the Academy? The hymns, prayers, Bible-readings? What about the Academy's required weekly church attendance and Bible study?[133] What about the Congregationalists who dominated the founding, administration, mission, campus, and required religious elements?[134] What about the YMCA meetings and lectures at the Academy?[135]

What about the revivals, evangelists, Gospel meetings, prayer meetings, Bible studies, and conversions that garnered so much attention among the churches and townspeople?[136]

What about the nearby influence at Northfield, Massachusetts of the famous Dwight L. Moody—evangelist, preacher, teacher, revivalist, YMCA leader, Christian Endeavor writer and speaker, Mt. Hermon School founder, and leader of the Student Christian Movement?[137]

Did all of these concentrated Christian elements work to fill Dr. Bob's mind with salient Bible truths to which he returned when he resumed extensive Bible study, made his decision to pray for sobriety at the home of T. Henry Williams, met Bill Wilson at the home of Henrietta Seiberling, and had his last drink on June 10, 1935?[138]

The reader will find and be able to use the tools in the companion resource binders and the Dr. Bob Core Library— partly located in an interim home here on Maui and partly in their new secure and accessible location at the North

---

[133] Beck, *A Proud Tradition*, 39; Russell, *Bare Hands*, 10-12.
[134] Fairbanks, et. al., *Sketch*, 2-15, 20-21, 52-54, 56, 60-61, 69-73.
[135] Fairbanks, et. al., *Sketch*, 61: ". . . the positive influence of the churches, the Young Men's Christian Association, and the Athenaeum and Art Gallery, make an unusual combination of collateral educational forces. . . ." See also: Stone, *St. Johnsbury Illustrated*, 63-66.
[136] Nutting, *Becoming the United Church of Christ*, 224: "increase in Sabbath School enrollment. For the first time we get report of Societies of Christian Endeavor."
[137] Stone, *The Vermont of Today*, Vol. II, 860-63.
[138] See Dick B., *Henrietta B. Seiberling: Ohio's Lady with a Cause*, 4th ed. (Kihei, HI: Paradises Research Publications, Inc., 2006).

Congregational Church (UCC) on Main Street in St. Johnsbury. That library will contain many of the books and documents cited in this resource volume. A reader will be able to decide on the answers for himself or herself. Or to pursue these questions further. Our job is to lay out the resources, point to the dots, and let the facts do the connecting if this seems possible, reasonable, and purposeful.

Connecting the "Whole" (the Akron A.A. Pioneer Program) to the Historical Dots Representing the Individual St. Johnsbury Factors That Might Have Impacted on Dr. Bob's Akron Statements, Work with Others, Program Ideas, and Successes

As has been the objective in my previous titles, the job is to start with the facts. Not legends. Not guesses. Not revised accounts! Not deleted and substituted materials. Not self-made, concocted supposed descriptions of A.A. or its "creed." And our voluminous companion binders, the books and materials in the North Congregational Church Dr. Bob Core Library, and the extensive statements in this title contain several approaches. The first is to list what the A.A. founders and early pioneers themselves had to say about the Creator, the Bible, Jesus Christ, prayer, quiet time, God's guidance, obedience, and religious association. Next to persuade the readers to avail themselves of whatever historical materials might eventually be given and added to the permanent, accessible, free location in at North Congregational Church of St. Johnsbury, a suitable recovery archive which is hospitable to early A.A.'s Christian fellowship roots and history. Then to seek their support for lodging all the needed resources free so that they can be seen, studied, and learned initially from our core library—which is growing frequently with each new inquiry, acquisition, and internet search we make. Then to invite visits to the core library at its ultimate North Congregational Church location, and also to the boyhood premises, the Town, the Town archives, library, churches, and academy to see for themselves. Then to define what is to be seen and learned from a solid look at the St. Johnsbury of Dr. Bob's youth. These are the stage settings.

But the lessons are to be learned from the various "dots" which represent factors that could and probably did have a bearing on Dr.

Bob's intense relationship with, and studies about, his Heavenly Father, Jesus Christ, the gift of the Holy Spirit, the Bible, conversions, prayer, healing, daily devotionals, and Christian literature.

The Primary Influences Being Examined to Find Detailed Evidence

The following are some of the primary factors that could have influenced Dr. Bob's life. The documentation accompanies the discussions both before, after, and in, this chapter:

REVIVALS IN VERMONT: The "Great Awakening" of 1875 in the Congregational Church.

Dr. Bob was not born until 1879. But, as we have mentioned and cited above, an enormous Christian awakening was begun in Vermont only a few years before his birth. The decimation and slumber that occurred in the churches due to the Civil War led to a somber group of "elite" church going people who seemed to have lost touch with the awakenings and revivals that had characterized an earlier period. But things changed. Church records describe an uprising of concern, energy, and fervor unlike anything previously seen in Vermont. Beginning in 1875, there occurred what came to be called "The Great Awakening" in St. Johnsbury. It was spurred by a new vitality in the YMCA and its community-wide evangelism, as well as the support of Vermont leaders—among them the important Fairbanks family of St. Johnsbury. There was a revitalized and widespread series of efforts to "save souls," promote prayer, study the Bible, rejuvenate churches and church life, and effectuate revivals, evangelist talks, and Gospel meetings. Though other prior events had earned the terms "First Great Awakening" and "Second Great Awakening," these were over well before the Vermont events which began in 1875. And you will find the whole St. Johnsbury scene depicted in this title, in the core library, and in my resource binder on this subject.[139]

---

[139] John E. Nutting, *Becoming the United Church of Christ in Vermont 1795-1995* (Burlington, VT: The Vermont Conference of the United Church of Christ, 1995), 206-07.

One example of itinerant ministry pops up in the history records about Rev. William Withington Thayer (1809-1881). Rev. Thayer moved to St. Johnsbury, Vermont, shortly after having been a pastor in Lyndon, Vermont, for six years. ". . . Declining all subsequent invitations to settle, but preaching considerably at St. Johnsbury and elsewhere, and being for several years specially connected with the Home Missionary work. In 1870 he became the Librarian of the newly establish Athenaeum at St. Johnsbury—donated by a Fairbanks family member; and Thayer held the position ten years."[140]

RELEVANCE OF EVANGELIST DWIGHT L. MOODY: *The widespread interests, contacts, and personal work of the famous evangelist Dwight L. Moody.*

Dwight L. Moody had some special connections with Vermont revivalism. He pointed the YMCA toward a new program of personal work, revivals, and conversions. He founded the Mt. Hermon School at nearby Northfield, Massachusetts. Students from St. Johnsbury Academy (which Bob attended) funded an appeal for the purpose of sending a delegation of five to represent the Academy at the interscholastic convention held at Northfield, Massachusetts, by Mr. Moody in June during Bob Smith's Junior Year.[141] Moody perfected his ideas on evangelism and revivals. He had relatives in St. Johnsbury. So far, we have documented that at least one St. Johnsbury leader came to Northfield to spend time with and help Moody.[142] And

---

[140] *Minutes of the Eighty-Third Annual Meeting of the General Convention of Congregational Ministers and Churches of Vermont, Held at Rutland, June, 1878. Sixtieth Annual Report of the Vermont Domestic Missionary Society, and Fifty-Eighth Annual Report of the Vermont Education Society* (Montpelier, Vermont: Printed at the Vermont Chronicle Office, 1878), 49. : http://books.google.com/books?id=hP4QAAAAIAAJ&pg=RA5-PA16&dq=%

[141] *The Academy Student* at St.. Johnsbury Academy, 76.

[142] Major Whittle--a "former associate" of, "and lifelong fellow-worker" with Moody--records in his diary of September, 1875, that during the two weeks that he and Philip Paul (P. P.) Bliss spent with Moody beginning September 8, 1875, "Many brethren from different parts of the country came and went while we were there, among them Stuart, of Philadelphia; Rowland, Dodge, and McBurney, of New York; Remington, of Fall River; Moore, of Boston; Fairbanks, of Vermont, and others." William R. Moody, *The Life of Dwight L. Moody by His Son* (New York: Fleming H. Revell, 1900), 261. And Franklin Fairbanks was a trustee of Moody's Northfield Seminary. See, for example: Jacob G. Ullery, comp., *Men of Vermont* (Brattleboro, VT: Transcript Publishing, 1894), 128.

the revival theme was greatly aided by Moody's prestige, ideas, colleagues, and leadership.[143]

SIGNFICANCE OF THE FAIRBANKS FAMILY OF ST. JOHNSBURY: *The immense prestige, philanthropy, and Christian activity of the Fairbanks family of St. Johnsbury.*

The story has many facets, and you will find them in this title and in my Fairbanks resource binder and core library books. Erastus and Thaddeus Fairbanks founded a business which revolved around the platform scale that became needed, famous, and widespread in use around the world. Thaddeus Fairbanks invented that platform scale. In time, almost everyone in the family of his parents and their immediate descendents became involved in the Fairbanks business. A third brother Joseph joined in before long. Without doubt, the business made the Fairbanks people very wealthy. They expanded their business. They were strong and dedicated adherents to the Congregational Faith and its churches. Many of the Fairbanks people became ordained ministers. Some were pastors in St. Johnsbury. Family member Horace Fairbanks (Governor the State of Vermont) was chairman of the North Congregational Church building committee. He and his brother Franklin produced the funds to complete the building—their contribution far exceeding the 400 pledges from church members. Fairbanks family members donated the money to erect a building for the Young Men's Christian Association. They donated the money to construct the Fairbanks Museum—across the street from the North Congregational Church. They donated the money to erect the Athenaeum—the town library and adjunct to the local Academy. They founded the St. Johnsbury Academy and filled it with their religious requirements and expectations. All Academy Trustees—like the Fairbanks people themselves—were required to be members of a Congregational Church. Thaddeus was considered the Academy's founder, and another Fairbanks was its long-time headmaster. Bending to the intentions of the founders, the Academy required students to attend weekly church and Bible study. Daily Chapel attendance was required. Many of the Academy buildings and dormitories were erected or donated by Fairbanks people. Fairbanks family members were leaders in the Vermont YMCA, and the YMCA

---

[143] See James F. Findlay, Jr., *Dwight L. Moody: American Evangelist 1837-1899* (Chicago: The University of Chicago Press, 1969).

regularly held lectures at the Academy. In fact, some of the town-wide revivals spilled over into the Academy's facilities. Graduation ceremonies began and ended there with prayer and were often accompanied by a sermon. The curricula contained requirements of Christian education, morality, and Bible study. The Fairbanks family was deep into public service and philanthropy. Members served as Governors of Vermont, as legislators of Vermont, and on educational boards in Vermont. They served as trustees and leaders of St. Johnsbury Academy, leaders in the YMCA, and donors of funds to missions—domestic and international—and of funds for Bibles and to help young men in seminaries and to help indigent ministers. They served in many capacities in the state, county, and local Congregational conventions, associations, and churches. And they aided the Christian Endeavor Society, to which Dr. Bob belonged. In short, you can scarcely walk a block in the center of the little town without bumping into something built, donated by, run by, or related to the ubiquitous Fairbanks clan. Their influence was enormous in most of the activities and places that impacted on the lives of Judge Walter Smith, his wife Susan Holbrook Smith, and their son Robert Holbrook Smith. All the Smiths inevitably came in touch with a Fairbanks—whether in church, Sunday school, prayer meetings, revivals, conversions, the St. Johnsbury Academy, the YMCA, mission work, women's groups, government and community service, politics, and business. The Fairbanks people were towered role models of Christian ethics, morality, worship, benevolence, witness, fellowship, service, and education. You can find the documentation of these facts in this title and in the companion binders.

The great concern of the Fairbanks people—stressed by the remarks, services, and positions of the three brothers (Deacon Erastus, Thaddeus, and Joseph P.)—is perhaps best exemplified by some treasures from correspondence by Joseph P. which is quoted here:

> I have spent this day in my room, and it has not been without its consolations. In the study of that precious treasure, God's Word, and in holding communion with Him, there is a satisfaction which the world cannot give; . . . . I have followed you as you have gone up to the house of God. I have seen you listening to the anthem, and joining in the exercise of prayer. I have met with you in the Sabbath school, and tried to catch the

low hum of the recitations. . . . I have concluded to write a communication to the Sabbath school. . . . The following is the communication referred to, addressed, "To the Teachers and Scholars of the St. Johnsbury Plain Sabbath School": . . . . It is now about the hour that you are assembled for your usual Sabbath exercises and prayer; the song of praise and the instructions of the Bible are attended to without disturbance; and the plan of salvation through Jesus Christ is presented for your contemplation and acceptance . . . . It is not uncharitable to suppose that very little true religion exists in this community. . . .

What selfish creatures too, we are! The great object for which all created beings should unite their energies is the promotion of the glory of God. And yet how our first thoughts centre on self. What matters it whether life or death, health or sickness, abundance or want, are my lot, provided the glory of God is promoted by my joy or suffering? If the glory of God is our chief object, we are pursuing the great design of our existence, and fulfilling the will of our heavenly Father, and we may safely leave consequences to Him. . . . Lord Jesus, strengthen me and all of us, that henceforth we may live, not unto ourselves, but unto Thee.

[There follows a description of what Joseph P. Fairbanks wrote "for the public journals," and the following are among the listed subjects: (1) On the increase of ministers; a second article on the increase of ministers (in February, to enlist interest in the concert of prayer for colleges); (2) Education Society as a means of raising up ministers; (3) The amount of aid to be given to indigent young men preparing for the ministry; (4) Whose duty is it? (a paper for the better support of the clergy; (5) What is essential to render prayer effectual?; (6) Family prayer; (7) What shall be done? (a plea to promote temperance, virtue, and intelligence); (8) What has been done? (a paper on temperance); (9) Duties in regard to slavery; and (10) Take notes of sermons.

May 14, 1854. Dear E.: I suppose you are now in your little room, perhaps engaged in reading your Bible, or in your evening devotions. . . . I am often filled with wonder at the continued blessings poured out upon us while we are so unmindful of the Giver. . . . Why are we taught the way of salvation and assured of the blessed Savior's love, while the great mass of our race are going down the broad road, without ever having the glad news of salvation? . . . . I would like to have you write me what constitutes your Sunday reading. I hope the Bible will be the principal book for the Sabbath, and that you will read it with earnest attention, seeking to learn from every verse what duty is required of you, or what truth is taught."[144]

You can legitimately ask if there was a resident of St. Johnsbury, Vermont, in the period from 1875 to 1898 whose life was not materially impacted by the doings of one Fairbanks or another. Just walk from Dr. Bob's birthplace on Summer Street to Main Street one block down. There you will find the enormous North Congregational Church along with a host of other churches, and learn that one of the Fairbanks family became a pastor of the nearby South Congregational Church. You will learn that most of the Fairbanks people were deeply involved in North Church including the construction of its buildings. Across the street from the North Church lies the Fairbanks Museum donated by the family. Down Main Street, a short distance away, is the Athenaeum—the town library donated by a Fairbanks and stocked with books donated by Fairbanks people. Still farther come the host of St. Johnsbury Academy buildings—there largely because of the benevolence of the Fairbanks people. Even the YMCA building, now destroyed because of fire, was a donation from the Fairbanks people. This is not to mention the number of Fairbanks business enterprises which brought jobs, revenue, and wealth to the community—hemp, pig iron, scales, banking, and even railroad development. Prayers meetings were held in the Fairbanks plant itself during the hot and heavy revival days of the Awakening period. Judge Smith was involved in banks where Fairbanks people had served. And even Dr. Bob worked for the Fairbanks company after Bob's graduation from St. Johnsbury Academy.[145]

---

[144] Samuel H. Taylor, *A Memorial of Joseph P. Fairbanks* (Riverside, 1865).
[145] Arthur F. Stone. *St. Johnsbury Illustrated: A Review of the Town's Business, Social, Literary, and Educational Facilities, with Glimpses of Picturesque Surroundings* (St. Johnsbury, VT: Caledonian Pres—C.M. Stone & Company,

THE INFLUENTIAL FACTORS FLOWING FROM AND IN DR. BOB'S FAMILY: *The family of Judge Walter Perrin Smith, Dr. Bob's father*

It appears that the depth of the Smith family's St. Johnsbury involvement has never been fully or adequately plumbed—particularly as that involvement may have been related to Dr. Bob's later reflections on his youth. Supporting citations will follow. And one thing is clear—the Smith family was Congregationalist to the core; for there didn't appear to be a day that one or the other of the family members was not involved in some local, area, or state Congregational Church work.

The Judge: Let's begin with the Judge. He received a fine education, went to law school, became a lawyer, and practiced law in St. Johnsbury. He served as state's attorney, a state legislator, and a superintendent of schools.[146] Judge Smith was also a lay spiritual leader of North Congregational Church as a life-time Deacon, beginning in 1902;[147] a superintendent of the Sunday school, and taught in the Sunday school beginning in 1890.[148] The Sunday School teaching allegedly continued for 40 years.[149] He was an examiner for St. Johnsbury Academy;[150] a local YMCA president and chairman,[151] and also an elected Judge of the Probate Court situated in St.

1891); Charles Edward Russell. *Bare Hands and Stone Walls: Some Recollections of a Side-Line Reformer* (NY: Charles Scribner's Sons, 1933), 8-25; Claire Dunne Johnson. *"I See By The Paper..." An Informal History of St. Johnsbury* (St. Johnsbury, VT: The Cowles Press, 1987); Richard Beck. *A Proud Tradition A Bright Future: A Sesquicentennial History of St. Johnsbury Academy* (St. Johnsbury, VT: St. Johnsbury Academy, 1992), 5-25; Claire Dunne Johnson. *Images of America: St. Johnsbury* (Dover, NH: Arcadia Publishing, 1996).
[146] *DR. BOB*, 9.
[147] Stone, *North Congregational Church*, 86. Letter from Bob Swartz, church archivist, dated October 25, 2007.
[148] North Congregational Church *Year Book* 1890, p. 4.
[149] *DR. BOB*, 9. Other statements place the duration of his teaching at 30 years.
[150] *St. Johnsbury Academy Catalogue* for 1873, p. 22.
[151] Walter P. Smith is listed as YMCA "President or Chairman" for Saint Johnsbury. *Year Book of the Young Men's Christian Associations of North America, for the year 1896* (Published by The International Committee, 1896), 128.

Johnsbury.[152] He was associated with some of the banking interests held by the Fairbanks family.[153]

Bob's Mother: The wife and mother Susan Amanda [Holbrook] Smith has been given short and undeserved shrift by historians. Over and over they have minimized her life work and important role in Bob's life. They tended to dismiss her as a strictly religious, woman who merely "busied herself" in church and social affairs. But the facts tell us a great deal more. Mrs. Smith attended and graduated from St. Johnsbury Academy.[154] She became a teacher there for years 1875 and 1876.[155]. Academy records show that she delivered several important addresses about the school and its history.[156] She became a member of the Executive Committee of the Alumni Association in 1892.[157] She wrote two chapters of the Academy History.[158] She was a member of the Vermont Library Board's Board of Library Commissioners.[159] She was President of the St. Johnsbury Women's Congregationalist Club.[160] And she was a member of the American Home Missionary Society.[161] A biography characterized her as "an active worker in the beneficent and educational activities of the times."[162] Her activities at

---

[152] *DR. BOB,* 9. Further details on his status as Probate Judge follow later in the text.
[153] Stone, *St. Johnsbury Illustrated,* 15; Jacob G. Ullery, *Men of Vermont: An Illustrated Biographical History of Vermonters and Sons of Vermont* (Brattleboro, VT: Transcript Publishing Company, 1804), 370-71.
[154] *St. Johnsbury Academy Catalogue* for 1874, 9, lists Susie A. Holbrook as a member of Senior Advanced Class. At page 45, it lists Susie E. Holbrook (Mrs. W. P. Smith) of St. Johnsbury as a Graduate. [Note: "Susie A." (for "Susan Amanda") is correct..
[155] *St. Johnsbury Academy Catalogue,* 93 lists Mrs. W. P. Smith of the Class of '74 as teacher for 1875-1876.
[156] *Semi-Centennial of St. Johnsbury Academy* (1892), 57.
[157] *Semi-Centennial of St. Johnsbury Academy* (1892), 57.
[158] Arthur F. Fairbanks, et. al. *An Historical Sketch of the St. Johnsbury Academy 1942-1922,* n.d., p. v.
[159] Albert Nelson Marquis, *Who's Who in New England* ( ), 994, "Smith, Susan Holbrook."
[160] Marquis, *Who's Who in New England,* 994.
[161] Letter from Ken B. to Taylor Reed regarding Reed's article "Alcoholics Anonymous Rooted in St. Johnsbury Institutions" in *The Caledonian-Record,* online edition, October 12, 2007, and monograph of C.S. Smith, *An Historical Sketch of Home Missionary Work in Vermont, By the Congregational Churches* (Montpelier: Press of the Watchman Publishing Company, 1893)
[162] William H. Jeffrey, *Successful Vermonters* (East Burke, VT: The Historical Publishing Company, 1904), 98.

North St. Johnsbury Congregational Church included participation in a church quartet,[163] extensive work in women's matters, addresses on church history,[164] service as a Sunday school teacher,[165] Assistant Superintendent of the Sunday School,[166] Superintendent of the Intermediate Department,[167] and work with domestic missions.[168] She was a very much involved and mentioned North Congregational Church member.[169]

Bob, the son: Then there was Bob [Specific citations will be found below.]. For now, we simply point to Dr. Bob's own statements that he attended North Congregational Church, going with his family to Sunday Morning worship, afternoon Sunday school, Sunday evening services, and Wednesday prayer meetings (the latter, occasionally). Also was active in Christian Endeavor Society meetings of North Congregational Church. The church archivist wrote us that Bob was first listed in the North Church Year Book in 1880, recorded as attending the church Sunday school, and then last listed in the church Year Book for 1914. At St. Johnsbury Academy, he was a member and Manager of the Glee Club.[170] He participated in debates there.[171] He belonged to the Adelphian literary society there.[172] Each week, he regularly attended the required Sabbath church service and Bible service.[173] He attended Chapel every day—an event described by a student as follows: "Attendance at morning prayers was sternly

---

[163] Stone, *North Congregational Church*, 64.
[164] Stone, *North Congregational Church*, 68.
[165] Letter from Bob Swartz, North Congregational Church, St. Johnsbury, Archivist, October 25, 2007.
[166] Letter from Swartz, Oct. 25, 2007.
[167] Letter from Swartz, Oct 25, 2007.
[168] Letter from Ken B. to Taylor Reed regarding Reed's article "Alcoholics Anonymous Rooted in St. Johnsbury Institutions" in *The Caledonian-Record,* online edition, October 12, 2007, and monograph of C.S. Smith, *An Historical Sketch of Home Missionary Work in Vermont, By the Congregational Churches* (Montpelier: Press of the Watchman Publishing Company, 1893)
[169] Arthur Fairbanks, Lemuel S. Hastings, James F. Colby, Susan H. Smith, Joseph Fairbanks, Charles H. Merrill, and Wendell P. Stafford *An Historical Sketch of St. Johnsbury Academy 1842-1922* (St. Johnsbury, VT: Trustees of the St. Johnsbury Academy, n.d.)
[170] *The Academy Student*, February, 1898, 50.
[171] *The Academy Student*, February, 1898, 45.
[172] *The Academy Student*, February, 1898, 45.
[173] *St. Johnsbury Academy Catalog,* General Information, 18.

exacted of each and all—no excuses. Besides the reading of scriptures, the hymns, and the prayers, the man of science, the principal or some visiting clergyman usually said a few words of reproof upon the sins of youth or of exhortation to godliness."[174] Bob Smith was President of the Junior Class.[175] He delivered the Oration at his own graduation ceremony.[176] He seemed never to have forgotten his St. Johnsbury training in conversion, prayer, the Bible, church, Sunday school, and the Academy. Nor the principles of love and service he learned from Christian Endeavor. Considering his family's acknowledged immense participation in church and Christian activities, it is hard to imagine that much of this did not spill on and over the young Bob at the hands of his talented parents.[177]

DR. BOB'S CHURCH: *North Congregational Church, St. Johnsbury*

Several previous searchers in quest of Dr. Bob's church life came back to me [Dick B.] virtually empty-handed. And this prompted my son and me to visit the North Congregational Church itself, go inside the church, interview its current pastor, contact its archivist, and review its records. And the records are hardly non-existent. In fact, they go back over 100 years. We cite them elsewhere.

As stated, Mr. and Mrs. Walter Smith were first listed in the church yearbook for 1878. The two became members on May 7, 1883. North Congregational Church, St. Johnsbury, was organized on April 7, 1825, and known then as the "Second Congregational Church." The present building is the fourth edifice to house North Congregational Church. The church prospered to the point that in February, 1877, members met with Rev. Henry W. Jones to discuss the new building. A canvassing committee had 400 pledges for a four-year-period within six weeks. A building committee was appointed with then-State of Vermont Governor Horace Fairbanks as its chairman. Church

---

[174] Charles Edward Russell, *Bare Hands and Stone Walls* (NY: Charles Scribner's Sons, 1933), 11.
[175] *The Academy Student,* February, 1898, 76.
[176] St. Johnsbury Academy Commencement Exercises for the Class of 1898 records: "ORATION-The 'Crank' in History, ROBERT HOLBROOK SMITH, St. Johnsbury."
[177] Specific historical documents are also cited in later portions of the text devoted to each of Dr. Bob's activities.

members had raised about $37,000; and the Fairbanks brothers Horace and Franklin contracted to construct the new building; and through the estate of Erastus Fairbanks the church builders secured somewhere between $50,000 to $125,00 to complete the building. Horace and Franklin Fairbanks presented the church with a 3,004 pound bell for the platform of its 1470 foot tower.[178]

It is almost impossible not to credit the influence on Bob Smith of his relationship with his family's Congregational church. By his own statement, attendance alone was extensive—worship Sunday morning, instruction at Sunday School in the afternoon, the service on Sunday evening; and sometimes Wednesday evening prayer meeting. To these activities, he specifically mentioned and added the Monday evening Christian Endeavor meeting—which required weekly attendance. Other North Congregational Church activities were also in progress—outreach to other churches, union meetings with other churches, revivals, visits by evangelists, YMCA Gospel meetings, Christian Endeavor activities. We have yet to learn just how much influence the pastor himself had on the ideas and actions of Bob.

DR. BOB AND HIS SUNDAY SCHOOL:

There is yet to be found enough additional information on the content of North Church Sunday School teaching. Church records state that both of Dr. Bob's parents taught in that Sunday School for many years. Also that several members of the Fairbanks family were involved as superintendents and teachers. Church records do list Bob as attending. There was an International Congregational Sunday School class guide in wide use in Congregationalist churches. And a Fairbanks family member was involved in that work.[179]

The Sunday school goal for the Vermont Congregational churches was set forth as follows in their Sabbath School Report contained in the minutes of the 1872 conference:

> We are taught to labor directly for the conversion of souls, with the expectation of success. In all their work for Christ, Christians should have a definite object in view, as definite as

---

[178] Supporting citations can be found in subsequent chapters.
[179] Stone, *North Congregational Church*, 58-62.

any secular work, ad labor directly for the accomplishment of that object. The great object of the Sabbath School teacher should be to bring his scholars to Christ, and then instruct them, so that they shall become intelligent, efficient Bible Christians. His prayers and labors, in school or out, should have this distinctly in view. To use the words of Dr. J. Hall, "Setting Jesus Christ fully, simply, distinctly, kindly, earnestly before the child, and accompanying the presentation with payer for the power of the Holy Spirit, is the great work of the Sabbath School teacher."[180]

More can and will be revealed!

THE PASTOR'S ROLE: *Mentioned but not fully amplified.*

Three pastors headed the flock at North Congregational Church during the key years of Dr. Bob's youth. Did they ever come to dine with the Judge Smith family? Did they counsel any of the family members on any subject? Is there correspondence? How much did the pastors participate in the Christian Endeavor Society meeting? There is a note in the church history that they substantially influenced and inspired the lives of Christian Endeavor participants.[181] What was the relationship of Mr. and Mrs. Smith with governing elders? There may be many more records; and, if there are, we will give it the old school try in obtaining them. Suffice it to say that we have received excellent cooperation from Pastor Jay Sprout and church archivist Bob Swartz.

THE CHURCH'S YOUNG PEOPLE'S GROUP: *The Christian Endeavor Society*

Founded at the Williston Congregational Church in Portland, Maine, in February 1881, shortly after Bob was born, the Christian Endeavor Movement spread like wild fire across Maine, Vermont, Massachusetts, and then around the globe. Several key points in the program seem directly related to the ideas Dr. Bob brought with him from his youth to Akron and its spiritual program: Confession of Christ, Bible study meetings, Prayer meetings, Conversion Meetings,

---

[180] *Minutes of the Seventy-Seventh Annual Meeting of the General Convention of Vermont, 1872*, Sabbath School Report, 21-22.
[181] Stone, *North Congregational Church*, 69-70.

Topical discussions, Quiet Hour and attendant practices, social and Christian fellowship, and the oft-mentioned principles of "love and service." Detailed newsletters, guidebooks, and other literature laid out a rigorous program of Christian service, and particularly loyalty to the local church.[182] In fact, as our Christian Endeavor resources show, the church deacons were part of the Christian Endeavor church governance; and that, of course, included Judge Walter Perrin Smith. Our Christian Endeavor binder and core library books describe the entire Christian Endeavor program in great detail. To a lesser degree, so does our chapter in this volume.

YMCA: *The Young Men's Christian Association*

It seems abundantly clear that the Vermont YMCA, during the vital "Great Awakening" period beginning in early 1875, was a far different organization than the YMCA today. The YMCA influence and the participation of its young people were evident from at least 1870 forward. The thrust of the YMCA ministry was to work with all denominations, outside of the church framework, community-wide and state-wide, and to organize and catalyze revivals, evangelistic speakers, church union activities, winning souls to Christ, and conducting lectures and concerts in the churches, the YMCA building itself (beginning in 1885), the community, and the St. Johnsbury Academy. Its vibrant outreach in Vermont from the 1875 period onward to 1898 was immense.[183] Dwight L. Moody, his Massachusetts colleagues, YMCA field workers, and youth committees appear to have been influential on the churches and communities. The reports on Vermont Congregational work mention the employment of four lady evangelists, including a Miss Lydia Hartig and a Miss Nellie Barnes. Reports state:

> Early in the winter the attention of the Secretary was called to the Training School for Christian Workers in Northfield, Mass., and to what had been done by the young ladies connected with this school in holding district meetings and

---

[182] Dick B. *The James Club and the Original A.A. Program's Absolute Essentials*, 127-57.

[183] Nutting, *Becoming the United Church of Christ*, 206: "Gratitude for the Young Men's Christian Association 'great gathering to the fold of Christ during the year [1875] . . . bid the committee God's speed in their work.'"

assisting in pastoral visitation under the direction of the minister of the village church. . . . Two young ladies were chosen from the school to make the trial. They were sent first into the Northern part of the State to work in a double field. The results of the labors of Miss Hartig and Miss Barnes in their first fields, and the interest which this new move in missions aroused, both within and outside the State, were such that the Directors of the Society [Vermont Domestic Missionary Society] decided to employ two more in this special service from the same school. . . . A good comment on the wok of the district evangelists has been given in the report of the pastor at Tyson: "The interest in religion has not been so deep and so widespread for many years, and has already resulted in several well-marked conversions, in an increase of seven to the Church on confession, with several more to be received soon, and in an immense change for the better in the way in which evangelical religion is regarded in the community."[184]

Fairbanks people were involved with these—particularly Colonel Franklin Fairbanks.[185] Both St. Albans and St. Johnsbury employed trained women workers in 1894.[186] "Union meeting held for three weeks at St. Johnsbury with an evangelist [in 1885] with gratifying results. Societies of Christian Endeavor at both churches . . . and the work of the Young Men's Christian Association, under the fresh impetus of the gift of new and elegant building is well taken up by young men."[187] There were great conversion successes in Vermont and in St. Johnsbury.[188] YMCA people played a part as "Y" people conducted Gospel meetings, revivals, lectures, and concerts.[189] And they converted many to Jesus Christ as Lord and Savior.[190]

---

[184] Nutting, *Becoming the United Church of Christ*, 235-37.
[185] Nutting, *Becoming the United Church of Christ*, 247.
[186] Nutting, *Becoming the United Church of Christ*, 240.
[187] Nutting, *Becoming the United Church of Christ*, 222.
[188] Nutting, *Becoming the United Church of Christ*, 227: "Increase in conversions due in part to supplemental work of evangelists. . . . Instead of being jealous of evangelists, pastors are ready to thank God for them."
[189] Nutting, *Becoming the United Church of Christ*, 226: "Revivals have occurred to nearly a score of churches . . . usually with the help of neighboring pastors or evangelists. The last years have been in Vermont years of unusually quickened life and spiritual blessing. The Holy Spirit in reviving power has visited a larger number

ST. JOHNSBURY ACADEMY:

At the time of the Smith family members' participation, St. Johnsbury Academy embraced Congregationalism from top to bottom. Religious requirements were spelled out in the grant deeds from the dedicated Congregationalist Fairbanks family members, and carried out by Fairbanks family members as founders, trustees, officers, headmasters, and teachers.[191] As stated, trustees were required to be Congregational members.[192] Daily Chapel was a must. A Weekly church service and a weekly Bible service were musts. And the educational focus certainly included Christian moral standards, ethics, and practices.[193] There were required textbooks on Bible study and Christianity. Prayers and sermons were a part of many of the assemblies, including graduations. As stated, Dr. Bob was into the Academy up to his ears—parental involvement in exams, teaching, history presentations, alumni activities.[194] As shown, young Bob was in the Glee Club and became Manager. He participated in debates. He belonged to one of the literary societies. He was President of the Junior Class. He is mentioned several times in school records, catalogues, and notes. And he delivered the Oration at his graduation. It appears quite likely that the

---

of churches than before for a long period. . . due to the expectancy of faith and direct application of the Word and personal appeals. . . . Special reference to YMCA and Young People's Societies and Societies for Christian Endeavor and Children's Day coming to be generally observed. . ."

[190] Nutting, *Becoming the United Church of Christ*, 206: "St. Johnsbury has been the center of the work [in 1875], not only for the churches of this Conference but also for the northeastern part of the state. . . What shall be done to save souls? Meanwhile the same fire burned in the hearts of laymen and Christian women."

[191] Fairbanks et al., *St. Johnsbury Academy*, 3, 6-11, 9-19, 25, 68, 101-03, 104-05. St. Johnsbury Academy Catalog for 1874, 1878, 1892

[192] Fairbanks et al., *St. Johnsbury Academy*, 9: "Therefore it is hereby provided, as the condition of the validity of this deed, that the Trustees of the aforesaid St. Johnsbury Academy shall be men of piety, & members in regular standing of some orthodox Congregational church, or churches, holding the doctrines essentially of the Westminster Shorter Catechism."

[193] Fairbanks et al., *St. Johnsbury Academy*, 9: Trustees and their associates and successors were enjoined to adopt measures "[t]o make the Institution a school of moral and religious instruction [meaning] that the fundamental doctrines of the Bible be taught, & the great duties of repentance & faith, be urged upon the attention of the school."

[194] Fairbanks et al., *An Historical Sketch of the St. Johnsbury Academy 1942-1922*, v, 56, 71, 106.

religious atmosphere that permeated campus doings had insured an effect on Dr. Bob's continued exposure to the Bible, prayer, church, and daily devotions.[195]

REVIVALS:

History records enormous revival activity and conversion in Vermont beginning in 1875.[196] As stated, many in St. Johnsbury called it the "Great Awakening" of 1875.[197] Evangelism, revival meetings, Gospel meetings, and conversions were conducted with such success that in the little town of St. Johnsbury—with an estimated population of between 4,600 and 5,800—one huge crowd was composed of 1,500 people and another crowd at St. Johnsbury Academy numbered 1,700 people.[198] Meetings were held in North Church, South Church, and St. Johnsbury Academy; and the YMCA leaders and lay people were extremely active in the community-wide outreach.[199] Actual records were kept of the number of conversions that resulted.[200] North Church had its share.[201] See the year by year, frequent reports on these revivals and those who evangelized.[202] See also the YMCA reports on the successes of revival efforts.

EVANGELISTS:

We know that the famed Evangelist Dwight L. Moody did not personally speak in St. Johnsbury during the initial months of the "Great Awakening" period (i.e., from February through May of

---

[195] Arthur Fairbanks, Lemuel S. Hastings, James F. Colby. Susan Holbrook Smith, Joseph Fairbanks, Charles H. Merrill, and Wendell P. Stafford, *An Historical Sketch of St. Johnsbury Academy 1842-1922* (St. Johnsbury Academy, n.d.).
[196] Nutting, *Becoming the United Church of Christ*, 206-07;
[197] See, for example, Stone, *North Congregational Church*, 30-31.
[198] The population of the township of St. Johnsbury, Vermont, was 4,665 in 1870 and 5,800 in 1880. See: *The Encyclopaedia Britannica: A Dictionary of Arts, Sciences, and General Literature*, 9th ed.—popular reprint, Volume XXI (New York: Henry G. Allen, 1888), 176; s.v. "St. Johnsbury."
[199] Stone, *North Congregational Church*, 30-31.
[200] Stone, *North Congregational Church*, 30-31.
[201] Stone, *North Congregational Church*, 30-31.
[202] *Nutting. Becoming the United Church of Christ, 206-07, 209, 213, 222, 224, 226-32, 234-42, 246-49.*

1875).[203] But history does record his being the sparkplug of new YMCA activity just prior thereto. Also that his revival methods had become a guide. For example, the "anxious" seats of the Charles G. Finney practices, were replaced—in large part—with Moody's private and personal "inquiry" preliminaries. History tells us also that people visited his nearby school and colleagues at Mt. Hermon, Massachusetts, where students were being trained in evangelism. There are ample records of lay evangelists who came to St. Johnsbury to lead revival activities.[204] And there are ample records of YMCA Gospel meetings held in the community. There were also itinerant revivalists who visited and preached.[205] We have yet to locate any direct evidence of Smith family participation though it seems unlikely that they were not touched by the scene because it was everywhere evident—though North Congregational Church, St. Johnsbury, was reputedly sufficiently strong that its people did a good deal of the community outreach, community-wide participation, and help for weaker Congregational churches and their conversions in nearby areas.

GOSPEL MEETINGS:

As discussed in the previous chapter, part of the revival activity took the form of Gospel meetings where YMCA workers were out and about in the community to "save souls."[206] Their accounts actually record the number of people converted at various meetings. As you look through the Congregational Church reports, you can see that there were several different groups, including the YMCA, that were working for conversions: The YMCA itself, the Vermont Domestic Missionary people, even Dwight L. Moody in several larger communities,[207] and from the local church folds themselves, the Christian Endeavor Societies.

---

[203] Moody was preaching in the United Kingdom from June of 1873 until he left England for America on August 14, 1875. See Edith L. Blumhofer and Randall Balmer, eds., *Modern Christian Revivals* (Urbana, Ill.: University of Illinois Press, 1993), 124; and William R. Moody, *The Life of Dwight L. Moody by His Son* (New York: Fleming H. Revell, 1900), 252.
[204] *North Congregational Church*, 30-31. See also the previous accounts of Ira Sankey.
[205] See the remarks about Rev. Thayer and his preaching at St. Johnsbury before he finally became associated with the Athenaeum.
[206] Nutting, *Becoming the United Church of Christ*, 207, 209, 212, 215, 222, 226.
[207] Nutting, *Becoming the United Church of Christ*, 215.

PRAYER MEETINGS:

Prayer, people rising in prayer, and prayer meetings were frequently mentioned in connection with North Congregational Church, with South Congregational Church, with revival meetings, with YMCA outreach, with conversions, and with events at St. Johnsbury Academy. The fever was so high that some of the prayer meetings were actually held in the rooms of the Fairbanks business enterprise itself.[208]

BIBLE STUDIES:

The Christian Endeavor Society meetings attended by Dr. Bob featured the Bible, memorization of Bible verses, and recitation of portions of the Bible. Often some meetings were called Bible study meetings.[209] The avowed mission of the North Congregational Church Sunday school was to teach young people the Word of God.[210] The focus of Christian Endeavor was to utilize and practice it. Recall too that a weekly Bible study meeting was also required of every St. Johnsbury Academy student, together with prayer and Bible-readings at the daily Chapel exercises. We have included a great deal of specifics on Christian Endeavor principles and practices because they so closely resemble those of the early Akron A.A. Christian Fellowship from 1935 through 1938.

REQUIRED CHURCH AND CHAPEL ATTENDANCE:

In a single remark about his church, Sunday school, and Christian Endeavor attendance as a youngster, Dr. Bob used the expression "more or less forced" to go. As already shown, the correlative exposure he had to the religious fervor of his family, his church, and his community has been grossly understated and needs to be

---

[208] Edward T. Fairbanks. *The Town of St. Johnsbury Vermont: A Review of One Hundred Twenty-five Years to the Anniversary Pageant 1912* (St. Johnsbury, VT: The Cowles Press, 1914), 316.
[209] See the extensive chapter on Christian Endeavor principles and practices.
[210] *North Congregational Church*, 57: "As soon as our church was organized in 1825 the little band started a Sabbath School. Later this became known as the Sunday School, and today the Church School, but though the name changed, the purpose through all the years was the same, the study of the world's best-seller, the Bible."

considered along with the other statement. The severe temper of the "more or less forced" remark was countered in small part by his other statement that he had had "excellent training" as a youngster. And part of that training was the required daily chapel attendance and required weekly church and Bible study meeting attendance established by St. Johnsbury Academy.

THE CALEDONIAN (TOWN NEWSPAPER):

As our research discloses, even the Town newspaper was in the pious hands of the Congregationalist Fairbanks family. Two generations of Deacon Erastus's family were not only involved in the North Congregational Church, but also were involved in owning, editing, and publishing the widely known newspaper for Caledonia County, of which St. Johnsbury was a part. The newspaper and its past issues present excellent accounts of almost every activity relevant to Dr. Bob's youth, the "Great Awakening" of 1875 in St. Johnsbury, and the Town of St. Johnsbury itself.

THE COMMUNITY CHANGES BETWEEN 1875 AND 1898:

The attempt in the companion binders is not to document what happened in the hearts of the people of St. Johnsbury, nor how many actually were saved and became Christian students of the Bible. This, even though many of the reports do provide lots of specific numbers. It is to show the intensity of community activity and how it moved from sober, somber, apathy to large gatherings, community-wide effort, and increased conversions and church attendance. This is best covered by listing the changes in the YMCA, the churches, the schools, the revivals, and the religious communities in this period. Records of the Congregational Churches, the Young Men's Christian Association, Vermont Historical Society, St. Johnsbury Academy, North Congregational Church, the Athenaeum, the Fairbanks Museum, and other entities tell of a dramatic change in the activities, lives, happiness, and involvement of St. Johnsbury people during the exciting Awakening period and the next two decades. And we will refer to, and document as many as we can.

The Influences As They Pertained to Cure of Alcoholism

As the quotes at the beginning of this title indicate, in the beginning years of A.A. in Akron, both Bill Wilson and Dr. Bob Smith talked frequently and explicitly about the Lord Jesus Christ and about their Heavenly Father. They indicated solid belief that alcoholism could be cured and that salvation—because of the work of the Great Physician [as Bill and countless others called Jesus Christ]—could bring about relief from alcoholism.[211]

Having seen his grandfather Willie Wilson cured of alcoholism by conversion, and having himself attended temperance and revival meetings as well as daily chapel at Burr and Burton Academy, Bill Wilson sought the same solution many years later at the Calvary Rescue Mission in New York where he gave his life to Christ and soon called on the "Great Physician" to deliver him. Several biographies have now made it clear that Bill had attended revival and temperance meetings in his youth.[212]

Vermont Congregationalists were strong supporters of the temperance movement.[213] The Fairbanks family members were involved.[214] The YMCA was promoting temperance. Christian Endeavor people were not far behind.[215] Dwight L. Moody tendered the conversion solution and supported the temperance movement. And so did the town-wide St. Johnsbury meetings at and after the "Great Awakening" of 1875.

The YMCA itself was even more vigorous. And so were their St. Johnsbury meetings. One of Moody's biographers attempted to define the tone:

> Moody also gave unswerving support to the crusade against intemperance. . . . This fight had long been considered a special

---

[211] Dick B., *The Conversion of Bill W.: More on the Creator's Role in Early A.A.* (Kihei, HI: Paradise Research Publications, Inc., 2006).
[212] Dick B., *The Conversion of Bill W.*
[213] The minutes of the conferences, recording activity of the churches during the 1875 to 1895. period contain many references. And see Nutting, *Becoming the United Church of Christ*, 222, 226.
[214] Nutting, *Becoming the United Church of Christ*, 222, 226.
[215] Clark, *Christian Endeavor in All Lands*, 499-500.

concern of evangelical Protestants. . . . According to the average temperance worker, elimination of "demon rum" promised an end to such widespread social ills as poverty, crime, insanity, divorce, and the general disintegration of the American family. The evangelist supported the movement chiefly by incorporating meetings devoted exclusively to temperance in his revival campaigns. In his major crusades of the seventies he held such meetings once a week, usually modeled after the familiar prayer meetings that all church people had frequented at one time or another. Often these services included lengthy testimony from reformed drunkards, each one attesting to the work of revivals and the Christian faith in helping to shatter the power of John Barleycorn over his life. . . .

Moody was not as single-minded, however, about the matter as were the most ardent advocates of total abstinence. The primary aim of a confirmed crusader. . . .was to get people to sign the pledge of abstention. Religious faith was designed primarily to stiffen the will, thereby preserving the pledge. In contrast, Moody never mentioned the pledge. Instead he reversed the order of precedence, always making the conversion experience primary, abstinence a manifestation of that experience. To preach temperance and no more was to go only halfway in solving personal problems. Salvation of men's souls was the only true cure for drunkards. One participant in a revival campaign in Massachusetts saw this distinction clearly: "To drinking men, as to everybody else," he said, Moody's one message was "Believe on the Lord Jesus Christ and thou shalt be saved" . . . in any case Moody remained fully identified with the anti-liquor forces throughout his adult years.[216]

Just as bringing people to salvation through insisting that they "believe on the Lord Jesus Christ" was key in the days of Dr. Bob's youth, so it was in early Akron A.A. where every new A.A. was required to do what Dr. Bob had long ago done in his youth and what Bill Wilson had done at the altar in the Calvary Rescue Mission. They accepted Jesus Christ as their Lord and Savior, confessed and proclaimed they had

---

[216] Findlay, *Dwight L. Moody*, 281-83.

been born again, and were converted to Christianity in the very way the Bible prescribed for those seeking a new birth.[217]

Conversion

Our mission here is not to discuss at length or to debate the subject of conversion and the cure of alcoholism. But the subject warrants some initial understanding amidst the plethora of psychological and scientific discussions about what a conversion is or isn't. And perhaps the best starting point is to emphasize that which even the debaters and analysts tend to accept: People have been cured of alcoholism by conversion to Christianity![218] And that is important largely because conversion as a solution impacted on Bill Wilson, on Dr. Bob, and on the initial "surrenders" to Christ that were mandatory and commonplace in early Akron A.A.

Conversion and Bill Wilson: In order to see where "conversion" entered the A.A. scene in the case of Bill Wilson, let's briefly look at that picture as it is discussed in detail in my title, *The Conversion of Bill W.*[219] To emphasize our own documentation, I will cite the historical confirmation in the works of other scholars. First, there is the widely reported account of the conversion of Bill Wilson's drunkard grandfather Willie Wilson in a dramatic experience at the top of Mount Aeolus in East Dorset, Vermont, followed by Willie's charge to the altar at the town Congregational church, his proclamation that he had been saved, and his subsequent continued sobriety for some eight years until death.[220] Second there are the long discussions by Bill Wilson with his psychiatrist William D. Silkworth, M.D., when Silkworth emphatically assured Wilson that the Great Physician Jesus Christ could cure him.[221] Wilson then went to the altar at Calvary Rescue Mission in New York, made a decision for Christ, and soon

---

[217] See Dick B., *A New Way In*.
[218] See Clinebell, *Understanding and Counseling*.
[219] Dick B., *The Conversion of Bill W.: More on the Creator's Role in Early A.A.* (Kihei, HI: Paradise Research Publications, Inc., 2006)
[220] Francis Hartigan: *A Biography of Alcoholics Anonymous Cofounder Bill Wilson* (NY: St. Martin's Press, 2000), 10-11.
[221] Dale Mitchel, *Silkworth: The Little Doctor Who Loved Drunks* (MN: Hazelden, 2002), 11-12, 34, 44-51, 159; Bill W. *My First Forty Years* (MN: Hazelden, 2000), 145.

declared he had been born again.[222] Bill immediately went around telling people that the Lord had cured him of his terrible disease.[223] And for sure, he never drank again. Years later, Bill was to repeat his conviction about "conversion" when he wrote Dr. Carl Jung to tell him that Jung's prescription of conversion had made conversions available in A.A. "on an almost wholesale basis."[224]

Conversion and Dr. Bob: Since most of this title is devoted to reporting the conversion of hundreds of people, at mass meetings and in churches, in St. Johnsbury, Vermont, we need say little about the many ways and times in which Dr. Bob was the hearer of accounts of conversions—by lay people in the Young Men's Christian Association, by Christian Endeavorers, by lay evangelists, by preachers, and by missionary people. You will also see here how much talk there was in his Sunday school about saving souls. You will see that entire meetings in Dr. Bob's Christian Endeavor Society were emphasizing conversions at the close of meetings. There was no surprise, then, when Dr. Bob launched out in Akron at the time the new program was developing, and insisted that newcomers accept Christ.[225]

Conversion and some of A.A.'s influential pre-founders: There were many whose books on or about conversion and spiritual cures had a telling influence on Dr. Bob, and to some extent, on Bill Wilson. And while these intellectuals might have been in disagreement about what conversion was, how it was accomplished, why it worked, and the duration of its effectiveness, these people established a phalanx of evidence that alcoholics were cured by conversion. They included: (1) James H. Leuba;[226] (2) E. D. Starbuck;[227] (3) William James;[228] (4) T.

---

[222] "Lois Remembers: Searcy, Ebby, Bill & Early Days." Recorded in Dallas Texas, June 29, 1973, Moore, OK: Sooner Cassette, Side One; Bill W., *My First Forty Years*, 147.
[223] *Alcoholics Anonymous*, 4th ed., 191.
[224] *Pass It On* (NY: Alcoholics Anonymous World Services, Inc., 1984),
[225] Jared C. Lobdell, *This Strange Illness: Alcoholism and Bill W.* (NY: Aldine De Gruyter, 2004), 84-85; Dick B, *A New Way In: Reaching the Heart of a Child of God in Recovery with His Own, Powerful Historical Roots* (Kihei, HI: Paradise Research Publications, Inc., 2006), 11; *Introduction to the Sources and Founding of Alcoholics Anonymous* (Kihei, HI: Paradise Research Publications, Inc., 2007), 18.
[226] James H. Leuba, "A Study in the Psychology of Religious Phenomena" *The American Journal of Psychology,* Vol. VII., April, 1896., No. 3.

S. Arthur;[229] (5) Mary Baker Eddy;[230] (6) Dwight L. Moody;[231] (7) Billy Sunday;[232] (8) Carl Gustav Jung; (9) William D. Silkworth;[233] (10) George A. Coe;[234] and (11) L. W. Grensted,[235] There were and are a host of others who believed that alcoholism could be cured by conversion.[236]

The countless conceded conversion cures: Many writers have discussed conversion and the cure of alcoholism. Perhaps The Reverend Canon L.W. Grensted came closest to categorizing the writings and viewpoints. He discussed the theories of Freud, Adler, James, Jung, and Leuba, among others. He covered and endorsed the veracity of the cures claimed at Lourdes and in Christian Science testimonies, as well as cures involving no Christian aspects at all. He makes a case for the existence of God, the existence of cures, and the special nature of those he distinguishes from the psychological recognitions. He credits elements of suggestion, faith, and love but contradicts the views of Leuba and others that such cures have no basis in divine power. But one will do much better from an evidence standpoint by simply reading my extensive studies of healings and cures throughout the ages. Science likes to dismiss these testimonies and histories as "anecdotal," but the volumes and volumes of accounts certainly provide plenty of conversion-cure proofs throughout the ages. I have hardly found convincing the limited attempts of

---

[227] E. D. Starbuck, *The Psychology of Religion* (NY: Scribner's, 1903).
[228] William James, *The Varieties of Religious Experience* (NY: Vintage Books/The Library of America, 1990).
[229] T. S. Arthur, *Strong Drink: The Curse and The Cure* (San Francisco, CA: Hubbard Brothers, 1877).
[230] Mary Baker Eddy, *Science and Health with Key to the Scriptures* (Boston: Published by the Trustees under the will of Mary Baker Eddy, 1916).
[231] James F. Findlay, Jr., *Dwight L. Moody: American Evangelist 1837-1899* (Chicago: The University of Chicago Press, 1969).
[232] William T. Ellis, *Billy Sunday: The Man and His Message* (Chicago: Moody Press, 1959).
[233] Mitchel, *Silkworth*.
[234] George A. Coe, *The Spiritual Life* (NY: 1900).
[235] L. W. Grensted, *Psychology and God: A Study of the Implications of Recent Psychology For Religious Belief and Practice Being the Bampton Lectures for 1930* (London: Longman's Green and Co.,, 1931).
[236] *Alcohol, Science and Society*, "Twenty-nine Lectures with Discussions as Given at the Yale Summer School of Alcohol Studies" (New Haven, CT: Quarterly Journal of Studies on Alcohol, 1945), 267, 269-85, 403-18, 437-60; Dick B. *A New Way In*, 56-70.

psychologists and psychiatrists to compartmentalize and look in the mind for divine presence and power. Moreover, psychologists, psychiatrists, and psychotherapists have many ways of defining, differentiating; and drawing only on the material, adopted by and premised upon their own scientific definitions. The discussions appear to require a belief that God could not possibly perform miracles, let alone cure an alcoholic. It strikes me that, since I have been cured of alcoholism by the power of God, as have thousands and thousands of others, I would prefer to start where early AAs started: Neither medicine nor psychiatry had relieved alcoholics with predictable or substantial certainty. Nor have they today despite the expenditure of billions for research, treatment, pharmaceuticals, and "psycho-neuro-religio" analyses.

Oddly, while claiming ultimately that alcoholism cures by God were disputable and perhaps specious, William James nonetheless cited all kinds of cases and even coined the psychological definition for conversion that is even in use today. James had a definition that is frequently quoted, even though James was neither a theologian nor a clergyman.[237] Carl Jung posited that alcoholism could be cured by conversion,[238] but his definition of conversion has been dismissed as non-Biblical. by those who have critiqued Jung's thesis.[239] Billy Sunday had a simple definition based on Romans 10:9.[240] Shoemaker quoted both the William James definition and Romans 10:9—apparently believing the two were compatible.[241] Leuba ascribed the conversions to affective disorders that had been relieved but then attributed to religious ideas and power consistent with the patient's belief.[242] Others spoke of "sudden or ("gradual") educational" conversions.[243] Still others spoke of a mystical "Other" or "Something"—a position common with that of some present-day

---

[237] Samuel M. Shoemaker, Jr., *Realizing Religion* (NY: Association Press, 1929), 22.
[238] Dick B., *The Conversion of Bill W.*, 125-26; *Pass It On*, 382-86.
[239] Leslie D. Weatherhead, *Psychology, Religion and Healing* (NY: Abingdon-Cokesbury Press, 1951), 287.
[240] William T. Ellis, *Billy Sunday: The Man and His Message* (Chicago: Moody Press, 1959), 181-82.
[241] Samuel M. Shoemaker, Jr., *Realizing Religion*, 22; and *If I Be Lifted Up*, 81-83.
[242] James Leuba, "Studies in the Psychology of Religious Phenomena," *American Journal of Psychology*, 1896.
[243] Shoemaker, *Realizing Religion*, 27.

analyses.[244] Still others spoke of some supposed difference between "Gospel" conversions and other conversions.[245] And I have cited some examples of such comments in my footnote. But I think it fair to say that the conversions experienced by Bill at the Calvary Mission altar and by Bob in his youth in the Congregational Church were quite simply what followed from their belief in God and their acceptance of Jesus Christ as Lord and Savior. Their belief and actions were based on belief in the accuracy and integrity of the Bible and its many records of healing and cures in Jesus' name—not merely on some inexplicable eradication of a mental disorder followed by attribution based on religious beliefs. Seemingly all the critical writings concede that cures occurred. They also conceded that many cures came to those who turned to God in the name of Jesus Christ. Yet none could do ought but cite the possibility of other explanations. Not proof of the explanations, just theories. And none dealt with the accuracy and integrity of clear-cut Biblical healing accounts at the hands of Jesus, Peter, Paul, Phillip, and other followers of Jesus as the Way. The healings by born-again believers, as reported in the Book of Acts, were founded on the belief that he who confesses with his mouth that Jesus is Lord and believes in his heart that God raised Jesus from the dead fulfills the Bible's requirement for salvation and new birth (John 3:16, Romans 10:9). As well as the assured power of the Holy Spirit that became available on Pentecost just as Jesus had promised in Acts 1 and 2. In fact, in 1 Corinthians 15:1-8, the Apostle Paul explained "the gospel which I preached unto you, which also ye have received, and wherein ye stand; by which also are ye saved."

Specifics in the reports scholars did examine: The time and place spread of those who were studied and described as having been converted and healed includes Augustine, Brother Lawrence, Jerry McAuley, S. H. Hadley, John B. Gough, Charles G. Finney, John Nelson, David Brainerd, Eleanor Emerson, Henry Alline, Colonel James Gardiner, Jonathan Edwards, Adolphe Monod, Billy Bray, Rev. John H. Livingston, Rev. Jeremiah Hallock, and Rev. A. Nettleton. The reader can sort through the writings of Leuba, Starbuck, James,

---

[244] L.W. Grensted, *Psychology and God: A Study of Recent Psychology for Religious Belief and Practice, Being the Bampton Lectures for 1930* (London: Longmans, Green and Co., 1931), 80.
[245] Jared C. Lobdell, *This Strange Illness: Alcoholism and Bill W.* (NY: Aldine De Gruyter, 2004), 44.

Arthur, Eddy, Moody, and Sunday to see the cases reported and studied by these people.[246]

Contemporary accounts of cure by conversion: You may also want to see my extensive studies of the cure of alcoholism by the power of God with specific citations to the varied examples, time periods, and backdrops—including specific early A.A. statements and testimonies.[247]

Even if one were to sort out and set aside cures attributable to all the psychological theories propounded by James, Starbuck, Leuba, and others, he would still have to deal with two things: (1) The accuracy and integrity of the Bible; and the results sought and attained by those who relied on it. (2) The clear-cut healings by the power of God that are described throughout the Bible and relied upon by contemporary healers. Let's just take one, of many examples in the Book of Acts. Peter explained the word which was published throughout all Judaea:

> How God anointed Jesus of Nazareth with the Holy Ghost and with power: who went about doing good and healing all that were oppressed of the devil; for God was with him. And we are witnesses of all things which he did both in the land of the Jews and in Jerusalem . . . (Acts 10: 38-39)

Relevance

Why this excursion into conversion as we look at Dr. Bob's youth? There is a very simple reason.

---

[246] For an extensive review of these early writings, see Jared Lobdell's *Strange Illness*; Bill Pittman, *A.A. The Way It Began* (Seattle: Glen Abbey Books, 1988); Leslie D. Weatherhead, *Psychology, Religion and Healing* (NY: Abingdon-Cokesbury, 1951); Howard Clinebell, *Understanding and Counseling Persons with Alcohol, Drug, and Behavioral Addictions*. Rev. and enl. ed. (Nashville: Abingdon Press, 1998).
[247] Dick B., *When Early AAs Were Cured and Why*, 3rd ed. (Kihei, HI: Paradise Research Publications, Inc., 2006); and Dick B., *Cured!: Proven Help for Alcoholics and Addicts*, 2d ed. (Kihei, HI: Paradise Research Publications, Inc., 2006).

Dr. Bob and Bill formulated a program in Akron that required conversion as a condition of membership.[248] We have already covered the source of Bill Wilson's conviction that conversion was the solution to alcoholism.[249] That is the message Bill undoubtedly carried to Dr. Bob when they met in Akron.[250] On the other hand, because that message was deliberately eliminated from the Shoemaker-oriented program that Bill published four years later in the Big Book, the other half of the equation has been ignored. Bill had seen conversion at work with his grandfather Willie's conversion and cure. He had heard the Carl Jung conversion prescription from his friend Ebby Thacher. Bill had gone to the altar and Calvary Rescue Mission and been converted. And he had verified his own conversion experience by reading the William James book at Towns Hospital. Bottom line: Bill never drank again.

That's the Wilson side of the conversion picture. But what were the basic Bible ideas that Bill and Dr. Bob put in their pioneer program that had such great success? How and why was conversion mandated in the program that Bill and Bob developed? And the complete answer involves the other side of the conversion picture—the history unearthed and disclosed in this book. Very probably most AAs, most counselors, most clergymen, most psychologists, most historians, most scientists, and most researchers have not had the slightest clue to Dr. Bob's immersion in conversion as a youngster. Immersion through his family, his church, his Sunday School, his Christian Endeavor activities, the YMCA, his four years at St. Johnsbury Academy, and through the conversion atmosphere that had permeated St. Johnsbury as a community largely as the result of the "Great Awakening" of 1875.

Put the two together—Wilson's conversion idea and Dr. Bob's conversion background—and you will understand why it was that conversion to Christ was an essential element of the program they founded in 1935. Without a recitation of those the historical facts and details, your beliefs will be doubted. Without them, you will probably be pelted with all the usual remarks about "spiritual but not religious,"

---

[248] Dick B., *A New Way In: Telling the Truth* (Kihei, HI: Paradise Research Publications, Inc., 2006), 11.
[249] Dick B., *The Conversion of Bill W.*
[250] *Alcoholics Anonymous*, 4th ed., 191

"higher powers," and "inclusiveness." And sometimes—though they represent the real founding of Alcoholics Anonymous—you will hear: "Aw, that's not A.A." All well and good if you like, but you will not understand either the relevance or the depth in importance of early A.A.'s conversion picture if you succumb to the nonsense.

"Your Heavenly Father will never let you down!"
Alcoholics Anonymous, 4th ed., p. 181

3
A.A.'s Dr. Bob and His St. Johnsbury, Vermont, Roots

What can seekers see and find if they decide to visit to the actual building specified as Dr. Bob's birthplace and boyhood home in St. Johnsbury, Vermont? If they allow enough time, they will get far more than they ever bargained for. Of course, they can see a beautiful fall leaves display if they go there in the autumn. Also, to be sure, they can search out and enjoy the nearby ski resorts if they go there in the winter. They can visit the many historical and scenic locations in the state of Vermont.[251] They can see a very unique and quaint village that became a center of Vermont business prosperity, Christian revival and evangelism, and profound Congregational church activity.[252] And they can frequent nearby antique stores and used book-store resources.[253]

Yes, but what about A.A.? Why go to Dr. Bob's home town after all these years just to see where A.A.'s cofounder was born and raised? You will be amazed at just how much A.A. history you can see, study, and learn. Actually, literally thousands go to Founders Day in Akron each year not only to hear the speakers, but primarily to view Dr. Bob's Home, tombstone, the King School meeting place, Henrietta Seiberling's Gate House, the T. Henry Williams Home, St. Thomas Hospital, King School, and a couple of other sites. I've done it several times. But St. Johnsbury will offer you far more than a drive-by tour of Akron. If, you are seeking a similar town-tour experience in St.

---

[251] Arthur F. Stone. *The Vermont of Today: With Its Historic Background, Attractions and People.* Vol. II (NY: Lewis Historical Publishing Company, Inc., 1929)—the Green Mountains Tour—(pp. 875-91).
[252] Arthur F. Stone, comp., *St. Johnsbury Illustrated: A Review of the Town's Business, Social, Literary, and Educational Facilities, with Glimpses of Picturesque Surroundings* (St. Johnsbury, VT: Caledonian Press—C.M. Stone & Company, 1891); Claire Dunne Johnson. *Images of America: St. Johnsbury* (Dover, NH: Arcadia Publishing, 1996).
[253] *St Johnsbury, Vermont: Maple Center of the World*, (St. Johnsbury, VT: The St. Johnsbury Chamber of Commerce, 1981).

Johnsbury, you may find inspiration in the massive buildings and village's pre-occupation with churches, libraries, museums, YMCA activity, and educational supremacy. A religious and educational supremacy founded by three Fairbanks brothers who insisted on a Christian atmosphere in every town resource they touched—Congregational to the core. Both the Fairbanks family members—all Christians, Congregational church leaders, YMCA leaders, and proponents of Christian education—and the Smith family members (who held the same convictions), lived their lives in a very religious village whose principal leaders were dedicated servants of the Creator and His son Jesus Christ.

The answer as to why AAs and those "in recovery" would go to St. Johnsbury can and should be much more rewarding, fulfilling, and satisfying. Particularly if they are trying to get a handle on how the earliest AAs "found" God, established a relationship with Him, and moved on to the abundant and eternal life that the Good Book promised to those who become children of the living Creator.

That answer can be found underlined, supported, and available for all alcoholics, addicts, families of the afflicted, historians, professionals, clergy, recovery workers, and recovery history students. You would go there to learn as much as possible about what Robert Holbrook Smith, M.D., brought with him from St. Johnsbury, Vermont, to Akron, Ohio. And hence exactly what had enabled drunks and others to discover what God could and would do for the alcoholic who still suffers when God is sought. Hebrews 11:6 states God's view of the matter quite well:

> But without faith, *it is* impossible to please *him* [God], for he that cometh to God must believe that he is and *that* he is a rewarder of them that diligently seek him. (KJV)

The St. Johnsbury of Dr. Bob's youth is replete with testimony to the diligence and zeal that could be found among its residents earnestly seeking sonship and fellowship with the Creator.

Let's say you want to know how the Bible got from St. Johnsbury to Akron and became embedded in the Christian Fellowship founded there in 1935. Let's say you want to know where early AAs learned about the power of the Creator to heal them, guide them, and bless them. Let's say you want to know the reason for early A.A. conversions and "surrenders" to Jesus Christ on their path to a relationship with Almighty God. Let's say you wonder if the converted alcoholic is "powerless" to resist temptation, relapse, and more drinking and disasters. Let's say you wonder why early AAs talked about the Bible, the Ten Commandments, the Sermon on the Mount, the Book of James, 1 Corinthians 13, love, service, elimination of sin, prayer, quiet time, and fellowship with like-minded believers. Let's say you still erroneously think that all this came from the Oxford Group to Akron and then was simply rejected largely because of A.A. distaste for the Oxford Group. Let's say you think that none of this is relevant to the bottom line task of the real alcoholic in A.A. today—which is to trust God, clean house, and help others. Both *Anne Smith's Journal* and Bill Wilson's Big Book tell you that you can't give away what you haven't got. Let's say you are bewildered about being told to form your own idea of "a" god, a "not-god;" or of a power that is a radiator. Or to swallow the undefined "spiritual but not religious idea;" or to select and name your "higher power" as a light bulb; or to forget the availability of "cure" and buy into the new thought that relapse is considered OK and virtually inevitable today.

I'll hazard a guess that you won't find the answers to these things even in the exciting secular events that occur in Akron each year. The speakers won't talk about them. The hospitable keepers of the sites know little about them and will speak even less on the subject. The Home and the tombstone are unable to talk about conversion, cure, and the early Christian Fellowship. Nor is the privately-owned T. Henry Williams house. Nor the Seiberling Gate Lodge. Nor the St. Thomas Hospital ward. Nor the King School. And if they could talk, the atmosphere is such that these topics would not even be very welcome either in Akron or in A.A. today. I've gone there many times, and I love it. But I have never learned one thing about Dr. Bob's youth, training, beliefs, and translated convictions by going there. There is an exception to that statement. If you buy the AA of Akron pamphlets from the Intergroup office, or if you see the exhibits manned by A.A. historian and archivist Ray G. at Dr. Bob's Home during Founders Day activities, you will get a head start. Nevertheless, these are the things that St. Johnsbury had to offer—and still does.

If these things are bothering you as your ponder healing of your own affliction or about your own ability to carry a message of real hope to the alcoholic or addict who still suffers, you would go there to see just how much of the early A.A. program can be traced to its real spiritual beginnings in Vermont. You would go there to see if there really were places at church, Sunday School, prayer service, Wednesday prayer meetings, the YMCA, and Christian Endeavor where Dr. Bob learned. You'd go there to see if St. Johnsbury Academy really did require daily chapel and weekly church and Bible study attendance. You would go there to see if the message about our Heavenly Father was rooted in the excellent training in the Bible that Dr. Bob said he had received there as a youngster. You would go there to discover the roots of the movement Dr. Bob Smith and Bill Wilson co-founded years later—roots that produced a documented 75%-93% success rate among seemingly hopeless, medically incurable, real alcoholics who thoroughly followed the early A.A. path to a relationship with God. You would find, from this book, from the resource binders, from the Dr. Bob Core Library books at North Congregational Church, and from the archival materials at the church, the museum, the Athenaeum, and the Academy a host of historical materials you never dreamed existed or were relevant to A.A. You would come to understand how and why the pioneers believed they could be healed and were cured! And why they said so! Quite simply, you'd see how it came to be that they believed that God is, and that He would heal them if they sought Him--diligently[254] And obeyed Him—diligently.[255]

The Treasures in Dr. Bob's Birthplace and Boyhood Home, North Congregational Church, Christian Endeavor Society, St. Johnsbury Academy

Dr. Bob's Birthplace and Boyhood Home: Today's Dr. Bob's birthplace and boyhood home (at the corner of Center and Summer

---

[254] Hebrews 11:6—believe that God is, and that he is a rewarder of them that diligently seek Him
[255] Exodus 15:26—"And [the LORD] said, If thou wilt diligently hearken to the voice of the LORD thy God, and wilt do that which is right in his sight, and wilt give ear to his commandments, and keep all his statutes, I will put none of these diseases upon thee, which I have brought upon the Egyptians: for I *am* the LORD that healeth thee." Psalm 103:2-3—"Bless the LORD, O my soul, and forget not all his benefits: Who forgiveth all thine iniquities; who healeth all thy diseases."

Streets, not far from North Congregational Church, St. Johnsbury) is managed as a non-profit, drop-in recovery center. Its address is 297 Summer Street, St. Johnsbury, Vermont 05819. The building is owned by a hospital organization. Its paid staff and volunteers host regular A.A. and other meetings and provide counseling and referral services.[256] There have been D.U.I. and similar programs there. The center is run by directors, a paid staff of four, and numerous volunteers. It also serves as a drop-in center for people in recovery. It has expressed a desire to improve Dr. Bob's birthplace and boyhood home, refurbish Dr. Bob's bedroom, and, to a yet to be planned and defined degree, establish an information center and library which can tell visitors about Dr. Bob, his youth, and the Town of St. Johnsbury. Should it choose to do so, it could help others to recognize the recovery potential available to the afflicted by informing them about Dr. Bob's religious connections and excellent Bible training in St. Johnsbury, and how his education impacted on the astonishingly-successful early A.A. program developed in Akron, Ohio, starting in 1935. It could also point visitors to the easy walk down to Main Street and to North Congregational Church, the museum, the library, and the Academy. To do that, the people there would need to have the historical resources, steep themselves in the facts, and be willing to explain the history to those who happen by. That is a service they can render to visitors. But you can simply go to the Dr. Bob Core Library at North Congregational Church and get all the information, directions, and education about A.A. and its historical roots that you could possibly absorb. It's accessible, open, friendly, and free.

You can also find out for yourself by reading our new titles, based on extensive research. You can do it by continued monitoring of our www.DrBob.info website. Or you can go there when our binders and core library are housed in the new, well-stewarded, accessible location. Or you can go there and utilize the many facts and resources in this title, and yourself trudge the evidentiary path at St. Johnsbury—mostly located in a three block walk on Main Street..

North Congregational Church, St. Johnsbury: You will find more details and specific citations about the church and its relevant history elsewhere. Suffice it to say here that Dr. Bob and his parents regularly

---

[256] Kingdom Recover Center Pamphlet: *Bringing People & Recovery Together: Drop-in Center Information, Socialization, Education, and Referrals.*

attended services at this church at least four times a week. They were much involved—the father as a life-time deacon, Sunday school superintendent, and long-time Sunday School teacher there. The mother as a choir member, Sunday school superintendent and teacher, missions worker, leader in church women's organizations, and historian. Bob's father, Judge Walter Perrin Smith, sat on the Caledonia County (Vermont) Probate Court. The Judge served as a superintendent of St. Johnsbury schools, examiner at St. Johnsbury Academy,[257] where his wife taught and his son matriculated, and he was a YMCA president. Bob's mother has been incorrectly characterized as a stern, church-going lady who busied herself with the countless social and religious activities of North Congregational Church, St. Johnsbury. She was said to have believed the way to success and salvation lay through strict parental supervision, no-nonsense education, and regular spiritual devotion. But her actual story tells us much, much more. As we have mentioned, Mrs. Walter Smith had graduated from and taught at St. Johnsbury Academy.[258] She was on its alumni executive committee.[259] She wrote two chapters of its official history book.[260] She delivered at least one address on the history of St. Johnsbury Academy.[261] She was also president of a Women's Club,[262] was a member of the Vermont Library Commission,[263] and was involved in domestic mission work.[264] The facts are in the St. Johnsbury church library for all to see.

The Christian Endeavor Society: Founded on February 2, 1881, at the Williston Congregational Church in Portland, Maine, less than a year-and-a-half after Dr. Bob was born on August 8, 1879, this movement spread across New England and then around the world, attaining a

---

[257] *St. Johnsbury Academy Catalogue* for 1873, p. 22.
[258] Fairbanks et al., *An Historical Sketch*, 106.
[259] Fairbanks et al., *St. Johnsbury Academy*, 71.
[260] Fairbanks et al., *An Historical Sketch*, p. v.
[261] Fairbanks et al., *An Historical Sketch*, 71.
[262] Marquis, *Who's Who in New England*, 994.
[263] Albert Nelson Marquis, *Who's Who in New England* ( ), 994, "Smith, Susan Holbrook."
[264] Letter from Ken B. to Taylor Reed regarding Reed's article "Alcoholics Anonymous Rooted in St. Johnsbury Institutions" in *The Caledonian-Record*, online edition, October 12, 2007, and monograph of C.S. Smith, *An Historical Sketch of Home Missionary Work in Vermont, By the Congregational Churches* (Montpelier: Press of the Watchman Publishing Company, 1893)

membership of 3.5 million at its apex.[265] Dr. Bob said he had received "excellent training" in the "Good Book" as a youngster—at his church, Christian Endeavor, and (as history shows) at St. Johnsbury Academy. Actually, the Christian Endeavor Society supported the local church, was self-governing, and self-supporting. It insisted on confession of Jesus Christ, individual and also weekly Bible study at its meetings, prayer meetings, conversion meetings, Quiet Hour, and discussion of religious topics. It also had the (later-to-be A.A.) slogan of "love and service."[266] The facts are in this title, our binders, the library, and our other writings. They could and should be in St. Johnsbury; and the most important and helpful books will be there and more.

St. Johnsbury Academy: In 1894, Dr. Bob entered St. Johnsbury Academy as a fifteen-year-old. "The Academy was founded in 1842 by the three Fairbanks brothers [Erastus, Thaddeus, and Joseph], local residents and manufacturers, to provide 'intellectual, moral, and religious training for their own children and the children of the community.'"[267] We have shown that the Fairbanks people were devout Congregationalists—several of them ministers. They saw to it that Christian education, morals, and training were part and parcel of the founding, administration, and activities of this independent secondary school. The Academy required daily chapel and required weekly church and Bible study attendance. On his graduation in 1898, Dr. Bob delivered the commencement Oration and then went to Dartmouth College for four years. The Academy is still alive with those who know the facts and with the archives and literature which tells them.

Research Potential in St. Johnsbury. On our recent trip to St. Johnsbury, my son Ken and I actually studied a number of the records and resources in St Johnsbury about the neglected story of Dr. Bob's "excellent training" in the Good Book "as a youngster." And we now

---

[265] "Christian Endeavor," *Time Magazine,* July 11, 1927: http://www.time.com/time/magazine/article/0,9171,929339,00.html ; accessed on November 4, 2007.

[266] See, for example: "Platform of Principles," *The New York Times*, July 11, 1892: http://query.nytimes.com/gst/abstract.html?res=9906E4D61631E033A25752C1A9619C94639ED7CF ; accessed 11/4/07.

[267] "St. Johnsbury Academy, St. Johnsbury, Vermont": http://denoweb.petersons.com/ccc92/display_pdf?p_instance_id=156127.pdf; accessed 11/4/07.

know there are innumerable sources for research and acquisition of information at St. Johnsbury Academy, the St. Johnsbury Athenaeum (the local library), the Fairbanks Museum and Planetarium, and at North Congregational Church, and the Town of St. Johnsbury itself. Additional information is obtainable from various Congregational and United Church of Christ publications and archives. Some is available in nearby Burlington, Vermont. Also from the Vermont Historical Society, the University of Vermont, and extensive Congregational and YMCA materials. There are also a good many diaries and memoirs to be checked. We believe—based on an interview with the minister at North Congregational Church, St. Johnsbury, and interviews with archivists in the town--that there is still much to be learned at St. Johnsbury Academy, and from Christian Endeavor records at North Congregational Church, St. Johnsbury (and perhaps elsewhere, as well)--particularly from journals of meetings, so common in Bob's days, as well as from his Sunday school regimen. The little village abounds with places to search for A.A.-related history apparently never yet tracked. We have already assembled and placed in our core library titles by distinguished St. Johnsbury historians, Vermont historians, Congregational church historians, North Congregational Church historians, YMCA historians, Temperance historians, and several important biographies, genealogies, and histories of the Fairbanks family, the Smiths, and Vermont's religious leaders. We cite them frequently in this title and in the resource binders. We've gone to great lengths to acquire, study, and make them available.

Highlights of
Our Dr. Bob History Companion Resource Volumes

This title is an explanatory book about the scope, purpose, and contents of the many resource collections in binders and core library books and materials which contain much-needed information and history. Those volumes are headed for a responsible, well-stewarded, permanent location right in St. Johnsbury Vermont at Dr. Bob's church. Meanwhile, they will be stewarded, studied, and expanded. And this is a summary of what the binders presently contain:

- Complete, carefully-researched and annotated evidentiary materials detailing: the birth, birthplace and boyhood home, and genealogy of Dr. Bob; key statements of A.A. founders about A.A's roots; the St. Johnsbury, Vermont of Dr. Bob's youth; key information about the Judge Walter Perrin Smith family and its prominence in the affairs of St. Johnsbury's governmental, judicial, business, educational, church, and religious life; the significant influence of the Fairbanks Family on the community and on the activities of the Smiths; the North Congregational Church, St. Johnsbury; its Sunday School; the Christian Endeavor Society; the Young Men's Christian Association; Vermont Congregationalism; and St. Johnsbury Academy--where Judge Smith conducted examinations; where Mrs. Walter P. Smith graduated and became a teacher and historian of the Academy and a leader in its alumni activities, and where there was stress on Bible study, Bible-readings, prayers, hymns, church attendance, daily Chapel, conversion, moral and religious training; and studies of Christian texts; the St. Johnsbury Athenaeum (town library); the Fairbanks Museum and Planetarium; the influence of St. Johnsbury ideas on the early A.A. program; the early A.A. program and the recognizable influence of Dr. Bob's younger days; and more. And many photographs!

- Key statements of the first three AAs—Bill Wilson, Dr. Bob Smith, and attorney Bill Dotson—which make several points abundantly clear about pioneer A.A.: (1) Abstinence was first in objective. (2) Reliance on the Creator was a necessity. (3) Confession of Christ (i.e., conversion) was the way to a relationship with God. (4) Study of the Bible (the Good Book) was absolutely essential to the early A.A. program. (5) Prayer and Quiet Time were daily fare. (6) Love and Service became the motto. (7) Working with other alcoholics and bringing them the message of God's healing and cure was required. (8) Religious and social comradeship were recommended. (9) Attendance at a church of one's choice was also recommended. (10) Early AAs were cured of their alcoholism by the power of God and so stated for almost a decade after A.A.'s founding in 1935.

- Dr. Bob's birth certificate and a picture of Dr. Bob's birthplace and boyhood home on 297 Summer Street in St. Johnsbury. There is a brief history of Dr. Bob's birthplace and boyhood home and of the Town of St. Johnsbury itself. Then pictures of the St. Johnsbury Dr. Bob saw—North Congregational Church, St. Johnsbury; the Young Men's Christian Association building, the Fairbanks Museum and Planetarium, the St. Johnsbury Athenaeum, the court house, the Fairbanks scales plant, various Fairbanks residences, and St. Johnsbury Academy. Lots of photos and pictures of all these places in the early days.

- A large section on the Fairbanks Family. As so many have already written, no picture of St. Johnsbury would be complete without adequate background on the Fairbanks people. The whole family was immersed in Congregationalism and deeply religious. The Fairbanks's became famous and very wealthy from the invention of the Fairbanks platform scale by Thaddeus Fairbanks. Their public service and dedication to Christian and moral education were everywhere evident—the North Congregational Church, St. Johnsbury, was served by them in a myriad of ways; they donated most of the Town's principal landmark buildings—the North Congregational Church, the Fairbanks Museum and Planetarium, the St. Johnsbury Athenaeum, the YMCA building, and numerous buildings connected with St. Johnsbury Academy—which the family founded. Various Fairbanks's served in the Fairbanks business; in the Congregational churches of the community, as well as district and state conferences; in Sunday School teaching; in YMCA work; in revivals and missionary work; and in about every aspect of the St. Johnsbury Academy—where many held positions as trustees and officers. They served as clergy, headmasters, deacons, teachers, school superintendents, legislators, military officers, and—in two cases—as Governors of the State of Vermont.

- Abundant information on the Smith family: Ancestry, marriages, births, Congregational church activities, Christian Endeavor involvement, participation in revivals and evangelism, Sunday School involvement, YMCA participation, musical interests and involvements, the Judge's position in various government positions, and Mrs. Walter Smith's teaching, writing, speaking, and alumni work at the Academy.

- North Congregational Church, St. Johnsbury, information. This church was a key influence in Dr. Bob's life and ultimately on the A.A. program itself. The entire family attended that church four, and sometimes five, times each week—for worship, Sunday School, Bible study, and prayer. The church had a vibrant relationship with the Christian Endeavor Society to which Dr. Bob belonged. The North Church led the way in many conversions, revivals, and Gospel meetings. It also worked with the YMCA, evangelists, and revivals. Judge Smith was a life-time Deacon (lay spiritual leader) of the church and taught Sunday school there for over 30 years. Mrs. Smith was prominent in many church committees and activities. The history of the church and what it did is presented from the church's records and from Congregational and United Church of Christ sources. The present North Church building was financed largely by the Fairbanks family and constructed by two of its members. Church leaders have helped immensely in assembling facts.

- Information about Vermont Congregationalism and what it did in the churches, with youth, with unions, with Christian Endeavor, with the YMCA, with revivals, conversions, and evangelism, with Sunday Schools, and with the principles of autonomy, self-governance, and self-support. Moreover, 1875—just four years before Dr. Bob's birth in 1879--was called the "Great Awakening" in St. Johnsbury and the surrounding communities in Vermont.[268] St. Johnsbury Historian Claire Dunne Johnson wrote:

    > The year 1875 saw the beginning of the "Great Awakening," so-called, a tremendous surge of a new religious fervor, initiated here by the Y.M.C.A there were great mass meetings at the churches and even at the scale shops. Prayer meetings and hymn-sings were attended by great numbers of people, and various

---

[268] Stone, *North Congregational Church, St. Johnsbury, Vermont: 1825-1942* (St. Johnsbury, VT: North Congregational Church, 1942), 31, 32.

religious groups in town were inspired to build their own churches.[269]

- Conversion was a major objective and achievement. Enlargement of church membership accompanied the saving of souls. You can scarcely pick up a book, report, or history of Dr. Bob's Vermont days without seeing frequent mention of: (1) Conversions. (2) The concern about "saving souls." (3) The importance of bringing people to Christ.

- Considerable information on the Christian Endeavor Society, which was in full flower in Vermont—including in St. Johnsbury—within four-to-six years of its founding in Maine in 1881. The principles of confession of Christ, Bible study meetings, prayer meetings, conversion meetings, the Quiet Hour (and "Comrades of the Quiet Hour), topical discussions, reading of literature, social and religious comradeship, and church attendance—as well as Christian Endeavor's motto of "Love and Service"--can be found in the Akron A.A. founded at Dr. Bob and Anne Smith's home in 1935. Included in the St. Johnsbury core library are an immense number of articles written by Dick B. on the Christian Endeavor Society, its principles and practices, and its evident contribution to early A.A.'s spiritual program of recovery.

- St. Johnsbury Athenaeum information. It was a library donated to the community by the Fairbanks's. It served as the town library and an adjunct to St. Johnsbury Academy educational outreach. Many a St. Johnsbury Academy graduating class had its picture taken on the steps of the St. Johnsbury Athenaeum—although, it should be noted, Dr. Bob's graduating class picture in 1898 was taken on the steps of North Congregational Church, St. Johnsbury.

- Information on the Fairbanks Museum and Planetarium. It too was donated to the community by the Fairbanks's and still stands as the repository of many archival and historical

---

[269] Claire Dunne Johnson. *"I See By The Paper. . ." An Informal History of St. Johnsbury* (St Johnsbury, VT: The Cowles Press, 1987), 84.

treasures—in addition to its function as a museum and a planetarium. It also served as an adjunct to the St. Johnsbury Academy educational outreach.

- YMCA-related information. The YMCA occupied a special place in St. Johnsbury religious life. It conducted lectures at St. Johnsbury Academy. It conducted concerts, even in the churches. It organized revivals, conversions, and evangelist visits. Many of its activities were coordinated directly with the churches, and occurred while Christian Endeavor and (perhaps) other youth activities were in progress. Conversion to Christ was a key mission. The YMCA building (which was destroyed by fire in 1984) was donated in 1885 to the community by the Fairbanks family.

- Information on St. Johnsbury Academy. This institution is a virtually-unmentioned part of the Dr. Bob/A.A. picture. The Fairbanks's were Congregationalists. They founded St. Johnsbury Academy and specified the necessity for Christian and moral education. They required in their deeds that all Trustees be members of a Congregational Church. Church attendance and Bible study were required of students once a week. Chapel attendance was required daily. Graduation ceremonies were opened with prayer, closed with prayer, and often involved a sermon by an ordained minister. Courses in Christian materials, with Bible study and other biblical texts, were required. YMCA lectures were frequently given there. Judge Smith was an examiner.[270] Mrs. Smith was a graduate, then a teacher, then a frequent speaker, then an historian, and also a member of the executive committee of the alumni. The school records are replete with accounts of Dr. Bob's participation. His attendance card, yearly class status, membership in the Glee Club, Managing the Glee Club, membership in the Adelphian Literary Society, participation in debates, presidency of his Junior Class, his oration at his own commencement exercise, and class notes and prophecy are presented. In fact, thanks to the diligent work and research of the archivist there, we probably have more information about

---

[270] *St. Johnsbury Academy Catalogue* for 1873, p. 22.

the Smiths and the Academy than on any other Dr. Bob subject.

- Cure of alcoholism information. The cure of alcoholism by the power of God was an accepted fact in early A.A. The original drafts of A.A.'s basic text boasted at first that "never" had a person failed who had thoroughly followed the path which led to a relationship with God. The clear statements that God's power had cured the pioneers can still be found in A.A.'s own literature concerning Bill Wilson, Dr. Bob, and A.A. Number Three. Unique to our resource volume on the cures is the collection of hundreds of newspaper and magazine materials for more than a decade after A.A. founding—in all of which AAs said there was a cure, alcoholism could be cured, and that they had been cured. We have included copies of the news articles so stating. Yet, despite this overwhelming evidence, A.A. "leaders" and "trusted servants" today, and most of the recovery community, have adopted the bizarre idea that alcoholism *cannot* be cured. This despite a decade of testimonies to the contrary.[271]

- Information on the original Akron A.A. program. Elements of the original Akron program of recovery are described in some detail, largely from A.A.'s own early literature.[272] They have been thoroughly covered in a number of Dick B. books already published. They make the conclusive case—beyond a reasonable doubt—that early AAs achieved a documented 75%-93% success rate among seemingly-hopeless, "medically incurable," real alcoholics who thoroughly followed the A.A. path to a relationship with, and reliance on, the Creator of the heavens and the earth. And for the assurances that they could, see, for example: Genesis 1:1; Exodus 15:26; Psalm 103:3; and 3 John 2.

---

[271] See Dick B., Cured: Proven Help for Alcoholics and Addicts (Kihei, HI: Paradise Research Publications, 2003).
[272] Dick B. *The James Club and the Original A.A. Program's Absolute Essentials*, 4th ed. (Kihei, HI: Paradise Research Publications, Inc., 2005), 119-25.

The Place to Start: Key Remarks by A.A. Founders and Pioneers about Conversion, the "Great Physician," the "Good Book," the Power of God, the Cure of Alcoholism, and Service to Others

The Founding of A.A. and Its Astonishing Success Rates

Based on eighteen years of almost-continuous research, analysis, and publication, our series of companion binders is intended to be a resource. The resource will make available in raw form the findings which trace the path of A.A. cofounder Dr. Robert H. Smith's enormous spiritual growth and contributions to the field of alcoholism recovery programs and cures. Its purpose is to set the record straight—with documented evidence—on the true religious origins, biblical foundations, and basic ideas of the early A.A. Christian Fellowship of Akron, Ohio.

The original, early, pioneer A.A. fellowship was founded by Bill Wilson of New York (often called "Bill W.") and Dr. Robert Smith of Akron (often called "Dr. Bob"). The date was June 10, 1935. The place was the residence of Dr. Bob and his wife Anne Smith and their children ("Smitty" and Sue) at 855 Ardmore Avenue, in Akron. The first A.A. *group* was founded in 1935 when Akron attorney, Bill Dotson, was cured of alcoholism and marched from the Akron City Hospital to join Bill W. and Dr. Bob in the "alcoholic squad" (as it was then often called). In his last major talk to AAs, Dr. Bob said: There was no basic text. There were no "Twelve Steps." There simply was what Dr. Bob often called the "Christian Fellowship," which took its basic ideas from the study of the Bible—appropriately dubbed the "Good Book."

The following key remarks by the first three AAs make very clear the roots, the basic ideas, and the principles of that early Akron pioneer program.

And just why is this almost forgotten earliest program and the founders' remarks about it so important? The answer lies in the documented, 75%-93% success rate it achieved among seemingly hopeless, "medically incurable," real alcoholics who thoroughly followed the path that the pioneers marked out. Where's the proof? Where do you find the documentation? Again, you start with the founders and the incorporation of their statements in A.A.'s own "Conference Approved" literature. Moreover, you can go to the Griffith Library, located at the Wilson House grounds in East Dorset, Vermont, where Bill Wilson was born and raised. And you can see the rosters, the names, the dates, and the sobriety records of A.A.'s first forty. Among those forty pioneers—who were primarily from the Akron Area—fifty percent had maintained continuous sobriety, and twenty-five percent had "slipped" but had returned to attain sobriety. We have included the documented study by scholar Richard K. in our "cured" resource binder. Perhaps even more important, the early A.A. men declared consistently that they had been "cured" of alcoholism. Cured by the power of the Creator. By 1939, the success rate and the growth of A.A. skyrocketed largely because of the leadership of one of Dr. Bob's sponsees—Clarence H. Snyder. In Cleveland, records showed there was a ninety-three percent success rate; and the A.A. fellowship there grew faster than in any part of the United States—it went from one group to thirty in a year.[273]

The Christian Religious Elements from Dr. Bob's Early Life and Bill W.'s Many Earlier Comments and Experiences

This is the documented account of the real, early, "original," pioneer A.A. program and of the specific ideas that arose out of the "excellent training" (as Dr. Bob put it) in the Good Book that Dr. Bob had received as a youngster in St. Johnsbury, Vermont. You will see all the elements of that early St. Johnsbury religious backdrop in the companion resource binders. To that backdrop, Bill Wilson brought two highly important elements of the pioneer A.A. religious program: (1) Conversion as the cure. (2) Service as the means of evangelizing and maintaining the cure, and of perpetuating the two fundamental elements of love and service—the latter being the motto of the Christian Endeavor of Dr. Bob's youth in St. Johnsbury.

---

[273] These 93% and 30 group figures are documented in A.A.'s own *DR. BOB and the Good Old timers*; in Mitch K.'s *How It Worked*; and in my own title, *That Amazing Grace*. They are discussed in more detail at a later point here.

But first, let's see how the first three AAs—Bill Wilson, Dr. Bob Smith, and Bill Dotson--painted the picture accurately with their recorded remarks.

What the First Three AAs Had to Say

Bill W.: A.A. cofounder Bill Wilson led off with his early comments about the three elements he brought to the early Akron program scene—(1) Conversion and the new birth as essential to the solution of alcoholism. (2) Cure as the result. (3) Service and help for other alcoholics as the action required for consummation of purpose.

- First, as to Bill Wilson's conversion and rebirth, resultant cure, and "golden text" message:

  Bill's grandfather Willie Wilson had been converted and cured in East Dorset years before A.A. Grandpa Willie never drank again after he was saved.[274]

  Professor William James had confirmed the efficacy of such conversion cures, citing the findings and accounts of Dr. Edwin D. Starbuck, Revivalist Charles G. Finney, Professor James Leuba, and psychology Professor George A. Coe, together with the dramatic conversion cures of Jerry M'Auley, S. H. Hadley and many others in similar cases.[275]

  Following the conversion example evident in the life of his friend Edwin T. Thacher (called "Ebby"), Bill also went to the Calvary Rescue Mission in New York.[276] He knelt at the

---

[274] Susan Cheever, *My Name Is Bill: Bill Wilson—His Life and the Creation of Alcoholics Anonymous* (New York: Washington Square Press, 2004), 17; Dick B., *The Conversion of Bill W.: More on the Creator's Role in Early A.A.* (Kihei, HI: Paradise Research Publications, Inc., 2006), 25-26, 41, 117-18, xii; and Bill Wilson, *Bill W.: My First 40 Years: An Autobiography by the Cofounder of Alcoholics Anonymous* (Center City, MN: Hazelden, 2000), 6.

[275] William James, *The Varieties of Religious Experience* (New York, NY: Vintage Books/The Library of America, 1990), 348, 435, 448-54, 177-200, 204-22, 237-38; and Mel B., *New Wine: The Spiritual Roots of the Twelve Step Miracle* (Center City, MN: Hazelden, 1991), 52-56, 83-88, 127-41.

[276] Dick B., *The Conversion of Bill W.,* 45-50, 84-88.

altar with a Brother who prayed with him.[277] In the words of his wife Lois, "And he went up, and really, in very great sincerity, did hand over his life over to Christ."[278] Reverend Sam Shoemaker's wife phrased it as she had witnessed it: Bill "made his decision for Christ."[279] After that, Bill twice wrote in his autobiography, "For sure I was born again."[280]

Shortly after his conversion at the Calvary Rescue Mission, Bill returned to boozing and was drinking heavily again for another two or three days. But things had changed. One writer conjectured that "something had changed in the way Bill drank."[281] For one thing, during what had been his third hospitalization at Towns Hospital in New York, Bill had had important conversations with his psychiatrist there—William D. Silkworth, M.D. Silkworth's biographer observed:

> Silkworth has not been given the appropriate credit for his position on spiritual conversion, particularly as it may relate to true Christian benefits. Several sources, including Norman Vincent Peale in his book *The Positive Power of Jesus Christ*, agree that it was Dr. Silkworth who used the term "The Great Physician" to explain the need in recovery for a relationship with Jesus Christ. . . . In the formation of AA, Wilson initially insisted on references to God and Jesus, as

---

[277] Dick B., *The Conversion of Bill W.*, 88-94; *"Pass It On": The Story of Bill Wilson and How the A.A. Message Reached the World* (New York, NY: Alcoholics Anonymous World Services, Inc., 1984), 116-19; and Bill Wilson, *Bill W.: My First 40 Years*, 136-37.

[278] "Lois Remembers: Searcy, Ebby, Bill Early Days." Recorded in Dallas, Texas, June 29, 1973, Moore, OK: Sooner Cassette, Side One; and Dick B., *The Conversion of Bill W.*, 61.

[279] Dick B., *The Akron Genesis of Alcoholics Anonymous*. Newton ed. (Kihei, HI: Paradise Research Publications, Inc., 1998), 157-58; and *New Light on Alcoholism: God, Sam Shoemaker, and A.A.* Pittsburgh ed. (Kihei, HI: Paradise Research Publications, Inc., 1999), 233-34, 359.

[280] Bill Wilson, *Bill W.: My First 40 Years*, 147; Dick B., *The Conversion of Bill W.*, 110; and William Wilson, *W. G. Wilson Recollections* (pp. 103 and 130 of a manuscript dated September 1, 1954) personally inspected by Dick B. at Stepping Stones Archives. Note: The phrase "For sure I'd been born again" appeared in two separate places in two separate documents.

[281] Cheever, *My Name is Bill*, 117.

well as the Great Physician. . . . Silkworth challenged the alcoholic with an ultimatum. Once hopeless, the alcoholic would grasp hold of any chance of sobriety. Silkworth, a medical doctor, challenged the alcoholic with a spiritual conversion and a relationship with God as part of the program of recovery.[282]

Heading out in 1934, immediately after his Calvary Mission conversion, Bill had remembered his hours of discussion with Dr. Silkworth on the subject of the "Great Physician." The discussion had occurred during Bill's third hospitalization period at Towns Hospital where Silkworth was chief psychiatrist.[283] After the Mission experience and his continued drinking, Bill reflected:

> But what of the Great Physician? For a brief moment, I suppose, the last trace of my obstinacy was crushed out as the abyss yawned.[284]

Bill had been hit hard by his friend Ebby Thacher's flat statement that God had done for him what he could not do for himself. It had evidently produced Bill's conclusion that Ebby had truly had been saved and was reborn at the Calvary Mission.[285] Indeed, following his own altar experience, Bill had written his brother-in-law, "I've got religion."[286] These were also the first words that Bill's friend Ebby uttered to Bill at Bill's apartment after Ebby had been converted at the Calvary Rescue Mission altar.[287] Ebby's telling words to Bill are recorded in Bill's personal story in each of the four editions of the A.A. basic text.

---

[282] Dale Mitchel, *Silkworth: The Little Doctor Who Loved Drunks* (Center City, MN: Hazelden, 2002), 50; Dick B., *The Conversion of Bill W.*, 50-76; and Norman Vincent Peale, *The Positive Power of Jesus Christ: Life-changing Adventures in Faith* (Carmel, NY: Guideposts, 1980), 60-62.
[283] Mitchel, *Silkworth*, 44-55.
[284] Wilson, *My First 40 Years*, 145.
[285] Dick B., *The Conversion of Bill W.*, 48-49; and Francis Hartigan, *Bill W.: A Biography of Alcoholics Anonymous Co-founder Bill Wilson* (New York: Thomas Dunne Books, 2000), 49, 59.
[286] Dick B., *The Conversion of Bill W.*, 95.
[287] *"Pass It On,"* 111.

And Bill concluded the following as to Ebby:

> Nevertheless here I was sitting opposite a man who talked about a personal God, who told me how he had found Him, who described to me how I might do the same thing and who convinced me utterly that something had come into his life which had accomplished a miracle. The man was transformed, there was no denying he had been reborn.[288]

Moving toward his final Towns Hospital treatments, Bill appeared to be clinging to his conclusion that Ebby had been reborn, that he (Bill) had been reborn, and that Dr. William D. Silkworth had assured him that the "Great Physician" (Jesus Christ) could therefore cure him—just as He seemed to have relieved Ebby of his alcoholism. Thus Bill had told his wife Lois that he "had found the answer."[289] A.A.'s official biography said Bill came to the hospital waving a bottle and telling the doctor, "Well this time, I've found something."[290]

Bill began to put his thoughts into action. In his own words: "I remember saying to myself, 'I'll do anything, anything at all. If there be a Great Physician, I'll call on him.'"[291] Almost immediately, he cried out to God for help. His conversion experience was very similar to that which his grandfather Willie Wilson had had some years before at Bill's hometown of East Dorset, Vermont.[292]

---

[288] From lines 935-42 of the manuscript I found and copied at Stepping Stones Archives. The manuscript was titled, "Bill Wilson's Original Story." See Dick B., *Turning Point: A History of Early A.A.'s Spiritual Roots and Successes* (Kihei, HI: Paradise Research Publications, Inc., 1997), 99-100.
[289] Matthew J. Raphael, *Bill W. and Mr. Wilson: The Legend and the Life of A.A.'s Co-founder* (Amherst: University of Massachusetts Press, 2000), 78.
[290] *"Pass It On,"* 120.
[291] Wilson, *My First 40 Years, 145.*
[292] Wilson, *My First 40 Years, 145-46;* Cheever, *My Name is Bill,* 17; and Dick B., *The Conversion of Bill W.,* 133-35.

Having actually had this Towns Hospital conversion *experience*, Bill consulted Dr. Silkworth, and was told by Silkworth and Bill's wife Lois that he had had a genuine conversion. To be absolutely certain, Bill then spent almost a day studying the William James book, *The Varieties of Religious Experience*.[293] This study produced his belief that the William James accounts of conversion cures validated his own cure. And, like his grandfather, Bill never drank again.

Dr. Silkworth and Dr. Norman Vincent Peale had become very good friends. And Silkworth and his wife once held their church membership at Marble Collegiate Church in New York.[294] Peale wrote extensively on how Dr. Silkworth had told a man named Charles, who later became a member of Marble Collegiate, that the Great Physician Jesus Christ could cure his alcoholism.[295] And now Bill Wilson had joined the ranks. He also wanted to tell others about it. On his discharge from the Towns Hospital, Bill immediately began searching out drunks at Towns Hospital, in Oxford Group meetings, and at the Rescue Mission in an attempt to convert them.

A.A.'s basic text appears to contain a concise sample statement by Bill in his own words of the message he attempted to carry:

> Henrietta [Dotson], the Lord has been so wonderful to me, curing me of this terrible disease that I just want to keep talking about it and telling people.[296]

That Bill maintained his message seems evident from the following account by a Cleveland member:

---

[293] Dick B., *The Conversion of Bill W.*, 96-98.
[294] Mitchel, *Silkworth*, 51.
[295] Peale, *The Positive Power*, 60-62; and Mitchel, *Silkworth*, 11-12, 44-45, 47, 50-51.
[296] *Alcoholics Anonymous*, 4th ed. (New York: Alcoholics Anonymous World Services, Inc., 2001), 191

... [W]hen I came home Clarence [Snyder] was sitting on the davenport with Bill W. I do not recollect the specific conversation that went on but I believe I did challenge Bill to tell me something about A.A. and I do recall one other thing: I wanted to know what this was that worked so many wonders, and hanging over the mantel was a picture of Gethsemane and Bill pointed to it and said, "There it is. . ."[297]

But as a fervent herald and messenger, Bill failed to get anyone sober in the first six months, and very few in the period thereafter. Both Bill and his wife Lois so stated on many occasions.[298]

Nonetheless, Bill brought his message to Akron and to his first meeting with Dr. Bob—who, as will be seen here,—was thoroughly acquainted with conversions. In fact, the necessity for the conversion solution was soon incorporated in the first pioneer Christian program where new people were required to surrender to Jesus Christ in a ceremony that took place in all of early Akron A.A.'s weekly fellowship meetings. I have personally verified this procedure by means of four eye-witness accounts. The first is that of Clarence H. Snyder, who got sober in 1938, and details his "surrender to Christ." You can find it discussed in my title *That Amazing Grace*, in Mitch K.'s title *How It Worked*, and in Lobdell's *This Strange Illness* at page 84. The second eye-witness account is that of A.A. pioneer J. D. Holmes. His verification is in the form of complaints about how they "made" him surrender to Jesus Christ. His story can be found on the Hindsfoot Foundation web site. The third eye=witness is Larry Bauer who took great pains both to

---

[297] *Alcoholics Anonymous*, 3rd ed. (New York: Alcoholics Anonymous World Services, Inc., 1976), 216-17.
[298] *Alcoholics Anonymous Comes of Age,* p. 65: "At the end of six months nobody had sobered up. And, believe me, I had tried them by the score;" after Bob got back from Akron, he and Lois tried again, and he said, "As it turned out, we did not sober up a single one," p.73. Lois Wilson said of Bill's witnessing, "Although he had not permanently sobered up anyone in New York, simply trying to help others had kept him from even thinking of drinking." *Lois Remembers* (NY: Al-Anon Family Group Headquarters, Inc, 1987), 95.

write and then to telephone me (Dick B.) to refute the idea that they had "anointed with oil" and Bauer stated emphatically that he had been taken upstairs and "gotten born-again." The final eye-witness was Ed Andy, an old-timer from Lorain, Ohio. I was privy to a phone conversation between Ed, Danny Whitmore, and myself where Andy stated: "They wouldn't let you in unless you accepted Jesus Christ." In other words, conversion was mandatory in the early program.

There was an additional and vital element, however, that Bill contributed to the early A.A. pioneer program developed in Akron. That element was helping other alcoholics!

- Second, to be sure, Bill could and did attest to his conversion and new birth. He could and did attest to his own cure. His words are set forth on page 191 of even the latest edition of the A.A. basic text. Bill carried the matter one vital step further. He wanted to help other drunks be cured by the very same conversion solution. In fact, as late as January 23, 1961, Bill contacted and wrote the famous Swiss psychiatrist Dr. Carl Gustav Jung, who has been credited with being the founder of the A.A. conversion solution:

  > ... [I]t was about 1931 that he [Rowland Hazard] became your patient. I believe he remained under your care for perhaps a year. . . . To his great consternation, he soon relapsed into intoxication. Certain that you were his 'court of last resort,' he again returned to your care. There followed the conversation between you that was to become the first link in the chain of events that led to the founding of Alcoholics Anonymous. . . . First of all, you frankly told him of his hopelessness, so far as any further medical or psychiatric treatment might be concerned. This candid and humble statement of yours was beyond doubt the first foundation stone upon which our Society has been built. . . . When he then asked you if there was any hope, you told him there might be, provided he could become the subject of a spiritual or religious

experience—in short, a *genuine conversion*. . . . [Rowland Hazard] did find a conversion experience that released him for the time being from his compulsion to drink. . . . This concept proved to be the foundation of such success as Alcoholics Anonymous has since achieved. This has made conversion experience . . . available on an almost wholesale basis.[299]

- Third, with conversion and cure as part of his firm conviction as to the solution, Bill had brought one other vital factor to the table when he first met Dr. Bob in Akron. In fact, Bill was relentless in his pursuit of this factor. It was "service." In all editions of A.A.'s basic text, Bill had written:

> Our very lives, as ex-problem drinkers, depend upon our constant thought of others and how we may help meet their needs.[300]
>
> Practical experience shows that nothing will so much insure immunity from drinking as intensive work with other alcoholics. It works when other activities fail. . . . Carry this message to other alcoholics! You can help when others fail.[301]
>
> Burn the idea into the consciousness of every man that he can get well regardless of anyone. The only condition is that he trust in God and clean house.[302]

I believe it is more than fair to say that **Bill's three principal contributions** to early A.A. (accompanied as they were by his diligent perseverance) were: (1) **Conversion**—the idea that Bill had seen at work in his own grandfather's life, and then in his own. (2) **Cure through conversion**—the idea that he had seen to be effective in his own life, suggested by Dr. Carl Jung, suggested by Dr. William Silkworth, and—to Bill's mind—affirmed by the studies of Professor

---

[299] "*Pass It On*, 382-83 (emphasis added).
[300] *Alcoholics Anonymous*, 4th ed., 20.
[301] *Alcoholics Anonymous*, 4th ed., 89
[302] *Alcoholics Anonymous*, 4th ed., 98.

William James. (3) **Service to those still suffering**—the idea that he had seen at work in the Salvation Army, the Rescue Missions, the YMCA, and certainly in the Oxford Group with which he had been associated. This third "service" concept became a cardinal, and perhaps unique, factor in A.A.'s own spiritual recovery program and successes—working with others by carrying the message of how the Creator could help them get well.

Dr. Bob: Dr. Bob was clearly familiar with all three factors—conversion, cure, and service. They were part and parcel of his pre-drinking training. But the last point rang a bell with Dr. Bob whose early Christian Endeavor days had embraced "love and service" as their motto. Why, then, had Dr. Bob descended so deeply into alcoholism when he knew about conversion, cure, and service? I have no difficulty with this question: Drunks on a roll are hardly busy thinking about conversion or cure or service. And certainly about consequences—consequences that others can tell them a hundred times are inevitable. They are intent on succumbing to temptation—they are intent on getting the next drink, followed by the next drunk, followed by the next disaster, followed by the blind return to the same activities and results. Some have swallowed the current meeting-room-philosophy and idle chatter that alcoholism is doing the same thing over and over and expecting the result to be different. But not in my book. This definition ignores reality. If it has any merit, it should be rephrased that alcoholism is doing the same thing over and over despite knowing the result will be exactly the same. That's the insanity. Knowing the result. Yet wildly, irresponsibly, and relentlessly pursuing the cause. Dr. Bob knew the problem. He knew the consequences. And, as Dr. Silkworth explained so well in A.A.'s basic text, the venerable Dr. Bob rose yet another time to get in trouble. And if Wilson's message had a real impact—and Dr. Bob said Bill knew what he was talking about—it was Bill's ability to portray both the insanity and the solution Bill had found.

Simply stated—until he met Bill Wilson in 1935—Dr. Bob had not wanted to quit drinking despite its ruinous consequences in his own life. He had remarked to his good friend Henrietta Seiberling: "Henri, I think I'm just one of those *want*-to-want-to guys."[303] On the other

---

[303] *DR. BOB*, 59.

hand, his new-found acquaintance, Bill Wilson, *had* wanted to quit. Bill had taken specific action. He went to the altar. He called on the Great Physician for help. Bill had quit. He never drank again. And Bill was tendering conversion, cure, and service as the roots of his own sobriety. But obviously more was needed because Bill had failed utterly in his witnessing efforts with others.

Dr. Bob had never applied or given "service" to other alcoholics as part of his religious program of conversion, reliance on the Creator, obedience to God's will, Bible study, prayer, Quiet Hour, church, and religious comradeship. Nor had Bob applied and combined the two cardinal principals: (1) Abstinence, and (2) Then turning to the Creator for help. Why? I believe and have often said that the answer is simple. Unlike Bill—when he staggered to the Calvary Mission altar and then called out to the Great Physician for help at Towns Hospital, Dr. Bob had not yet wanted to quit drinking badly enough to do whatever it took. Again: Dr. Bob never wanted to quit drinking, and the inevitable result of his obsession and craving was that he pursued that which he did want—drink!

On Bill's service idea, Dr. Bob had this to say of his first conversation with Bill:

> "What did the man [Bill Wilson] do or say that was different from what others had done or said?" It must be remembered that I had read a great deal and talked to everyone who knew, or thought they knew, anything about the subject of alcoholism. But this was a man who had experienced many years of frightful drinking, who had had most all of the drunkard's experiences known to man, but who had been cured by the very means I had been trying to employ, that is to say the spiritual approach. He gave me information about the subject of alcoholism which was undoubtedly helpful. Of far more importance was the fact that he was the first living human with whom I had ever talked who knew what he was talking about in regard to alcoholism from actual experience. In other

words, he talked my language. He knew all the answers, and certainly not because he had picked them up in his reading."[304]

"Now the interesting part of all this is not the sordid details, but the situation that we two fellows were in. We had both been associated with the Oxford Group, Bill in New York, for five months, and I in Akron, for two and a half years. Bill had acquired their idea of service.

"I had not, but I had done an immense amount of reading they had recommended. I had refreshed my memory of the Good Book, and I had had excellent training in that as a youngster. . . . I had done all the things that those good people told me to do. . . . But the one thing that they hadn't told me was the one thing that Bill did that Sunday—attempt to be helpful to somebody else."[305]

Bill W., Dr. Bob, and Bill D. on the Cure of Alcoholism by the Power of the Creator: It is probably enough in this resource book to point out that Bill Wilson (AA Number One), Dr. Bob Smith (AA Number Two), and Bill Dotson of Akron (AA Number Three) are each recorded in A.A.'s basic text as stating that they had been cured of alcoholism.[306]

---

[304] *Alcoholics Anonymous*, 4th ed., 180.
[305] *The Co-founders of Alcoholics Anonymous: Biographical sketches: Their last major talks* (New York: Alcoholics Anonymous World Services, Inc., 1972, 1975), 11-12.
[306] *Alcoholics Anonymous*, 4th ed.: Bill Wilson said the "Lord has been so wonderful to me, curing me. . ." p. 191. Dr. Bob stated that Bill Wilson "had been cured." p. 180. Dr. Bob told the nurse at Akron's City Hospital "that he and a man from New York had a cure for alcoholism." p. 188. Bill Dotson said, "That sentence, "The Lord has been so wonderful to me, curing me of this terrible disease, that I just want to keep telling people about it," has been a sort of golden text for the A.A. program and for me." p. 191. None of the three ever had another drink.

On to Dr. Bob's Spiritual Tools from St. Johnsbury, Vermont

This chapter just concluded gives you a taste of the how, what, and why of its many companion resource volumes. The real need for the voluminous, accompanying content is to let the reader examine for himself or herself the actual spiritual tools laid at Dr. Bob's feet in St. Johnsbury. And, to that end, we move on to the details.

"Your Heavenly Father will never let you down!"
Alcoholics Anonymous, 4th ed., p. 181

4
Dr. Bob's Birthplace, Boyhood Home, and Youth

A picture of Dr. Bob's birthplace is included in our resource binder. Also a copy his birth certificate. Also several other photographs of Bob, Anne Smith (his wife), Bill Wilson, the founders and their wives, the entire group, and the children of Dr. Bob and Anne Smith. These come from the collection of my good friend Dennis Wayne Cassidy, a top flight A.A. historian who just passed on and made his whole collection available to me. This chapter simply summarizes the details about the Smith family whose members (the Judge, his wife Susan, and Bob) lived at the Summer Street home in St. Johnsbury.

Following are the Smith details:

- Robert Holbrook Smith was born in his family's home at 297 Summer Street in St. Johnsbury, Vermont.[307]

- His date of birth was August 8, 1879. His date of death was November 16, 1950.[308]

- His parents were Judge Walter Perrin Smith and Susan Amanda (Holbrook) Smith.[309]

- Walter P. Smith and Susan A. Holbrook were married in Lyndon, Vermont, on August 15, 1876.[310]

---

[307] *DR. BOB and the Good Oldtimers* (NY: Alcoholics Anonymous World Services, Inc., 1980), 9.
[308] *DR. BOB*, 9, 348.
[309] William H. Jeffrey, *Successful Vermonters* (East Burke, VT: The Historical Publishing Company, 1904), 98.
[310] Stone, *St. Johnsbury Illustrated*, 15.

- Included in the resource binders are the genealogies of the Smith and Holbrook families. To be noted is the fact that Susan Amanda Holbrook's father, Perley Rogers Holbrook, was a physician (M.D.).[311]

- Bob had an older foster sister named Amanda Northrup who later became a history professor at Hunter College, New York.[312]

- Records make clear that Bob:

    From childhood through high school, regularly attended three North Congregational Church, St. Johnsbury, services on each Sunday of each week [313] (the Sunday attendance involved morning church worship, Sunday school in the afternoon, and Sunday evening service); and Bob often attended the Wednesday evening prayer meeting.[314]

    Regularly participated in that church's Monday night Christian Endeavor Society meetings.[315]

    Catalogues, school records, Class Notes, and student news articles make it clear that Bob Smith:

    Attended St. Johnsbury Academy from 1894 to 1898.[316]

---

[311] Jeffrey, Successful Vermonters, 98; John Lawrence, *The Genealogy of the Family of John Lawrence, of Wisset, in Suffolk, England, and of Watertown and Groton, Massachusetts Continued to the Present Year* (Printed for the Author, 1876—The Riverside Press, Cambridge: Printed by H. O. Houghton and Company), 25.
[312] *DR. BOB*, 12, 14.
[313] *St Johnsbury Academy Catalogue*, 20.
[314] *Alcoholics Anonymous*, 4th ed., 172.
[315] *Alcoholics Anonymous*, 4th ed., 172.
[316] *Catalogues of St. Johnsbury Academy for the Academic Years* ending 1895, 1896, 1897, 1998, provided to the authors for inspection and with copies in our resource binder.

Was "required to attend one church service and a Bible service regularly on the Sabbath..."[317]

Managed the St. Johnsbury Academy Glee Club and sang in its concerts.[318]

Had access to the St. Johnsbury Athenaeum library and the Academy library; and The Adelphian and The Athenaeum literary societies which afford "special facilities for improvement in composition and debate."[319]

Was to be given "religious instruction... not intended [to provide] the inculcation of a sectarian creed, but that the fundamental Doctrine of the Bible will be taught, and the great duties of Repentance and Faith urged upon the attention of the school."[320]

Belonged to the Adelphian Literary Society at the Academy.[321]

---

[317] See: Richard Beck. *A Proud Tradition A Bright Future: A Sesquicentennial History of St. Johnsbury Academy* (St. Johnsbury, VT: St. Johnsbury Academy, 1976), 7, 14, 16-17, 19. 30, 34, 270, 272-74; Charles Edward Russell. *Bare Hands and Stone Walls: Some Recollections of a Side-Line Reformer* (NY: Charles Scribner's Sons, 1933), 7, 11-15; and Fairbanks, *Sketch*, 15, 60-61.

[318] *The Academy Student* for October 1897, 34 recorded that Smith had provided the music (a medley) for an Athenaeum meeting, and was Second Director of the Adelphians who presented the program. The Academy Student, p. 50 stated in its School Notes, "Robert Smith is business manager of the Glee Club;" At page 51, it stated,
The Glee Club is leading the singing in chapel and already a great improvement can be noticed in that part of our morning service;" and our resource binder contains a copy of the "Grand Concert By the Academy Glee Club".... Assisted by the Y.M.C.A. Orchestra. Members of the Glee Club... Robert H. Smith... Robert H. Smith, Manager. The event was to be held Friday Evening, March 4th, 1898 at Eight O'clock, at Academy Hall.

[319] *St. Johnsbury Academy Catalogue* for 1873, 21.

[320] First formal announcement of the opening and purpose of the Academy, *St. Johnsbury Academy*, 15.

[321] *The Academy Student* for 1898, 45, record a debate for January 22, with the following subject for discussion and result: "Resolved that a large accumulation of personal wealth is detrimental to society." The affirmative was defended by Newell and Smith, and the negative by Fairbanks and Stone."

Participated in debates at St. Johnsbury Academy where the Academy history stated: "There was public speaking in the form of orations and debates both before the school at chapel exercises by members of the senior and middle classes, and in public exhibitions of these classes, and of the Adelphian and Athenian societies."[322]

Delivered the Oration at his own graduation ceremony.[323]

Stated he had received excellent training in the Bible as a youngster.[And very convincing support for his statement can be identified in the extensive indoctrination emanating to him from the North Congregational Church, St. Johnsbury; its Sunday School, and its active Christian Endeavor Society. Also, therefore, in his involvement in the regular Bible studies, prayer meetings, conversions, and Quiet Hour observances of the Christian Endeavor Society. Also in St. Johnsbury Academy's required daily morning prayers, reading of the scriptures, and hymns; required Sabbath attendance upon church and Sunday school (verified by a signed affirmation by the student of his or her attendance); required prayers and Bible reading at the required daily Chapel; its graduation prayers and sermons; its offering of YMCA lectures, religious education studies, and Christian textbooks. Not to be overlooked is the emphasis which the Congregational church placed on Bible education in the home; and both of Bob's parents were much involved in teaching at the North Congregational Church, St. Johnsbury].[324]

---

[322] *St. Johnsbury Academy*, 67.

[323] When my son Ken and I visited the Academy library in this year (2007), the archivist dug out the commencement program for Dr. Bob's graduating class. She made a copy. And it lists Dr. Bob as delivering the commencement Oration.

[324] See: Richard Beck. *A Proud Tradition A Bright Future: A Sesquicentennial History of St. Johnsbury Academy* (St. Johnsbury, VT: St. Johnsbury Academy, 1976), 7, 14, 16-17, 19. 30, 34, 270, 272-74; Charles Edward Russell. *Bare Hands*

One Academy historian adds this to the school scene:

> Smith's unusually frequent church attendance also drew the attention of his Academy classmates. His Class of 1898's Class Day program, containing the Class Prophecy, predicted that "after leaving college," he would become "a professional fisherman," then "settle down" as "Rev. Robert H. Smith, pastor of a church in Paunee, Ohio."[325]

May have been a participant in the innumerable reported Christian revivals, conversions, evangelistic meetings, Gospel meetings, YMCA meetings, and Christian Endeavor outreaches that figured prominently throughout the years of his youth in St. Johnsbury, which we have bracketed as 1881 to 1898.

Could reasonably be expected to have had contact with the godly Fairbanks family members so deeply involved in Christian activities, Christian education, revivals, conversions, churches, the YMCA, and the St. Johnsbury Academy. The Fairbanks family was very substantially involved in the North Congregational Church, St. Johnsbury, from the very first—founding the church; serving as deacons, and as Sunday School teachers and superintendents; serving on the building committees; participating in the construction of the present church edifice; and actually singing in the choir. Many of the family members were Christian ministers. Many were involved in the YMCA and the town revivals. And most were heavily involved in the Christian setting at St. Johnsbury Academy. Even the Fairbanks deeds to St. Johnsbury Academy imposed

---

and Stone Walls: Some Recollections of a Side-Line Reformer (NY: Charles Scribner's Sons, 1933), 7, 11-15; and Fairbanks, *Sketch*, 15, 60-61.
[325] Beck, *A Proud Tradition*, 49.

school requirements as to religion and Congregationalism.[326]

- Walter Perrin Smith (Bob's father) was born at Hardwick in Caledonia County, Vermont, on November 4, 1841, and was:

    Prepared for college at the Hardwick and Morrisville academies and graduated from the University of Vermont in 1867. He studied law at the University of Michigan and with Powers & Gleed at Morrisville, and was admitted to the Lamoille county bar at the May term, 1869. He formed a partnership in St. Johnsbury with Hon. Jonathan Ross and practiced law until December, 1882.
    Elected Probate Judge of the Caledonia district in 1882 and held that position during Bob Smith's youth.[327]

    A Deacon of the North Congregational Church, St. Johnsbury, and was listed in books of the time as "influential in the political and religious life of St. Johnsbury."[328]

    A Sunday school teacher at the North Congregational Church, St. Johnsbury, for at least thirty years.[329]

    With his family (including Bob)—who were all members of the church—regularly attended Sunday Morning services, Sunday School in the afternoon,

---

[326] Claire Dunne Johnson, *Images of America: St. Johnsbury* (Dover, NH: Arcadia Publishing, 1996), 10-13, 23-30, 38, 69; Claire Dunne Johnson. *"I See By The Paper . . ." An Informal History of St. Johnsbury* (St. Johnsbury, VT: The Cowles Press, 1987), 26-27, 33, 37-39, 42, 56-59, 75-76, 84-87, 91, 95, 100-04, 129, 139, 165, 180-81, 203; Fairbanks et al., *Sketch*, iii-v, 2-15, 20-22, 56, 60-61, 68-74, 101-06; and Stone, *St. Johnsbury Illustrated* (entire vol.)
[327] Stone, *St. Johnsbury Illustrated*, 15. As to the Probate Courts, see Arthur F. Stone, *The Vermont of Today: With Its Historic Background, Attractions and People*, Vol. I (NY: Lewis Historical Publishing Company, Inc., 1929), 346; and as to the Caledonia County Courts and Courthouse, see Stone, *The Vermont of Today*, Vol. I, 354.
[328] Stone, *North Congregational Church. . . . 1825-1942*, 86-87.
[329] *DR. BOB*, 9.

Sunday evening services, and Wednesday prayer meetings.

An Examiner at St. Johnsbury Academy, which Bob Smith attended and from which Bob graduated in 1898.[330]

A president and chairman of the local YMCA.[331]

State's attorney for Caledonia County from 1874-76. Elected to the legislature representing St. Johnsbury in 1880 and 1882; and served on the judiciary and other important committees. He served as superintendent of the village schools.[332]

For several years a director in Merchants National Bank of St. Johnsbury; a director of the First National Bank; and a trustee, member of the board of investors, and vice-president, of Passumpsic Savings Bank.[333]

"An able and effective debater, he has frequently taken the stump during national elections, and delivered addresses on memorial and other public occasions."[334]

"Judge Smith has ever been influential in the political and religious life of St. Johnsbury. . . . He is a member of the North Congregational church."[335]

President of Carrick Bros. Granite Co.[336]

---

[330] *St. Johnsbury Academy Catalogue* for 1873, p. 22.
[331] Walter P. Smith is listed as YMCA "President or Chairman" for Saint Johnsbury. *Year Book of the Young Men's Christian Associations of North America, for the year 1896* (New York: Published by The International Committee, 1896), 128.
[332] Stone, *St. Johnsbury Illustrated*, 15.
[333] Stone, *St. Johnsbury Illustrated*, 15, 90.
[334] William H. Jeffrey, *Successful Vermonters* (East Burke, VT: The Historical Publishing Company, 1904), 98.
[335] Jeffrey, *Successful Vermonters*, 98.
[336] Jacob G. Ullery, comp., *Men of Vermont: An Illustrated Biographical History of Vermonters and Sons of Vermont* (Brattleboro, VT: Transcript Publishing Company, 1894), 371.

In politics, always a Republican, and in religious faith, a Congregationalist.[337]

- Susan Amanda (Holbrook) Smith (Bob's mother) was born in Hardwick, Vermont, on June 26, 1855, daughter of Perley Rogers Holbrook, M.D., and Maria Louisa (Lawrence) Holbrook, and was:

    A student of private schools.

    A graduate of St. Johnsbury Academy in 1874; and a teacher at St. Johnsbury Academy for two years.[338]

    Author and editor of two of the eight chapters of An Historical Sketch of St. Johnsbury Academy 1842-1922[339]

    Member of the Board of Library Commissioners of Vermont.[340]

    President of St. Johnsbury Woman's Club, 1896-98[341]

    Member of North Congregational Church, St. Johnsbury.

    Sunday School teacher there beginning in 1890

---

[337] Ullery, *Men of Vermont*, 371.
[338] Fairbanks et al., eds., *An Historical Sketch of St. Johnsbury Academy 1842-1922*, 106.
[339] Fairbanks et al., eds., *An Historical Sketch of St. Johnsbury Academy 1842-1922*, 48-77.
[340] Albert Nelson Marquis, *Who's Who in New England* ( ), 994, "Smith, Susan Holbrook."
[341] Previous discussions in this title, as well as their accompanying footnotes, document the remainder of the positions held and taken by Mrs. W. P. Smith—president of the St. Johnsbury Women's Club, member of St. Johnsbury Congregational Church, Sunday School teacher, superintendent of two different departments of the church school, reporter to the church on its young people's groups, the Christian Endeavor Society, and participant in the church quartet [*North Congregational Church*, p. 64], and member of the Home Missionary Society.

From 1892, superintendent of the home department of the church.

Later, the head of the intermediate and primary departments of the Sunday School.

In 1888, a participant in the musical activities of the church, becoming part of a double quartet.

A "reporter"--at the church's centennial banquet--on the many activities organized by the church: (1) the St. Johnsbury Female Cent Society--which furnished the church, equipped the pulpit, bought the Bible, furnished the communion table, and donated to the American Board of foreign missions; (2) the Women's Sewing Society; (3) the Juvenile Sewing Society; (4) the Ladies' Missionary Society; (5) the Ladies' Benevolent Society; (6) the Girl's Benevolent Circle; (7) Christian Helpers; (8) "Do Ye the Next Thing"; and (9) sixty years of young people's societies, including Pioneer Band, Misses Circle, King's Daughters, Busy Bee Society, Young People's Guild, and Round Table Circle.

One who reported to the church, "The Christian Endeavor Society which started in 1887 has continued throughout the years as the leading young people's organization. . . ." In 1891, she said, there was a Junior Society of Christian Endeavor.

Not only a teacher at the St. Johnsbury Academy; but was also a member of the Alumni Association executive committee; was a speaker at several important historical celebrations at St. Johnsbury Academy; and author of two chapters of its official history.[342]

---

[342] Fairbanks et al., *Sketch*, v., 56, 71

- Bob Smith met his bride-to-be (Miss Anne Ripley, a student at Wellesley) at a dance in the St. Johnsbury Academy gym; this was at a time Anne was spending a holiday with a college friend.[343]. Many years later, said to be about 17 years, the two were married at the home of Anne's mother in Illinois on January 15, 1915.[344] Dr. Bob and Anne then took up residence in Akron, Ohio.[345]

- Dr. Bob loved St. Johnsbury so much that he made a point of visiting family and friends there each year and was insistent, at the time of his impending death, that he be taken there for one final trip.[346]

---

[343] *DR. BOB*, 16.
[344] *DR. BOB*, 29, 16..
[345] *DR. BOB*, 29.
[346] *DR. BOB*, 339-40.

> "Your Heavenly Father will never let you down!"
> *Alcoholics Anonymous*, 4th ed., p. 181

5
North Congregational Church, St. Johnsbury

Worship, Sunday School, Missions, Revivals, Evangelism, Town Meetings, Christian Endeavor, YMCA

The Key Time Period: 1875-1898

The time period that receives the greatest attention in this resource volume begins with what is called in North Congregational Church, St. Johnsbury, records, "The Great Awakening" of 1875.[347] It ends with Robert Holbrook Smith's graduation from St. Johnsbury Academy in 1898. For this would be the period where the Smith family church—North Congregational Church, St. Johnsbury—could have contributed to what "Dr. Bob" said was the "excellent training" he had received in the "Good Book" (i.e., the Bible) "as a youngster."[348]

Vermont, Its Churches, the YMCA, and Others Are Part of the Picture

The St. Johnsbury Congregational doings in the period of "The Great Awakening" of 1875, and the decade-and-a-half thereafter, are not an isolated group of activities. Although there had been revivals before in Vermont and elsewhere, the religious impact had waned severely during the Civil War. The Civil War decimated the YMCA and the

---

[347] Arthur Fairbanks Stone, *North Congregational Church, St. Johnsbury, Vermont: 1825-1942* (St. Johnsbury, VT: North Congregational Church, 1942), 31, 32.
[348] Dr. Bob's actual statement, according to the AA Grapevine transcript, was: "I had refreshed my memory of the Good Book, and I had had excellent training in that as a youngster." See: "Dr. Bob's Last Major Talk: An Excerpt," *AA Grapevine*, November 2003 (online source: AA Grapevine Digital Archive, # 157): http://aagrapevine.org/da/browsesearchresult.php?da=q%3Apolis&pg=16 ; accessed on 10/31/07.

membership roles of Vermont churches, and it also left them all a rather restrained, somber, and unenthusiastic body of Christians. And the time had come for things to change. And change they did—dramatically and remarkably. They changed through the instrumentalities of members of the Fairbanks family, the YMCA, people in the North Congregational Church, St. Johnsbury, and the young people in the Christian Endeavor Society of that church.

Dr. Bob and North Congregational Church, St. Johnsbury, Itself

First, a word or two about North Congregational Church, St. Johnsbury, Vermont, itself. The church was organized on April 7, 1825, and known then as the "Second Congregational Church." The First Congregational Church (the mother church) was in St. Johnsbury Center and organized on November 21, 1809. The present building on Main Street is the fourth edifice to house North Congregational Church, St. Johnsbury. The men who supervised construction of its predecessor building were the three brothers, Erastus, Thaddeus, and Joseph Fairbanks. When it came time for the present building to be erected, several young men proposed, in February 1877, that another building be erected. Soon there were 400 pledges. A building committee was appointed with then-State of Vermont Governor Horace Fairbanks as its chairman. Fairbanks family members Horace and Franklin took the construction contract and raised a very substantial part of the needed money from the estate of Erastus Fairbanks. The tower of the church rises 140 feet. And Horace and Franklin Fairbanks presented the bell which weighs 3,004 pounds. The church architecture much resembles the other town buildings—the Fairbanks Museum and Planetarium, the YMCA building (destroyed by fire in 1984), the St. Johnsbury Athenaeum (town library), and structures at St. Johnsbury Academy—all of which were donated, financed, or in some way constructed in large part, by the philanthropic expenditures of St. Johnsbury's famous and wealthy Fairbanks family members who had made the Fairbanks platform scale world-renowned and an industrial necessity throughout the world.[349]

---

[349] Pamphlet of North Congregational Church, United Church of Christ, St. Johnsbury, Vermont, provided by its archivist Bob Swartz to the authors on October 25, 2007, titled "History of North Congregational Church."

The blue, hardbound, church history book of North Congregational Church, St. Johnsbury, contains much additional information.[350] The council that organized the church met in the home of Major Joseph Fairbanks on April 7, 1825, and listed Joseph Fairbanks as one of the original "members in regular standing in this church." These people gave their assent to the Articles of Faith and The Covenant included in this volume. In 1874, a special committee headed by Franklin Fairbanks proposed changing "pew rentals" and inaugurating "free church sittings." Rev. Henry W. Jones became pastor in 1875 and served until October 8, 1885. In 1877, the church became, by name, the North Congregational Church, St. Johnsbury; and as the church neared completion, four of the children of Erastus Fairbanks added their gifts—Emily Fairbanks Goodell gave the pulpit Bible; Horace Fairbanks and Franklin Fairbanks gave the bell; and a sister-in-law of Erastus (Miss Sarah Crossman) presented the church with large photographs of the first five pastors. Records showed that, during the tenure of Rev. Henry Jones, and by 1878, there had been an "increase in attendance at the morning service, Sunday School, the Sunday evening service and the Wednesday evening prayer meeting" (all of which were mentioned by Dr. Bob as being part of his regular weekly participation in the church).[351]

The "Great Awakening" of 1875

The North Congregational Church, St. Johnsbury, church history book has a section, beginning on page 30, with the heading "The Great Awakening." Its importance is so great and is so related to Dr. Bob's family and his youth that it is here quoted almost in full:

> Foremost in the time and importance of Mr. Jones' pastorate was the greatest revival this town has ever witnessed. It is significant that it began, continued and ended with a consecrated group of laymen that won men and women and young people to Christ with no technique of a professional evangelist, but with the Holy Spirit working through

---

[350] Stone, *North Congregational Church, St. Johnsbury, Vermont: 1825-1942* (St. Johnsbury, VT: North Congregational Church, 1942). The church's pastor showed us this book in the church's archives room and also allowed us to make copies of a number of pages from it.
[351] Stone, *North Congregational Church, St. Johnsbury, Vermont: 1825-1942* ( ).

convincing appeals of laymen for all to lead the Christian life. Early in 1875 the State Young Men's Christian Association were making a religious canvass of Vermont. On February 6 two of the committee [and others] . . . met a group at Town Hall in the afternoon where plans were outlined for a series of gospel meetings. The following Sunday afternoon another meeting was held in the Town Hall with a meeting in the South church in the evening. When at the latter place 42 persons rose for prayers there was no doubt but that the day of Pentecost had fully come. On Monday evening at the North church, 57 rose for prayers. Both on Monday and Tuesday, meetings for inquirers were held in the North church vestry preceding the mass meeting in the auditorium of the church. A few weeks later two more Massachusetts laymen . . . arrived. Twelve hundred people filled the South church on a weekday evening at which 140 rose for prayers. Meetings were held at the Avenue House hall and twice at the Fairbanks scale factory. . . . On March 27 [the laymen] . . . came back here. . . . As no church was large enough to hold the throngs that had been coming to these services, the climax in attendance and results was reached on March 28 when 1400 people crowded Academy hall and its passage ways, while 300 held an overflow meeting in old Number 10. More than 100 rose for prayers at this meeting. . . . Noonday prayer meetings were started and sponsored by the Y. M. C. A. that continued for several years. Laymen conducted meetings in two rural schools. All the churches had much larger attendance at the Wednesday evening prayer meetings, the number at the North church rising from an average of 40 to more than 150, As a result of this great awakening, 109 joined the North church in 1875. At the May communion 54 joined on confession of faith. . . . [352]

More on the "Great Awakening" of 1875 and North Congregational Church, St. Johnsbury. The *Minutes of the Eightieth Annual Meeting of the General Convention of Congregational Ministers and Churches of Vermont, Held at Bennington, June 1875,* had this to say:

---

[352] Stone, *North Congregational Church . . . 1825-1942,* 30-31.

The work had not long continued at St. Johnsbury before the surrounding towns began to feel its influence and the influence, too, of the Spirit, and to demand similar labor. Accordingly, in the latter part of the February and March, Gospel meetings, conducted chiefly by Mr. J.T. Quimby of Thetford, assisted by helpers from St. Johnsbury, were held in East Burke, West Concord, Danville, Lyndon, East St. Johnsbury, Lyndonville, Passumpsic and West Burke. Later, nearly every other town and village in the county has had one or more series of such meetings, conducted generally by brethren from Vermont. A genuine and marked revival interest has attended and followed labor in every place visited. . . . The church in Danville reports rather a low state of religious feeling till the Gospel meetings March 1st, but since great prosperity, although no additions are reported. June 1st thirty-eight united with the church and more will follow. There have been more than one hundred conversions in the town.[353]

From nearly or quite nearly every Conference, and from a large proportion of the churches of the State, grateful mention is made of the work of the Young Men's Christian Associations. . . . The calls for Gospel meetings from the towns of the State have been greatly multiplied, there is a large number of workers, and these as a class are older and more efficient, having come nearer the Lord in personal experience. Over ninety places have been visited. . . . [E]xtensive revival has usually resulted. Conversions have taken place in almost every town, nearly a thousand persons have followed after their close. . . . The work has probably been most fruitful among the young. . . . This class has been readily reached by the Gospel workers, and when converted they have themselves readily found and entered the field of labor. . . . There has been a delightful atmosphere in St. Johnsbury Academy during the year, and several conversions at different times. . . . [A]t Burr and Burton Seminary [later attended by A.A. cofounder Bill

---

[353] *Minutes of the Eightieth Annual Meeting of the General Convention of Congregational Ministers and Churches of Vermont, Held at Bennington, June 1875. Fifty-seventh Annual Report of the Vermont Domestic Missionary Society, and Fifty-fifth Annual Report of the Vermont Education Society* (Montpelier: J. & J.M. Poland, Steam Printers, 1875), 27-31.

Wilson] and other schools, a like state of religious feeling has existed.[354]

The Sunday School Factor

As North Congregational Church, St. Johnsbury, was organized, the organizers started a Sabbath School which later became known as the Sunday School. The "purpose through all the years was the same, the study of the world's best-seller, the Bible." Deacon Erastus Fairbanks became its second superintendent.[355] Judge Walter Smith taught in that Sunday school for some thirty years; and Mrs. Walter Smith served as an assistant superintendent and then superintendent of an intermediate group. The subscribers to the Sunday School Covenant included Erastus Fairbanks as Superintendent and Joseph P. Fairbanks as Teacher. Among other things, they pledged themselves:

> . . . [T]o avail ourselves of every opportunity and every incident to lead them to the only Saviour of lost sinners—and that we will labor to entertain at all times a lively sense of the value of the Soul; and that we will daily wait on God in fervent prayer, for the School collectively and for the scholars in our several classes individually; beseeching Him to bless our humble efforts, and to send down the Holy Spirit and gather all these into the fold of Christ. . . .[356]

There were monthly Sunday School concerts where there were "holy songs and lisping hymns of praise, their Scripture recitations and instructive addresses an prayers." From 1861 until his death in 1895, Col. Franklin Fairbanks was the superintendent. For many years the Sunday School met at 1:45 PM every Sunday afternoon in the year, closing around 3 o'clock. At the opening exercises the entire school joined in the singing at this devotional service. Then the younger classes assembled in the chapel, all studying the international lessons. Promptly at 2:30 the bell brought the chapel group back to the auditorium. Here the superintendent closed the service with his interpretation of the day's lesson. Col. Fairbanks was for some years a member of the International Lesson committee. Under Col Fairbanks's

---

[354] *Minutes of the Eightieth Annual Meeting . . . 1875*, 75, 76.
[355] Stone, *North Congregational Church, . . . 1825-1942*, 57.
[356] Stone, *North Congregational Church, . . . 1825-1942*, 58.

administration in 1892, the home department was started with Mrs. Walter P. Smith as superintendent. This kept many in touch with the work of the school and stimulated home study of the Word. In 1908, Mrs. Walter P. Smith became the head of the intermediate and primary departments. Before Horace Fairbanks died in 1888 he created a trust which provided for the gift of beautiful books every year to each child of the primary and intermediate departments of the Sunday School who attended morning worship regularly and kept the text of the sermon in a text book.[357]

The Stone Family and North Congregational Church, St. Johnsbury

Here is some background information about the Stone family and North Congregational Church, St. Johnsbury, from several sources.

> Passing to a later consideration of the highlights of this period [i.e., 1875-1885, when Rev. Henry W. Jones was pastor of North Congregational Church, St. Johnsbury], . . . the first to be noted was the election of a committee consisting of the pastor, F. B. Denio, and Mrs. C. M. Stone to edit and publish a new church manual. . . . About this time [in 1875] a new office was created, that of registrar. The first for many years was Mrs. C. M. Stone, whose husband was clerk of the church, . . .[358]

> Sarah Fairbanks Stone (1831-1909) was the daughter of Gov. Erastus and Lois Crossman [or, more accurately, "Crosman"] Fairbanks and was born on June 13th, 1831. She received her education from the St. Johnsbury Academy, Round Hill Institute, and the Mt. Holyoke Seminary, which she graduated from in 1851. She taught briefly at the St. Johnsbury Academy, as an assistant to Headmaster James K. Colby. She married Charles Marshall Stone on May 4, 1858. She joined the North

---

[357] Stone, *North Congregational Church, . . . 1825-1942*, 61-64.
[358] Stone, *North Congregational Church, St. Johnsbury, Vermont, 1825-1942* ( ), 27.] "Mrs. C. M. Stone" was Sarah Fairbanks (1831-1909). She was born on June 30, 1831, in Saint Johnsbury, Caledonia, Vermont. Her parents were Erastus Fairbanks and Lois Crosman. She married Charles Marshall Stone on May 4, 1858. Their children were: Mary E. Stone, Arthur Fairbanks Stone, Philip H. Stone, Emily Louise Stone. See Fairbanks, *Genealogy of the Fairbanks Family*, 330.

Congregational Church in 1850 and was an active member, holding several positions. She was one of the founding members of the St. Johnsbury Woman's Club. Her obituary (Box 1: Folder 19) reports that 'during the 25 years which her husband edited the Caledonian she was a frequent though often unknown contributor to its columns.' She and Charles Marshall had four children - Arthur Fairbanks Stone, Mary E. Stone, a third child, and Emily Louise Stone (who died at the age of 20 months). Sarah Fairbanks Stone died on March 11, 1909.[359]

Charles Marshall Stone (1833-1890) was born on April 18, 1833 to Charles Stone and Sarah Wells of Lyndonville. At the age of 17 he left his father's farm to work as an apprentice at the Caledonian Record in St. Johnsbury, with its founder A.G. Chadwick. The paper changed hands several times until 1857, when C. M. Stone, then a partner, bought out George Rand to maintain sole interest of the paper. He died on March 12, 1890.[360]

Charles and Sarah Stone had a son, Arthur Fairbanks Stone, who succeeded his parents in several capacities. Arthur, grandson of Deacon Erastus Fairbanks, was a member of North Congregational Church. He became a clerk of that church. And he became editor and publisher of the *Caledonian Record* on the death of his father, Charles Marshall Stone.[361]

---

[359] "Inventory of the Stone family papers, 1849-1998" (The University of Vermont: UVM Libraries: Special Collections): http://cdi.uvm.edu/findingaids/viewEAD.xql?pid=stone.ead.xml; accessed 02/10/08]
[360] "Inventory of the Stone family papers, 1849-1998" (The University of Vermont: UVM Libraries: Special Collections): http://cdi.uvm.edu/findingaids/viewEAD.xql?pid=stone.ead.xml; accessed 02/10/08]
[361] For more information on Arthur Fairbanks Stone, see: "Inventory of the Stone family papers, 1849-1998" (The University of Vermont: UVM Libraries: Special Collections): http://cdi.uvm.edu/findingaids/viewEAD.xql?pid=stone.ead.xml; accessed 02/10/08]

Women in the Home Missions Work

In 1888, Mrs. Henry Fairbanks of St. Johnsbury, Vermont, is listed as the Chairman of Committee for the Woman's Aid to A.M.A. [the American Missionary Association].[362]

In the January of 1889, Mrs. W. P. Fairbanks is listed as the Treasurer of the Woman's Home Missionary Union, and as having received $60.00 from "St. Johnsbury, W. H. M. S., North Ch., for A. H. M. S., to const. Mrs. Horace Fairbanks, Mrs. C. M. Stone, and Mrs. T. M. Howard, L. Ms. of W. H. M. U."[363]

In December of 1889, Mrs. Wm. P. Fairbanks of St. Johnsbury was Treasurer of the Woman's Home Missionary Union in Vermont, which is listed as a Woman's State Organization co-operating with the American Missionary Association.[364]

In 1895, "Mrs. William P. Fairbanks, is still listed as Treasurer for Woman's Work for the Woman's Home Missionary Union of Vermont.[365]

As noted, Dr. Bob's mother, Mrs. Walter P. Smith, was also involved in the women's missionary work.[366]

---

[362] *The American Missionary*, Vol. XLII. April, 1888. No. 4. : http://www.fullbooks.com/The-American-Missionary-Vol-XLII-April-1888.html ; accessed: 11/08/07.

[363] *The Home Missionary*: For the Year Ending April, 1889, Vol. LXI (New York: American Home Missionary Society, 1889), 440-41: http://books.google.com/books?id=WasPAAAAIAAJ&pg=PA441&lpg=PA441&dq=%22cm+stone%22+missionary&source=web&ots=5KBpseVmS4&sig=zltgu5MPuFeBMfFJJWXBdIvbLe8#PPP7,M1 ; accessed: 11/08/07.

[364] According to *The American Missionary*, Volume 43, No. 12, December, 1889: http://www.ihaystack.com/authors/v/various/00016172_american_missionary_volume_43_no_12_december_1889/00016172_english_ascii_p007.htm ; accessed: 11/08/07.

[365] *The American Missionary*, Volume 49, No. 3, March, 1895: http://www.ihaystack.com/authors/v/various/00015887_the_american_missionary_volume_49_no_3_march_1895/00015887_english_ascii_p003.htm ; accessed: 11/08/07.

[366] Letter from Ken B. to Taylor Reed regarding Reed's article "Alcoholics Anonymous Rooted in St. Johnsbury Institutions" in *The Caledonian-Record,* online edition, October 12, 2007, and monograph of C.S. Smith, *An Historical Sketch of*

A New Pastor and Added Zip in 1885

The Rev. Dr. Charles M. Lamson became the seventh pastor.[367] On October 8, 1885, at his installation, he was given "the right hand of fellowship by Rev. Dr. Edward T. Fairbanks, and the prayer by Rev. Henry Fairbanks." The North Congregational Church, St. Johnsbury, church history book records several important facts: "Through the next eight years both the pastor and the people were 'joyfully happy and nobly useful,' inspired to greater service by fine leadership."[368] "The average attendance at the morning service was 402 with an average of 263 at the evening service. The church was well organized from the oldest to the youngest. Besides the Christian Endeavor Society of which Miss Lillian M. Pearl was secretary-treasurer, there was a Girls' Missionary Band and a Boys' Missionary Society." "The Sunday School had a membership of 330 and the average attendance at the week day prayer meeting was 80."[369]

There was a famous choir in St. Johnsbury which included George and Horace Fairbanks. There followed a small choir. By 1881, there was a quartette choir; and "[i]n 1888 there is the first appearance of a double quartet which included . . . Mrs. Walter P. Smith."[370] At a centennial banquet, Mrs. Walter P. Smith told of the women who organized themselves into the "St. Johnsbury Female Cent Society" and raised money to furnish the church, equip the pulpit, buy the Bible, furnish the communion table, and give to the American Board of foreign missions. She told of the formation of the Women's Sewing Society, a Juvenile Sewing Society, a Ladies' Missionary Society, and other benevolent young people's societies.[371]

Home Missionary Work in Vermont, by the Congregational Churches (Montpelier: Press of the Watchman Publishing Company, 1893).
[367] Lamson took over from Rev. Henry W. Jones, who served from 1875 to 1885. See: Fairbanks, *The Town of St. Johnsbury*, 307.
[368] Lamson, who served as pastor of North Congregational Church, St. Johnsbury, from 1885 to 1894, was replaced by Albert H. Heath, who served from 1894 to 1899. See: Fairbanks, *The Town of St. Johnsbury*, 307.
[369] Stone, *North Congregational Church, . . . 1825-1942*, 38-39.
[370] Stone, *North Congregational Church, . . . 1825-1942*, 64.
[371] Stone, *North Congregational Church, . . . 1825-1942*, 68-70.

Dr. Bob and the Christian Endeavor Society

The North Congregational Church, St. Johnsbury, church history book specifically says, "The Christian Endeavor Society [in which Dr. Bob was active] which started in 1887 [in the St. Johnsbury Church] has continued through the years as the leading young people's organization and many an adult of today has vivid memories of the influence of the pastors, their wives and other leaders who inspired them in their formative years."[372]

Members of the Fairbanks Family and Judge Walter Smith

The North Congregational Church, St. Johnsbury, church history book lists the Deacons and names Franklin Fairbanks and Walter P. Smith. It lists the Sunday School Superintendents and names Erastus Fairbanks, Joseph P. Fairbanks, Horace Fairbanks, and Franklin Fairbanks.[373]

Arthur Fairbanks Stone was one of the grand sons of Erastus Fairbanks. And Arthur Stone returned to St. Johnsbury to become editor and publisher of the town newspaper, the *Caledonian*; and, in addition, served as clerk for the North Congregational Church.

Several comments should be made about other Congregational activities related to St. Johnsbury. The first concerns the Vermont Domestic Missionary Society. Much of the work had to do with "an alarming weakness of many churches in smaller towns due to emigration." Employment of theological students for summer work with churches was involved. However, Vermont records state, "From two-thirds to three-fourths of all the churches now existing in the state have been founded or at some time aided by our state missionary society, including not a few which have grown to strength and prominence. Many others, still weak, have been kept from extinction. . . ." Not surprisingly, the Society was filled with Fairbanks efforts. Erastus Fairbanks was president from 1849-1865; Franklin Fairbanks

---

[372] Stone, *North Congregational Church, . . . 1825-1942*, 69-70. "Christian Endeavor was founded in Portland, Maine in 1881 by Canadian born Dr. Francis E. Clark at the Williston Congregational Church." Christian Endeavor International web site: http://www.christianendeavor.com/index.cfm?PAGE_ID=34 ; accessed 10/31/07.
[373] Stone, *North Congregational Church*, 86-87.

from 1877-84; and Rev. Henry Fairbanks from 1884-1914. Another effort to strengthen the Congregational churches can be credited largely to the Fairbanks family. In 1856, in accordance with the bequest of Joseph P. Fairbanks of St. Johnsbury, two funds came under the responsibility of the Congregational Convention, the income to be used, in one case, for "the aid of pious young men in a course of preparation for the ministry," and in the other, "to be given to disabled and needy clergymen of Vermont." One fund was called the Fairbanks Board of Education; and the other the Fairbanks Board for the Relief of Ministers—expanded to aid also the widows and orphans of ministers. The *Vermont Missionary* first appeared as a four-page monthly sheet in November 1889 as the organ of the Vermont Missionary Society. The Vermont Branch of the Women's Board of Missions was organized in 1872 and the Woman's Home Missionary Union in 1888. There are extensive lists containing the names and tenure of ministers serving the churches of Vermont.[374] The relevance to Dr. Bob's training and beliefs of these other elements in Congregational Church life is probably easier to explain by reference to other volumes of the Fairbanks Family, the Fairbanks concern for the Congregational Church, its ministers, and its young men and their education. In other words, the Vermont Congregational Churches and North Congregational Church, St. Johnsbury, were demonstrably stronger as the result of the "Great Awakening" of 1875 and all the domestic missionary work, YMCA collaboration, revivals, and Fairbanks religious and educational stipulations concerning the YMCA and St. Johnsbury Academy. Christian youth workers, Christian trustees, Christian church attendance, chapel, and prayer, and support of revivals and conversions were everywhere evident in the period following the "Great Awakening." And St. Johnsbury, its Fairbanks family, and North Congregational Church, St. Johnsbury, were strong parts of the work.

The involvement of the Smith family in North Congregational Church, St. Johnsbury, is covered elsewhere. Suffice it to remember again here that: (1) Judge Smith was a Deacon, a Sunday School Superintendent, and taught Sunday School there for over 30 years. (2) His wife Susan was in a church quartet. She taught Sunday School. She was

---

[374] John M. Comstock, *The Congregational Churches of Vermont and Their Ministry 1762-1942 Historical and Statistical* (St. Johnsbury, VT: The Cowles Press, Inc., 1942), 15-21, 24-25, 28, 153, 181, 250.

superintendent of two different Sunday School groups. She was much involved in women's affairs and domestic missions.[375] And she rendered papers on the church history. (3) Young Bob was listed as a member and as a Sunday School student; and he himself verified his intense involvement in four services a week, as well as his participation in the Christian Endeavor Society of the church.

There is an old saw about the young man who was upset, in his youth, about how little his father knew about most important things. Years later, he concluded, after listening carefully to his father's remarks and views, that "the old man has sure learned a lot since I was a young boy."

Parallel might be Dr. Bob' possible and supposed distaste for church as a youngster. This speculative thinking has very little evidence of such distaste. But it was a heavy requirement in those days for a young boy to have to attend church services four times a week and Christian Endeavor on Mondays. It was a heavy load to listen to incessant talk about Temperance, Anti-Saloon movements, and sin. It was a heavy requirement for a high school student at St. Johnsbury Academy to attend daily chapel, do a required church service each week, and also do a mandatory Bible study or prayer meeting. Add to that the prayers and sermon at graduation, and St. Johnsbury Academy's stress on moral and religious education. You might get a picture of how a high-spirited, young, college student might recall and re-think all the "burdensome" religious education as he plunged into the depths of heavy drinking and partying—later into unqualified alcoholism. If a distaste for religious and church matters did develop, it could well have been a correlative counter-part of desired license and freedom of action—even unabashed lawlessness such as that which accompanied the Prohibition era. But let's consider what happened to Dr. Bob when the going got really tough—in the home, in the medical practice, in the pocketbook, in the reputation, and in the self-degradation. Remember, that without really wanting to quit drinking, Dr. Bob began what some have called a spiritual quest. That, however, is hardly an adequate

---

[375] Letter from Ken B. to Taylor Reed regarding Reed's article "Alcoholics Anonymous Rooted in St. Johnsbury Institutions" in *The Caledonian-Record*, online edition, October 12, 2007, and monograph of C.S. Smith, *An Historical Sketch of Home Missionary Work in Vermont, By the Congregational Churches* (Montpelier: Press of the Watchman Publishing Company, 1893)

description or a perceptive understanding of the alleged "quest." For Dr. Bob returned to reading the entire Bible several times. He revved up his prayer life. He joined a church. He participated in Oxford Group meetings. And he drank! Why? For the very simple reason that he wanted to—he still thought he could beat the game.

But then came the prayer on the carpet at the behest of Henrietta Seiberling and his own admission of alcoholism, followed by the miraculous arrival of a Bill Wilson on the hunt.[376] And in practically no time at all, Dr. Bob was returning to the training and memories of his youth—he and his wife in church, kids in Sunday School, regular Bible study, prayer three times a day, and extensive use of devotionals and extensive reading of Christian literature on God, Jesus Christ, the Bible, prayer, healing, love, and Oxford Group ideas. "Immense" was the word he used to describe his reading. Immense was the word others used to describe the vast number of books in his home. And regular was his insistent distribution of these books for others to study, return, and be queried about.[377] To me, the actual facts describe a desperate man who well remembered his religious past, readily picked up the tools he had learned how to wield, and tried to "beat the game" while playing it the "old school way." To me, that describes conduct typical of an alcoholic. Bill Wilson explained it well in the chapter "More About Alcoholism." Trip, no trip. Oath, no oath, Whiskey to beer. Quit, no cessation. That's an apt description of the seemingly helpless insanity. Dr. Silkworth told Bill Wilson that the Great Physician could cure him. Bill signed pledge after pledge to quit in the family Bible. But Bill didn't quit until he wanted to; and he didn't call on the Great Physician until after his conversion, until Ebby Thacher had held out a solution of real merit, and until Bill had pounded down a few more drinks on the way to the hospital and the visit to the Great Physician. It reminds me of the well-known stories about the penitents on the way to Duffy's in Calistoga. They gulped down some last drinks on the way, and they looked forward to the morning "hummers" which insured they would still be able to drink. Yet Duffy himself became on of the greatest speakers on the A.A. circuit. He knew what alcoholics did, and he had planted a sign in the yard: "God could and would if He were sought."

---

[376] See these books by Dick B.: *Henrietta B. Seiberling*; *Dr. Bob and His Library*; *Good Morning*; and *The Akron Genesis*.
[377] See Dick B., *Dr. Bob and His Library*.

I think Bob's son Smitty may have described Dr. Bob belated biblical revival pretty well. He told me that his dad was averse to "sky pilots"—ministers. He also told me that Dr. Bob preferred the "message to the messenger." And both characterizations, if warranted and accurate, would explain the thrust—and return to youthful days—of the emphasis on meetings—revival, Bible, and prayer; acceptance of Christ in a biblical way, reliance on the Creator, Quiet Time (the Quiet Hour of his Christian Endeavor days), with love and service to others. Anything, perhaps, but the church devotion which had characterized his early years with his family in Vermont. Church, as you will note, was recommended in Akron but not required. When the Akron program was mapped out by the former church-goer Bob and the no-church goer Bill, it certainly picked up all the church tools, but not the church. The message that Dr. Bob had learned took precedence over the necessity for a man of the cloth as messenger in importance. And the pastor's role took a back seat to fervent prayer, Bible study, conversions, fellowship, and witness.

The Church Is Only One Part of a Larger Spiritual Picture

In this and other segments, we will review the many factors which were involved in Dr. Bob's "excellent training" in the "Good Book" "as a youngster." His own family were a large influence. It would seem that the ubiquitous Fairbanks people were everywhere involved in the places Dr. Bob frequented. They were stalwart, dedicated, outreaching Congregationalist Christian role models. They exemplified non-profit, charitable, love and service. They talked Christian principles. And they were everywhere that Dr. Bob's family members and he were present—the church, the Sunday School, the St. Johnsbury Athenaeum, the YMCA, the revivals, the Gospel meetings, and the St. Johnsbury Academy. The YMCA was intensely involved in community-wide outreach. The Vermont Domestic Missionary Society was intensely involved in strengthening churches with state-wide unions, meetings, itinerant ministers, young volunteers, publications, and soul-saving. It would appear that North Congregational Church, St. Johnsbury, didn't need the strengthening as a church, but it had already been buttressed in its building, its Sunday School, and its outreach by Fairbanks activity. St. Johnsbury had become a strong center for spreading the "Great Awakening" of 1875. Many Fairbanks family members were part of Dr. Bob's church. Christian Endeavor was acclaimed as the hottest young people's group of the time. The town revivals, Gospel meetings, and evangelistic work touched many (if not all) of the churches and seemingly every resident of the town itself. Lastly, the St. Johnsbury Academy, founded by the Fairbanks brothers, loomed large as an influence. Conversions were innumerable. The whole atmosphere was Congregational. The Fairbanks people were Congregationalists. The Smiths individually were involved with the St. Johnsbury Academy and were Congregationalists. The YMCA conducted affairs in the town and at the St. Johnsbury Academy, and Judge Smith and many of the Fairbanks people were involved in both. The Vermont Domestic Missionary Society appeared to be a pet of the Fairbanks leaders, and it was a special interest of Mrs. Smith's.[378]

There are plenty of dots to look at before you connect them up and find the pervasive influence of the Creator, Jesus Christ, the Bible, conversion, fellowship, and witness in Dr. Bob's younger years. Each segment criss-crosses the whole and points up the parts and their interrelationship.

North Congregational Church *Year Book*, January, 1902

One of the documents we acquired during the course of our research was a copy of a North Congregational Church, St. Johnsbury, *Year Book*, dated January, 1902. Even though the *Year Book* bears a date three-plus years after Bob Smith graduated from St. Johnsbury Academy in 1898, young Bob did go to work for the E. & T. Fairbanks & Company in St. Johnsbury for a couple of years after he graduated from the Academy. And the *Year Book* covers either the period of his continued church attendance, or contains facts so relevant to his training that we will set forth some major portions of it. Suffice it to say that the Directory lists the following church members at page 23, in the following fashion:

---

[378] Letter from Ken B. to Taylor Reed regarding Reed's article "Alcoholics Anonymous Rooted in St. Johnsbury Institutions" in *The Caledonian-Record,* online edition, October 12, 2007, and monograph of C.S. Smith, *An Historical Sketch of Home Missionary Work in Vermont, By the Congregational Churches* (Montpelier: Press of the Watchman Publishing Company, 1893)

Smith, Walter P., m. 20 Summer [the address of the home at that time]
Smith, Mrs. Susan H., m
Smith, Robert H.

ORDINANCES OF THE CHURCH

The Ordinances of The Church on the back of the front cover are particularly informative and say:

"LORD'S DAY.
"Morning Service, 10:30 a.m.
Sunday School, 12 m.
Junior Christian Endeavor Society, 3:30 p.m.
Christian Endeavor Society, 6:15 p.m.
Evening Service, 7 p.m.
The Sacrament of the Lord's Supper will be administered on the first Lord's Day in January, March, May, July, September and November

"WEEK DAY.
"Mid-week Service, Wednesday evening, 7:30 o'clock
Preparatory Service on the Wednesday evening preceding the Lord's Supper. The North and South Churches unite in this service.
Woman's Prayer Meeting, Friday afternoon at 4 o'clock. For other services see the appointments of the various societies of the Church. The members of this Church are respectfully urged to avoid, as far as possible, making social or other engagements for Wednesday evenings, which would interfere with their attendance upon the regular meetings for conference and prayer. Let this evening in the week be considered as always engaged in advance for this important service. There are five other evenings for our pleasure of business; let us give Wednesday evenings to Christ and the Church."

OFFICERS AND COMMITTEES

"Pastor—Rev. Edward M. Chapman
Deacons--. . . . Walter P. Smith, term expires January, 1908. . . .
Executive Committee—The Pastor, Deacons, Clerk, Sunday School Superintendent. . . .

Committee on Home Charity—The Pastor, Mrs. T.M. Howard, Mrs. C.M. Stone, Mrs. W. P. Smith, E.T. Ide

SUNDAY SCHOOL...

Teachers in the Adult Department. . . . Mrs. W. P. Smith. . . .

WOMAN'S ASSOCIATION

President, Mrs. J. L. Perkins; First Vice President, Mrs. W. P. Smith

SENIOR CHRISTIAN ENDEAVOR

. . . Committees, Lookout . . . Prayer Meeting . . . Social . . . Missionary.

JUNIOR SOCIETY OF CHRISTIAN ENDEAVOR

. . . Chairman Lookout Committee . . . Chairman Prayer Meeting Committee . . . Chairman Social Committee . . . Chairman Missionary Committee.

TREASURER'S REPORT

Benevolent Contributions [lists contributions for the following in specified amounts:] Committee on Home Charity, Congregational Home Missionary Society, American Missionary Assn., Vermont Domestic Missionary Assn., Congregational Education Society, International Institute, Congregational Sunday School and Publishing Society, Vermont Bible Society, St. Johnsbury YMCA

TOPICS FOR MID-WEEK SERVICES

Since there are topics for each week, we here list some samples—and in almost every case, there are correlative Bible verses: (1) Misconceptions about Religion. (2) The Beauty and Strength of Righteousness. (3) Success Through Self-Sacrifice. (4) The Way into the Kingdom—citing "The New Birth and the Great Gift, John 3:1-21." (5) True religion. (6) The Mission of Christ. (7) The Sabbath. (8) The Ethics of the Blessed Life. (9) Christ's Message to Men. (10)

Saving Life and Losing It. (11) The Duty of Forgiveness. (12) Spiritual Freedom. (13) The Works of God Manifested. (14) Slighting God's Invitations. (15) The Pledge of Immortality. (16) Jesus in the Home. (16) Christ the King. (17) Christ the Judge. (18) Remembering Christ. (19) The Holy Spirit. (20) Christ the Redeemer. (21) The Living Christ.

The Comparison with Early Akron A.A.

It's for sure that Bill Wilson didn't bring to Akron any of the training, topics, studies, principles or practices that are mentioned above. Nor did the Oxford Group entertain such a program or bestow it on the early AAs in 1935.

Let's leave St. Johnsbury Academy, Christian Endeavor, the YMCA, the revivals, and the daily chapels to one side. If you look at the sheer enormity of religious discipline of which Dr. Bob himself spoke and which is evident in the foregoing materials on North Congregational Church alone, you can hardly doubt that our "Heavenly Father" (as Dr. bob called Him), His son Jesus Christ (which was the core of the church training), the gift of the Holy Spirit, the Bible, Bible studies, prayer meetings, conversions to Christ, and teachings and topics having to do with the Bible and Christ were a part of Dr. Bob's daily fare and that each can be identified in the simple rudiments of the Akron program which Bill and Bob founded and of which Bob was leader.

"Your Heavenly Father will never let you down!"
Alcoholics Anonymous, 4th ed., p. 181

6
The Christian Endeavor Society
and
Its Legacy to Alcoholics Anonymous

Dr. Bob attended North Congregational Church, St. Johnsbury.[379] That church had a vibrant Christian Endeavor Society supporting the church, beginning in 1887, when Dr. Bob was about eight years old.[380]

---

[379] Dr. Bob's parents [Walter P. Smith and Susan H. Smith (= Mrs. Walter P. Smith)] are first mentioned in the North Congregational Church, St. Johnsbury, *Year Book for 1878*, on page 13 (approximately one year before Dr. Bob was born on August 8, 1879), according to a letter to Dick B. dated October 25, 2007, from Bob Swartz, the church's archivist.

[380] "The Christian Endeavor Society which started in 1887 [i.e., in North Congregational Church, St. Johnsbury] has continued through the years as the leading young people's organization. . . . In 1891 [when Dr. Bob was about 12 years old], and again in 1921, there was a Junior Society of Christian Endeavor which later merged into a larger society." *North Congregational Church, St. Johnsbury, Vermont, 1825-1942* (   ), 69, 70.

An interesting comment appears in Nutting's *Becoming the United Church of Christ in Vermont, 1795-1995*, which seems to imply that the Society of Christian Endeavor might even have become active at North Congregational Church, St. Johnsbury, as early as 1885: "Union meeting held for three weeks at St. Johnsbury with an evangelist with gratifying results. Societies of Christian Endeavor at both churches . . ." ; John E. Nutting, *Becoming the United Church of Christ in Vermont, 1795-1995* (Burlington, VT: The Vermont Conference of the United Church of Christ, 1996), 222.

Nutting also records another important comment in the "State of Religion in the Churches" section of the report for 1886 about when Societies of Christian Endeavor became active in Vermont: "For the first time [i.e., in 1886] we get reports of Societies of Christian Endeavor (first organized four year [sic] ago). Now twenty churches have them." Nutting, *Becoming the United Church of Christ*, 224.

"Christian Endeavor was founded in Portland, Maine in 1881 by Canadian born Dr. Francis E. Clark at the Williston Congregational Church." http://www.christianendeavor.com/index.cfm?PAGE_ID=34 ; accessed 11/5/07.

According to a report given at the seventh National Convention of Societies of Christian Endeavor, held on July 5, 1888, in Chicago, Illinois (which was called to order by President W. J. Van Patten of Burlington, Vermont), there were at this time 110 Societies of Christian Endeavor in Vermont. See: "Christian Workers.

Dr. Bob's father, as a Deacon, was an Honorary Member of Christian Endeavor. And Dr. Bob not only said he had received excellent training in the Bible as a youngster, but also stated that he had attended the North Congregational Church, St. Johnsbury, regularly for Sunday morning worship, afternoon Sunday School, and the evening service, as well as the Wednesday prayer meeting on occasion. In the same context, it is not difficult to see the Christian and biblical principles he acquired from his church and Christian Endeavor. Nor that there is

---

Convention of the Societies of Christian Endeavor," *The New York Times*, July 6, 1888, page 3.

"The first meeting of the Vermont Christian Endeavor Union was held at Burlington December 14, 1886, and was fortunate in having present both President F. E. Clark and Secretary Ward. Forty societies were reported, and showed by the number of their delegates what a power the society had already become in the State.

"The first president of the Vermont Christian Endeavor Union was Professor G. H. Perkins, of Burlington, elected December 14, 1886. . . . The fifth Convention [in 1890] was held at St. Johnsbury, and Rev. P. McMillan, of Woodstock, was elected president." Francis E. Clark, *World Wide Endeavor: The Story of the Young People's Society of Christian Endeavor: From the Beginning and in All Lands* (Philadelphia: Gillespie, Metzgar & Kelley, 1895), 515.

"One of these names [that we have not noticed before in the records of Christian Endeavor] is that of Hon. W. J. Van Patten, of Burlington, Vt., a prominent layman, connected with the Winooski Avenue Church [of Burlington, Vermont], whose society stands fifth on the recorded list, being formed Dec. 5, 1881.

"It was due to Mr. Van Patten's influence that this fifth society was formed, . . .

"At the [second] convention already described he [Mr. Van Patten] appears as a member of the finance committee most appropriately, for it was due largely to his generosity and ample pocketbook placed at the disposal of the society that its principles during its first two years were spread broadcast. . . .

"[In his paper read at this second convention on 'Ways and Means of Enlarging the Work of the Young People's Society of Christian Endeavor,] . . . Mr. Van Patten . . . said: 'Our societies differ from Young Men's Christian Associations in this: We are denominational, while they are not. Work done for one of our societies is done for one denomination, while work done for an association is done for all denominations.'

"Mr. Van Patten . . . is . . . an earnest advocate and supporter of the Young Men's Christian Association. He has given a very large sum of money for the erection of a beautiful association building in Burlington, the city of which he is now the honored mayor." Clark, *World Wide Endeavor*, 125, 126.

"Mr. W. J. Van Patten . . . [was] the most liberal friend of the Christian Endeavor movement in its earliest days, . . ." Clark, *World Wide Endeavor*, 192.

"[At the third convention—also known as the fourth convention—held on October 22, 1884, in Lowell, Mass.,] [T]wo [places] in Vermont [were represented]—Chester and Burlington.

"Vermont had seven societies, . . ." Clark, *World Wide Endeavor*, 145.

strong evidence that he wound up transmitting the principles and practices of his youth to the major principles and practices of early A.A. in Akron.

Abundant books, articles, and records tell us exactly what Christian Endeavor, Vermont Christian Endeavor, and the North Congregational Church Christian Endeavor required, did, and accomplished.[381]

The Christian Endeavor Manual, prepared by the founder of Christian Endeavor, Rev. Francis Edward Clark, D.D., is one of several books and manuals that lay out the salient features of the movement, its history, its pledge, its prayer meetings, its consecration services, its lines of committee work, its Quiet Hour, and its other activities.

A revival of religion in the Williston Congregational Church of Portland, Maine, produced the founding of the Christian Endeavor Society on February 2, 1881, by some young converts and a few others. By the autumn of 1881 and the early months of winter, there were several vigorous societies in Maine, Vermont, and Massachusetts.

The founder, Dr. Francis Clark, wrote that the fundamental principles of the Christian Endeavor Society were four: (1) Confession of Christ; (2) Service for Christ; (3) Fellowship with Christ's people; and (4)

---

[381] See: (1) Francis E. Clark, *Christian Endeavor in All Lands: A Record of Twenty-five Years of Progress* (Boston, MA: The United Society of Christian Endeavor, 1906); (2) Francis Edward Clark, *The Christian Endeavor Manual* (Boston, MA: The United Christian Endeavor Society, 1903); (3) Amos R. Wells, *Expert Endeavor: A Text-Book of Christian Endeavor Methods and Principles for the Use of Classes and of Candidates for the Title of "C.E.E.-Christian Endeavor Expert"* (Boston, MA: United Society of Christian Endeavor, 1911); (4) John Franklin Cowan, *New Life in the Old Prayer Meeting* (NY: Fleming H. Revell Company, 1906); (5) John M. Comstock, *The Congregational Churches of Vermont and Their Ministry, 1762-1942: Historical and Statistical* (St. Johnsbury, VT: The Cowles Press, Inc., 1942); (6) John E. Nutting, *Becoming the United Church of Christ of Christ in Vermont, 1795-1995* (Burlington, VT: The Vermont Conference of the United Church of Christ, 1996); (7) Stone *North Congregational Church: St. Johnsbury, Vermont 1825-1942*; (8) Charles M. Sheldon, *In His Steps* (NJ: Spire Books, Fleming H. Revell Company, 1963); and (9) James DeForest Murch, *Successful C.E. Prayer-meetings* (Cincinnati, OH: The Standard Publishing Company, 1930).

Loyalty to Christ's church. And millions of young people conscientiously promised to read the Bible and to pray every day. Private devotion was stimulated by the "Quiet Hour." Its "Pentecostal Sign" was "Let the redeemed of the Lord say so." Christian Endeavor was a society which knew no denominational lines, no national boundaries, and no sectarian names of denominational shibboleths— with the motto, "For Christ and the Church."

The whole history of the movement established that the society "is in the church, and of the church, and for the church," and that it is peculiarly and essentially a church organization. It differed from the Young Men's Christian Associations and the Young Women's Christian Associations, whose work was necessarily in a sense outside the churches, though in close sympathy with them. The YMCA and YWCA existed for the whole community and not primarily for the individual church. Their work was to rescue young men and women of the whole city, and to provide, so far as possible, a home for the unchurched. Their responsibility was largely for those outside of the churches, while the Christian Endeavor movement existed largely for those within the churches or those who might be brought within the radius of some local church influence. But the history of Christian Endeavor, of the Congregational Churches, and of the YMCA of Vermont shows frequent cooperation in the moves to convert others to Christ.

The pastor, deacons, elders or stewards, and Sunday-school superintendent, if not active members were *ex officiis* honorary members of Christian Endeavor. The Society was under the control of the official board of the church.

The active member promised not only to make it the rule of his life to pray and read the Bible daily, and to support his own church loyally, but also to be present at, and to take some part, aside from singing, in every Christian Endeavor prayer-meeting, unless prevented by a reason which he could conscientiously "give to the Master."

Much effort was given to obtaining new members.

One of the most important and original features of the Christian Endeavor movement was the prayer-meeting pledge or covenant. The covenant was said to have two sides and two parties to the agreement: "The Christ in whom we trust furnishes the strength; we promise in obedience, "Trusting in the Lord Jesus Christ for strength, I promise Him." The covenant contained six definite promises that relate to the Christian life:

- (1) I will read the Bible.[382]

- (2) I will pray.[383]

- (3) I will support my own church.[384]

- (4) I will attend the weekly prayer-meeting of the society.[385]

- (5) I will take some part in it, aside from singing.[386]

- (6) I will perform a special duty at the consecration meeting if obliged to be absent.

---

[382] In early A.A., the Bible was stressed as reading matter. In fact, Dr. Bob stated that A.A.'s basic ideas came from the Bible and that the "absolutely essential" parts were the Book of James, Jesus' Sermon on the Mount, and 1 Corinthians 13. Discussing reading, Dr. Bob's wife Anne wrote in her spiritual journal that all reading should be guided, that the Bible was the main sourcebook, and that not a day should pass without reading it.

[383] In his chapter "More Prayer in the prayer meeting," Rev. J.F. Cowan felt it appropriate to analyze prayer into some of its constituents as Dwight Moody did. Cowan listed Adoration, Confession, Restitution, Thanksgiving, Forgiveness, Unity, Faith, Petition, and Submission. Cowan, *New Life in the Old Prayer Meetings*. Anne Smith laid out similar definitions for AAs and their families in the journal she shared with them in morning quiet hour sessions.

[384] In early A.A. attendance at a church of one's choice each week was recommended but not required. And Dr. Bob and Anne Smith attended the West Side Presbyterian Church in Akron during the early A.A. years.

[385] Early AAs had only one "regular" meeting each week. It was held at the home of T. Henry and Clarace Williams in Akron. And these meetings were called "old fashioned prayer meetings." Dr. Bob's son described them as "old fashioned revival meetings."

[386] Even in today's A.A. meetings, newcomers are urged to get "commitments." These include making coffee, setting up chairs, being a greeter, cleaning up after a meeting, and other duties such as serving as Secretary, Treasurer, Chairperson, or General Service Representative.

- The Covenant was said to be Scriptural: Said they, we are told to "pray without ceasing"; "search the Scriptures"; "confess Christ before men"; "to be about our Father's business;" "grow in grace"; "follow in the footsteps of Jesus Christ"; and "I will do what he would have me do."

- The Society of Christian Endeavor centered about the prayer-meeting. Every meeting had its topic with many Scripture references and abundant helps. Believers were encouraged to give testimony like Paul's: "I know that in me dwelleth no good thing"; "I know whom I have believed"; "I know that all things work together for good to them that love God"; and "I know that I have a building of God, a house not made with hands." The CE prayer-meeting aimed to be eminently a meeting of prayer. It began with prayer and closed with a prayer of benediction, had "seasons of prayer" in the course of a meeting, and often the "chain of prayer," where prayers of one were followed in succession by another's. Prayer for the meeting; meditation on the subject of the meeting; and study of the Bible passages which related to the topic were all important.

- "Drawing the net" was the phrase that emphasized giving the unconverted an opportunity to express their decision for or against Christ—also in special meetings of a revival nature. Sometimes the question, "Will you now and here decide for Christ and express that decision?"

- Endeavorers were urged that "wherever it is possible the pastor close each meeting, whether consecration or other, with a few earnest words." Sometimes the meetings allowed the last five minutes of the hour to the pastor. At that time, he often invited decisions for Christ.

- A "Good Prayer-Meeting" was said to assure the following; and it can be seen from the descriptions by Dr. Bob's wife Anne that the principles were followed::

- (1) Every one takes part.[387]

- (2) The spirit of prayer manifestly exists.[388]

- (3) Souls are saved.[389]

- (4) You to leave "with a heart aglow."[390]

---

[387] Early A.A. meetings were described by Dorothy S.M. as "old fashioned prayer meetings" and also by Dr. Bob's son Smitty (on the telephone to me) as "old fashioned revival meetings." Those present made it clear that all participated in the prayers. *DR. BOB*, 101.

[388] Anne Smith wrote: "We have ceased to believe in the power of God which can save. We do not sincerely believe in prayer. . . . Is it not written that prayer is inevitably answered? What do you do when you pray? . . . That we4 are so in touch with the Holy Spirit that He can give us at that moment a message that is accurate and adequate. . . . pray that Spirit may tell you what to pray for. . . . A way to find God's will not to change it." Dick B., *Anne Smith's Journal, 1933-1939*, 3rd ed. (Kihei, HI: Paradise Research Publications, Inc., 1998), 114.

[389] Though the records went undescribed and undiscussed for many years, recently it has been abundantly established from the mouths of four early A.A. pioneers that leading people to Christ was part and parcel of the upstairs "real surrenders." Those who attested and are mentioned in several of my titles were Larry Bauer, J.D. Holmes, Ed Andy, and Clarence H. Snyder. Larry Bauer personally wrote me and phoned me, stating that he had been taken upstairs and "got born again." As reported in Hinds Foundation literature, J.D. Holmes complained about being led to Christ as an oldtimer. I listed to Ed Andy state on the telephone that they "wouldn't let you in unless you accepted Jesus Christ." And I personally heard from Clarence Snyder's wife Grace Snyder, and also read in Mitch K.'s biography of Snyder, that Clarence specifically described the prayers by which the old timers led him to accept Jesus Christ as his Lord and Savior. Anne Smith wrote: "The moment we ourselves are saved, we must set ourselves to saving others. The way Christ became the Atoning Lamb was by his hanging on the Cross and dying there. And Christianity for me means to dedicated myself to serve others even unto death." Dick B., *Anne Smith's Journal, 1933-1939*, 3rd ed. (Kihei, HI: Paradise Research Publications, Inc., 1998), 85.

[390] Of the early meetings, Anne Smith wrote: "Never let your zeal flag; maintain the spiritual glow." She cited the Moffatt Translation, and the King James Version of Romans 12:11 reads; "Not slothful in business; fervent in spirit; serving the Lord." Dick B., *Anne Smith's Journal, 1933-1939*, 3rd ed., 79.

- (5) "You anticipate eagerly the next one."

- (6) "The singing is brisk, yet thoughtful."

- (7) "The leader forgets self and remembers Christ."[391]

- (8) There has been "much preparation."[392]

- (9) "Our Saviour is present, and everyone knows it."[393]

- (10) Every one has a copy of the weekly topics with the suggested Bible-readings.[394]

- (11) Members will give careful preparation and Bible-study on the topic of the meeting.[395]

The Comrades of the Quiet Hour, a part of Christian Endeavor, consisted of all persons that were willing to sign the following covenant: "Trusting in the Lord Jesus Christ for strength, I will make it the rule of my life to set apart at least fifteen minutes every day, if possible in the early morning, for quiet meditation and direct communion with God." The Quiet Hour, they said, would reveal the Lord to them in four ways:

---

[391] Anne Smith wrote in her journal: "Don't try, but trust. . . . We find release not by our own efforts but by what Christ does for us and in us when we open every area of our lives to Him." Dick B., *Anne Smith's Journal*, 11.

[392] As discussed in the next footnote, the preparation for the Akron Wednesday meeting was such that the leaders asked God what they should say, and who should say it. In short, an entire meeting was devoted to preparation.

[393] Anne Smith wrote: "seek the in-dwelling presence of Christ; dedicate body, soul, and spirit; pray that the Holy Spirit may take charge; have the attitude of 'Speak Lord for Thy Servant Heareth. . .'" Dick B. *Anne Smith's Journal, 1933-1939*, 111.

[394] At the "regular" Wednesday evening pioneer fellowship meeting, topics were presented and discussed. *DR. BOB*, 100, 137-42; and on the preceding Monday, Dr. Bob and the other elders would ask God's guidance as to who should lead the forthcoming Wednesday meeting and as to what the topic should be. *DR. BOB*, 137-39.

[395] Anne Smith wrote: "The method of holding Quiet Time varies some with each individual. All include prayer and Bible reading and study and patient listening to God." Dick B., *Anne Smith's Journal, 1933-1939*, 106.

- (1) through the thoughtful reading of the Word of God and devotional books, which may supplement the Word and make it plainer;[396]

- (2) through prayer and supplication;[397]

- (3) and above all through meditation and realization of the presence of a personal God in Christ Jesus;[398] and

- (4) and by the power of the Holy Spirit working in their hearts.[399]

There are abundant resources documenting each of the foregoing statements. And we have taken particular care to note the parallels between the Christian Endeavor instructions and the practices in Akron as detailed in *DR. BOB and the Good Oldtimers* and *Anne Smith's Journal*. Probably the most helpful details as to the Christian Endeavor Society are these:

Francis E. Clark, *Christian Endeavor in All Lands: A Record of Twenty-Five Years of Progress* (Boston, MA: The United Society of Christian Endeavor, 1906).

Francis E. Clark, *Memories of Many Men in Many Lands: An Autobiography* (Boston: United Society of Christian Endeavor, 1922).

Amos R. Wells, *Expert Endeavor: A Text-book of Christian Endeavor Methods and Principles* (Boston: International Society of Christian Endeavor, 1911).

---

[396] The Bible was open and read at the early A.A. meetings; and they also used devotionals such as *The Upper Room, My Utmost for His Highest*, and *The Runner's Bible*. See Dick B. *The Akron Genesis of Alcoholics Anonymous*, 181-215.

[397] Anne Smith's daughter Sue Smith Windows describes in *Children of the Healer* how people would gather at the Smith home in the morning and, led by Anne Smith, would hear the Bible, pray, seek guidance, and discuss the practices. Smith and Windows. *Children of the Healer*, 43-44.

[398] Dick B. *Anne Smith's Journal, 1933-1939*, 57-62.

[399] Dick B. *Anne Smith's Journal*, 1933-1939, 111.

The John E. Nutting compilation of the history of the churches of Vermont contains reference after reference to the vitality and outreach of the Christian Endeavor Society in the towns of Vermont.[400] These societies were mentioned regularly in company with the state of the Vermont Congregational Churches, their vitality, growth, and activity. In short, the impact of the society was felt exactly where it was intended to be felt—in the church.

Relevance to Early A.A.

We will not detail here the points we make at great length in other segments. Though there have been those who have attempted to tie the early Akron A.A. program far too closely to the Oxford Group, the fact is that the almost wholesale adoption of the life-changing principles of the Oxford Group into the Alcoholics Anonymous basic text was not done until 1939—four years after Akron A.A. was founded and had developed its original, Christian, spiritual program of recovery. The Oxford Group program, and the teachings of Rev. Samuel M. Shoemaker to Bill Wilson (author of the basic text), have not been given the credit they deserve for the immense part of their contribution to Bill Wilson's 1939 book venture.[401] And a few words about Bill Wilson's resurrection of Oxford Group ideas in the body of his 1939 text are in order.

As I have pointed out in my studies of the Oxford Group and Shoemaker contributions, many of the Oxford Group ideas derived from sources similar to those of Vermont Congregationalism and even more directly from the ideas of some of the Christian Endeavor Society mentors such as Dwight L. Moody, John R. Mott, F. B. Meyer, and Henry Drummond. However, these "progenitor" forces as I have described them in my Oxford Group writings, were in place and influencing Congregationalism, Christian Endeavor, the YMCA, the Student Christian Movement, and Moody's Mt. Hermon schools and students long before the Oxford Group or its founder became involved

---

[400] Nutting, *Becoming the United Church of Christ in Vermont*, 222, 24, 26-27, 33-34. 38, 40-42, 47, 50, 53.
[401] Dick B., *The Oxford Group and Alcoholics Anonymous: A Design for Living That Works*, 2d ed. (Kihei: HI: Paradise Research Publications, Inc., 1998); *New Light on Alcoholism: God, Sam Shoemaker and A.A.*, 2d ed. (Kihei, HI: Paradise Research Publications, 1999).

in life-changing. And the New England revivals, evangelism, Gospel meetings, saving of souls, conversions, Bible study meetings, prayer meetings, and Sunday school teachings and techniques bear no significant relation to the life-changing ideas of Oxford Group founder Dr. Frank N.D. Buchman.

The twenty-eight Oxford Group principles that impacted on Bill Wilson's Big Book and Twelve Steps centered on the following major ideas: (1) God had a plan, and man's basic duty was to fit himself into that plan. (2) Sin was the barrier that separated man from God. (3) Sin had to be "cut-out" through surrender and life-changing practices—Confidence, Confession, Conviction, Conversion, and Continuance. Plus Restitution (4) Sin was the problem. Jesus Christ was the cure. The result was a miracle. The Power was that of Jesus Christ. (5) Quiet Time was the means by which man grew spiritually in the process—Bible study, two-way prayer, journaling, and checking. (6) Adherence to the "moral standards" laid out by Dr. Robert E. Speer as the uncompromising absolute principles taught by Jesus—honesty, purity, unselfishness, and love. (7) Fellowship with accompanying loyalty and team work were essentials in the outreach team work. (8) Witness (called "sharing for witness") was the duty to carry the message to someone else whose life needed change.

The principles of New England Congregationalism—embraced by North Congregational Church, St. Johnsbury (which Dr. Bob attended in his youth), the Congregational denomination, and Christian Endeavor—were much more simple: (1) There was a strong focus on church worship, Sunday School, evening services, and mid-week prayer meetings. (2) Belief in God was requisite. (3) Salvation through Jesus Christ and Jesus Christ only was the Way. (4) Elimination of sinful conduct—particularly use of intoxicating liquor—was a large concern.. (5) Bible study meetings were vital. (6) Old fashioned prayer, revival, conversion, and Gospel meetings took particular prominence during the "Great Awakening" of 1875 and thereafter among Congregational churches. (7) Intense Bible reading was done in the home, in the church, in Christian Endeavor, in the YMCA, and in St. Johnsbury Academy. (8) Converting others to Christ by intense personal work was everywhere manifest in church reports of the period..

While there are similarities, Dr. Bob's Congregationalist approach that was translated to the early A.A. program was incredibly simple—and closely resembled his own "excellent training" in the Bible as a youngster. It simply called for: (1) abstinence and resisting temptation—an adaptation from the Salvation Army, the Rescue Missions, YMCA, and Temperance viewpoints; (2) reliance on the Creator and conversion to Jesus Christ; (3) obedience to God by eliminating sinful conduct and replacing it with the walk of love; (4) growing in fellowship with and understanding of God and His son through Bible study, prayer, and seeking God's guidance in a Quiet Hour; and (5) helping others get cured of alcoholism by the power of God.

Church was recommended, but not required. Fellowship with like-minded believers was also recommended, but not required.

Compare the two sets of ideas—those of the Oxford Group and those of Vermont Congregationalism—if you will: The Oxford Group mission was world-changing through life-changing. It was connected with no denomination—while Congregationalism and that Congregational denomination dominated the Vermont scene in Bob's life. The <u>Oxford Group required no acceptance of Christ</u>—while Congregationalism was dedicated to saving souls by conversion to Christ. In fact, the Oxford Group particularly spurned the word "conversion" and opted for the expression "change." While the Bible could be seen in the Oxford Group picture, Frank Buchman had to hire "Bible teachers" to speak to and teach his businessmen's groups; and there was no Oxford Group emphasis or focus on the Book of James, Jesus' Sermon on the Mount, and 1 Corinthians 13 such as that advocated by Dr Bob and Akron. The Oxford Group's "Two-way prayer" was another Oxford Group hybrid and catch-phrase. It was not Biblical. And it was hardly the equivalent of Congregational or early Akron old fashioned group prayer meetings, group Bible study meetings, group Gospel meetings, or group revival and conversion meetings. Nor did the Oxford Group's "world changing through life-changing" resemble the Christian Endeavor's primary and oft-declared stress on confession of Christ, daily Bible study, daily prayer, and a Quiet Hour for individuals. And "For church!" Nor did the Oxford Group trade on the Biblical "love and service" phraseology of

Christian Endeavor—a slogan that seems to have spilled over directly into Dr. Bob's own language.

Bill Wilson patently attempted to distance A.A. language from biblical language and from Christianity.[402] Bill Wilson specifically, expressly, and intentionally dumped what was called the dogma and doctrines of the Missions. The following remarks illustrate the point;

> Ruth Hock (the secretary who prepared the Big Book manuscript told of the beginning stages of the big dump. She related:) "Fitz insisted that the book should express Christian doctrines and use Biblical terms and expressions. . . . Fitz was for going all the way with 'God.'"[403]
>
> Bill Wilson said of A.A.'s southern Friend, that he, Fitz M.: "wanted a fairly religious book infused with some of the dogma we had picked up from the churches and missions which had tried to help us."[404]
>
> A.A. historian Francis Hartigan contended: "New York members also provoked a confrontation over the use of the word 'God' in the Twelve Steps, with Hank and Fitz M. taking opposite sides. Hank, who wasn't religious, wanted to leave God out entirely and instead refer to the 'spiritual nature' of the recovery the steps were designed to bring about. Fitz, whose father was a minister, thought the Steps should reflect explicitly Christian doctrine."[405] And that "Bill may have included some heavily Christian wording in his early drafts of the Big Book"[406]
>
> Wilson said: "The problem of the Steps has been to broaden and deepen them, both for newcomers and oldtimers. . . . How

---

[402] *Alcoholics Anonymous Comes of Age: A Brief History of A.A.* (NY: Alcoholics Anonymous World Services, Inc., 1967), 17, 162-64.
[403] *Pass It On* (NY: Alcoholics Anonymous World Services, Inc., 1984), 199; Dick B. *The Conversion of Bill W.*, 104.
[404] Bill W., "Where did the 12 Steps come from?" *A.A. Grapevine*, July, 1953; Dick B. *A New Way Out: New Path—Familiar Road Signs—Our Creator's Guidance* (Kihei, HI: Paradise Research Publications, 1006), 6, 30.
[405] Dick B. *The Conversion of Bill W.*, 106.
[406] Dick B. *The Conversion of Bill W.*, 106.

to widen the opening so it seems right and reasonable to enter there and at the same time avoid distractions, distortions, and the certain prejudices of all who may read, seems fairly much of an assignment."[407]

Lois Wilson, in *Lois Remembers,* chimed in: "Finally it was agreed that the book should present a universal spiritual program, not a specific religious one, since all drunks were not Christian."[408]

Out went the Bible and Jesus Christ. Out went 400 to 800 pages of the Big Book manuscript which were, according to Bill and Parkhurst's secretary Ruth Hock, simply trashed material . . . and were "mostly Christian in tone and content."[409]

With that trashing went mention of the Bible, Jesus Christ, plus all exclusive mention of the one, true, living God of the Bible as Creator. Also, all mention of salvation, the saving of souls, and conversion to Jesus Christ as Lord and Savior. There was no suggestion of the previously required Bible study, prayer, and conversion meetings. Bill's references to a "god" were mixed with New Thought "Universal Mind," "Czar of the Universe," and similar expressions. Also, with New Thought talk of some "higher power"—an expression whose existence went back at least as far as the writings of New Thought proponent Ralph Waldo Trine prior to 1900, William James and his "higher powers" in 1900, as well as Emmet Fox and his "higher power" of the 1930's. Some such language had appeared in Oxford Group writings such as Victor Kitchen's *I Was a Pagan* and Shoemaker's talk of a "Force greater than ourselves." It most certainly was a far cry from the explicit and capitalized biblical words for God that Bill, for some reason—perhaps his own conscience—still repeatedly included in the Big Book—Creator, Maker, Father, Father of lights, Spirit, and God.

All this to illustrate that Dr. Bob's undeviating references to his "Heavenly Father," the "Good Book," "God," and Jesus as the "Master" and "Lord" put miles of distance between the God, Jesus,

---

[407] Dick B. *The Conversion of Bill W.*, 103.
[408] Dick B. *A New Way Out*, 40-41.
[409] Dick B. *A New Way Out*, 40.

and Bible of Dr. Bob's Christian Endeavor Society and youth on the one hand, and the compromised language of the Oxford Group, Sam Shoemaker, and Wilson's own basic text published in 1939 by the Works Publishing Company of New Jersey, and known as *Alcoholics Anonymous*, on the other hand.

Even Dr. Bob's simple, compelling, and oft-quoted statement about the Twelve Steps placed him squarely in his St. Johnsbury and Christian Endeavor roots and training as a youngster. A key A.A. "Conference Approved" pamphlet states: "Dr. Bob firmly believed that 'love and service' are the cornerstones of Alcoholics Anonymous."[410] Christian Endeavor leaders had long and often characterized the phrase "love and service" as a key to understanding Christian Endeavor.[411]

Here is an enlightening discussion of the Vermont Christian Endeavor Union by E. G. Osgood its State President in 1895:

> The first meeting of the Vermont Christian Endeavor Union was held at Burlington December 14, 1886, and was fortunate in having present both President F. E. Clark and Secretary Ward. Forty societies were reported, and showed by the number of their delegates what a power the society had already become in the State.
>
> The first president of the Vermont Christian Endeavor Union was Professor G. H. Perkins, of Burlington, elected December 14, 1886. Rev. J. L. Sewall, then of Milton was elected the second president at St. Albans November 1, 1887, where an interesting meeting was held with encouraging reports of progress. The third Convention was held at Montpelier December 5, 1888, and Rev. Geo. A. Smith, of St. Albans, was elected president. The fourth Convention was held at Rutland. Mr. J. W. Sault, of St. Albans, was made president. The fifth Convention was held at St. Johnsbury, and Rev. P. McMillan,

---

[410] *The Co-Founders of Alcoholics Anonymous*, 9.
[411] Amos R. Wells. *Expert Endeavor*, 65; Founder Francis E. Clark wrote: "Christian Endeavor is a watch Whose mainspring is love, Whose movement is service, Whose hands point to heavenly joys on the dial of eternity." Clark, *Christian Endeavor in All Lands*, 326.

of Woodstock, was elected president. The sixth Convention was held at Brattleboro, and Rev. Z. Martin, of Bennington, was elected president. The seventh Convention was held in Bennington. Rev. T. G. Thompson, of Burlington, was chosen president. The eighth Convention was held at Barre, when Mr. E. G. Osgood, of Bellows Falls, was elected president. The ninth Convention was held at Newport, and Mr. E. G. Osgood was re-elected president.

We now have more than three hundred societies in our Union.[412]

Christian Endeavor Conferences[413]

"The first conference was held in the Williston [Congregational] Church [at Portland, Maine], June 2, 1882. There were six societies represented . . ."[414]

"A large growth over the preceding year was reported at the second conference, in June, 1883, showing 63 societies with a membership of 2,630. . . . Seventeen of these societies were in Maine, 11 in Massachusetts, 41 in all New-England; while of the other 12, 5 were in New York and the rest scattered throughout the West, . . ." "Second Annual Conference of the Young People's Society of Christian

---

[412] [From: Francis E. Clark, *World Wide Endeavor: The Story of the Young People's Society of Christian Endeavor: From the Beginning and in All Lands* (Philadelphia: Gillespie, Metzgar & Kelley, 1895), 515 ; http://books.google.com/books?id=VBmRQCj0aZUC&printsec=frontcover&dq=%22Christian+Endeavor%22+Johnsbury ; accessed 12/13/07.]

[413] The following review of the early growth of Christian Endeavor is extracted from: ". . . How the Christian Endeavor Movement Has Spread. Starting in a Modest Church Eleven Years Ago, It Now Extends over Christendom—Purposes and Principles Outlined," *The New York Times*, July 11, 1892 [Section: Christian Endeavor Extra, Page CEE12]: http://query.nytimes.com/gst/abstract.html?res=9D02E3D61631E033A25752C1A9619C94639ED7CF ; Accessed 11/5/07.

[414] "The second society [i.e., after Williston, Maine—note that this is not the "second convention"] was established in Newburyport, Mass., . . . in the same year the movement originated [i.e., in 1881]."

Endeavor, held at Payson Memorial church, Portland, Me., June 7th, 1883."[415]

"The fourth [third!?] convention was held Oct. 22, 1884, in Kirk Street Church, Lowell, [Massachusetts] . . ."[416]

"The next National Convention convened July 9 and 10, 1885, at Ocean Park, a seaside resort near Old Orchard Beach, Me., . . . The idea of securing a General Secretary, . . . was broached; . . . [A]nd, perhaps, more important than all, the 'United Society of Christian Endeavor' was founded and incorporated under the laws of Maine. At this convention Mr. Van Patten was chosen President . . .

"The society had now grown to 253 societies, with 14,892 members in all parts of the country. They had begun to be reported in foreign lands also, and news came of flourishing Christian Endeavor Societies in Foo-Chow, Honolulu, and other foreign lands. . . .

". . . Headquarters of the United Society were established at S Beacon Street, Boston, but were soon removed to more commodious rooms at 50 Bromfield Street."

"In the Summer of 1887, at the Saratoga Convention, the Rev. F. E. Clark was chosen President of the United Society and editor of Christian Endeavor literature, . . ."

"The conventions of 1886 and 1887, both held at Saratoga Springs . . . were attended, the first by 1,000 and the second by 2,000 delegates."

"The seventh annual convention was held at Chicago July 5-8, 1888. Over 5,000 delegates were present from thirty-three States and Territories."

"The eighth annual convention was held at Philadelphia July 9-11, 1889. Over 6,500 delegates were present, . . ."

---

[415] Joseph Williamson, *A Bibliography of the State of Maine from the Earliest Period to 1891, in Two Volumes: Volume II* (Portland [, Maine]: The Thurston Print, 1896), 668

[416] This convention seems to have been referred to by Clark as the "third convention." See: Francis E. Clark, *World Wide Endeavor: The Story of the Young People's Society of Christian Endeavor: From the Beginning and in All Lands* (Philadelphia: Gillespie, Metzgar & Kelley, 1895), 145.

"The ninth annual convention was held at St. Louis, Mo., June 12-15, 1890. Over 8,000 delegates were present . . ."

". . . [T]he tenth surpassed them all. It was held at Minneapolis, July 9-12, 1891. Over 14,000 delegates were present, . . . Among the eminent men who addressed the convention were . . . Ira D. Sankey, the Gospel singer. . . .

"Christian Endeavor Societies are found in thirty evangelical denominations, the Presbyterians leading the list with 4,500 societies, and the Congregationalists, Baptists, Methodists, and Christians standing next in the order named. Among these are reported 1,200 junior societies, . . .

"The year 1890-91 saw the substantial settlement in most quarters of the agitation for separate denominational societies to the exclusion of the Christian Endeavor name and interdenominational fellowship."

According to the report of John Willis Baer, the General Secretary of the United Society of Christian Endeavor, given for him at the eleventh National Convention of Christian Endeavor by J. M. Hill:

> In 1881 [the year Christian Endeavor was founded], there were 2 societies;
> in 1882, 7;
> 1883, 56;
> 1884, 156;
> 1885, 253;
> 1886, 850;
> 1887, 2,314;
> 1888, 4,879;
> 1889, 7,672;
> 1890, 11,013;
> last year [= 1891] at Minneapolis, 16, 274; and
> to-day [= 1892], after eleven years, . . . there are regularly reported societies to the number of 21,080, . . .
> This recorded list is absolutely correct, so far as we know;[417]

---

[417] "Secretary Baer's Report: Wonderful Increase of the Christian Endeavor Societies," *The New York Times*, July 11, 1892.

The Christian Endeavor Pledge

Though the precise words differ here and there, the Christian Endeavor Pledge is near, dear, and fundamental to every Christian Endeavor member. For example, my son Ken and I went from Maui to Washington, D.C. where I was invited to speak at the 125th Anniversary of the Society. We visited United States Senator Daniel Akaka of Hawaii to apprise him of our recovery work. At the conclusion of our visit, the Senator quietly said to my son Ken, "I was raised in Christian Endeavor." For many years, the Senator had previously directed the choir at the famous Congregational church in the capital area. On our return, I contacted an elderly woman in Honolulu to ask her about Christian Endeavor in Hawaii since I had learned from my research that Hawaii was an important growth area for the world-wide society. She commented to me: "I am very active in Christian Endeavor, particularly in women's affairs. I still remember very well our pledge."

Rev. Francis Clark wrote, "The following forms of the covenant pledge are used, and many others embodying the same idea. It will be seen by these forms that it is flexible enough to be adapted to different circumstances. . . The form used in most societies is as follows:

Active Member's Pledge.

Trusting in the Lord Jesus Christ for strength, I promise Him that I will strive to do whatever He would like to have me do; that I will make it the rule of my life to pray and to read the Bible every day, and to support my own church in every way, especially by attending all her regular Sunday and midweek services, unless prevented by some reason which I can conscientiously give to my Saviour; and that, just so far as I know how, throughout my whole life, I will endeavor to lead a Christian life. As an active member I promise to be true to all my duties, to be present at and to take some part, aside from singing, in every Christian Endeavor prayer-meeting, unless hindered b some reason which I can conscientiously give to my Lord and Master. If obliged to be absent from the monthly consecration-meeting of the society, I will, if possible, send at least a verse of Scripture to be read in response to my name at the roll-call.[418]

Amos R. Wells, Editorial Secretary of the United Society of Christian Endeavor, wrote the Expert Endeavor manual, and stated the following in Chapter II concerning "The Pledge":

> **What is our Christian Endeavor pledge?** It is a standard of character and action which we promise to try to reach.
>
> **Is the pledge compulsory?** No one is obliged to join the society. Every Endeavorer takes the pledge because he wishes to, believing that it will help him in his Christian life. . . .
>
> **What are the standards set up in the pledge that is used by the large majority of the societies?** As to the individual life, that the Endeavorer will try to do whatever Christ would have him do; that he will make it the rule of his life to pray and read the Bible every day; that he will try to lead a Christian life as long as he lives. As to the society, that he will try to be true to all his duties, especially in taking some part, aside from singing, in every Christian Endeavor prayer meeting and sending some message to the consecration meeting if he is absent. As to the church, that he will support it in every way, especially by attending all the regular Sunday and midweek services.
>
> **Do we promise to do these things?** No; but only to try to do them, trusting in Christ for strength. . . .
>
> **Does the pledge create new duties?** Not one. Every item of the pledge is already a duty for every one that pretends to be a follower of Christ. . . .
>
> **Does the pledge make Bible-reading, prayer, and prayer-meeting testimony a duty when they should be a privilege?** It holds us to them as a duty, and so gives them a chance to become a privilege. . . .

---

[418] Clark, *Christian Endeavor in All Lands,* 250-52.

In this spirit, how shall we keep our promise to pray daily? By setting apart a regular time for communing with our Father, and by spending some worthy amount of time in this blessed employment. Try early morning, and at least fifteen minutes, as a Comrade of the Quiet Hour.

How shall we keep our promise of daily Bible-reading? Not by reading a hasty verse when we are sleepy and about to go to bed, but by reading generous portions of the Holy Writ, often in connection with some illuminating commentary, and by thinking about what we have read till it becomes a part of our lives. . . .

What is the most important part of the pledge? The first sentence. It sums up all our promises: to try to do Christ's will; and all our resources: the unfailing strength of Jesus Christ."[419]

DR. BOB and the Good Oldtimers has long been the only A.A. history book, other than segments of the Big Book itself, that I have studied, analyzed, and enthusiastically recommended to A.A. sponsees, newcomers, and Christians. In fact, Grace Snyder (widow of Clarence H. Snyder) told me that Clarence had intended to write a history of A.A. And I have copies of the first segments of his proposed book. However, according to Grace, Clarence was sufficiently satisfied with the *DR. BOB* book that Clarence abandoned his plans for a separate book. On the other hand, it was his custom to provide a free copy of the *DR. BOB* book to the newcomers who attended the Snyder retreats over the years.

Analysis of the foregoing Christian Endeavor materials has made it quite clear just how much the practices in Christian Endeavor, of which Dr. Bob spoke, can be seen in the pages of *DR. BOB and the Good Oldtimers* and in the verified practices which personified early Akron A.A.'s pioneer Christian fellowship. In fact, thanks to the thoughtfulness and caring of the late Dennis Wayne Cassidy, we now have the actual manuscript (with ink addictions and editing) that A.A.

---

[419] Amos R. Wells, *"A Text-book of Christian Endeavor Methods and Principles: For the Use of Classes and of Candidates for the Title of "C.E.E."—"Christian Endeavor Expert"* (Boston: United Society of Christian Endeavor, 1911), 13-16.

staffer Niles Peebles prepared for A.A. publication. The reader of this title is invited to read the *DR. BOB* book from cover to cover, and then to review the materials in our present title. We believe you will depart from the effort believing for sure that Dr. Bob's training became the foundation for what he and the pioneers did years later in the new Akron recovery program—long before the Big Book was published.

A Look at the Early A.A. Program that Bill W. and Dr. Bob Founded in 1935

When Bill Wilson met Dr. Bob Smith at Henrietta Seiberling's Gate Lodge Home in Akron on Mother's Day of 1935, each man had some strong alcoholism recovery factors stored away in his mind.

Bill Wilson brought to the table three major spiritual ideas that Dr. Bob had simply not implemented in his previous Christian walk. (1) The first idea: Because of the deadly, downward spiral of drunkenness, relief does and cannot come by willpower or human aid alone. (2) The second idea: The experience of Dr. Carl Gustav Jung established the efficacy of conversion as a cure, and the experience of Dr. William D. Silkworth the efficacy of relying on the Great Physician (Jesus Christ) to be cured. (3) The third idea: The vital importance of telling others still suffering about the healing that can be achieved through the power of God. In a very real sense, Bill's convictions were embodied in the so-called "abs's" he put in his Big Book just after his description of the Twelve Steps, and in the message he gave on page 191 of the 4th edition: "Henrietta, the Lord has been so wonderful to me curing me of this terrible disease that I just want to keep telling people about it."[420] Dr. Bob brought to the table the totality of his Christian upbringing and what he called his "excellent training" in the Bible as a youngster in St. Johnsbury, Vermont. These principles and practices were, for the most part, not those of the Oxford Group with which both Bill and Bob had been "associated" as Dr. Bob put it. Dr. Bob had not implemented the principles for the very simple reason that he called himself a "want to, want to" guy, and simply did not want to quit drinking. Bill Wilson was really not conversant with Bob's Congregational, Christian

---

[420] See Dick B., *The Conversion of Bill W.* (Kihei, HI: Paradise Research Publications, 2006). (Information on this title is available on the Dick B. web site: http://www.dickb.com/conversion.shtml).

Endeavor, and YMCA ideas. Moreover, Bill had been totally unsuccessful in getting anyone sober until he met and joined with Dr. Bob.[421]

Bill moved into the Smith home in Akron for the entire summer of 1935. Bill and Bob had lengthy discussions until the wee hours of the morning each day. We know that Anne Smith (Dr. Bob's wife) read the Bible to the two men each day. We know that the two men drew their basic ideas from the Bible. And we know that Anne Smith wrote down in her journal and shared with all the pioneers the elements of the Oxford Group and Bible principles being used. But little has been said about what Dr. Bob really contributed personally or from his youth or from the Bible to the simple early program that had such remarkable successes.

From his parents, his North Congregational Church, his Sunday school, his Bible study and prayer meetings, his participation in the Christian Endeavor Society, his touching base with the activities of the YMCA of which his father was a local president, and the rigorous daily chapel and required Bible study and church attendance of his St. Johnsbury Academy, Dr. Bob was fully equipped to develop a program of recovery, using Bill's contributions, and using the Christian Endeavor ideas of Dr. Bob's youth. Thus, from St. Johnsbury, Dr. Bob brought some clearly defined ideas from his youth: (1) Abstinence—the cardinal point of the Temperance people, including Congregationals and Christian Endeavorers. (2) Reliance on the Creator and conversion to Jesus Christ. (3) Obedience to God's will. (4) Growth in fellowship through prayer, Bible study, Quiet Hour, and the reading of Christian literature. (5) Reaching out to others in love and service.

Yet the origin of these basic ideas from the Bible, and particularly from St. Johnsbury, has not, until recently, even been mentioned by AAs, recovery writers, or historians—perhaps largely because Dr. Bob in his usual reticence and modesty simply did not discuss them. And so it has become important to search out, report, document, and disseminate A.A.'s Christian Endeavor Factor via the Biblical training and Christian upbringing Dr. Bob received as a youth in St. Johnsbury.

---

[421] See *DR. BOB and the Good Oldtimers* (New York: Alcoholics Anonymous World Services, 1980).

A Look at the New Dr. Bob Core Library Now Being Put in Place at North Congregational Church, St. Johnsbury

Prior to this year, there never has been a library devoted exclusively to the when, where, what, how, and why of the basic Biblical contributions made by Dr. Bob from his youthful training to the Akron Pioneer A.A. Christian Fellowship he and Bill Wilson founded in 1935 and which brought the hope and reality of cure to so many of the seemingly hopeless, medically incurable alcoholics willing to join a fellowship of like-minded believers who really tried to get well by the power of God.

The new library will, as this article covers, contain substantial background on A.A.'s Christian Endeavor roots. I have covered some of the material in my earlier published titles such as *Dr. Bob and His Library, 3rd ed.; The Books Early AAs Read for Spiritual Growth, 7th ed., The James Club and the Original A.A. Program's Absolute Essentials, When Early AAs Were Cured and Why, The Good Book-Big Book Guidebook, Real Twelve Step Fellowship History*, and *Introduction to the Sources and Founding of Alcoholics Anonymous*.

To make the resource comprehensive, useful, and accurate, the library will also include materials on: (1) The "Great Awakening" of 1875 in St. Johnsbury. (2) Dr. Bob and the Smith Family. (3) The Fairbanks Family of St. Johnsbury and its predominant influences and activities. (4) The North Congregational Church of St. Johnsbury. (5) Revivals, evangelism, and conversions during the period from 1875 to and including Dr. Bob's graduation from St. Johnsbury Academy in 1898. (6) The Christian Endeavor Society to which Dr. Bob belonged and what it did. (7) Vermont Congregationalism and Missionary Work during Bob's years as a youngster. (8) The activities and influence of the Young Men's Christian Association. (9) The impact of the evangelist Dwight L. Moody. (10) St. Johnsbury Academy and the significant contribution of the Smiths—father, mother, and Bob at that period. (11) The Town of St. Johnsbury. (12) St. Johnsbury as Dr. Bob knew it as a youth—his boyhood home and birthplace, the North Congregational Church, the Fairbanks Museum, the YMCA building, the Athenaeum (town library), the courthouse, and the many buildings at St. Johnsbury Academy. (13) The relevant A.A. and historical literature. (14) Items from the Dennis Wayne Cassidy memorial historical collection of A.A. history. (15) Photographs, manuscripts, and memorabilia. (16) 20-plus binders with abundant additional historical resource data prepared by Dick B. and Ken B. (17) All of the 28 volume Dick B. Historical Reference Title set. (18) Two new books by Dick B. on Dr. Bob's youth and also his biography. (19) The tie between St. Johnsbury and Akron. (20) The evidence of the documented, 75%-to-93% success rate of Akron pioneers among the seemingly-hopeless, medically-incurable, real alcoholics who went to every length to establish their relationship and fellowship with their Creator and His son Jesus Christ. (21) The original Akron program, and (22) More as it is acquired, analyzed, and publicized.

If, as, and when its acquisition, analysis, documentation, publication, and dissemination—along with shipping and handling costs—has been funded by benefactors whose contributions are already being made and who will be joined by others, the great majority of the books and materials for the library will be placed in North Congregational Church over the next months of 2008.

Christian Endeavor Literature for the Dr. Bob Core Library

In the course of my (Dick B.'s) writing, I have read, studied, and acquired a number of basic Christian Endeavor books and materials. And these will be in the library.

I was invited to be a principal speaker at the 125th Anniversary Convention of Christian Endeavor International at the Cannon Office Building in Washington, D.C. There I located the present-day leaders of Christian Endeavor and also saw literature I did not have. Timothy Eldred, Executive Director of Christian Endeavor International, graciously agreed to make available to me some of the major Christian Endeavor books located at its headquarters in Michigan.

Those Christian Endeavor books have now been acquired, and they will be in the new core library at North Congregational Church.

A bibliography of those books to be placed in the library is set forth below. And the books themselves contain an enormous number of references to United Christian Endeavor Society literature and recommended reading. So also do my books and the binders being placed at North Congregational Church. Some of the books have already been discussed at length elsewhere, but the entire collected books are listed below--with appropriate additional quotes, comments, and references.

The Christian Endeavor Bibliography of Books Being Placed in St. Johnsbury

We have added a number of quotes which will prove useful in utilizing the library books and seeing their relevance to the Alcoholics Anonymous Christian Fellowship program.

The Books Just Acquired from Christian Endeavor International—a Panoply of Writings

Brain, Bell M. *Fifty Missionary Programmes.* Boston: United Society of Christian Endeavor, 1901, 13-14. (Brain describes the typical Scripture Lesson and Prayer at an "ideal missionary meeting" where "the Bible is used as 'the sword of the Spirit,' the all-powerful Word of God, which according to his promise shall not return unto him void;" and also "the 'Great Commission,' as recorded in the four Gospels and the book of Acts".)

_____. *Weapons for Temperance Warfare.* Boston: United Society of Christian Endeavor, 1897, 14-15, 17-24, 40-47, 81-82. (Brain describes "pledge-signing;" the devotional service of the temperance meeting—the Scripture lesson, the prayer, and the hymns, with ample simple texts, Bible readings, and Bible testings; innumerable quotations from Shakespeare, Milton, William Penn, Spurgeon, John B. Gough, St. Augustine, Luther, John Adams, Father Matthew, Frances E. Willard, and others; and "An Evening With John B. Gough, programming the Scripture Lesson, Prayer, Roll-Call, Solo, Anecdotes, and personal reminiscences).

Chaplin, W. Knight. *Francis E. Clark: Founder of the Y.P.S.C.E.* Boston: United Society of Christian Endeavor, n.d.

Clark, Francis E. *World Wide Endeavor: The Story of The Young People's Society of Christian Endeavor From the Beginning and in All Lands.* Philadelphia: Gillespie, Metzger & Kelley, 1895.

The Church in Relation to Its Own Christian Endeavor Society

"The Society of Christian Endeavor started with another conception of the prayer-meeting. It was not a place for instruction from man so much as for instruction from Go. It was not the place for the exposition of a body of divinity or for indoctrination in the fine points of theology. It was a place for *practice* rather than preaching, for inspiration and fellowship rather than for instruction. A place for participation of all the average two-talent people, rather than of the exceptional ten-talent man and woman.

"The idea of instruction was not ignored, but the leaders of this new society contended that the prayer-meeting was not the place for instruction in the ordinary sense of the word, and that there is ample room for instruction in other services of the church.

"The Sunday morning service is for instruction. The Sunday evening service is for instruction. The Sunday-school is for instruction. The pastor's catechetical class if for instruction. The missionary concert is for instruction. The religious newspaper is for instruction. In fact, there are few departments of church life which have not this for their central idea. But the Christian Endeavor Society has always believed that the prayer-meeting was for another order of service, and that this other service is quite as necessary to the development of spiritual activities as the service of instruction.

And so it happens that the whole idea of participation is changed. There is something for Thomas and Harry and Mary and Susan to do, as well as for their respective and respected fathers and mothers. . . . It is not sufficient for them to confess Christ before men by baptism and by publicly joining the church of Christ, but frequent, nay, constant, confession of Him alone insures their growth in grace. . . he can rise to his feet and say: 'I love Him because He first loved me.' He can offer the Publican's trembling prayer, 'God be merciful to me a sinner,' or the Psalmist's humble petition, ' Create within me a clean heart, O God.' . . . . They can at least repeat a verse of Scripture or a favorite hymn which expresses their heart's devotion. . . . In short, the society of Christian Endeavor is built upon this radical idea, that in the prayer-meeting there is a place for every one; a word, a testimony, or a prayer; that it is a necessary part of the Christian life to confess the Lord, and that no one can grow in grace as he should when he neglects this aid to an outspoken Christian life." (68-69)

The Church and the Society of Christian Endeavor

"What, pray, is the church? I am speaking now of the local organization. Is it a certain number of the older members? Is it the congregation that gathers to hear the pastor's Sunday morning sermon or to engage in the evening service? Is it the mid-week prayer meeting? Yes, it is all these and more. The church is the local body of Christ's followers who worship Sunday morning and Sunday evening. The church is the people at prayer in the mid-week service. The Sunday-school is the church giving and receiving instruction. . . The missionary society is the church praying and giving for the advancement and extension of the Kingdom of God. The Christian Endeavor Society is the church training and being trained for practical service in the kingdom" (185)

[Note: Dr. Bob and his parents were involved in all these, as our documentation in our new resource book and in the resource binders being placed in the Dr. Bob Core Library makes quite clear.]

The Y.M.C.A. and the Society of Christian Endeavor

"The Y.M.C.A. can hardly be called a sister of the society without forcing language and bringing a smile to the bearded face of many a Y.M.C.A. brother, but yet the relationship between the Y.M.C.A. and the Society of Christian Endeavor has always been considered a family relationship. They occupy different fields, and they both recognize the fact. The association is for the community at large, the society for the individual church. Th3e association is necessarily undenominational, the society is necessarily inter-denominational. The association can acknowledge allegiance to no one church, the association [*sic* – but meaning "society"] must acknowledge allegiance to some one church; and yet, though they occupy different positions, each is doing an invaluable work which the other cannot accomplish. . . . But, as I have said, they can in many ways mutually aid one another; as the receptions which are given by the associations to the societies, and by the societies to the associations, have been proved. Some of the best workers among the secretaries of the Y.M.C.A. have been trained in the Christian Endeavor Society for their future work, and some of the most earnest advocates and eloquent speakers at Endeavor conventions have been leading Y.M.C.A. workers" (191)

[Note: Dr. Bob's father was a deacon in the North Congregational Church, superintendent of and teacher in its Sunday school, as well as a regular attender at the church. He was also president of the local Y.M.C.A. The Fairbanks family members were deeply involved in the North Congregational Church and in the Y.M.C.A., donating to the building of the church and of the Y.M.C.A. They held offices in both organizations. The Y.M.C.A. lay leaders were prominent in the "Great Awakening" of 1875 in St. Johnsbury. The Y.M.C.A. conducted lectures and concerts at North Congregational Church; and it also conducted lectures at St. Johnsbury Academy]

Clements, John R. *The Francis E. Clark Year Book: A Collection of Living Paragraphs From Addresses, Books, and Magazine*

Articles by the Founder of the Young People's Society of Christian Endeavor. Boston: United Society of Christian Endeavor, 1904. The quotes following give a real picture of Clark's role and views:

QUIET HOUR--Prayer, Bible study, Asking guidance

March 19: None of us have, perhaps, Henry Drummond's wit, learning or natural charm of manner; but we may have the chief quality that made his character so uplifting and inspiration to multitudes. I have said much in these letters of late about "the morning watch." I ventured even to recommend in my annual address at San Francisco the observance of this daily quiet time alone with God. I know of no other school than this in which the lesson of Drummond's life can be learned (42).

March 20: To-morrow morning rise an hour earlier than usual. You will be tired and sleepy? No doubt. You will wish to turn over for another nap? I do not doubt it. But no matter; overcome drowsy nature for once, at least; and a good hour before breakfast, and before the rest of the family are stirring, be dressed and ready for a talk with the King. The joy of the appointment he is waiting to keep with you is worth the extra exertion a thousand times over.

Take your Bible, your own Bible, the one with marks and references, and comments in your own handwriting, and go, if possible, into a room quite by yourself. Open your Bible to the fourteenth chapter of John, and read a chapter or two from there on, slowly, meditatively, lifting up you heart, and saying frequently as you read, "O Lord, open thou my eyes that I may understand." Perhaps you will not get through half a chapter, so full of new and wondrous meaning will each verse be as you dwell upon it, the new light from heaven illuminating the page. No matter. All the better, indeed. The spirit of Christ is in every verse. There is food enough in any verse for a morning meal (43).

March 29: Giving God a chance at you; that is the meaning of the Quiet Hour. Parents, teachers, friends, books, newspapers, business, pleasure, all these have a chance at us. Should we not also give God a chance at us? (48).

June 12: "Practicing the presence of God." It involves going away by one's self. It involves a daily quiet hour with God. It involves a putting away of all known sin. It involves a searching of the heart for the rebellious life-guard who would keep some of the apartments of the soul closed to the entrance of the King (71).

OBEYING GOD'S WILL--Eliminating sinful conduct, walking in the light

July 9: Confess, repent, forsake sin; and the darkness will flee away, and God's light will flood your soul (80).

July 19: Why are we banded together? Why do we keep the Quiet Hour? Only that we may receive a blessing in our own hearts? Only that we may know the joy of communion with God? Yes, for this, and for much more—even that we may bring a blessing upon others, that we may offer the fervent, effectual prayer that availeth much (83).

FELLOWSHIP WITH LIKE-MINDED BELIEVERS-- Avoiding slipper people and slippery places

August 22: If your companion, though he be your best friend, cause you to stumble; if he leads you into bad ways; if he makes you careless and thoughtless, and indifferent of the good, and complacent of the evil, cast him off, flee from him as Joseph fled out of the way of temptation, though you leave the very garment by which he seeks to hold you in the clutches of the tempter (96).

October 9: . . . . There are multitudes in whose ears have been sounding as with cataract roar this tremendous truth spoken by the voice of God himself: "Obey my voice, and I will be your

God, and ye shall be my people;" and yet they have never heard it (114).

BRINGING OTHERS TO CHRIST BY WITNESSING--
converting them

November 9: I believe the great danger in these days is not of asking people too often to decide for Christ, or of asking it in an unwise, perfunctory, or unpleasant way, but of not giving the invitation at all (127).

December 4: I look upon it as one of the first duties of a child of God to tell the glad news to others, "Let the redeemed of the Lord, say so" (138).

Growth in Understanding and Fellowship through Prayer and Devotional Reading of the Good Book

December 19: Meditation shows us that God is the source of supply for all our needs. "My soul thirsteth for God, for the living God." Prayer digs a channel straight and true to this source of supply. "Ask, and ye shall receive." Devotional reading of the Word of God keeps the channel from becoming clogged with selfishness and self-seeking. It keeps us from simply teasing God for material blessings and nothing more. "My God shall supply all your need."

Poling, Reverend Daniel A. *Dr. Poling's Radio Talks with Questions and Answers.* NY: George H. Doran Company, 1927.

[See the quotations from Dr. Poling in the review of A.A. principles below]

Wells, Amos R. *Expert Endeavor: A Textbook of Christian Endeavor Methods and Principles* Boston: United Society of Christian Endeavor, 1911.

Prayer Meetings

"What are the results that we may gain from the prayer meeting? They are five: original l thought on religious subjects; open committal to the cause of Christ; the helpful expression of Christian thought and experience; the cultivation of the spirit of worship through public prayer and through singing; the guidance of others along all these lines of service and life" (9)

Bible-Reading, Prayer, and Prayer-Meeting Testimony a Duty

"Does the pledge make Bible-reading, prayer, and prayer-meeting testimony a duty when they should be a privilege? It holds us to them as a duty, and so gives them a chance to become a privilege" (14-15).

The Principles of Christian Endeavor

"Definite standards of service, and definite commitment to those standards. Open confession of Christ, and speaking for Him according to ability and opportunity. The cultivation of the devotional life b regular prayer and Bible-study. Training in Christian service by a variety of committee work. Loyalty to the church and regular attendance upon the church services. Generous giving to Christian work. Christian citizenship. Interdenominational fellowship, and the promotion of peace and goodwill among the nations of the world" (20)

Relationship with the Church Sunday School

"It is twofold: to help the Sunday school through the Christian Endeavor society, and to help the Christian Endeavor society through the Sunday school" (81)

"The Sunday school is for Bible-study; the Christian Endeavor society, for religious training. The first is for impression, and the second for expression. The Christian Endeavor society has no time for teaching the Bible, and the Sunday school has no time for training in prayer-meeting testimony, in public prayers, in mission-study, in the leading of meetings, in the conduct of business meetings, in the many activities of the Christian Endeavor committees and officers" (84)

Temperance Work by Endeavorers

". . . . They may engage actively in temperance campaigns, holding mass-meetings, organizing temperance parades, with striking banners and transparencies, circulating temperance leaflets, and working to get out the full temperance vote. They may get up a society temperance pledge to be signed by all the members and then framed, each new member signing it as he enters" (95)

The Quiet Hour

"It is a regular time spent daily in quiet communion with God and meditation on the Bible, and the greatest themes of life and destiny" (125)

_____. *The Officers' Handbook: A Guide for Officers in Young People's Societies, with Chapters on Parliamentary Law and Other Useful Themes.* Boston: United Society of Christian Endeavor, 1900, 1911.

Doing Our Father's Business

"And our Christian Endeavor business should be done in the very best way. We are 'about our Father's business'" (7)

Daily Prayer and Daily Bible Reading

"Private devotion is the fourth plank of our society platform— daily prayer and daily Bible-reading" (12)

INTERDENOMINATIONAL FELLOWSHIP

"Sixth and last in the list of Christian Endeavor principles is the interdenominational fellowship. Christian Endeavor has developed a very complete and beautiful system of unions—city, county, State, national, and world-wide. In most communities, these unions are the only rallying centers for the Christians of all faiths" (14)

Relation to the Autonomous Church

"This society, being a part of the church, owes allegiance only and altogether to the church with which it is connected. The Pastors, Elders, Deacons, Stewards, and Sunday-school Superintendent, if not active members, shall be, *ex officiis*, honorary members" (30)

_____. *The Young People's Pastor*. Boston: United Society of Christian Endeavor, 1905.

Inviting a Decision for Christ
"There is one purpose for which I wish our pastors would more frequently assume the leadership of our prayer meetings, and that is to 'draw the net.' If the meeting has been an impressive one, and the pastor thinks that some have been moved are usually indifferent, why should he not at the close simply take charge of affairs for a few minutes, and give an invitation for Christian decisions? Thus every Endeavor meeting would be a possible revival. To watch for signs of spiritual awakening, and take prompt advantage of them, is the pastor's blessed task, and the Endeavor prayer meeting gives him a superb opportunity for it" (15-16).

[OBEDIENCE TO GOD'S WILL, DAILY PRAYER, DAILY BIBLE-READING]
"What are promised here? Eight things:--
    1. An attempt to do Christ's entire will.
    2. Daily prayer as a rule of life.
    3. Daily Bible-reading as the rule of life. . ." (73)

Those Books Previously Acquired by, and Discussed, in Other Dick B. Titles, Articles

Clark, Francis E. *Christian Endeavor in All Lands*. Boston: The United Society of Christian Endeavor, 1906. And here were some key quotes relevant to the Akron A.A. program:

Trust in God; Obedience to His Will, Growth through Prayer and Reading in Order to Serve

"Christian Endeavor is a school Teaching us to trust and obey, To read and pray. To serve; Christ and the church in every way" (326)

Love And Service

"Bear with me if I rehearse once more the fundamental necessary features of this world-wide movement. . .—
    Confession, Service, Fellowship, Fidelity.
    Confession of our love for Christ.
    Proof of it by our service for Him.
    Fellowship with those who love Him.
    Fidelity to our regiment in which we fight for Him" (100)
"Christian Endeavor is a watch Whose mainspring is love, Whose movement is service, Whose hands point to heavenly joys on the dial of eternity" (326)

Non Denominational, Non Sectarian

"Here at last in the history of Christianity is an organization that is confined to no one sect, no one nation, no one language. . . . There are absolutely no denominational barriers which Christian Endeavor cannot surmount. There is no one of the many folds of the one Shepherd where the Society is not at home, and has not found its rightful home" (615, 618).

For the Salvation of Man

"Christian Endeavor does not ask a man whether he lives in Africa, in India, China, or America. It does not ask him whether he be clothed with a black skin, a white, a tawny, or a red one. Christian Endeavor stands first, last, and always for the salvation of man" (341)

_____. *Memories of Many Men in Many Lands: An Autobiography.* Boston: United Society of Christian Endeavor, 1922

Cowan, John Franklin. *New Life in the Old Prayer Meeting.* NY: Fleming H. Revell Company, 1906.

Murch, James DeForest. *Successful C.E. Prayer-Meetings.* Cincinnati, OH: The Standard Publishing Company, 1930.

Sheldon, Charles M. *In His Steps.* Nashville: Boardman Press, 1935.

Wells, Amos R. *Expert Endeavor: A Textbook of Christian Endeavor Methods and Principles.* Boston: United Society of Christian Endeavor, 1911.

Review of the Original Akron 5-Point Program and Correlative Christian Endeavor Sources

1. Abstinence: The Temperance position and pledge advocated by:

Christian Endeavor (Brain, *Weapons,* pp. 41-47)

"Every moderate drinker could abandon the cup if he would; every inebriate would if he could—John B. Gough" (42)

2. Reliance on the Creature and becoming His child through a decision for Christ:

Christian Endeavor (*Dr. Poling's Radio Talks*)

"For man is man and God is God" (48)

"The word "meek" here means whole-hearted submission to the will of God. In the original the word means bowed down or brought low, with humble as a derived meaning. In the sense of whole-hearted submission to the will of God, it may be applied, of course, to Moses, who, however imperious he was, did give himself unreservedly to the will of Jehovah" (48)

"How do we lose our fear of God? By knowing Him. . . . We know God at least through Jesus, His Son; know Him through Jesus, know Him as long-suffering and generous, sacrificial and kind, know Him as the omnipotent Father of us all" (102)

"How shall we escape if we neglect so great salvation? Salvation offered once and for all—salvation, triumph in Christ? . . . . How is the salvation achieved? Not by purchase. Not by blood inheritance. Not by right of earthly stations. It is the prerequisite of no office. It is the crown land of no temporal authority. What can mortal man do to secure his salvation? Mortal man can do only and just what God bids him do. He can repent and believe. He can arise and follow Christ as Matthew did, and as have all others who have achieved the great distinction" (162-63)

Christian Endeavor (Clark, *Memories of Many Men in Many Lands*)

"The corner stone of Christian Endeavor is not a theological doctrine, but a covenant of service: 'Trusting in the Lord Jesus Christ for strength, I promise Him that I will strive to do whatever He would like to have me do'." (688)

3. Obedience to the Creator's will

Christian Endeavor (Clements, *The Francis E. Clark Year Book*)

"There are multitudes in whose ears have been sounding with cataract roar this tremendous truth spoken by the voice of God himself: 'Obey my voice, and I will be your God, and ye shall be my people...'" (114)

"When we seek first the kingdom of God, other things will be added. Only when we love the Lord our God with all or might shall we love our neighbors as ourselves" (12)

Christian Endeavor (*Dr. Poling's Radio Talks*)

"What do you think the phrase 'pure religion' means? I think that it means exactly what James has said; namely, "pure religion and undefiled before God and the Father is this: to visit the fatherless and widows in their affliction, and to keep himself unspotted from the world"; in other words, to live a clean life personally, and then to minister to one's fellows. Pure religion is *being* and *doing* the will of the heavenly Father" (265)

[Note: the Book of James was the favorite of early AAs and considered "absolutely essential" to their program. This particular verse—James 1:27—is quoted in one of the AA of Akron pamphlets commissioned by Dr. Bob to enable AAs to gain a simple, "blue collar" understanding of the real A.A. program].

4. Growth in understanding and Fellowship through Prayer, Bible study, Quiet Hour, Reading

Christian Endeavor (Wells, *Expert Endeavor*)

"What is meant by 'the Quiet Hour'? It is the regular time spent daily in quiet communion with God and meditation on the Bible, and the greatest themes of life and destiny. In the pledge we promise to make it the rule of our lives to pray and read the Bible every day. The Quiet Hour simply makes this pledge a little more definite. . . . Why is it best to observe the Quiet Hour in the same place, as a rule? Because the surroundings will come to suggest devout thoughts and will put the spirit in the mood for helpful meditation and prayer. . . . Why is it best to set a minimum of fifteen minutes? Because we do not usually give enough time to such exercises, and they are so brief that nothing comes of the. . . . What may well be the beginning of every Quiet Hour? To remind ourselves that God is present. To say over and over to ourselves, 'God is here. Christ is by my side. The all-seeing, the all-powerful, the all-loving One is in this room. . . . Reading the Bible, the message from this present Father and Saviour. Read it in large portions. . . . What other helps shall we find for our Quiet Hour? Bible commentaries, especially those of a devotional turn, and books by the great masters of devotional writing, such as Jeremy Taylor, Fenelon, Thomas a Kempis, Meyer. . . and the great hymn writers, What will fill out and complete your Quiet Hour? Much prayer—loving and faith-filled talk with the Father; and much meditation—peaceful waiting to hear what the Father has to say to us" (128)

[Note: If you study *DR. BOB and the Good Oldtimers* as well as my titles, *Good Morning* and *The Akron*

Genesis, you will see how closely Dr. Bob followed these suggestions in his prayer life three times a day]

5. Witnessing to others in word and deed through love and service.

    Christian Endeavor (Clements, *The Francis E. Clark Year Book)*

        "I look upon it as one of the first duties of a child of God to tell the glad news to others. 'Let he redeemed of the Lord say so" (138)

    Christian Endeavor (Clements, *The Young People's Pastor*)

        "Christian Endeavor has always been true to it noble motto, 'For Christ and the Church.' (101)

    Christian Endeavor (Wells, *Expert Endeavor*)

        "What is meant by being a Christian? Accepting Christ openly as one's Saviour from sin and the Master of one's life" (119)

    Christian Endeavor (Murch, *Successful C. E. Prayer-Meetings*)

        "An Evangelistic Meeting—Pattern your program after that of a modern revival meeting. A live leader of song should have charge of the music. The songs should be of soul-winning. Have a number of church-members to give brief testimonies and urge the young people to make decisions for Christ. The minister should be invited to make a closing exhortation and hear the confessions of faith, if such is the usual order. Personal work prior to the meeting itself will make it more effective in every way" (pp. 66-67)

        "A Front-seat Meeting—Or this might be called a Reconsecrating Meeting. With 'Trusting in the Lord Jesus for Strength,' as the central theme, have a number of talks, urging every member to loyalty. At the close of the service, let your minister give an invitation to all those who want to reconsecrate themselves to their C.E. pledge to come forward and occupy the front seats. Those who wish to accept Christ as their personal Saviour should be included in this invitation. Those who have taken the front seats should then kneel in prayer" (72)

"A Testimony Meeting—Obviously the leading characteristic of a prayer-meeting should be the testimony. The leader and the chairman of the prayer-meeting committee should. . . urge them to use their tongues for Christ in this meeting better than ever before. The way to get this done is not to preach to these Endeavourers. . ." (88)

Christian Endeavor (Clark, *Christian Endeavor in All Lands*)

"In fact, he came to see that the order of our Lord's life-motto could not be reversed, but that those who should be won for the Christian life must *minister,* and not merely be ministered unto" (28)

"Another universal principle of Christian Endeavor is *constant service*" (96)

Note: These five "musts" of early A.A. (which can be found, item by item, in numerous Christian Endeavor books, writings, and talks) were summarized by Frank Amos to John D. Rockefeller, Jr. after the Amos visit to Akron and investigation of its principles, practices, and results. The specifics can be found in A.A.'s "Conference Approved" *DR. BOB and the Good Oldtimers*, pp. 131, 136.

The Importance to Recovery of the Christian Endeavor Factor

A.A. is not a Christian Fellowship today. Nor will it become one as over seventy years of evolutionary changes have made quite clear. On the other hand, it certainly was a Christian Fellowship at its inception as Dr. Bob often pointed out. The importance of this history is not about what A.A. could or should or might become today. The importance lies in the fact that almost no AAs today know this history. You won't find it in the ever-growing body of biographies of cofounder Bill Wilson (except in my recent title, *The Conversion of Bill W.*). You won't find it in A.A.'s "Conference Approved" literature except to the extent that tiny teasers exist in Dr. Bob's personal story in the Big Book, in DR. BOB and the Good Oldtimers, in the memorial issue on his death (RHS), and in the published account of his last major address to AAs in 1948 found in the Co-founders pamphlet published by A.A. World services.

Should this history, including the Christian Endeavor roots of A.A., be allowed to die out? We don't think so. In fact, the absence of these facts has given rise to all sorts of compromises, diversions, speculations, and revisions by the A.A. leadership hierarchy, by historians and commentaries, and by members themselves. Far worse, the lack of the history has led to the manufacture of a new program that hardly claims a success anywhere near that of the early program. The new program espouses bizarre ideas that A.A. is "spiritual but not religious." It espouses the idea that A.A. was originally a part of and grew out of the Oxford Group—which it did not, though that factor is important in understanding the history and the Big Book. It espouses the idea that the very mention of "God," "Jesus Christ," the "Bible," and "Christianity" will drive newcomers out of the rooms and get them drunk and that it is, to some old-timers, a repugnant attempt to force "religion" down their throats. It espouses the idea that a newcomer or an old-timer can believe in any "power" he or she likes. That "power," they say, can be a Light Bulb, a Radiator, Gertrude, Ralph, a Coke bottle, a chair, a table, a rock, the Big Dipper, Santa Claus, Him, Her, It, Somebody, Something, or nothing at all—if that is the member's choice. It espouses the idea that the manufacture, shaping, and conception of this power can be at the whim of the member. It flatly contradicts most of the basic Bible ideas which, according to Dr. Bob and Bill Wilson, were the foundation for A.A. principles and practices.

At the heart of the need for the early history lies the absurdity of ignoring it. Long before there was an Oxford Group, an A.A., or a Light Bulb "power," the idea that alcoholism could be cured by divine aid was in full flower among those that believed. I say full flower because it was embraced by the still-successful Salvation Army, the still-successful rescue missions, the early Y.M.C.A. precepts, and even by the Temperance Movement as it was lead by Christian figures. When Bill and Bob first formed A.A., they firmly declared that the underlying philosophy of A.A. was contained in Jesus' sermon on the mount. They declared that the Book of James in the Bible was their favorite. The favored the principles of love found in 1 Corinthians 13. They used all kinds of Christian devotionals like the Upper Room, My Utmost for His Highest, The Imitation of Christ, The Meaning of Prayer, and The Runner's Bible. They were handed and read all kinds of Christian literature such as the King James Version of the Bible, the E. Stanley Jones books such as The Christ of the Mount, the Henry Drummond book The Greatest Thing in the World, the Glenn Clark books such as The Soul's Sincere Desire, the Emmet Fox books such as The Sermon on the Mount, Toyohiko Kagawa's book on Love, Harry Emerson Fosdick's books on The Meaning of Faith and The Meaning of Service, Unity books on prayer, Mary Baker Eddy's Science and Health with Key to the Scriptures, and a host of others. See Dick B., The Books Early AAs Read for Spiritual Growth, Dr. Bob and His Library, and Anne Smith's Journal. They also read numerous Oxford Group books, books by Rev. Samuel Shoemaker, books by Norman Vincent Peale, and Roman Catholic Books such as St. Augustine's Confessions.

Let's consider what the early AAs embraced, largely from Christian Endeavor, from the ideas of Dr. Bob's youth, from the Bible, from Bill's experiences with conversion, and from Dr. William D. Silkworth's ideas about Jesus Christ as the Great Physician and about the nature of alcoholism: (1) Abstinence. (2) Resisting temptation. (3) Hospitalization. (4) Reliance on the Creator. (5) Acceptance of Jesus Christ as Lord and Saviour. (6) Daily Bible study. (7) Daily prayer. (8) Daily Quiet Hour. (9) Recovery in the homes among fellowshipping Christians. (10) Old fashioned prayer meetings—which Dr. Bob's son likened to "Old fashioned revival meetings." (11) Seeking God's guidance. (12) Obeying God's will by walking in love and eliminating sinful conduct. (13) Optional attendance at a church of one's own choice. (14) Vigorous outreach to still-suffering alcoholics to help them get straightened out in the same way. This outreach was done for no pay.

Is this the A.A. you know today? Is this the therapy you receive today? Is this what your treatment program teaches and embraces? Is this the message you carry to a newcomer you are trying to help?

It's important to acknowledge that you can quit drinking without A.A. or a 12 Step fellowship. You can quit drinking with medical, psychological, religious, therapeutic, pharmacological, nutritional, mutual therapy help. You can. People do. They also quit as participants in present day A.A. and 12 Step fellowships; in Christian recovery programs; in Christian-track programs; in Salvation Army rehabs; in missions; in City Team facilities; in Teen Challenge; and in a host of other ways. To deny this is to deny factual evidence. The key is whether one wishes to trust God and go the old school A.A. way or some other way. It's a matter of choice. But you don't have a choice if you don't know and are told that you shouldn't know or pass the information along. You should know. You may apply it. And, if it works, you ought to pass it along to someone who has been unable to quit on his own, has been unable to receive help through any human power, and who is attracted by Dr. Bob's assurance that: "Your Heavenly Father will never let you down!"

The outstanding fact is that there was a documented, 75%-to-93% success rate among seemingly-hopeless, medically-incurable, real alcoholics who bent every effort to establish a relationship and fellowship with their Creator and His son Jesus Christ. That's available today. Dr. Bob learned it in his youth, applied it when he really decided to quit drinking, and spent the rest of his life helping others to learn and apply it.

> "Your Heavenly Father will never let you down!"
> *Alcoholics Anonymous*, 4th ed., 181

7
St. Johnsbury Academy

**Its Congregational Roots; the Fairbanks Influence; and the Impact on the Smith Family—
Judge Walter P. Smith an examiner;
Susan Holbrook Smith, a graduate, alumni leader, teacher, speaker, and historian; and
Bob Smith ("Dr. Bob"), a student, debater, Glee Club member and manager, orator, and graduate**

Historical Resources

In our St. Johnsbury visit, my son Ken and I met and worked with the delightful Academy archivist and poured over catalogs, student newspaper items, and other records. Not only did we find a great deal of material on the mission and outreach of the Academy itself, but we were surprised to find a great deal of material on Dr. Bob and his family. We found the records of his mother's attendance at and graduation from the Academy. We found the records of her becoming a teacher there. She became much involved in alumni association activities. There was also extensive material showing that she had been a speaker at a number of celebrations and actually wrote two chapters of a classic description of the Academy. There was a record that showed Judge Smith had conducted examinations at the Academy. And there was a surprising amount of material on Dr. Bob himself—records of his being a student; pictures of him as a student; his own graduation program showing that he occupied the coveted spot of graduation Orator, indications that he was a debater and member of a literary society, and records of his participation in and being manager of the Glee Club. There were several class notes mentioning Bob, and there was a picture of his graduating class with him in the picture. In a few words, then, the Smiths—all of them—were much involved in the St. Johnsbury Academy and recognized in its still available papers.

Three Histories of St. Johnsbury Academy

Perhaps the most authoritative Academy history is a 124-page history book, titled *An Historical Sketch of St. Johnsbury Academy 1842-1922*. Its editors were Arthur Fairbanks, Lemuel S. Hastings, James F. Colby (the first headmaster), Mrs. Walter Perrin Smith (Bob's mother), Joseph Fairbanks, Charles H. Merrill, and Wendell P. Stafford. And we will refer to it in later portions of this chapter.

Next comes a brief portion of excerpts about St. Johnsbury Academy by an alumnus who, while he claimed extreme distaste for St. Johnsbury, its Fairbanks benefactors, and the Academy itself, discloses some important facts about the religious influences in St. Johnsbury and the rigorous religious training connected with the Academy.[422]

Finally, there is Richard Beck, who wrote a different type of history, titled *A Proud Tradition A Bright Future*.[423] Beck's work is lacking in details but valuable in some of the quotations he includes. It is noteworthy for a chapter on President Calvin Coolidge and Dr. Robert Holbrook Smith. Regrettably, as with so many of today's A.A. related histories, the author simply took his Dr. Bob material from A.A.'s *DR. BOB and the Good Oldtimers*, rather than doing his own research and setting forth a complete, accurate record about Dr. Bob. Moreover, his remarks indicate some strong opinions about what the school was and what it should be. However, we will refer to this also in later portions of this chapter. None of our remarks should be construed as undervaluing the Beck book as an historical resource.

The Beginnings

Beck quotes Richard G. Durnin, author of a 1968 doctoral dissertation, as follows:

---

[422] See Charles Edward Russell, *Bare Hands and Stone Walls: Some Recollections of a Side-Line Reformer* (NY: Charles Scribner's Sons, 1933).
[423] Richard Beck, *A Proud Tradition A Bright Future: A Sesquicentennial History of St. Johnsbury Academy* (St. Johnsbury, VT: St. Johnsbury Academy, 1992).

> The founders of the eighteenth century New England academies had several things in common. They were all part of Protestant Christianity (with strong Calvinist overtones), but which had been through a process of liberalization from the century before. . . . All of the men involved in founding these first academies were concerned with public and private morality; dutifulness in religion; devotion to family and the race; the Christian virtues; and useful knowledge, which then included classical languages.[424]

Beck adds:

> Not surprisingly, the hiring of ministers to serve as principals or headmasters was common. . . . The belief that a basic understanding of Christian (most often Protestant) doctrine was a necessity for mankind's continued progress was also evident in virtually all of the early New England academies' schedules, which almost invariably, included a brief devotional service at the start of each class day. This practice, which served as the origin of St. Johnsbury Academy's daily Chapel, was often accompanied with a requirement that all boarding students attend Sunday public worship services. Here too the Academy's founders followed the pattern identified by Durnin.[425]

Pointing to the way in which the Fairbanks family members had used the money and success achieved in their famous scales firm, Beck stated:

> As a group, the Fairbanks brothers perfectly represented the prototypical New England
> academy builders: devoutly religious in the Calvinist tradition, deeply committed to   societal progress, and wealthy enough to provide the institutions they believed would help lead the way to a better world.[426]

---

[424] Beck, *A Proud Tradition*, 6.
[425] Beck, *A Proud Tradition*, 6-7.
[426] Beck, *A Proud Tradition*, 9.

It was the Fairbanks brothers—Erastus, Thaddeus, and Joseph P. Fairbanks—who began, in 1842, laying out their plans for the Academy.

Arthur Fairbanks wrote:

> St. Johnsbury Academy, like so many other academies in New England, was founded in the interest of Christian education. . . . As the town grew and became a settled prosperous community, the tradition of the academy in association with the church asserted itself; and in 1842 the St. Johnsbury Academy was founded by three brothers: Erastus, Thaddeus, and Joseph Paddocks Fairbanks.
>
> All three brothers were men of marked ability, strong character, thorough integrity and high purpose. The material success of their manufacturing enterprise, though it contributed largely to the prosperity of the community, could not itself satisfy them, for they were men of Puritan stock and deep religious faith. They began early to make liberal gifts both of their income and of their personal services for religious, educational, and other philanthropic enterprises. Not the least important of these undertaking was the establishment of an Academy in St. Johnsbury for the intellectual, moral and religious training of boys and girls in northeastern Vermont.
>
> One family member approached James K. Colby, principal of Appleton Academy in New Ipswich, New Hampshire, about taking charge of the proposed institution. Thaddeus Fairbanks confirmed that the arrangements had been made. And on December 13, 1842, Colby taught his first class of 23 pupils, six being members of the Fairbanks family, in the Crossman House (owned by the Fairbanks brothers), south of the present courthouse.
>
> On November 16, 1843, Erastus, Thaddeus, Horace, and Joseph P. Fairbanks, along with Colby, organized a Vermont corporation with the stated purpose of "establishing and maintaining a Literary and Scientific Institution located near the South End of the St. Johnsbury Plain." The papers stated:

Said Institution shall be called and known by the name of The St. Johnsbury Academy.[427]

On December 6, 1843, Erastus, Thaddeus, and Joseph P. Fairbanks executed a deed of gift which, in part, stated the following:

> And the aforesaid Erastus Fairbanks, Thaddeus Fairbanks, and Joseph P. Fairbanks, believing that no system of education can be successful which does not recognize, the paramount importance of the Christian religion, & that no course of intellectual training in a public seminary, can fully develop the mental powers of the pupil & fit him for usefulness, except its ethics are founded upon Divine revelation.[428]

The deed further enjoined the Trustees, their associates, and successors in office that they adopt measures:

> To make the Institution a school of moral and religious instruction,--such instruction as contemplates the student's relation to a future state, and aims to secure his qualifications for it, in the cultivation of right affections & the conversion of the heart. By religious instruction is not intended, the inculcation of a sectarian creed, but that the fundamental doctrines of the Bible be taught, & the great duties of repentance & faith, be urged upon the attention of the school

> And believing that the foregoing injunctions can best be secured by a provision which shall perpetuate the election, as Trustees, of men whose religious views are in harmony with the foregoing & with each other,--Therefore it is hereby provided, as the condition of the validity of this deed, that the Trustees of the aforesaid Academy shall be men of piety, & members in regular standing of some orthodox Congregational church, or churches, holding the doctrines essentially of the Westminster Shorter Catechism."[429]

---

[427] Fairbanks et al., *Sketch*, 9.
[428] Fairbanks et al., *Sketch*, 9.
[429] Fairbanks et al., *Sketch*, 9.

Any sketch of the Academy thus makes it plain that homage is due the three Fairbanks brothers, both as its founders and as its upbuilders, since for nearly fifty years with scantiest aid from others they bore the entire burden of financial support, and by far the larger part of its present endowment has been derived from them and their descendents.[430]

In 1843, the school's annual *Catalogue of the Officers and Students*, stated:

> The scholars will be required to be subject to the supervision and direction of the instructor, not only in the school room, but in respect to their study hours, recreations, and conduct out of school. . . All members of the school will be required to attend meeting regularly on the Sabbath, where the teacher attends, except in cases where parents, or individuals of a suitable age to choose in such matters, request that attendance be elsewhere.[431]

Dr. Edward T. Fairbanks described the opening of school, about 1845:

> The great hand bell has been rung; every seat is filled; everyone is still; the master is in that high chair which no inferior man could gracefully occupy. . . . On the wall behind the great theoretical chart on the mater's right is his assistant, John P. Fisk, never lacking force. . . . On the other side is the eldest of a well-known sisterhood of teachers, Miss Catherine McKeen. . . . After scripture and prayer and some weighty words about self-respect and truthfulness, the classes are called off. . .[432]

Arthur Fairbanks stated: In 1856, a list of textbooks listed Paley's Natural Theology. "The same year the Greek New Testament is mentioned as one of the 'texts,' which was at this time one of the college requirements for admission at Dartmouth. The advanced

---

[430] Fairbanks et. al. S*ketch*, 10.
[431] Beck, *A Proud Tradition*, 19.
[432] Fairbanks et al., *Sketch*, 20-21.

character of many of these textbooks indicates work of a high order for a secondary school."[433]

In 1871, Rev. Homer Taylor Fuller became principal of the Academy. He had studied for the ministry at Andover Theological Academy and later at Union Theological Seminary, from which he was graduated in May, 1869. He was pastor of the Congregational Church in Pehtigo, Wisconsin. A new Principal, Fuller still maintained the strict Colby disciplining, both in and out of the classroom. Beck quotes the following remembrance of someone named Stone:

> Attendance at church Sunday morning and also Sunday School were compulsory.[434]

According to the record of an August 22, 1881 trustees meeting, the funds from Erastus Fairbanks' estate were donated with the understanding that "The Principal of the Academy shall attend the South Church and the other teachers, gentlemen and lady, shall be divided equally as nearly as may be, between the North and South Churches, so long as the two churches exist as organized bodies."[435]

In 1885, Rev. Fuller acceded to the request of Thaddeus Fairbanks and sent him substance of what Fuller had said at the recent graduating exercises. Praising the Academy, Fairbanks wrote:

> The fact that St. Johnsbury is a rare location for such a school. It is not in the vicinity of another larger town or city which has superior attractions or allurements for the young. It is large enough both to be independent of the Academy and at the same time to assist its work by the atmosphere it affords it. This atmosphere of refinement and of moral and Christian sympathy and purpose is not surpassed. . . . The thorough enforcement of the liquor prohibitory law of the state, he industry and good character and so good example of the residents of the village, the positive influence of the churches, the Young Men's Christian Association, and the Athenaeum and Art Gallery, make an unusual combination of collateral educational forces. .

---

[433] Fairbanks et. al. *Sketch*, 21.
[434] Beck, *A Proud Tradition*, 30.
[435] Beck, *A Proud Tradition*, 34.

. . The twin purpose of the Academy kept constantly in mind by both trustees and teachers is to keep before the pupils both a high and fine type of Christian character and the highest standard of intellectual discipline and attainment, or in other words to make earnest Christians and good scholars.[436]

The year of 1877 is to be remembered for the holding of the first meeting of the Alumni Association which had been organized the previous year. The meeting occupied the entire afternoon and with its oration by Judge Alonzo chronicles by Mrs. S. T. Brooks and its poem by Mrs. W. P. Smith made an auspicious beginning.[437]

The Period of Dr. Bob's Matriculation at St. Johnsbury Academy

Elsewhere we have pointed out that Dr. Bob's activity at the Academy pops up in many different areas. The foregoing discussion indicates the degree of Christian emphasis—daily chapel, required church and Sunday School attendance, scripture and prayers at opening of classes, required Biblical texts including the New Testament, and sermons and prayers on graduation.

Dr. Bob belonged to and managed the Glee Club. He was a member of a literary society. He participated in orations and debates both before the school at chapel exercises and in public exhibitions of these classes. He attended weekly prayer meetings.[438]

In June of 1892, the Academy observed its Semi-Centennial. This was in the hands of a committee appointed by the Alumni Association—with which Dr. Bob's mother was much involved, according to the current archivist.[439] The exercises were held in the Music Hall; and the

---

[436] Fairbanks et al., *Sketches*, 60-61.
[437] From page 56 of *St. Johnsbury Academy* in binder.
[438] Fairbanks et al., *Sketches*, 67.
[439] From page 57 of the Semi-Centennial of St. Johnsbury Academy, 1892 Alumni Secretary's Report states: "The fourteenth annual meeting of the St. Johnsbury Academy Alumni Association was held on the morning of Friday, June 24, 1892. . . . Executive Committee F.A. Dakin, Mrs. C.P Carpenter, W. P. Stafford, Mrs. W. P. Smith, Frank H. Brooks, all of St. Johnsbury."

history of the Academy was given by Revered Edward T. Fairbanks, and of the second quarter century by Mrs. Walter P. Smith, both of St. Johnsbury.[440]

In our resource binders are the class notes about Dr. Bob, his graduation program where he is listed as giving the Oration, and mention of his participation in literary society meetings and debates and in the Glee club.

Involvement of Fairbanks and Smith Families

We've previously listed various services of both the Fairbanks people and the Smith family—in North Congregational Church, in its Sunday School, in Christian Endeavor, in the YMCA, and in other community women's, library, and mission activities.

Here we will simply summarize what the Academy records show:

Trustees[441]

Erastus Fairbanks
Thaddeus Fairbanks
Joseph P. Fairbanks
Horace Fairbanks
Henry Fairbanks
Franklin Fairbanks
Edward T. Fairbanks

Presidents[442]

Erastus Fairbanks – 1847-1849
Thaddeus Fairbanks – 1849 – 1886
Henry Fairbanks – 1886 – 1918

---

[440] Fairbanks et al., *Sketches*, 71.
[441] Fairbanks et al., *Sketches* (Appendix I), 101.
[442] Fairbanks et al., *Sketches* (Appendix I), 102.

Secretaries[443]

J. P. Fairbanks – 1842 – 1846
Edward T. Fairbanks – 1882 – 1919

Treasurers[444]

J. P. Fairbanks (acting) – 1842 – 1846
Edward T. Fairbanks – 1882 – 1919

Assistant Teachers[445]

Rev. Henry Fairbanks – 1847
Sarah Fairbanks (Mrs. C. M. Stone) – 1852 – 1856
Emily Fairbanks – 1855, 1857
Rev. Edward T. Fairbanks – 1860
Emma J. Paddock (Mrs. James E. Taylor) – 1872 – 1875
Susan A. Holbrook (Mrs. W. P. Smith – Dr. Bob's mother) – 1875 - 1876[446]
Mary E. Stone – 1883
Lucy Fairbanks (Mrs. J. C. Alvord) – 1892

Dr. Charles E. Putney (1840-1920)

Mr. Putney was a teacher in the Academy for twenty-three years. . . . He was principal for fourteen years [from 1882 to 1896]. . . . Mr. Putney's influence was considerable in educational circles in the state. He served for several years as examiner of the normal schools . . . and also as president of the Caledonia County Association of teachers. He received the degree of Ph.D. from Dartmouth College in 1884. He was active in the work of the local YMCA and served as its president. But the institution dearest to his heart was the church. Notwithstanding the heavy burden of his Academy position, he was a deacon in the South Church, always conducted a large class in its Sunday School and was a faithful attendant of the mid-week meeting. He not only maintained

---

[443] Fairbanks et al., *Sketches* (Appendix I), 103.
[444] Fairbanks et al., *Sketches* (Appendix I), 103.
[445] Fairbanks et al., *Sketches* (Appendix II), 104-07.
[446] Catalogue in binder, page 93: "1875-76: Susan A. Holbrook [Class of '74]. (Mrs. W. P. Smith). St. Johnsbury.

the religious traditions on which the Academy was founded, but recognized that it was in the church that these traditions found their source and inspiration.[447]

Academy Picture of Dr. Bob and Boyhood Home

Between pages 64 and 65 of the Beck book is a group of pictures. In the middle of the group is a picture of Dr. Bob, and below it is a picture of his birthplace and boyhood home. The caption says:

> Dr. Robert Holbrook Smith (left), a St. Johnsbury-born member of the Class of 1898 who turned his all but certain early death into the birth of Alcoholics Anonymous, is pictured here in his graduation photograph from Dartmouth College in 1902. Dr. Bob's birthplace and boyhood home (below) located on Summer Street, was rededicated and opened to the public during the summer of 1992.[448]

Academy Lists of Students

For 1874, the Academy archivist provided the listing:

> Ladies. Senior Advanced Class. Susan A. Holbrook. Lyndon (Dr. Bob's mother)

For 1895, the Academy archivist provided the listing:

> Sub-Junior Class. Robert H. Smith. St. Johnsbury. 20 Summer St. [now numbered 297]

For 1896, she provided:

> Junior Class. Robert H. Smith. St. Johnsbury. 20 Summer St.

---

[447] Fairbanks et al., *Sketches*, 74-75. The Vice Principal of St. Johnsbury Academy from 1883 to 1895 was Audubon L. Hardy. See Claude M. Fuess, *Calvin Coolidge: The Man from Vermont* (Boston: Little, Brown, 1940), 40
[448] Beck, *A Proud Tradition*, 64-65.

For 1897, she provided:

> MIDDLE CLASS. Robert H. Smith. St. Johnsbury. 20 Summer Street.

For 1898, she provided:

> Senior Class. Robert H. Smith. St. Johnsbury. 20 Summer Street
>
> Grand Concert by the Academy Glee Club. Friday Evening. March 4th, 1898 at eight o'clock, Academy Hall. Members of the Glee Club. Robert H. Smith. Robert H. Smith, Manager.
>
> Robert Smith is business manager of the Glee Club.[449]
>
> The Societies. ADELPHIAN. . . . The subject for discussion Jan. 22 was: 'Resolved that a large accumulation of personal wealth is detrimental to society.' The affirmative was defended by Newell and Smith, and the negative by Fairbanks and Stone. The board of decision was not of one mind but decided for the negative.[450]

From the 1872 School Catalogue in our resource binder:

> All members of the school are required to attend one church service and a Bible service regularly on the Sabbath, and, unless with their parents, with the Principal, except when his consent to attend elsewhere is previously obtained. Denominational preferences of parents and guardians should be expressed in writing to the Principal.

From the 1873 School Catalogue in our resource binder:

> EXAMINATIONS: These are both oral and written. Public examinations occur at least twice in each year, and private examinations of many classes are held monthly. The

---

[449] *The Academy Student* (1898), 50.
[450] *The Academy Student* (1898), 45.

committees for the last public examinations were as follows . . . SECOND TERM. Walter P. Smith, Esq.

From the 1874 School Catalogue in our resource binder:

> GRADUATES. 1874. Susan E. [sic] Holbrook (Mrs. W.P. Smith).[451] St. Johnsbury.

From *The Academy Student*, the Academy newspaper, are the following concerning Bob [Bob was a member of the Adelphian Society]:

> . . . [T]he following program was carried out: Music, Medley . . . R. Smith. . . . NOTE: The writer thinks that Smith's medley is so good that it ought to be printed in the STUDENT. Saturday evening . . . the following officers were elected for the coming term . . . Second Director . . . R. Smith.[452]

> The Glee Club is leading the singing in chapel and already a great improvement can be noticed in that part of our morning service.[453]

From the Commencement Exercises Program for the Class of 1898. Opened with Prayer:

> ORATION – The 'Crank' in History. Robert Holbrook Smith, St. Johnsbury. . . . BENEDICTION.

A Somewhat-Sour Academy Alumnus: Charles Edward Russell

Charles Edward Russell (1860-1941), the famous Pulitzer Prize-winning writer, Socialist, and "muckraker" born in Davenport, Iowa, attended St. Johnsbury Academy. He graduated in 1881, only six years after the "Great Awakening" of 1875 in St. Johnsbury. Miraldi

---

[451] Dr. Bob's mother's maiden name was "Susan Amanda Holbrook."
[452] *The Academy Student* (1897), 34.
[453] *The Academy Student* (1898), 51

provides some important information about Russell's religious background in his biography of Russell:

> Russell was brought up in a Christian Evangelical household; his grandfather was a Baptist preacher; his father the Sunday school superintendent and one of the leading officials in Iowa's Young Men's Christian Association. They were all temperance advocates, and his father was reputed to have never tasted alcohol in his life.[454]

Russell's first comment about St. Johnsbury in his autobiography touches upon St. Johnsbury's religious orientation:

> About that time [i.e., around 1880, just before Russell left Iowa for St. Johnsbury at age 19] the religious press, with which most households were richly supplied, had much to say about the flawless orthodoxy and superior instruction dispensed at St. Johnsbury, Vermont, Academy, and thither it was decided to ship me to be bettered by special courses in Latin, political economy, and history.[455]

Miraldi adds the St. Johnsbury Academy perspective on the "morality" and lack of "temptations" in the Town of St. Johnsbury:

> The village, St. Johnsbury Academy proudly pointed out, was "widely known for the intelligence, public spirit and high-toned morality of its people." In fact, the academy boasted, St. Johnsbury was perfectly located: "Temptations are comparatively few, and incentives to culture are many and strong."[456]

Miraldi also notes that the strong religious orientation of St. Johnsbury Academy became a problem for Russell.

---

[454] Robert Miraldi, *The Pen Is Mightier: The Muckraking Life of Charles Edward Russell* (New York Palgrave Macmillan, 2003), 23.
[455] Charles Edward Russell, *Bare Hands and Stone Walls: Some Recollections of a Side-Line Reformer* (New York: Charles Scribner's Sons, 1933), 7.
[456] Miraldi, *The Pen Is Mightier,* 23.

But the piety of St. Johnsbury Academy—whose 1881 catalogue points out that 'good manners and morals are as important as mere intellectual acquisition'—was too much for the cutup from Davenport to take.[457]

Miraldi adds further:

> Occasional excitement about ideas, . . . could not make up for the insufferable discipline and rules of behavior that so rankled Russell. He disagreed with the maxims expressed in the academy's student guidebook which noted: "The rules of the school are not arbitrary or unnecessarily strict, but simply sufficient to protect pupils in the proper disposal of their time [and] to guard against temptations."[458]

If one can get past Russell's somewhat-negative perspective, there is much to learn from Russell about the religious environment in the Town of St. Johnsbury, and at St. Johnsbury Academy in particular, around the time of Dr. Bob's birth.

Here is how Russell describes where he stayed in St. Johnsbury:

> That part of the town I was to inhabit, called St. Johnsbury Plain, stretched for half a mile along a hillside shelf or plateau that was the legacy of an old glacial river. Three hundred feet below it, the silvery, idyllic Passumpsic [River], . . . The Academy buildings and dormitory stood at the south end of the plateau. So did the Academy boarding house, where I came to rest, and where from the one window of my room I looked eastward up a long winding valley . . .[459]

Russell's thorough description of the people of the Town of St. Johnsbury in 1880 is insightful.

> But the people that dwelt in this favored spot seemed to me for a long time merely enigmatic. The transition from the frank, outspoken, headlong, main-strength West was too abrupt.

---

[457] Miraldi, *The Pen Is Mightier*, 23.
[458] Miraldi, *The Pen Is Mightier*, 24.
[459] Russell, *Bare Hands and Stone Walls*, 8-9.

Where I lived nobody cared much for appearances and everybody moved more or less in the open; but here reigned the iron restraint of the invariable convention. It seemed to me at first that the Vermonters were chillier than their climate and the east wind that blew down their valleys had turned their marrow, if any, to ice. Their poise of an extreme reserve, their coldly formal greetings, their plain horror of the outré and the novel, their suspicion of strangers, in contrast with the hearty manners to which I had been accustomed, seemed unendurable. They had a fashion of speech that with its slow, deliberate drawl wearied me into an acute resentment. They said "he-ow" for "how" and "ke-ow" for "cow," and spoke of the Deity as "Ge-od." My own name was translated into "Russ-yell," which on the ball field was not so far out of the way, but when it came to "Love-yell" for the quiet Aldus Lovell that was my chum and confidant, I felt that even unintentional burlesque had gone too far. Despite all protests, they insisted upon calling my native state "Ee-oh-ah," and their way of looking me over with a cool and unhasting appraisal gave me the fantods. From what was said to be the common topic of their conversation, I thought they were making mental estimates of my probable worth in coinage of the realm. It was months before my dull perceptions sensed the fact that with these hill-folk the outward was only a mask. Under their frozen exterior no other people were more kindly, friendly, neighborly, and good to know, and I think I could cite no other community in this country blessed with an equal variety of the permanently sterling. In truth, the people there wore austerity as they wore their painfully formal Sunday clothes, in obedience to some tribal tradition unmeaning and inept; if they were close bargainers they were usually upright; and if day by day they seemed absorbed in trafficking they as sedulously maintained a standard of general culture, high and rare.[460]

The reader may want to consider at this point whether the religious conversions of approximately 1,500 of the townspeople of St. Johnsbury during the "Great Awakening" of 1875--about one-third of

---

[460] Russell, *Bare Hands and Stone Walls*, 9-10.

its residents at the time[461]--may have influenced the residents to the point that Russell could state that he "could cite no other community in this country blessed with an equal variety of *the permanently sterling*" (emphasis added).

Russell moves on to a discussion of his views of St. Johnsbury Academy and starts out on a fairly positive note.

> The Academy was in many ways an admirable institution. All the instructors were experts, and what was more worth, all were enthusiasts, each in his own line. The man of science seemed to me to know more than any one human being ought to be allowed to know; . . . he was able by mental gymnastics to reconcile perfectly the materialistic cynicism of the leading lights of his time with the ideology of what is called revealed religion, . . . Others of the faculty were of his pattern for ability and integrity. . . . Everything was as good as the best and the discipline was so relentless and granitic that it would have filled Jonathan Edwards with a recondite joy, . . .[462]

Miraldi provides some additional background information about St. Johnsbury Academy and Russell's classes.

> Founded in 1842, St. Johnsbury Academy was a coeducational preparatory school, essentially a four-year high school to prepare students for college; it cost the Russells about $500—for room, board, and tuition—to send Charles Edward there for two years. Tuition was relatively low because, unknown to the Russells, the town's leading family, the Fairbankses, had just endowed the academy with a $100,000 gift. Russell was eventually impressed by the school's academic life. 'All the instructors were experts,' he wrote after studying Latin, Greek, French, and German, all indispensable tools for the correspondent who eventually traveled the world. He took lessons in English grammar, British literature and history,

---

[461] The population of the township of St. Johnsbury, Vermont, was 4,665 in 1870, and 5,800 in 1880. See: *The Encyclopaedia Britannica: A Dictionary of Arts, Sciences, and General Literature*, 9th ed.—popular reprint, Volume XXI (New York: Henry G. Allen, 1888), 176; s.v. "St. Johnsbury."
[462] Russell, *Bare Hands and Stone Walls*, 10.

European history, and political economy—a thorough a well-rounded course of study that helped make Russell an erudite adult.[463]

But when Russell presents his lengthy discussion of the religious environment and instruction at St. Johnsbury Academy—which things are of considerable importance as we endeavor to understand what Dr. Bob may have experienced during his four years of attendance at the Academy from 1894 to 1898—he is not so complimentary. He begins as follows:

> There may be devices more ingeniously conceived to keep in ever watchful care the walk, morals, conversation, and religious fervor of the young than those practiced in this bustling academe, but I do not know what they could be. With reason the advertisements stressed the fact of an argus-eyed supervision. The Academy dormitory, it is true, sheltered under one roof young men and young women students, but the prospectus hastened to reassure parents, alarmed, perhaps, by this architectural slip. It pointed out with emphasis that a solid wall of masonry from ground to roof effectually separated the sexes. The principal lived on one side of this wall and the assistant principal on the other, and either or both would have been sure to detect any outbreak of levity, as, for example, an attempt to tunnel the wall.[464]

Russell then turns to the topic of morning prayers at St. Johnsbury Academy.

> Attendance at morning prayers was sternly exacted of each and all—no excuses. Besides the reading of the scriptures, the hymns, and the prayers, the man of science, the principal or some visiting clergyman usually said a few words of reproof upon the sins of youth or of exhortation to godliness. While the prayer was on, the principal was accustomed to hold his hand over his eyes in such a way that he could see between his

---

[463] Miraldi, *The Pen is Mightier*, 23.
[464] Russell, *Bare Hands and Stone Walls*, 10-11.

fingers and note an unlucky student whose attitude bespoke not the required sanctification.[465]

Next, Russell discusses the evening curfew and the Wednesday night weekly prayer meeting at North Congregational Church, St. Johnsbury.

> At eight o'clock every evening the Academy bell rang and after that signal no student could be out of his or her room without the express permission of the principal—difficult to obtain, except on Wednesday night to attend the weekly prayer meeting at the North Congregational Church. It was customary for some member of the faculty to go about with careful scrutiny to learn of possible backsliders in this respect. As the Academy dormitory and Academy boarding house, which stood close by, could accommodate but a small part of the student body, the rest lodged variously about the town. This made a perfect supervision sometimes difficult, but the emergency was bravely met, one of the principals sometimes disguising himself with false whiskers that he might better pursue this branch of useful knowledge.[466]

He then covers "Sabbath attendance upon church" and "upon Sunday school":

> Sabbath attendance upon church was required of all, likewise upon Sunday school, and was obtained by compelling each student to make a virtual affidavit every Monday morning that he had not been remiss in his devotions. He must return to the principal a signed affirmation reading as follows:
>
>> "I, ..., do solemnly declare upon my honor that I attended the morning service at . . . . . . Church, on Sunday . . . ., that I was present at the beginning of the services and remained until the close. I also attended the Sunday school at the . . . . Church."[467]

---

[465] Russell, *Bare Hands and Stone Walls*, 11.
[466] Russell, *Bare Hands and Stone Walls*, 11-12.
[467] Russell, *Bare Hands and Stone Walls*, 12.

After the preceding review of the religious requirements of St. Johnsbury Academy, Russell states: "The whole thing reeked with piety; . . . ."[468] And upon noting that tobacco, liquor, playing cards, games of chance, and dancing were all forbidden, he sums up by characterizing the Academy's requirements as "intensive . . . religious formalism."[469]

As we noted earlier, if one can get past Russell's dislike of "piety" and "religious formalism," one can clearly see Russell's identification of the religious activities in which Dr. Bob had said he had participated growing up in St. Johnsbury.

---

[468] Russell, *Bare Hands and Stone Walls*, 12.
[469] Russell, *Bare Hands and Stone Walls*, 14.

"Your Heavenly Father will never let you down!"
Alcoholics Anonymous, 4th ed., 181

8
The Fairbanks Family of St. Johnsbury, Vermont

To say the name "Fairbanks" is practically synonymous with saying the name "St. Johnsbury, Vermont." This chapter will highlight most of the materials you can find in our resource binders and give you some idea of the stature, influence, and impact that this unusual family had on the town where Dr. Bob grew up. And very probably on Dr. Bob himself and on his immense interest in the Bible, prayer, and guidance.

Summary of the Fairbanks Family's Vermont, Congregational, YMCA, and St. Johnsbury Service

Organizers of the society that spawned North Congregational Church, St. Johnsbury, met in the home of Major Joseph Fairbanks (father of the three brothers Erastus Fairbanks, Thaddeus Fairbanks, and Joseph Paddock Fairbanks), adjourned to the Meeting House, and formed the new church on April 7, 1825. Joseph Fairbanks and his wife, Phebe (Paddock) Fairbanks, both were among those assenting to the Articles of Faith and the Covenant at the time of forming the new church. Joseph's son Erastus Fairbanks became a Deacon of the church, and two of Erastus's sons (Horace Fairbanks and Franklin Fairbanks) also became Deacons of the church. In addition, two of Joseph's sons (Erastus Fairbanks and Joseph Paddock Fairbanks) became Sunday School Superintendents, and two of Erastus's sons (Horace Fairbanks and Franklin Fairbanks) also became Sunday School Superintendents. The footnotes are set forth in the genealogy portion of this chapter; and they document the foregoing points, as well as the biographical information immediately following the summary paragraph

E. & T. Fairbanks Company formed and began marketing the platform scale invented by Thaddeus. Prosperity abounded, and the business gained world-wide importance.

Erastus Fairbanks (also referred to as Deacon Erastus Fairbanks), son of Joseph and Phebe:

> President of E & T. Fairbanks Company
> President of two railroad companies
> State of Vermont Legislator for the Town of St. Johnsbury and re-elected
> Governor of Vermont in 1852 and again in 1860
> Founded St. Johnsbury Academy, with his brother Thaddeus
> President of Vermont Domestic Missionary Society
> Corporate member for many years of American Board of Foreign Missions
> Supervised construction of North Congregational Church, St. Johnsbury, building
> Deacon of North Congregational Church, St. Johnsbury
> Superintendent of North Congregational Church, St. Johnsbury, Sunday School
> "From earliest manhood Gov. Fairbanks was a devoted, active, public-spirited Christian man. He was for fifty years a pillar in the home church, Congregational; and in later life a member and officer of many benevolent boards, which he supported by liberal contributions of money, time and personal service."[470]
> His endowments assist in maintaining the St. Johnsbury Athenaeum, the Museum of Natural Science, and North Congregational Church, St. Johnsbury.

In his article on Erastus Fairbanks, Newell makes a number of observations which are relevant here:

> Six generations of New England forbears were behind Erastus Fairbanks, he being in the direct descent from Jonathan Fayerbancke, who migrated to Boston in 1633 from

---

[470] Lorenzo Sayles Fairbanks, *Genealogy of the Fairbanks Family in America, 1633-1897* (Boston: Printed for the Author by the American Printing and Engraving Company, 1897), 329.

Yorkshire. He was born in Brimfield, Massachusetts, in 1792.[471]

[In] 1852, Erastus Fairbanks was elected Governor of Vermont. In his opinion, probably the most important legislative act which he, as governor strongly supported through the General Assembly was the prohibitory liquor law. Although this act remained substantially in force for fifty years, immediate repercussions and opposition brought about his defeat in the next election.[472]

A strict moralist, Fairbanks could be counted on in the exigencies of life to reveal his staunch Congregationalism. For fifty years he was a pillar of the Congregational Church; he served on many benevolent boards of his church, state and national, to which he was a liberal contributor of money and personal attention.[473]

Those closest to him knew that he firmly believed that he had been motivated in his solemn responsibility by a divine power. Inspired constantly by a deep sense of providential guidance, Erastus Fairbanks dedicated himself to the service of Vermont and the Union.[474]

... [I]t may be said of Governor Fairbanks that he died on that November day of 1864 in faith, not having received the promises, but having seen them afar off.[475]

Sir Thaddeus Fairbanks, son of Joseph and Phebe:

> Inventor of the Fairbanks Platform Scale
> Owner of 32 patents for scales, and also patents for a hemp machine, stoves, a cast-iron plough, a device for

---

[471] Graham S. Newell, "Erastus Fairbanks," in *Vermont History: The Proceedings of the Vermont Historical Society*, Volume XXXII, Number 2, April 1964 (Burlington, VT: Vermont Historical Society, 1964), 59.
[472] Newell, "Erastus Fairbanks," 60-61.
[473] Newell, "Erastus Fairbanks," 61.
[474] Newell, "Erastus Fairbanks," 64.
[475] Newell, "Erastus Fairbanks," 64.

creating draught, a stead heater, a feed water heater, and a refrigerator.

Manager of the St. Johnsbury Hemp Co.

President of E. & T. Fairbanks & Co.

He was knighted by the Emperor of Austria, the King of Siam, and the Bey of Tunis.

Aided scores of students to go through college.

With his brothers established the St. Johnsbury Academy, and for 20 years assumed its support, later contributing substantially to its endowment.

President of St. Johnsbury Academy

Gave a Professorship to Middlebury College and contributed to missionary objects and to many western colleges many thousands of dollars every year.

"Mr. Fairbanks reflected his Puritan ancestry in his character and tastes; pure, upright and conscientious, and, though exceedingly taciturn, an attractive, impressive man. A man of Christian faith, of spiritual insight and force, and of fine native gifts, he was successful above most men in his chosen lines of work. . . ."[476]

Joseph Paddock Fairbanks (1806-1855; one of the three sons of Joseph Fairbanks)

In 1826 he commenced the study of Law with his uncle, Judge Ephraim Paddock, of St. Johnsbury.[477]

"After he was admitted to the bar, he practiced law for one year with his uncle, Judge Paddock." He then opened his own office.[478]

"In 1828, he united with the Church on St. Johnsbury Plain [which was then known as "Second Congregational Church" and is today called "North Congregational Church, St. Johnsbury"], then under the pastoral care of Rev. James Johnson. He continued an exemplary and

---

[476] Fairbanks, *Genealogy of the Fairbanks Family*, 333.
[477] Samuel H. Taylor, *A Memorial of Joseph P. Fairbanks* (Riverside, 1865), 8. http://books.google.com/books?id=p0kOAAAAYAAJ&printsec=frontcover&dq=%22Joseph+P.+Fairbanks%22&ei=6fW2R4zFG4nUsgORxLyQBQ#PPA8-IA8,M1 ; accessed: 2/16/08.
[478] Taylor, *A Memorial of Joseph P. Fairbanks*, 9

useful member of it till 1852, when he transferred his relation to the South Church."[479]

He commenced trade in mercantile business at Troy, Vermont, early in April, 1832, with his cousin, Horace Paddock, of St. Johnsbury.[480]

"Shortly after he settled at Troy, . . . he commenced that system of benevolent effort for educating young men for the ministry in which he afterward took so deep an interest."[481]

Near the end of April, 1833, he joined his brothers Erastus and Thaddeus in the E. & T. Fairbanks company, working initially as a traveling salesperson for the newly-invented Fairbanks Platform Scales with the State of Maine as his territory.[482]

In June 1835 he married Miss Almira Taylor, daughter of Capt. James Taylor, of Derry, New Hampshire.[483]

"For a few years after his marriage Mr. Fairbanks resided a part of the time at St. Johnsbury, and a part at Waterville, Me., he having become associated with his brothers, and the business at the two places being conducted as a joint partnership. But it was his conviction that their business required that one of the company should reside

---

[479] Taylor, *A Memorial of Joseph P. Fairbanks*, 12. James Johnson was installed as Pastor of North Congregational Church, St. Johnsbury—which was originally incorporated as the Second Congregational Church—on February 28, 1827, and dismissed on May 3, 1838. Joseph P. Fairbanks was "received" as a member of North Congregational Church, St. Johnsbury, on January 13, 1828, and remained a member until October 16, 1851, when he became a member of South Congregational Church, St. Johnsbury. He was also Superintendent of the Sunday School at North Congregational Church, St. Johnsbury, from 1840 to 1850, and again (after a brief break) for a period during 1851. See "North Congregational Church, 1825-1877 list of Pastors, Deacons & Parishioners. Originally incorporated as the Second Congregational Church, Saint Johnsbury, Vermont": http://freepages.genealogy.rootsweb.com/~nekg3/church/church_st-jay-north-cong.htm ; accessed 2/17/08.

[480] Taylor, *A Memorial of Joseph P. Fairbanks*, 20.
[481] Taylor, *A Memorial of Joseph P. Fairbanks*, 25.
[482] Taylor, *A Memorial of Joseph P. Fairbanks*, 28.
[483] Taylor, *A Memorial of Joseph P. Fairbanks*, 34.

at Waterville. . . . [H]e made arrangements to reside their permanently."[484]

Based on the requests of his two brothers, however, he settled permanently at St. Johnsbury in the autumn of 1839 and hired a person to close his business in Maine.[485]

"In 1843, he united with his brothers in establishing the St. Johnsbury Academy."[486]

"In 1845, [he] . . . was chosen to represent his town in the State Legislature."[487]

He was elected as a Trustee of Middlebury College in 1850.[488]

He was the first President of the Passumpsic Bank.[489]

"He was prominent in promoting and sustaining the cause of Sabbath schools, of temperance, and education, and on these subjects wrote and delivered able addresses."[490]

He quietly left Bibles at the hotels where he would stop.[491]

"For aiding feeble churches, either in supporting the ministry or in building houses of worship, he contributed again and again."[492]

"He sought out indigent young men of piety and promise, and encouraged them to enter on a course of study for the ministry. These he either gave such assistance as they needed, or he loaned them money, to repay when they might be able."[493]

"At the time of his death [May 15, 1855, he (Joseph P. Fairbanks)] . . . was President of the Passumpsic Bank, the Vermont Education Society, the Caledonia County Bible Society; and . . . one of the Vice-Presidents of the American Peace Society, . . ."[494]

---

[484] Taylor, *A Memorial of Joseph P. Fairbanks*, 38.
[485] Taylor, *A Memorial of Joseph P. Fairbanks*, 41.
[486] Taylor, *A Memorial of Joseph P. Fairbanks*, 43.
[487] Taylor, *A Memorial of Joseph P. Fairbanks*, 45.
[488] Taylor, *A Memorial of Joseph P. Fairbanks*, 105.
[489] Taylor, *A Memorial of Joseph P. Fairbanks*, 111.
[490] Taylor, *A Memorial of Joseph P. Fairbanks*, 115.
[491] Taylor, *A Memorial of Joseph P. Fairbanks*, 121.
[492] Taylor, *A Memorial of Joseph P. Fairbanks*, 122.
[493] Taylor, *A Memorial of Joseph P. Fairbanks*, 122.
[494] Taylor, *A Memorial of Joseph P. Fairbanks*, 173.

Colonel Franklin Fairbanks, one of the children of Deacon Erastus Fairbanks:

> Educated in public schools of St. Johnsbury and at several academies.[495]
>
> Partner and superintendent of works in E. & T. Fairbanks & Co.[496]
>
> "In 1876, at the organization of the firm as a corporation he was elected vice-president, and at the death of his brother in 1888 he was made president and has held this office to the present [1894]."[497]
>
> Active in construction of the St. Johnsbury & Lake Champlain Rail Road; was vice-president and became president.[498]
>
> ". . . [E]llected by the Republican party as representative from St. Johnsbury to the state Legislature in 1870 and again in 1872, at the latter session being chosen speaker of the House."[499]
>
> Appointed aide-de-camp with the rank of Colonel by two governors. President of First National Bank of St. Johnsbury President of Ely Hoe & Fork Co.
>
> ". . . [T]rustee of the Northfield (Mass.) Seminary, the Soldiers' Home, the St. Johnsbury Academy, the Athenaeum, and Museum of Natural Science."[500]
>
> Presented the special committee report that changed the pew rental rules of North Church Was on the building committee, of which his brother Horace was chairman
>
> Joined his brother Horace in contracting to build the present North Church Was a Deacon of North Congregational Church, St. Johnsbury
>
> Was Sunday School Superintendent of North Congregational Church, St. Johnsbury, from 1861 until at least 1894.[501]
>
> Member of the International Lesson Committee for ten years[502]

---

[495] Ullery, *Men of Vermont*, 127.
[496] Ullery, *Men of Vermont*, 127.
[497] Ullery, *Men of Vermont*, 127.
[498] Ullery, *Men of Vermont*, 127.
[499] Ullery, *Men of Vermont*, 127.
[500] Ullery, *Men of Vermont*, 128.
[501] Ullery, *Men of Vermont*, 128.
[502] Ullery, *Men of Vermont*, 128.

> Erected and donated to the Town of St. Johnsbury the Fairbanks Museum of Natural Science which was dedicated in 1891.[503]
> Advisory Member of the International Committee of the YMCA for six years
> Delegate to Centennial Temperance Celebration in Philadelphia in 1885
> Received an honorary degree of A.M. from Dartmouth College.

George Fairbanks, one of the children of Deacon Erastus Fairbanks:

> Sang in the famous choir of the North Congregational Church, St. Johnsbury

Horace Fairbanks, one of the children of Deacon Erastus Fairbanks:

> Governor of Vermont
> Educated in the County Schools and Phillips Andover Academy.
> Delegate to two Republican National Conventions
> Presidential Elector in 1868
> President of Vermont Division of P & O Railroad
> Vice-president of First National Bank
> President of E. & T. Fairbanks & Co.
> Sang in the famous choir of the North Congregational Church, St. Johnsbury
> Headed the building committee for the present North Congregational Church building
> Contracted, along with his brother Franklin, to construct North Congregational Church and raised the bulk of the needed funds from the estate of Erastus Fairbanks
> Joined his brother Franklin in donating the bell in the church belfry
> Was a Sunday School Superintendent of the North Congregational Church

---

[503] Ullery, *Men of Vermont*, 128.

> Established a beneficial trust which provided for awarding books to Sunday School children who faithfully attended.
> Donated the St. Johnsbury Athenaeum (town library) to the Town of St. Johnsbury, stipulating that it remain free to the citizens of St. Johnsbury.

Emily Fairbanks Goodell, one of the children of Deacon Erastus

> Married Rev. Constans L. Goodell, D.D.
> Goodell graduated from the University of Vermont and Andover Theological Seminary
> Goodell ordained and installed pastor of South Church, New Britain, Ct.
> Then pastor of Pilgrim Congregational Church, St. Louis
> His biography says: "He was one of the most prominent of Congregational clergymen; a leader in educational and mission work; and in the National Council."[1]

Mary E. [Fairbanks] Stone, one of the granddaughters of Deacon Erastus

> Was the first president of the Young Ladies' Missionary Society in 1882.

Rev. Henry Fairbanks, Ph.D., son of Thaddeus Fairbanks

> Attended and graduated from St. Johnsbury Academy, Dartmouth (in 1853), and Andover Theological Seminary (in 1857) [504]
> Secretary of the corporation of E. & T. Fairbanks & Co.
> Professor of natural philosophy and later natural history at Dartmouth (1860-1869) [505]
> Secretary and later Vice-President of E. and T. Fairbanks & Co. [506]

---

[504] "Noyes Family," http://noyes.rootsweb.com/b304.htm ; accessed November 3, 2007.
[505] "Noyes Family," http://noyes.rootsweb.com/b304.htm ; accessed November 3, 2007.

First President, under its new constitution, of the (General) Convention of Congregational Ministers and Churches of Vermont[507]

Corporate member of American Board of Foreign Missions for 20 years[508]

Member of four of the National Councils of Congregational Churches[509]

Delegate to the International Council of Congregational Churches in London in 1891[510]

Trustee of Dartmouth College[511]

President of the Trustees of St. Johnsbury Academy for many years[512]

Member of Fairbanks Board of Education (for pious youth)

Treasurer of Fairbanks Education Board

President of Vermont Domestic Missionary Society[513]

Led the evangelistic work of the YMCA in the State of Vermont. "For some years after 1875 the State Convention of the YMCA carried on an effective evangelistic work in a large number of towns in Vermont, witnessing most marked religious revivals, with large additions to the churches, and Mr. Fairbanks was prominent in this work, after the first year having charge, and directing it as Secretary."[1]

In 1878, he received the honorary degree of Doctor of Philosophy."[514]

---

[506] "Noyes Family," http://noyes.rootsweb.com/b304.htm ; accessed November 3, 2007.
[507] "Noyes Family," http://noyes.rootsweb.com/b304.htm ; accessed November 3, 2007.
[508] "Noyes Family," http://noyes.rootsweb.com/b304.htm ; accessed November 3, 2007.
[509] "Noyes Family," http://noyes.rootsweb.com/b304.htm ; accessed November 3, 2007.
[510] "Noyes Family," http://noyes.rootsweb.com/b304.htm ; accessed November 3, 2007.
[511] "Noyes Family," http://noyes.rootsweb.com/b304.htm ; accessed November 3, 2007.
[512] "Noyes Family," http://noyes.rootsweb.com/b304.htm ; accessed November 3, 2007.
[513] "Noyes Family," http://noyes.rootsweb.com/b304.htm ; accessed November 3, 2007.

In 1885, erected the YMCA building and donated the western section to the YMCA

Chairman of the YMCA in St. Johnsbury

Congregational Minister ordained when in the missionary service; [515] in charge of a large number of home missionary fields, preaching and directing the vacation labor of students and others, and gathering up the fruits of their work.

Donated services to other communities as an itinerant minister

Owned the old family flintlock six feet and four inches long brought from England by Jonathan Fairbanks

Rev. Edward Taylor Fairbanks, D.D., son of Joseph Paddock Fairbanks

Educated at Yale College and Andover Theological Seminary

Pastor of First Congregational Church (St. Johnsbury Center), 1868-1874

Pastor of South Congregational Church, 1874-1902

Principal of St. Johnsbury's Union School

Librarian of St. Johnsbury Athenaeum

State Senator

Author, *The Town of St. Johnsbury, Vt., a Review of One Hundred Twenty-Five Years to the Anniversary Pageant 1912.* Rev. Edward T. Fairbanks devoted fifty-four years to the writing and completion of this history.

Honorary D.D. from the University of Vermont in 1893

Rev, Arthur Fairbanks, Ph.D., grandson of Thaddeus, son of Henry

Educated at St. Johnsbury and graduated from Dartmouth College, valedictorian of his class

Tutor in Greek in Dartmouth College

Asst. Prof. German and Logic at Dartmouth

---

[514] "Noyes Family," http://noyes.rootsweb.com/b304.htm ; accessed November 3, 2007.

[515] "Noyes Family," http://noyes.rootsweb.com/b304.htm ; accessed November 3, 2007.

Student in Union Theological Seminary, Yale Divinity School, Berlin and Freiburg where he received the degree of Ph. D.
Lecturer in Yale Divinity School, Instructor in Graduate Department of Yale University
Received Congregational ordination in South Congregational Church, St. Johnsbury.
Author

Robert Noyes Fairbanks, grandson of Thaddeus, son of Henry

Graduated from St. Johnsbury Academy and Dartmouth College
Employed in the scale business with the Fairbanks Company.

Partial Fairbanks Family Genealogy and Comments

Joseph Fairbanks (1763-1846) of Brimfield, Mass. [(Gen.) VI][516] & Phebe Paddock (1760-1853)
Born: November 1, 1763 in Sherborn, Middlesex, Massachusetts[517]
Married: to Phebe Paddock
Born: September 6, 1760
Died: May 5, 1853
Father: James Paddock of Holland, Mass.
Mother: Ann Paddock

---

[516] Some of the following information about the Fairbankses is condensed from Ellery Bicknell Crane, ed., *Historic Homes and Institutions and Genealogical and Personal Memoirs of Worcester County, Massachusetts, with a History of Worcester Society of Antiquity*, Vol. I, illus. (New York: The Lewis Publishing Company, 1907), 488-90.

[517] Lorenzo Sayles Fairbanks, *Genealogy of the Fairbanks Family in America, 1633-1897* (Boston: Printed for the Author by the American Printing and Engraving Company, 1897), 170. Lorenzo Sayles Fairbanks was a lawyer and Member of the New England Historic Genealogical Society, Boston, Mass.
http://books.google.com/books?id=rbJ3WLoOEo0C&dq=%22genealogy+of+the+fairbanks+family%22&pg=PP1&ots=9HbjOyy7UX&sig=gSO6EBFqOcmJmsVbIk-hKWXKtL4&prev=http://www.google.com/search%3Fsourceid%3Dnavclient%26ie%3DUTF-8%26rls%3DGGLF,GGLF:2005-31,GGLF:en%26q%3D%2522Genealogy%2Bof%2Bthe%2BFairbanks%2BFamily%2522&sa=X&oi=print&ct=title&cad=one-book-with-thumbnail#PPA1,M1 ;
Accessed via the Internet on 10/30/07 (and earlier in 10/07)

Moved: to St. Johnsbury (from Brimfield) in 1815 [where his brother-in-law, Judge Paddock, and his (Joseph's) son Erastus were already established]
Purchased: in St. Johnsbury "a small water-power, and timber with which he and his son [Thaddeus] build a dam, a saw mill, a grist mill, and wagon shop."[518]
Died: September 27, 1846
Children: Erastus Fairbanks, Thaddeus Fairbanks, and Joseph Paddock Fairbanks[519]

Erastus Fairbanks (1792-1864) [(Gen.) VII] & Lois Crosman (1792-1866)[520]
    Parents: Joseph Fairbanks & Phebe Paddock
    Born: October 28, 1792, at Brimfield, Mass.[521]
    Moved: to St. Johnsbury (alone) in 1812[522]
    Married: to Lois Crosman, of Peacham, on May 30, 1815
    Parents: Samuel and Lois (Chamberlain) Crosman
        Born: November 13, 1792
        Married: to Erastus Fairbanks
        Died: May 15, 1866
    Died: November 20, 1864, at St. Johnsbury
    1835: Erastus was "one of six men to be granted a charter for the Connecticut and Passumpsic Railroad . . . and was named president when the

---

[518] Fairbanks, *Genealogy*, 171.
[519] Fairbanks, *Genealogy*, 171.
[520] Sometimes misspelled "Lois Crossman."
[521] *The National Cyclopaedia of American Biography: Being the History of the United States As Illustrated in the Lives of the Founders, Builders, and Defenders of the Republic, . . . ,* Volume VIII (New York: James T. White & Company, 1900), 320-21.
  "After leaving school at seventeen, he taught two terms, and then became a student in the office of his uncle, Judge Ephraim Paddock, of St. Johnsbury, Vt." (p. 320)
  "Thaddeus was the inventor of the firm, while Erastus managed its finances." (p. 321)
[522] The "Fairbanks Papers" web page says Erastus left Brimfield, Mass. in 1811 and "operated a store in Barnet, Vermont." See "Fairbanks Papers: 1815-1889, Doc 1-5, Doc 95," Vermont Historical Society Library:
http://www.vermonthistory.org/arccat/findaid/fairbank.htm ; accessed via the Internet on October 30, 2007.

company was finally organized in 1846. He held that position until 1854."[523]

1836, 1837, and 1838: State Legislator representing St. Johnsbury

1842: "With his brothers he founded the St. Johnsbury Academy"[524]

1847: Erastus, Thaddeus, and Joseph Fairbanks supervised the construction of a new building for North Congregational Church, St. Johnsbury.[525]

1848 (approx.): President of Passumpsic Railroad from White River to St. J.

1852-1853: Elected Governor of Vermont (22nd gov. of VT)

1860-1861: Re-elected Governor of Vermont (27th gov. of VT)

[_____: "For many years he was president of the Vermont Domestic Missionary Board, and a member of the American Board of Commissioners for Foreign Missions."[526]

[1814-1864 (approx.): "fifty years active in the Congregational church"]

["From earliest manhood Gov. Fairbanks was a devoted, active, public-Spirited, christian [sic] man. He was for fifty years a pillar in the home church, Congregational; and

---

[523] "Fairbanks Papers": http://www.vermonthistory.org/arccat/findaid/fairbank.htm ; accessed 10/30/07.

[524] "With his brothers he founded the St. Johnsbury Academy; and his generous endowments still assist in maintaining the Athenaeum, Museum of Natural Science, and the North Congregational Church, St. Johnsbury." *The National Cyclopaedia*, 321

[525] "North Congregational Church, St. Johnsbury, Vermont": http://www.ourkingdom.com/our_region/religion/north_congregationial_church_st_johnsbury/index.php?id=2 ; accessed via the Internet on 10/30/07.

[526] *The National Cyclopaedia*, 321. "The American Board of Commissioners for Foreign Missions" may be the same organization as the "American Board of Foreign Missions." See "Fairbanks Papers": http://www.vermonthistory.org/arccat/findaid/fairbank.htm; accessed via the Internet on 10/30/07. This same source as states that Erastus was "active in the temperance movement."

in later life a member and officer of many benevolent boards, which he supported by liberal contributions of money, time and personal service."[527]

Children (9)[528]: Jane, George, Horace, Charles, Julia, Franklin, Sarah, Emily, Ellen

Jane Fairbanks (1816-1852)[529] and Ephraim Jewitt (____-1865)[530]

Parents: (Deacon) Erastus Fairbanks and Lois Crosman

Born: December 3, 1816, in St. Johnsbury, Caledonia, Vermont

Married: to Ephraim Jewett on January 26, 1837
Ephraim Jewett died on November 19, 1865

Died: March 29, 1852

Children: Edward Adams Jewett, Hibbard Jewett, Henry E. Jewett

Edward Adams Jewett (Born: July 18, 1838-____)[531]

---

[527] Fairbanks, *Genealogy of the Fairbanks Family*, 329.

[528] Erastus had eight children according to this source: "Governor's Information," National Governors Association: http://www.nga.org/portal/site/nga/menuitem.29fab9fb4add37305ddcbeeb501010a0/?vgnextoid=c68348c188cc6010VgnVCM1000001a01010aRCRD&vgnextchannel=e449a0ca9e3f1010VgnVCM1000001a01010aRCRD ; accessed: October 30, 2007. The "Fairbanks Papers" states that Erastus and Lois had nine (9) children: "Fairbanks Papers": http://www.vermonthistory.org/arccat/findaid/fairbank.htm: Accessed via the Internet on 10/30/07. Lorenzo Sayles Fairbanks identifies nine children: Fairbanks, *Genealogy of the Fairbanks Family*, 330.

[529] Fairbanks, *Genealogy of the Fairbanks Family*, 330. Locke states: "From an obituary notice, I subjoin the following:--'Distinguished alike for the purity, the simplicity and consistency of her Christian and social character; for her cheerful and active piety; for the lively interest she manifested in the welfare of others; and for the many nameless deeds of friendship which constitute an enduring monument to her praise.'" John Goodwin Locke, *Book of the Lockes: A Genealogical and Historical Record of the Descendants of William Locke, of Woburn, with an Appendix, Containing a History of the Lockes in England, also of the Family of John Locke, of Hampton, N. H., and Kindred Families and Individuals* (Boston: James Monroe and Company, 1853), 271-72.

[530] "[As of 1853,] Mr. Jewett is a merchant and postmaster of St. Johnsbury." Locke, *Book of the Lockes*, 272.

[531] Fairbanks, *Genealogy of the Fairbanks Family*, 330.

Hibbard Jewett (1840-1844)[532]
Born: July 19, 1840
Died: April 16, 1844

Henry Erastus Jewett[533]
Born: April 9, 1842
Married: to ____ on May 31, 1876
Children (4):
Occupation: Clergyman, Vacaville, Cal.

George Fairbanks (1819-1843)[534]
Parents: Erastus Fairbanks and Lois Crosman
Born: on January 21, 1819, in St. Johnsbury
Died: April 20, 1843 [or 1842?]

Horace Fairbanks, Gov. (1820-1888)[535] and Mary E. Taylor (1824-____)
Parents: Erastus Fairbanks and Lois Crosman
Born: on March 21, 1820, in Barnet, Vt.
Married: to Mary E. Taylor on August 9, 1849, in Derry, N. H.
Parents: James and Persis (Hemphill) Taylor
Born: on March 2, 1824, in Derry, N. H.
"Received an excellent academic education in the County Schools and Phillips Andover Academy"
Age 20: "became confidential clerk of E. & T. Fairbanks & Co."
"[S]oon admitted to partnership, and for 48 years held most important responsibilities in that firm, being more than half this period its President."
"[a] chief promoter of the Railway line from Portland to Ogdensburg via the White Mountain Notch, and President of the Vermont division."

---

[532] Fairbanks, *Genealogy of the Fairbanks Family*, 330.
[533] Fairbanks, *Genealogy of the Fairbanks Family*, 330.
[534] Fairbanks, *Genealogy of the Fairbanks Family*, 330.
[535] Fairbanks, *Genealogy of the Fairbanks Family*, 330, 562.

1871: Presented to the Town of St. Johnsbury the "Institution endowed and incorporated under the name of The St. Johnsbury Athenaeum."
1876-1878: Governor of Vermont
"He was large and noble in his liberality, a most loyal and lovable Christian, . . ."
Died: on March 17, 1888, in New York

Children: Helen Taylor Fairbanks, Agnes Fairbanks, Isabel Fairbanks
    Helen Taylor Fairbanks (1854-1864)[536]
        Parents: Horace Fairbanks and Mary E. Taylor
        Born: on December 17, 1854
        Died: on March 18, 1864
    Agnes Fairbanks (1860-____)[537] & Ashton R. Willard
        Parents: Horace Fairbanks and Mary E. Taylor
        Born: on August 12, 1860
        Married: to Ashton R. Willard on Sept. 19, 1888
        Resides (as of 1897) in Boston
        Children: Isabel Fairbanks and Theodora
        Isabel Fairbanks Willard (1893-1894)
            Born: on October 3, 1893
            Died: on July 20, 1894
    Theodora Willard (1897-____)
        Born: on March 26, 1897
    Isabel Fairbanks (1861-1891)[538] & Albert L. Farwell
        Parents: Horace Fairbanks and Mary E. Taylor
        Born: on November 6, 1861

---

[536] Fairbanks, *Genealogy of the Fairbanks Family*, 563.
[537] Fairbanks, *Genealogy of the Fairbanks Family*, 563.
[538] Fairbanks, *Genealogy of the Fairbanks Family*, 563.

Married: to Albert L. Farwell, of
St. Johnsbury, September,
1889
Died: on July 2, 1891

Charles Fairbanks (1821-1898)[539]
Parents: Erastus Fairbanks and Lois Crosman
Born: December 8, 1821, Barnet, Vt.
"Fitted for college at Phillips Academy, Andover, Mass., but owing to ill health did not pursue his school studies further."

Julia Fairbanks (1824-1884)[540] and John H. Paddock (____-____)
Parents: Erastus Fairbanks and Lois Crosman
Born: June 9, 1824
Married: on February 11, 1857, to John H. Paddock
Died: June 10, 1884
Children: None

Franklin Fairbanks, Col. (1828-1895)[541] and Frances A. Clapp (1831-____)
Parents: Erastus Fairbanks and Lois Crosman
Born: on June 18, 1828, in St. Johnsbury, Vermont
Married: to Frances A. Clapp on December 8, 1852
Parents: Rev. Sumner G. Clapp and Pamelia (Strong) Clapp, of St. Johnsbury
Born: on November 2, 1831, in Enfield, Mass.
Died: on April 24, 1895
At age 17, he began his connection with the scale business; For many years superintendent of the Corporation of E. & T. Fairbanks & Co., and after the death of his brother Horace in 1888, he succeeded to the presidency
1858: A member of the staff of Governor Hall
1860: A member of the staff of Gov. Erastus Fairbanks
1871-73: Represented St. Johnsbury in the State Legislature
1877: He received the honorary degree of A. M., from Dartmouth
1891: His collections were "shrined" in a building which was incorporated and presented to the town of St. Johnsbury

---

[539] Fairbanks, *Genealogy of the Fairbanks Family*, 330.
[540] Fairbanks, *Genealogy of the Fairbanks Family*, 330.
[541] Fairbanks, *Genealogy of the Fairbanks Family*, 330, 564 (especially).

under the designation of the Museum of Natural Science.[542]

"For more than 30 years he was superintendent of the North Church Sunday School, also for a long time a member of the International S. S. Lesson Committee. In these and other services to the interests of religion and of missions he worked with zeal, and added to the permanent influence of a useful Christian life."[543]

Children (4): Alfred, Mary Florence, Margaret, & Ellen Henrietta

Alfred Fairbanks[544]:
    Born: December 8, 1857
    Died: December 9, 1857

Mary Florence Fairbanks (1859-____)[545] & J. T. Herrick (____-____)
    Born: on July 26, 1859
    Married: to Dr. J. T. Herrick, of Springfield, Mass., on Sept. 8, 1886
    Child: Paul F. Herrick, Born July 19, 1887

Margaret Fairbanks (1862-1863)[546]
    Born: on July 29, 1862
    Died: on August 26, 1863

Ellen Henrietta Fairbanks (1872-____)[547] & Frank Hilliard Brooks (1868-____)
    Born: on August 18, 1872
    Married: to Frank H. Brooks, of St. Johnsbury, on January 29, 1896[548]

---

[542] Fairbanks, *Genealogy of the Fairbanks Family*, 565.
[543] Fairbanks, *Genealogy of the Fairbanks Family*, 565.
[544] Fairbanks, *Genealogy of the Fairbanks Family*, 565.
[545] Fairbanks, *Genealogy of the Fairbanks Family*, 565.
[546] Fairbanks, *Genealogy of the Fairbanks Family*, 565.
[547] Fairbanks, *Genealogy of the Fairbanks Family*, 565.
[548] According to *Who's Who in New England*, Frank Hilliard Brooks and Ellen H. Fairbanks were married on January 29, 1897. See Albert Nelson Marquis, ed., *Who's Who in New England: A Biographical Dictionary of Leading Living Men and Women of the States of Maine, New Hampshire, Vermont, Massachusetts, Rhode Island and Connecticut*, 2d ed. (Chicago: A. N. Marquis & Company, 1916), 163. Marquis also states concerning Mr. Brooks: "Identified with E. & T. Fairbanks & Co., 1886--; began as bookkeeper, dir., 1897, chmn. Exec. Com. of bd., 1910, pres., May, 1912--. . . . dir. 1st Nat. Bank, St. Johnsbury. Apptd., 1913, by Gov. Fletcher, mem. Bd. of Commrs. to investigate ednl. System of Vt.; also mem. of State Bd. of

Sarah Fairbanks (1831-1909)[549] & Charles Marshall Stone (1833-1890)
- Parents: Erastus Fairbanks and Lois Crosman
- Born: on June 30, 1831, in St. Johnsbury
- Married: On May 4, 1858, to Charles M. Stone, of Lyndon, Vt.[550]
- Died: March 11, 1909
- Children (4): Mary E., Arthur Fairbanks, Philip H. and Emily Louise
  - Mary E. Stone (Born: March 16, 1859-____)[551]
  - Arthur Fairbanks Stone (1870-1944)[552]
    - Born: March 1, 1870
    - Married: to Helen Lincoln on Jan. 1, 1890
    - Wrote: *North Congregational Church, St. Johnsbury, Vermont: 1825-1942*
    - Died: 1944
    - Children: 3
  - Philip H. Stone (Born: May 2, 1872-____)[553]
    - Born: May 2, 1872
    - Married: to Adeline M. Anderson, on January 8, 1896
  - Emily Louise Stone (1873-1895)[554]
    - Born: November 16, 1873
    - Died: August 1, 1895

Emily Fairbanks (1833-____) & Constans L. Goodell (1830-1886)[555]
- Parents: Erastus Fairbanks and
- Born: on March 4, 1833, in St. Johnsbury, Vt.[556]

Edn. Trustee St. Johnsbury Athenaeum, St. Johnsbury Acad., Vt. State Y.M.C.A., . . . Conglist. Clubs: Commercial, Sphinx."
[549] Fairbanks, *Genealogy of the Fairbanks Family*, 330.
[550] "Fairbanks and Keester": http://www.familyorigins.com/users/k/e/e/Louis-J-Keester/FAMO1-0001/d184.htm#P7470 ; accessed via the Internet on 10/30/07.
[551] Fairbanks, *Genealogy of the Fairbanks Family*, 330.
[552] Fairbanks, *Genealogy of the Fairbanks Family*, 330.
[553] Fairbanks, *Genealogy of the Fairbanks Family*, 330.
[554] Fairbanks, *Genealogy of the Fairbanks Family*, 330.
[555] Fairbanks, *Genealogy of the Fairbanks Family*, 331: "He was one of the most prominent of Congregational clergymen; a leader in educational and mission work, and in the National Council."
[556] "Fairbanks and Keester": http://www.familyorigins.com/users/k/e/e/Louis-J-Keester/FAMO1-0001/d134.htm ; accessed via the Internet on 10/30/07.

  Married: to Rev. Constans L. Goodell, D. D., on May 5,
   1859
  Parents: Aaron and Elvira (Bancroft) Goodell
  Born: March 16, 1830, in Calais, Vt.
  Attended: Bakersfield Academy
  1855: Graduated: University of Vermont
  1858: Graduated: Andover Theological
   Seminary
  1859: Ordained & Pastor: South Church, New
   Britain
  1872-1886: Pastor, Pilgrim Congregational
   Church, St. Louis, Mo.
  Died: on February 1, 1886
  Children (2): Oliver Fairbanks and Laura Oliver
   Fairbanks Goodell (Born: April 20, 1865)
    Laura Goodell (1869-____) & Frank H. Heald
    Born: April 1869
    Married: to Frank H. Heald
 Ellen Fairbanks (July 27, 1836-May 28, 1843)[557]
  Parents: Erastus Fairbanks and Lois Crosman
Thaddeus Fairbanks (1796-1886) & Lucy Peck Barker (1799-1866)
 [(Gen.) VII][558]
 Born: on January 17, 1796, in Brimfield, Mass.
 Moved: to St. Johnsbury with his father in 1815
 Married: to Lucy Peck Barker, a native of St. Johnsbury, on
  January 17, 1820.
  Lucy's parents: Barnabas Barker and Ruth Peck
  Born: on April 29, 1799
  Married: to Thaddeus Fairbanks
   "[Lucy's] father, Barnabas, came with his
   father, John, and the first settlers of the town,
   and in 1791 brought his bride, Ruth Peck, from
   Rehoboth, Mass., on a pillion behind him."[559]

---

[557] [Charles McEwen Hyde,] *Historical Celebration of the Town of Brimfield, Hampden County, Mass.; Wednesday, October 11, 1876, with the Historical Address of Rev. Charles M. Hyde, D. D., and Other Addresses, Letters, Documents, etc., Relating to the Early History of the Town* (Springfield, Mass.: The Clark W. Bryan Company, Printers, 1879), 191.
[558] Fairbanks, *Genealogy of the Fairbanks Family*, 331.
[559] Fairbanks, *Genealogy of the Fairbanks Family*, 333.

Died: on December 29, 1866, in St. Johnsbury
Died: April 12, 1886, in St. Johnsbury, Vt.
1823: Established a small iron foundry[560]
____: Joined by brother Erastus . . . under name of E. & T. Fairbanks.
1830: Patented a design for a platform scale[561]
1833: Erastus, Thaddeus, and their brother Joseph "formed E. and T. Fairbanks and Company to manufacture and sell the scales."[562]
1842: Established, with his brothers, the St. Johnsbury Academy.
["His [Thaddeus's] lack of early educational advantages was keenly felt by him, and he did what he could for others, aiding scores of students to go through college, and, in 1842, with his brothers establishing the St. Johnsbury Academy, of which for twenty years he alone assumed the support, and then contributed largely to its endowment, devoting some $200,000 to this institution alone. He also gave a Professorship to Middlebury College, and his contributions to missionary objects, and to many western colleges, amounted to many thousands every year."[563]
["Mr. Fairbanks reflected his Puritan ancestry in his character and tastes; pure, upright and conscientious, and, though exceedingly taciturn, an attractive, impressive man. A man of Christian faith, of spiritual insight and force, and of fine native gifts, . . ."[564]
Children:
Henry Fairbanks, Rev. (1830-____)[565] [(Gen.) VIII][566] & Annie S. Noyes (1845-1872)

---

[560] "Fairbanks Papers": http://www.vermonthistory.org/arccat/findaid/fairbank.htm; accessed 10/30/07.
[561] "Fairbanks Papers": http://www.vermonthistory.org/arccat/findaid/fairbank.htm ; accessed 10/30/07.
[562] "Fairbanks Papers": http://www.vermonthistory.org/arccat/findaid/fairbank.htm ; accessed 10/30/07.
[563] Fairbanks, *Genealogy of the Fairbanks Family*, 333.
[564] Fairbanks, *Genealogy of the Fairbanks Family*, 333.
[565] Fairbanks, *Genealogy of the Fairbanks Family*, 333. See also: John Howard Brown, ed., *The Cyclopaedia of American Biographies. Comprising the Men and Women of the United States Who Have Been Identified with the Growth of the*

Parents: Thaddeus and Lucy (Barker) Fairbanks
Born: on May 6, 1830, in St. Johnsbury
Married: to Annie S. Noyes in 1862 in Hanover, N. H.
> Father: Rev. Daniel James Noyes, D. D., professor of intellectual philosophy and political economy at Dartmouth College, Hanover, N. H.
> Mother: Jane M. (Aiken) Noyes
> Born: on June 14, 1845, in Concord, N. H.[567]
> Died: on September 11, 1872, in St. Johnsbury
Remarried: to Ruthy Page of Newport, Vt., on May 5, 1874, in St. Johnsbury[568]
> Parents: Phineas and Jacintha (Barker) Page
> Born: on July 14, 1852, in Newport, Vt.
1842: Henry's father (Thaddeus) and his uncles (Erastus & Joseph) established the St. Johnsbury Academy
1847: Graduated from St. Johnsbury Academy
1853: Graduated from Dartmouth
1856: Received degree of A.M. from Dartmouth
1857: Graduated from Andover Theological Seminary
1857-59: "He was a home missionary and conductor of vacation labors of theological students"[569]

Nation. In Seven Volumes. Vol. III: Ericsson-Hempstead. (Boston, Mass.: James H. Lamb, 1900), 30
[566] Fairbanks, *Genealogy of the Fairbanks Family*, 565.
[567] Fairbanks, *Genealogy of the Fairbanks Family*, 567.
[568] Fairbanks, *Genealogy of the Fairbanks Family*, 567.
[569] Brown, *The Cyclopaedia of American Biographies*, 30. Lorenzo Sayles Fairbanks states on this point: "He then took up work under the auspices of the Missionary Society, in behalf of the weakest churches in Vermont, and, visiting them, studied their individual needs, so that, having wide acquaintance with theological students, he was able to arrange summer vacation supplies for nearly forty, during three years, a work that resulted in bringing new life to many churches that were nearly extinct,

1858: Ordained when in the missionary service

1859-65: Professor of natural philosophy at Dartmouth

1865-68: Professor of natural history at Dartmouth

1868: "He returned to St. Johnsbury and devoted his time to perfecting various inventions and to local religious work as his health permitted. He led the evangelistic work of the YMCA of the state, was president of the State missionary society, president of St. Johnsbury Academy [for many years], a trustee of Dartmouth college from 1870, and a member of the International Congregational council, London, England, 1891. He was also elected vice-president of the E. & T. Fairbanks & Co. corporation."[570]

1880: Received degree of Ph.D. from Dartmouth.[571]

---

and in giving a permanent ministry to more than twenty." Fairbanks, *Genealogy of the Fairbanks Family*, 566.

[570] Brown, *The Cyclopaedia of American Biographies*, 30, 31. Lorenzo Sayles Fairbanks states: ". . . [A]fter his mother's death, he removed to St. Johnsbury with his family, joining his father." Fairbanks, *Genealogy of the Fairbanks Family*, 566.

Fairbanks continues by saying that Henry was "preaching wherever there was no other supply, and doing what he could for the general religious work of the denomination. He was the first President, under its new constitution, of the Convention of Congregational Ministers and Churches of Vt. and more recently and until now [i.e., 1897] President of the Vt. Domestic Missionary Society, to the work of which he devotes a good deal of time. For some years after 1875 the State Convention of the Y.M.C.A. carried on an effective evangelistic work in a large number of towns in Vermont, witnessing most marked religious revivals, with large additions to the churches, and Mr. Fairbanks was prominent in this work, after the first year having charge, and directing it as Secretary. He has for twenty years been a corporate member of the American Board (Foreign Missions), has been a member of four of the National Councils of Congregational Churches, and was a delegate to the International Council in London in 1891, . . ." Fairbanks, *Genealogy of the Fairbanks Family*, 566.

[571] Lorenzo Sayles Fairbanks states that Henry "twenty years later [i.e., 20 years after 1858 (= 1878?)] received the honorary degree of Doctor of Philosophy." Fairbanks, *Genealogy of the Fairbanks Family*, 567.

Children, first marriage [to Annie S. (Noyes) Fairbanks]:

Arthur Fairbanks, Rev. (1864-____)[572]
- Parents: Henry & Annie S. (Noyes) Fairbanks
- Born: on Nov. 13, 1864, at Hanover, N.H.
- Married: to Elizabeth Leland, May 2, 1889
  - Her parents: Andrew & Sarah (Lord) Moody
- 1882: Graduated from St. Johnsbury Acad.
- 1886: Graduated from Dartmouth college
- 1886-87: Tutor, later assistant professor, of German at Dartmouth
- 1889: Studied at the University of Berlin
- 1890: Ph.D. from the University of Freiburg
- 1894-98: Instructor, comparative religion, Yale [professor at Yale divinity School]
- 1899: Acting assistant professor of Greek philosophy at Cornell university

Robert Noyes Fairbanks (1866-____)
- Born: on November 19, 1866
- "Became connected with the New York office of the Fairbanks works."[573]

Lucy Fairbanks (1868-____)[574]
- Born: on October 15, 1868 [as of 1897]: "Is in Evangelistic work near St. Johnsbury"

---

[572] Brown, *The Cyclopaedia of American Biographies*, 29.
[573] Brown, *The Cyclopaedia of American Biographies*, 31.
[574] Fairbanks, *Genealogy of the Fairbanks Family*, 567.

Charlotte Fairbanks (1871-____)[575]
    Born: on December 11, 1871
    "She studied Chemistry and received the degree of Ph. D.; recently [as of 1897] appointed Assistant at Wellesley College"
Children, second marriage [to Ruthy Page Fairbanks]:
Albert Thaddeus Fairbanks (1876-1891)
    Born: on July 3, 1876
    Died: on December 16, 1891
Marion Fairbanks (1881-____)
    Born: on April 27, 1881
Dorothy Fairbanks (1887-____)
    Born: on March 9, 1887
Ruth Comfort Fairbanks (1892-1893)
    Born: on May 28, 1892
    Died: on September 16, 1893

Charlotte Fairbanks (1837-1869) & George N. Webber (1826-)
Parents: Thaddeus Fairbanks and Lucy Peck Barker[576]
Born: on June 1, 1837, in St. Johnsbury
Married: to Rev. George N. Webber, D. D.[577], on May 4, 1858
    Born: on August 27, 1826, in Woodstock, Conn.
    Married: to Charlotte Fairbanks
    Occupation: Pastor, St. Johnsbury, Vt.; Hartford, Conn.; and Lowell, Mass.; and Professor in Middlebury College, Vt.

---

[575] Fairbanks, *Genealogy of the Fairbanks Family*, 567.
[576] "Fairbanks and Keester" : http://www.familyorigins.com/users/k/e/e/Louis-J-Keester/FAMO1-0001/d123.htm#P7495 ; accessed 11/11/07.
[577] Fairbanks, *Genealogy of the Fairbanks Family*, 333.

Living in Northampton, Mass., as of 1897
Died: on March 29, 1869, in Middlebury, Vt.
Children (4): Agnes Fairbanks, Annie, Frederic Fairbanks, Lucy

Agnes Fairbanks Webber (1860-1863)[578]
Born: on October 7, 1860, in Hartford, Conn.
Died: on February 6, 1863, in Hartford, Conn.

Annie Webber (1863-____)[579] & Walter Maxwell
Born: July 30, 1863, in St. Johnsbury
Married: to Prof. Walter Maxwell, on August 19, 1889. {"Now [1897] of Honolulu, H. I."}
Children:
Max Maxwell
Clyde Maxwell

---

[578] Fairbanks, *Genealogy of the Fairbanks Family*, 333.
[579] Fairbanks, *Genealogy of the Fairbanks Family*, 333.

Frederic Fairbanks Webber (1865-____)[580] & Gertrude Hyde
- Born: on June 5, 1865, in Lowell, Mass.
- Married: to Gertrude Hyde
- Resides (1897): in St. Louis, Mo.

Lucy Webber (1867-____)[581] & William Northrup McMillan
- Born: on June 26, 1867, in St. Johnsbury
- Married: to William Northrup McMillan on May 12, 1894
- Resides (1897): in St. Louis, Mo.

Joseph Paddock Fairbanks (1806-1855) [(Gen.) VII][582] & Almira Taylor (1811-1883)
- Parents: Joseph Fairbanks and Phebe Paddock
- Born: on November 26, 1806, in Brimfield, Hampden, Massachusetts
- Occupation: Lawyer; then joined E. and T. Fairbanks and Co. in 1833
- Married: to Almira Taylor on June 12, 1835, in Derry, Rockingham, New Hampshire
- Died: on May 15, 1855, in St. Johnsbury, Caledonia, Vermont
- 1833: Was in partnership with [his brothers] in the scale manufacturing business 22 years to the time of his death
- ("He . . . was deeply religious and unsparing in his efforts for the good of men.")[583]

---

[580] Fairbanks, *Genealogy of the Fairbanks Family*, 334.
[581] Fairbanks, *Genealogy of the Fairbanks Family*, 334.
[582] Fairbanks, *Genealogy of the Fairbanks Family*, 334.
[583] Fairbanks, *Genealogy of the Fairbanks Family*, 334.

("He was influential in the Legislature, especially in securing the Passage of the Prohibitory Law and acts to improve the school system.")

["He sent out hundreds of pages of letters and press articles on almost every theme of current importance, such as . . . religious and political issues, the Sabbath, . . . temperance, education, missions, benevolence; . . ."[584]]

[". . . he was a leader in the founding of St. Johnsbury Academy." (p. 334)]

["He was aboundingly [end of page 334] and modestly benevolent, Distributing multitudes of gifts anonymously . . . ; his purse was open freely to every worthy cause; the larger part of his property was bequeathed to benevolent objects, religious and educational."[585]

Children (2)[586]: Edward Taylor Fairbanks and William Paddock Fairbanks

    Edward Taylor Fairbanks (1836-after 1897) & Emma Cornelia Taplin (1844-____)

        Parents: Joseph Paddock Fairbanks and Almira Taylor

        Born: May 12, 1836, in St. Johnsbury

        Educated at St. Johnsbury Academy and Phillips Andover Academy, Mass.[587]

        Educated at Yale College (class of 1859)

        Educated (also) at Andover Theological Seminary

        Married: to Emma Cornelia Taplin, on July 9, 1862, in Derry, New Hampshire, daughter of Guy C. and Sally M. Taplin, of Montpelier

        Ordained: Jan. 1, 1868, as pastor of the First Congregational Church of St. Johnsbury Center

---

[584] Fairbanks, *Genealogy of the Fairbanks Family*, 334.
[585] Fairbanks, *Genealogy of the Fairbanks Family*, 334-35.
[586] "Fairbanks and Keester" : http://www.familyorigins.com/users/k/e/e/Louis-J-Keester/FAMO1-0001/d159.htm#P3379 ; accessed 11/08/07.
[587] Hiram Carleton, comp. and ed., *Genealogical and Family History of the State of Vermont*, Vol. 1 ( ), 118

Pastor: From Jan. 30, 1874, to July 15, 1902, of the South Congregational church of St. Johnsbury[588]

Wrote the history of St. Johnsbury

["He has a responsible part in the management of the St. Johnsbury Academy, the Athenaeum and the Museum, and is foremost in all movements looking toward the welfare of his native town."[589]]

Connected with many educational and religious organizations

Child: One Cornelia Taylor Fairbanks (1876-____)

Born: on June 25, 1876, in St. Johnsbury

William Paddock Fairbanks (1840-1895) [(Generation VIII] and Rebecca Pike (1841-____)[590]

Parents: Joseph Paddock Fairbanks and Almira Taylor

Born: on July 27, 1840, in St. Johnsbury, Vermont

Married: to Rebecca Pike on April 18, 1861, in St. Johnsbury

Resided: in St. Johnsbury before 1888

Resided: in Mount Vernon, Westchester, NY, after 1888

Graduated from St. Johnsbury Academy

(Entered Dartmouth in 1858, but left to engage in business

[____ "He spent some years in the office of E. & T. Fairbanks & Company, was admitted to partnership and on the incorporation of the company in 1874 he was appointed secretary & treasurer."[591]

---

[588] Carleton, *Genealogical and Family History*, 118.
[589] Carleton, *Genealogical and Family History*, 118.
[590] "Fairbanks and Keester" : http://www.familyorigins.com/users/k/e/e/Louis-J-Keester/FAMO1-0001/d192.htm#P7511 ; accessed 11/08/07
[591] Carleton, *Genealogical and Family History*, 118.

(Also secretary and treasurer for the St. Johnsbury and Lake Champlain Railroad Company)
(While in Michigan, he was a member of Governor Pingree's staff
(Represented St. Johnsbury in the Legislature 1884-1886
(In 1888 he went to New York as secretary of the Fairbanks Company of the city, where he remained until his death.
("He was . . . benevolent and generous.")
Children (3): Almira Taylor, Mabel, Joseph

Almira Taylor Fairbanks (1865-____) & Herbert W. Blodgett ( )
    Born: February 12, 1865
    Married: to Herbert W. Blodgett of St. J. on Jan. 17, 1888
Donald F. Blodgett
    Born: June 6, 1895
Mabel Fairbanks (1871-____) & Birney A. Robinson ( )
[(Generation) IX]
    Born: August 14, 1871, at St. Johnsbury, Vermont
    Married: to Birney A. Robinson of Westford, VT, on October 23, 1895
Joseph (1881-)
    Born: December 12, 1881

"Your Heavenly Father will never let you down!"
Alcoholics Anonymous, 4th ed., p. 181

9
The Town of St. Johnsbury of Dr. Bob's Youth

For the visitors to the Town of St Johnsbury, and to 297 Summer Street in particular (where Dr. Bob was born and raised), our core resource binders contain plenty of information on the history of St. Johnsbury. Plenty of town maps. Plenty of information on excellent walks that one can take in St. Johnsbury to see the historic buildings, find the historical data, and chat with the appropriate stewards of the relevant archives at places such as North Congregational Church, St. Johnsbury, the Fairbanks Museum and Planetarium, the St. Johnsbury Athenaeum, and the St. Johnsbury Academy.

For our purposes, the reason for providing information about the Town of St. Johnsbury is to enable the visitor to learn for himself or herself the facts about: (1) Dr. Bob's youth; (2) the godly Christian leaders of the community; and (3) the host of different influences that poured out inspiration for the town's conversions, prayer gatherings, Bible studies, worship services, church attendance, chapel observances, Christian youth activities, revivals, and excellent Christian education at St. Johnsbury Academy. This information will start visitors on a possible quest to see how much the A.A. of Akron (founded in 1935) resembles the situation at the time of Dr. Bob's youth in the critical period of 1875 to 1898.

The St. Johnsbury buildings, then, are impressive, pretentious, and attractive; but they don't produce a new birth, the abundant life, or the fellowship, witness, prayer, and outreach that are part of real fellowship with the Father and with his Son. Nonetheless, individually and as a group, they harbor treasures of evidence showing what was available in Dr. Bob's youth.

A short walk from 297 Summer Street down one block to Main Street will show you just how available the Christian resources actually were in Dr. Bob's younger years.

Reaching Main Street, in the block below, turn left. Walk to the huge North Congregational Church, St. Johnsbury. It was founded by Fairbanks family members, constructed by Fairbanks brothers, funded out of the Erastus Fairbanks Estate, and frequented by generations of this dedicated Christian lineage of Congregational benefactors. The church bespeaks that Fairbanks family's love of the Creator, of his Son Jesus Christ as their Lord and Savior, of his Word (the Bible), and for all a church can offer to those who wish to share the love and fellowship. Even more important, the church today has a pastor and an archives committee. They are gracious and very helpful. There are church records which memorialize the activities of the church leaders—Fairbanks people, members of the Smith family, and Dr. Bob as the student. There is plenty still to be learned there about the pastors, the services, the prayer and Bible study activities, the committees, the revivals and evangelization meetings, the Sunday School agenda and classes, and the Christian Endeavor Society of that particular church. The church histories, archives, and other records depict a fervor of revival that characterized the 1880's and 1890's of Dr. Bob's youth. Our resource binders and historical books constitute the Dr. Bob Core Library located at North Congregational Church.

Walk across the street from North Congregational Church, St. Johnsbury, to which the Smith family belonged. Go into the Fairbanks Museum and Planetarium. Again the mark of Fairbanks benevolence and concern for others is evident. The Museum is large, beautiful, and filled with archival data along with the other collections and artifacts to be found there. The Museum contains historical records, bibliographies, and data about the community, the Fairbanks family, and even Dr. Robert Holbrook Smith. Including the *A.A. Grapevine*'s Memorial Issue issued at the time of Dr. Bob's death.

Move out on Main Street to the Town of St. Johnsbury building which contains offices of the fire department, of vital statistics, and of public officials. That's where we located and secured a certified copy of the birth certificate for Robert Holbrook Smith (Dr. Bob). And genealogy researchers know how much information can be obtained from public records and helpful public officials. They are nearby and easily contacted.

Just steps away is the St. Johnsbury Athenaeum. This enormous, ornate, period, architectural structure matches other buildings donated by the Fairbanks people [including North Congregational Church, the Fairbanks Museum and Planetarium, the YMCA building (destroyed by fire in 1984), and structures at St. Johnsbury Academy]. It also epitomizes the selfless benevolences of the Fairbanks family. It was donated to the Town of St. Johnsbury. The library within was itself, in large part, donated by the Fairbanks people. It is there that you can find all sorts of biographies, histories, and accounts of activities going on at the time of Dr. Bob's youth. A Fairbanks family member was long-time librarian at the facility. Today, there's a copy machine, a reference desk, ample catalog cards, and a staff to help with searches.

Across the street is the imposing court house building where Judge Smith officiated at the Caledonia County Probate Court. Next is the South Congregational Church which also included Fairbanks people in its midst and pulpit.

Finally, there is St. Johnsbury Academy, consisting of many buildings. It was founded by the Fairbanks brothers. One Fairbanks was President of the trustees. Others were trustees. One was Principal (headmaster) for many years. He often delivered sermons at graduations and other events. There was daily chapel, and the St. Johnsbury Academy heritage was Congregationalist to the core. Even the deeds granting the property contained religious requirements as to the administration of the school. There is a first-rate archivist who provided us with all kinds of records and data about St. Johnsbury Academy; Judge Smith; the substantial involvement of his wife as a graduate, teacher, speaker, and executive with the alumni association; and Robert Holbrook Smith himself—pictures of him as a student, a picture of his graduating class of 1898 (taken on the steps of North Congregational Church, St. Johnsbury), class notes, his membership in and management of the Glee Club, his membership in the literary society, and the curriculum in which he received his educational and some Christian training.

Unlike many other places of historical interest to AAs and recovery people, St. Johnsbury offers convenience at every turn. Good restaurants, fine hotel-motel accommodations, proximity of the historical locations, and lots of research resources.

In the latter realm, the following are available as to research tools. The following bibliographic list is based in part on information generously provided to the authors by the St. Johnsbury Academy Archivist and also includes other resource materials gathered and used by the authors and which will prove useful for the visitor:

Bibliography of books and materials in the St. Johnsbury area that pertain to the provenance of the up-bringing of Dr. Robert H. Smith, who graduated from St. Johnsbury Academy in 1898.

Books:

Balch, F., comp. A. *A Collection of Views in and around St. Johnsbury, Vermont.* St. Johnsbury, VT: Caledonian Press, 1900.

Beck, Richard, and Bradley F. Ashley. *A Proud Tradition, A Bright Future: A Sesquicentennial History of St. Johnsbury Academy.* St. Johnsbury, VT.: St. Johnsbury Academy, 1992.

Fairbanks, Edward T., and Daughters of the American Revolution. *The Town of St. Johnsbury, VT: A Review of One Hundred Twenty-Five Years to the Anniversary Pageant 1912.* St. Johnsbury, VT: The Cowles press, 1914.

Johnson, Claire D. *"I See by the Paper--": An Informal History of St. Johnsbury.* St. Johnsbury, VT: Cowles Press, 1987.

Johnson, Claire D. *"I See by the Paper—1920 to 1960": an Informal History of St. Johnsbury.* St. Johnsbury, VT: Cowles Press 1987.

Johnson, Claire D. *St. Johnsbury.* Dover, NH: Arcadia, 1996.

Russell, Charles E. *Bare Hands and Stone Walls: Some Recollections of a Side-Line Reformer.* New York: Charles Scribner's Sons, 1943.

Stone, Arthur F. *St. Johnsbury Illustrated: A Review of the Town's Business, Social, Literary, and Educational Facilities, with Glimpses of Picturesque Surroundings.* St. Johnsbury, VT: C. M. Stone & Company, 1891.

Yale, Allen R. *Ingenious & Enterprising Mechanics: A Case Study of Industrialization in Rural Vermont 1815-1900.* Ann Arbor, MI: UMI Dissertation Services, 1995.

ARCHIVAL MATERIAL:

Guide to Student Publications 1875 to Present. The Student newspaper. Student Publications. St. Johnsbury Academy Archives.
Guide to the Photograph Collection 1870 to Present. St. Johnsbury Academy Photographs. St. Johnsbury Academy Archives.
Guide to the St. Johnsbury Academy Catalogs 1843 to Present. St. Johnsbury Academy Archives.

Descriptive Pamphlet

St. Johnsbury Vermont: Maple Capital of the World. St. Johnsbury, VT: The St. Johnsbury Chamber of Commerce, 1981.

A University of Vermont Website Lead

http://cdi.uvm.edu/findingaids/browseEAD.xql?cat=all&rep=Johnsbury

Guides to Congregationalism in Vermont

Clark, Francis E. *The Christian Endeavor Manual.* Boston, MA: Christian Endeavor Society, 1903.
Comstock, John M. *The Congregational Churches of Vermont and Their Ministry 1762-1942.* St. Johnsbury, VT: The Cowles Press, Inc., 1942.
Nutting, John E. *Becoming the United Church of Christ in Vermont 1795-1995.* Burlington, VT: The Vermont Conference of the United Church of Christ, 1995.

The Young Men's Christian Association

Findlay, James F., Jr. *Dwight L. Moody: American Evangelist 1837-1899.* Chicago, IL: The University of Chicago Press, 1969.
Folger, Allen. *Twenty-Five Years As an Evangelist.* Boston: James H. Earle & Company, 1905.

Morse, Richard C. *My Life with Young Men: Fifty Years in the Young Men's Christian Association.* New York: Association Press, 1918.

Ober, Frank W., ed. *James Stokes: Pioneer of Young Men's Christian Associations by His Associates in More Than Half a Century of World Service to Young Men.* New York: Association Press, 1921.

The Jubilee of Work for Young Men in North America: A Report of the Jubilee Convention of North American Young Men's Christian Associations; Reports of the Commemorative Services of the Montreal and Boston Associations; A World Survey by Countries of the Association Movement. New York: The International Committee of Young Men's Christian Associations, 1901.

Fairbanks Family Data

Fairbanks, Lorenzo Sayles. *Genealogy of the Fairbanks Family in America, 1633-1897.* Boston, MA: American Printing and Engraving Company, 1897.

Giddings, Edward J. *American Christian Rulers or Religion and Men of Government.* NY: Bromfield & Company, 1890.

"Your Heavenly Father will never let you down!"
Alcoholics Anonymous, 4th ed, 181

10
The YMCA and St. Johnsbury, Vermont

The Founding of the YMCA and Its Purposes

In 1836, when George Williams (later, Sir George Williams) was about 16 years old and working as a sales assistant in a London draper's store, he gave his life to Jesus Christ, and began to pray and to seek God.[592] In 1844, Williams—together with a group of fellow drapers—founded the first Young Men's Christian Association (YMCA) in London, England, on June 6, 1844. Its purpose was "to substitute Bible study and prayer for life on the streets."[593] Cephas Brainerd states it this way:

> Young Men's Christian Associations had their origin in a desire to reach and save unconverted young men through the agency of converted men of the same age and class. This was the thought in the mind of George Williams when, in 1844, in the city of London, he organized the first Association.[594]

---

[592] Laurence L. Doggett, *History of the Young Men's Christian Association: Part I: The Founding of the Association, 1844-1855; Part II: The Confederation Period, 1855-1861* (New York: Association Press, 1922), 30.
[593] "History of the YMCA Movement": http://www.ymca.net/about_the_ymca/history_of_the_ymca.html ; accessed 11/30/07.
[594] Cephas Brainerd, "Young Men's Christian Associations," in Division IV. Christian Life. Tuesday, October 7, 1873. Fifth Section.—Christian Associations, in *Evangelical Alliance Conference, 1873: History, Essays, Orations, and Other Documents of the Sixth General Conference of the Evangelical Alliance, Held in New York, October 2-12, 1873*; Philip Schaff and S. Irenaeus Prime, eds. (New York: Harper & Brothers, 1874), 419.

"Brainerd's contact with the YMCA began in 1852 when at the age of 21 he joined the New York City association. He became a director of that association in 1857 and was its vice president from 1857-1859. During the early part of the Civil War he was active on the Army and Navy Committee of the association. Brainerd served as secretary general [sic] of the International Committee from 1867-1892,

As we have seen to some extent already, Bible studies, prayer meetings, and conversion efforts continued to be major focuses of the YMCA after it spread to North America.

The YMCA in North America

The first YMCA (local Association) in North America was established in Montreal, Canada, on November 25, 1851.[595] The first YMCA in the United States (and the second in North America) was established in Boston, Massachusetts, on December 29, 1851.[596] The Buffalo, New York, YMCA chapter—the third to be organized in North America—opened in June, 1852.[597]

Morse makes this important point about the local Associations of the YMCA:

---

during which he strongly influenced the character of the YMCA, including adopting an evangelical emphasis an a moderate attitude towards race relations." From: "Biography of Cephas Brainerd" in the "Cephas Brainerd: An Inventory of his papers" section of the Kautz Family YMCA Archives: http://64.233.167.104/search?q=cache:wMTJVZcAGZsJ:special.lib.umn.edu/findaid/html/ymca/yusa0015.phtml+%22Cephas+Brainerd%22&hl=en&ct=clnk&cd=1&gl=us ; accessed: 2/14/08.

    Richard C. Morse, who was from 1872 until 1915 the general secretary of the YMCA's (North American) Executive Committee (which later changed its name to the International Committee in 1879), says of Cephas Brainerd that he was "chairman for twenty five years (1867-1892) of the International Committee, . . ." See Richard C. Morse, *History of the North American Young Men's Christian Association* (New York: Association Press, 1919), 56. Morse, as general secretary, reported to Brainerd, as chairman.

    Cephas Brainerd is listed as "Chairman" of the "International Committee of Young Men's Christian Associations" in *Year Book of the Young Men's Christian Associations of North America for the Year 1892* (New York: Published by the International Committee, 1892), 3.

[595] "History of the YMCA Movement": http://www.ymca.net/about_the_ymca/history_of_the_ymca.html ; accessed 12/03/07.

[596] "History of the YMCA Movement": http://www.ymca.net/about_the_ymca/history_of_the_ymca.html ; accessed 11/30/07.

[597] Francis R. Kowsky, "Buffalo as an Architectural Museum: Young Men's Christian Association Building," 1983: http://preserve.bfn.org/bam/kowsky/ymca/index.html ; accessed: 12/03/07.

The origin of the Young Men's Christian Association dates from the beginning of the local Association, but its more orderly development and efficiency began later with the agencies of supervision which these local Associations created in conference and convention.[598]

The International Committee, "an organization of North American YMCA chapters concerned with the worldwide mission of the Association, came into existence" in Buffalo, New York, in 1854.[599] And it was also at Buffalo in 1854 that the first International Convention in North America met.[600]

Hopkins points out a significant weakness relative to the YMCA structure in its early years in North America:

> Within a few years of the establishment of YMCA work at the national level, it became clear that a single organization for the entire United States and Canada could not meet the needs of local associations for "mutual conference and discussion." Numerous district conventions had been held prior to the Civil War, and the idea of state and local meetings was proposed by the Executive Committee to the Philadelphia Convention of 1865. The concept was formally adopted the following year at the Albany Convention [of 1866], with the goal that conventions be held in every state and district.[601]

---

[598] Richard C. Morse, *My Life with Young Men: Fifty Years in the Young Men's Christian Association* (New York: Association Press, 1918), 435.
[599] Francis R. Kowsky, "Buffalo as an Architectural Museum: Young Men's Christian Association Building," 1983: http://preserve.bfn.org/bam/kowsky/ymca/index.html ; accessed: 12/03/07.
[600] Morse, *My Life with Young Men*, 435. Note also: ". . . [B]y the time the first 'Annual Convention of Young Men's Christian Associations of the United States and British Provinces' was held in 1854 there were fourteen American associations present." "Kautz Family YMCA Archives: YMCA National Level Research, Planning and Development: An Inventory of Miscellaneous Records," http://special.lib.umn.edu/findaid/html/ymca/yusa0034.phtml ; accessed: 12/03/07.
[601] ". . . [A] summary of material from C. Howard Hopkins, *History of the YMCA in North America* (New York: Association Press, 1951)." From: "Kautz Family YMCA Archives: YMCA State Committees: An Inventory of Their Records": http://special.lib.umn.edu/findaid/html/ymca/yusa0030.phtml ; accessed: 12/03/07. [See, especially pages 124-27 in the Hopkins book.] Note also: "Starting in 1854, annual national conventions, held under the auspices of the Executive Committee,

Brainerd identifies the two "distinctive features" of the YMCA in America:

1. It has been wholly undenominational, and based upon the belief that the average American young man, outside of church influence, was more open to the approaches of such an agency; and,
2. Work has been performed almost wholly by Christian laymen, because these were best fitted to carry it on; and, also, because the ministry could not under the limitations of human strength, as well as denominational exigencies, perform it.[602]

As we have noted, six churches—representing five denominations—worked together with the Vermont State YMCA Committee in presenting the "Gospel meetings" in St. Johnsbury in 1875. And the leaders of many of the meetings in St. Johnsbury were YMCA laymen from Boston.

YMCA State Conventions and State Committees

Hopkins continues by explaining what happened once the idea of having state conventions was adopted at the North American YMCA Convention at Albany in 1866:

> The first permanent state organization [of the Young Men's Christian Associations] was set up by delegates to a convention held in New Haven, Connecticut in May 1867. Other pioneers included . . . Vermont, and Ohio, all of which organized later in 1867. . . .
>
> The state committees worked closely with the International Committee, which rendered a wide variety of services to the states. Services included financial advising, coordination

---

were in charge of coordination on the national level. In 1879 the Executive Committee changed its name to the International Committee and in 1883 incorporated as the permanent, centralized agency for the American YMCA movement." "Kautz Family YMCA Archives," http://special.lib.umn.edu/findaid/html/ymca/yusa0034.phtml ; accessed: 12/03/07.
[602] Brainerd, "Young Men's Christian Associations," 420.

between two states working jointly, and the development of model constitutions, program outlines, and statements of purpose for state work. State organizations almost universally followed the structural organization of the parent agency, with an executive committee, an evangelical test of membership, the direct relation to local Associations, and incorporation including provision for property holding for local Associations.[603]

As Vermont and other states began to hold YMCA state conventions and form state committees beginning in 1867, their State Committees pursued their work in two considerably-different ways. S. A. Taggert, State Secretary of the Pennsylvania YMCA, put it this way at the North American YMCA Convention at Richmond in 1875:

> There are two distinct forms of effort that have been prosecuted by State Committees. *First*, the Evangelistic form, namely, a State Executive Committee, composed of godly men determined to form themselves into a praying band and go out to the Associations to preach Christ. . . . *Secondly*, we have in some of our State organizations the visits of men from different parts of the State to labor more distinctively for the Association. In Pennsylvania we do not neglect the Evangelistic effort, but we combine with it special work to reach and organize young men.[604] [Emphasis in the original]

Commenting on the remarks of Taggart and others at the 1875 North American YMCA convention, Cephas Brainerd stated the following at the same convention:

> In this broadening work, we see as never before, opportunities not only for enlargement, but for reform and improvement. You remember the interesting reports presented yesterday of

---

[603] ". . . [The information excerpted in the main text] is a summary of material from C. Howard Hopkins, *History of the YMCA in North America*, New York: Association Press, 1951." See: "YMCA State Committees: An Inventory of Their Records": http://special.lib.umn.edu/findaid/html/ymca/yusa0030.phtml ; accessed 11/30/07.
[604] *Proceedings of the Twentieth Annual Convention of the Young Men's Christian Associations of the United States and British Provinces, Held at Richmond, VA., May 26-30, 1875* (New York: Published by the Executive Committee, 1875), 40.

the work of the various State Committees. Wisdom in organization is well represented by the brethren from Pennsylvania. The vivid power and fervor of evangelistic work are exemplified and emphasized by the State Committees of New England. There is no conflict here. The Secretaries of Pennsylvania and Massachusetts are not at cross purposes in their work. Perhaps the discussion wore that appearance to some, but we want both these forms of effort—organization and evangelization.

Massachusetts—the old Bay State as they delight to call her—would not lose anything by the organization and the deep laid foundations of Ohio and Pennsylvania. Nor would Pennsylvania and Ohio lose anything if they took all the enthusiasm in lay work, the sweet songs and vigorous evangelism of the Committees of New England.

It is this blessed work of our Associations that has developed lay preachers more and *Moore* [referring to Henry M. Moore]. I can remember when our cause had very few Moores to preach Christ upon the platform, in the street and often in the pulpit. I can remember, too, when we sadly lacked the wise organizing energy exhibited by Mr. Taggart, the Secretary of Pennsylvania. But there are now many Taggarts and Moores in the work, though not so many Littlefields who can sing these beautiful songs."[605] [Emphasis in the original]

We noted earlier at length that the effort by YMCA laymen which led to the "Great Awakening" of 1875 in St. Johnsbury had begun with the work of Evangelist K. A. Burnell and Henry M. Moore in Massachusetts in 1872, had moved into New Hampshire in 1873, had proceeded into Vermont through the Vermont State YMCA

---

[605] *Proceedings of the Twentieth Annual Convention of the Young Men's Christian Associations of the United States and British Provinces, Held at Richmond, VA., May 26-30, 1875* (New York: Published by the Executive Committee, 1875), 59, 60.

"Littlefields" refers to "C. J. [probably Cyrus J.] Littlefield," who together with Robert K. Remington, Henry M. Moore, Francis O. Winslow, Sydney E. Bridgman, and Russell Sturgis, Jr., made up the "Massachusetts brethren" who put on the "Gospel meetings" which resulted in the "Great Awakening" of 1875 in St. Johnsbury. C. J. Littlefield was present at the 1875 North American YMCA Convention.

Convention at Norwich in late 1874, and had then spread to all of New England.

As reported in the 1882-1883 YMCA *Year Book*, "Corresponding Member" A. J. Howe of Montpelier, Vermont, gave the following report on the status of the YMCA in Vermont:

> At present the State has twenty Associations employing two general secretaries.
>
> The State Executive Committee numbers twenty. The Annual State Convention, held in Newport the first day of November, was in January followed by District Conferences in St. Johnsbury and Burlington; resulting, through the aid of Secretaries Ingersoll, Watkins and Wishard, in the appointment of general secretaries at St. Johnsbury and Burlington, . . .[606]

In the "List of State and Provincial Conventions Held Between June, 1881, and May, 1882," section of the 1882-1883 YMCA *Year Book*, the following data is provided for the Vermont YMCA State Convention held in Newport on November 1-2, 1881:[607]

Associations Represented:	9
Delegates:	19
Corresponding Members:	34
Money Expended during Year:	$856.59

The YMCA in St. Johnsbury, Vermont

The St. Johnsbury Association of the Young Men's Christian Association (YMCA) was formed on October 1, 1855.[608]

---

[606] No author, *Year Book of the Young Men's Christian Associations of the United States and Dominion of Canada for the Year 1882-1883* (New York: Published by the International Committee, 1882), 55.

[607] No author, *Year Book of the Young Men's Christian Associations of the United States and Dominion of Canada for the Year 1882-1883* (New York: Published by the International Committee, 1882), 16.

[608] Edward T. Fairbanks, *The Town of St Johnsbury VT: A Review of One Hundred Twenty-Five Years to the Anniversary Pageant 1912* (St. Johnsbury, VT: The Cowles Press, 1914), 317.

> Meetings were held in private houses to begin with, then in the [St. Johnsbury] Academy and the church vestries. Reorganization was made on a broader basis in 1858 with 41 new members; and again in 1867 [the year of the first State YMCA convention in Vermont], at which time a reading room was opened and a lecture course established which with passing years became famous.[609]

The YMCA was very much involved in the St. Johnsbury community. Within four years of the State Committee for the YMCA in Vermont's having come into existence, the Fourth Annual Convention of the Young Men's Christian Associations in Vermont was held on October 11-12, 1870, in St. Johnsbury.[610] The Fairbankses were leaders in the YMCA revivals, Gospel meetings, and conversions. Dr. Bob's father, Judge Smith, was a president and chairman of the local YMCA. Though destroyed by fire in 1984, the YMCA building—donated by a Fairbanks—was one of the many architectural buildings that made up the Fairbanks legacy. YMCA laymen from Massachusetts and representatives of the Vermont YMCA State Committee were able to lead many to Jesus Christ during the "Great Awakening" of 1875 in St. Johnsbury. They brought the churches together for revivals, prayer meetings, and Gospel meetings. Even Dwight L. Moody--a long-time YMCA member, former President of the Chicago YMCA, and life-long supporter of and fundraiser for the YMCA—may have played at least an indirect role in the spiritual welfare of St. Johnsbury. We will tell the story by pointing to the personalities involved.

In "Main Table—No. 1.—Reports of American Associations," presented in the 1882-1883 YMCA *Year Book*, the following

---

[609] Fairbanks, The Town of St. Johnsbury, 318.
[610] See, for example: (1) "Current Notes" in *The New York Times*, October 13, 1870, page 2: http://query.nytimes.com/gst/abstract.html?res=9D03E2DD1F3CE13BBC4B52DFB667838B669FDE ; accessed 12/01/07; and (2) *Young Men's Christian Associations. Proceedings of the Fourth Annual Convention of Young Men's Christian Associations in Vermont, Held at St. Johnsbury, Oct. 11th and 12th, 1870* (Published by the State Executive Committee; Burlington: R. S. Styles, Steam Book and Job Printer, 1870). Dwight L. Moody attended this convention.

information is provided for the St. Johnsbury, Vermont, YMCA Association for the calendar year 1883:[611]

President:	Chas. E. Putney[612]
General, Executive, or Corresponding Secretary:	Chas. H. Sage
Population of Town (latest Census):	4,500
Date of Organization:	1867
Total No. of Members:	311
No. of Active Members:	187
No. of Members on Committees:	142
Current Expenses last year:	$1,652

In "Table No. III.—Religious Meetings Not Exclusively for Young Men," presented in the 1882-1883 YMCA *Year Book*, the following information is provided for the St. Johnsbury, Vermont, YMCA Association for the calendar year 1883:[613]

In the Rooms:	Daily Meeting
	Gospel Meeting
Elsewhere:	Gospel Meeting
	3 Neighborhood or Out District Meetings

In "Table No. IV.—Reports of Religious Meetings for Young Men," presented in the 1882-1883 YMCA *Year Book*, the following information is provided for the St. Johnsbury, Vermont, YMCA Association for the calendar year 1883:[614]

Prayer Meetings—Average Attendance:	25
Bible Classes—Average Attendance:	9

---

[611] No author, *Year Book of the Young Men's Christian Associations of the United States and Dominion of Canada for the Year 1882-1883* (New York: Published by the International Committee, 1882), 131.

[612] Charles (Chas.) E. Putney had just become Principal of St. Johnsbury Academy.

[613] No author, *Year Book of the Young Men's Christian Associations of the United States and Dominion of Canada for the Year 1882-1883* (New York: Published by the International Committee, 1882), 145.

[614] No author, *Year Book of the Young Men's Christian Associations of the United States and Dominion of Canada for the Year 1882-1883* (New York: Published by the International Committee, 1882), 150.

Julius J. ("J. J.") Estey, the "Corresponding Member" for the State of Vermont YMCA in 1885, reported:

> The St. Johnsbury Association occupy new buildings of their own, with all modern conveniences. [This is a reference to the building erected by Rev. Henry Fairbanks.]

> At St. Johnsbury, Burlington, Rutland and Brattleboro, the same general secretaries are employed this year as last. No state secretary has been employed. The State work has been done under the direction of Mr. C. H. Sage, the general secretary of the St. Johnsbury Association, who is also secretary of the State Committee.[615]

Charles Edward ("C. E.") Putney and A. S. Hopkins

According to "Continuation of Official Reports Received by the Executive Committee, 1874-75," C. E. Putney is listed as the President for the YMCA of St. Johnsbury and A. S. Hopkins is listed as the Corresponding Secretary. The number of members of the St. Johnsbury YMCA is listed as "250."[616] In 1873, Charles E. Putney "became assistant principal in St. Johnsbury Academy under Mr. Homer T. Fuller [who became principal in February 1871 and resigned in 1882[617]], whom he succeeded in the principalship [sic]. In 1896 he resigned on account of ill health."[618]

---

[615] No author, 1885. *26th International Convention of Young Men's Christian Associations, Held at Atlanta, BA., May 13-17, 1885, and the Year Book for 1885* (New York: Published by the International Committee, 1885), xcii.

[616] *Proceedings of the Twentieth Annual Convention of the Young Men's Christian Associations of the United States and British Provinces, Held at Richmond, VA., May 26-30, 1875* (New York: Published by the Executive Committee, 1875), [page not numbered].

[617] C. E. Putney, "St. Johnsbury Academy" in George Gary Bush, *History of Education in Vermont*, No. 29; United States Bureau of Education. Circular of Information No. 4, 1900: *Contributions to American Education History*, ed., Herbert B. Adams (Washington: Government Printing Office, 1900), 124-30. http://books.google.com/books?id=lDoWAAAAIAAJ&pg=PA124&lpg=PA124&dq=%22C.+E.+Putney%22+Johnsbury&source=web&ots=JebV9Tu6uA&sig=QKfZ-x50EWqPua5191sfQgcsneo#PPP3,M1 ; accessed 2/17/08.

[618] [no author stated], Charles Edward Putney: An Appreciation (n.p.: Published by the Charles E. Putney Memorial Association, n.d.), 5, 6. Charles E. Putney is listed as "principal of St. Johnsbury academy and president of Y. M. C. A." in "Business

Henry Fairbanks of St. Johnsbury

"For some years after 1875 the State Convention of the Y. M. C. A. carried on an effective evangelistic work in a large number of towns in Vermont, witnessing most marked religious revivals, with large additions to the churches, and [Rev. Henry] Fairbanks [,Ph.D.,] was prominent in this work, after the first year having charge, and directing it as Secretary."[619]

Professor Henry Fairbanks, Franklin Fairbanks, and Horace Fairbanks are listed together in the "Sustaining Memberships and Other Subscriptions Received During 1883" section of the 1882-1883 YMCA *Year Book* as each having given $100.00.[620]

"The Young Men's Christian Association building in St. Johnsbury was erected by him [in 1885]."[621]

He was listed as a corresponding member from St. Johnsbury, Vermont—together with C. S. McGown—in "The Convention Personnel" section of *A Report of the Jubilee Convention of the North American Young Men's Christian Associations* in 1901.[622]

Directory: St. Johnsbury—Caledonia County, 1887-1888."
http://www.rootsweb.com/~vermont/BusinessDirectoryStJohnsburyCaledonia_2.html ; accessed 2/17/08.

[619] "Noyes Family," http://noyes.rootsweb.com/b304.htm ; accessed November 3, 2007.

[620] No author, *Year Book of the Young Men's Christian Associations of the United States and Dominion of Canada for the Year 1882-1883* (New York: Published by the International Committee, 1882) , 113.

[621] Distinguished biographers, eds., *The National Cyclopaedia of American Biography*, Volume X (New York: James T. White, 1909), 300; s.v.: "Fairbanks, Henry"

[622] No author, *The Jubilee of Work for Young Men in North America* (New York: The International Committee of Young Men's Christian Associations, 1901), 493.

Franklin Fairbanks of St. Johnsbury

Franklin Fairbanks of St. Johnsbury, Vermont, was listed in the "Sustaining Memberships and Other Subscriptions Received During 1881" section of 1882-1883 YMCA Year Book.[623]

Professor Henry Fairbanks, Franklin Fairbanks, and Horace Fairbanks are listed together in the "Sustaining Memberships and Other Subscriptions Received During 1883" section of the 1882-1883 YMCA *Year Book* as each having given $100.00.[624]

And he was elected on May 18, 1883, in Milwaukee, Wisconsin, as an "Advisory Member" of the International Committee of Young Men's Christian Associations.[625]

Dwight L. Moody

"On his seventeenth birthday (1854), Dwight Moody went to Boston to seek employment. He became a clerk in Holton's Shoe Store, his uncle's enterprise. One of the work requirements was attendance at the Mount Vernon Congregational Church, pastored by Edward Kirk. . . . [A] Sunday School teacher encouraged him along. One Saturday, April 21, 1855, the teacher, Edward Kimball, walked into the store [where Moody worked, spoke with him, and] . . . Moody knelt down and was converted."[626]

"1854: . . . [Dwight L. Moody] joins YMCA."[627]

---

[623] No author, *Year Book of the Young Men's Christian Associations of the United States and Dominion of Canada for the Year 1882-1883* (New York: Published by the International Committee, 1882), 61.

[624] No author, *Year Book of the Young Men's Christian Associations of the United States and Dominion of Canada for the Year 1882-1883* (New York: Published by the International Committee, 1882), 61. , 113.

[625] No author, *Year Book of the Young Men's Christian Associations of the United States and Dominion of Canada for the Year 1883-1884* (New York: Published by the International Committee, 1883), unnumbered page.

[626] "Biography of D.L. Moody" : http://www.believersweb.org/view.cfm?ID=82 ; accessed 11/03/07.

[627] "The Christian History Timeline: Dwight L. Moody (1873-1899) and His World" : http://ctlibrary.com/3674 ; accessed 11/3/07.

"In 1861 Moody became a city missionary [in Chicago] for the YMCA."[628]

"The Chicago Y.M.C.A. was moving ahead also, as Moody rose to its presidency from 1866 to 1869. He had a part in erecting the first Y.M.C.A. building in America when he supervised the erection of Farwell Hall in 1876, seating 3,000. That year he also held his first revival campaign in Philadelphia."[629]

"A second incident was the meeting of Ira A. Sankey, while attending a Y.M.C.A. convention in Indianapolis in July of 1870."[630]

"He arrived home August 14 [, 1875,] and hurried to Northfield to conduct a revival. His mother, many friends and relatives were saved there."[631]

"The Boston crusade was held January 28 to May 1, 1877 in a tabernacle seating 6,000. The years 1877-78 saw many smaller towns in New England states being reached."[632]

"Moody's interest in schools left him a lasting ministry. The forming of the Northfield Seminary (now Northfield School for Girls) in 1879, and the Mount Hermon Massachusetts School for Boys (1881) was the beginning."[633]

"In 1880 he started the famous Northfield Bible Conferences which continued until 1902, bringing some of the best speakers from both continents to the pulpit here. The world's first student conference was

---

[628] "Biography of D.L. Moody" : http://www.believersweb.org/view.cfm?ID=82 ; accessed 11/03/07.
[629] "Biography of D.L. Moody" : http://www.believersweb.org/view.cfm?ID=82 ; accessed 11/03/07.
[630] "Biography of D.L. Moody" : http://www.believersweb.org/view.cfm?ID=82 ; accessed 11/03/07.
[631] "Biography of D.L. Moody" : http://www.believersweb.org/view.cfm?ID=82 ; accessed 11/03/07.
[632] "Biography of D.L. Moody" : http://www.believersweb.org/view.cfm?ID=82 ; accessed 11/03/07.
[633] "Biography of D.L. Moody" : http://www.believersweb.org/view.cfm?ID=82 ; accessed 11/03/07.

held in 1885 and the Student Volunteer Movement started two years later as a natural outgrowth."⁶³⁴

"From 1884 on, his crusades were smaller and limited to October to April. He spent his summer months in Northfield, Massachusetts for study, rest, family and development of his schools."⁶³⁵

"From 1884-1886 he was in many of the smaller cities of the nation, remaining about three days in each place."⁶³⁶

Moody's friend, General Julius J. ("J. J.") Estey, the "Corresponding Member" for the State of Vermont YMCA in 1885, reported:

> The eighteenth [Vermont YMCA] State Convention was held in Brattleboro, October 10-12, 1884. Mr. D. L. Moody and Mr. H. L. Hastings, of Boston, Mr. Watkins of the International Committee, and State Secretaries Hall, Lawrence and [Allen] Folger [of New Hampshire], contributed valuable assistance toward making the Convention one of profit.⁶³⁷

"In 1898 Moody was chairman of the evangelistic department of the Army and Navy Christian Commission of the Y.M.C.A during the Spanish-American War."⁶³⁸

The Relevance to the Smith Family Activities

That YMCA people were much involved in the religious life of St. Johnsbury during the period of Dr. Bob's youth seems demonstrably clear. To the extent that the Smiths were directly involved with the

---

⁶³⁴ "Biography of D.L. Moody" : http://www.believersweb.org/view.cfm?ID=82 ; accessed 11/03/07.
⁶³⁵ "Biography of D.L. Moody" : http://www.believersweb.org/view.cfm?ID=82 ; accessed 11/03/07.
⁶³⁶ "Biography of D.L. Moody" : http://www.believersweb.org/view.cfm?ID=82 ; accessed 11/03/07.
⁶³⁷ No author, 1885. *26ᵗʰ International Convention of Young Men's Christian Associations, Held at Atltanta, BA., May 13-17, 1885, and the Year Book for 1885* (New York: Published by the International Committee, 1885), xcii.
⁶³⁸ "Biography of D.L. Moody" : http://www.believersweb.org/view.cfm?ID=82 ; accessed 11/03/07.

Fairbanks family members, they were exposed to YMCA interests; but research thus far has not unearthed any direct evidence to that effect.

The YMCA conducted concerts in North Congregational Church. It held revival meetings which involved North Congregational Church. It presented lectures at St. Johnsbury Academy. And there is evidence that it worked alongside Christian Endeavor in achieving conversions through revivals. But none of this can be directly linked to Dr. Bob as far as present research has disclosed. There was a YMCA secretary in St. Johnsbury. There was a YMCA building in St. Johnsbury—though it has since been destroyed by fire. There was a proximity between St. Johnsbury and nearby Northfield, Massachusetts, where Dwight Moody's people were training students to be lay evangelists. And there were links between Northfield, its Mt. Hermon School, and Vermont people. But, other than the fact that Judge Smith served as a President and chairman of the local YMCA, we have no way of knowing at this time whether young Bob's Smith training in the Bible, prayer, and Christianity involved only his church, his Christian Endeavor participation, and his days at St. Johnsbury Academy. Considering the small population of St. Johnsbury, it seems possible that paths crossed. But the dichotomy of energy between the YMCA and the denominational activities of churches was clear. So we leave it at that—worthy of mention, and worthy of further research. The reason has to do with the vigor and effective conversions in Vermont and in St. Johnsbury that was catalyzed by YMCA workers.

The Young Men's Christian Associations (YMCA) and St. Johnsbury

Partial Bibliography

Young Men's Christian Associations. Proceedings of the Fourth Annual Convention of Young Men's Christian Associations in Vermont, Held at St. Johnsbury, Oct. 11th and 12th, 1870. Published by the State Executive Committee. Burlington: R. S. Styles, Steam Book and Job Printer. 1870. 36pp.

Ninth Annual Convention of the Young Men's Christian Associations and Churches of Vermont, Held at The Congregational

Church, Royalton, September 13*th*, 14*th*, 15*th*, 1875. Burlington: R. S. Styles & Son, Steam Book and Job Printers. 26 pp.

First Annual Joint Convention of the Young Men's Christian Associations and Churches of Vermont and New Hampshire, at Keene, N. H., November 23-25. Burlington: Free Press Association, 1895. 57 pp.

Proceedings of the Annual National Convention, YMCA (June 1879).

Proceedings of the Fourteenth Annual Convention of the Young Men's Christian Associations of the United States and the British Provinces (Portland, Maine, July, 1869)

Laurence L. Doggett, *History of the Young Men's Christian Association* (New York: Association Press, 1922);

[Sherwood] Eddy, *A Century with Youth: A History of the Y.M.C.A. from 1844-1944* (New York: Association Press, 1944)

C. Howard Hopkins, *History of the Y.M.C.A. in North America* (New York: Association Press, 1951);

Richard C. Morse, *History of the North American Young Men's Christian Associations* (New York: Association Press, 1913).

Clarence P. Shedd, *History of the World's Alliance of Young Men's Christian Associations* (London: S.P.C.K., 1955)

William G. McLouglin, *Revivals, Awakenings, and Reform: An Essay on Religion and Social Change in America, 1607-1977* (Chicago: University of Chicago Press, 1978).

James F. Findlay, Jr., *Dwight L. Moody, American Evangelist, 1837-1899* (Chicago: University of Chicago Press, 1969).

"Your Heavenly Father will never let you down!"
Alcoholics Anonymous, 4th ed, 181

11
The Original, Akron A.A. Spiritual Program of Recovery

How easy it is for historians, scholars, trusted servants, and every-day drunks to get so wrapped up in trivia, controversy, criticism, and even socializing that they somehow misplace the most important and primary purpose, activity, and accomplishment of Alcoholics Anonymous.

Alcoholics Anonymous is about helping the person who still suffers. Not about your message. Not about mine. Not about your experience. Not about my experience. Not about our love and service. Not about how many meetings I attend, how many people you sponsor or that I sponsor, nor how many of "them" relapse or don't relapse. Bill Wilson propounded the "I am responsible" theme. And yet some are still calling A.A. a "selfish" program, a "spiritual" program, an "inclusive" program, and a "universal" program.

No. It is a fellowship of alcoholics banded together to maintain sobriety and to help the alcoholic who still suffers achieve sobriety. Specifically, it originally insisted on a trust in God.

Yet what about God—our Heavenly Father, the Creator of the heavens and the earth? Just what is the message we can carry about Him to the person who still suffers? The answer is that the new person can be cured of his alcoholism—just as Bill Wilson, Dr. Bob, and A.A. Number Three Bill Dotson all stated they were. Alcoholism can be cured, was cured, and is curable. And those who get wrapped up in the phrases "one-day-at-a-time," "daily reprieve", "in recovery," and "recovering" are ignoring the often read and quoted abc's of A.A.: "We were alcoholic and could not manage our own lives. Probably no human power could have relieved us of our alcoholism. God could and would if he were sought."

Before revisionists changed our language, A.A. was about helping the seemingly hopeless, medically incurable, real alcoholic to be cured. As one of the original Big Book covers stated, A.A. was the pathway to a cure. And the healer was God. That's how you helped the alcoholic who still suffered. You were to tell and show him what God had done for you. You asked him if he believed in God. And, if he did, Akron had a very simple program for showing him the path to the relationship with God that would give him victory, an abundant life, and everlasting life.

Many Claims. Many Errors. One Truth

When Was A.A. Founded?

You would think by now that everyone knew when A.A. began and where. Yet I was active in A.A. and its meetings for two or three years before I ever heard mention of the founding. Finally, I learned that the date was June 10, 1935--the date that Dr. Bob had his last drink. But that did not satisfy today's historians. They tinkered with dates and concluded that Dr. Bob didn't have his last drink on June 10th, that the medical convention to which he went in Atlantic City never occurred when AAs had heard it did, and that A.A. was founded on some other date thereabouts.

If you asked someone when George Washington cut down the cherry tree, just think how many different answers the historians might provide today. The best starting point would be to disclose that he didn't cut down the cherry tree. Does it matter? Today, we don't even seem to celebrate George's birthday and prefer lumping all our presidents together.

Well, AAs do care. It matters to them. So I set forth all the arguments and dates of our alleged founding long ago in my title, *The Akron Genesis of Alcoholics Anonymous.*[639] You can study them there if you like. Long after A.A. was founded, Lois Wilson still wrote that A.A. had been founded in 1934 when drunks were coming to the Wilson home in Brooklyn. Others wanted to date it when Ebby Thacher first carried the message to Bill Wilson in New York. T. Henry Williams

---

[639] Please see http://www.DickB.com/Akron.shtml for details on this title.

often said that A.A. started right on the carpet of his Palisades home in Akron when Dr. Bob, Henrietta Seiberling, and the others in the Oxford Group knelt and prayed for Dr. Bob's recovery. Still others like to date it as of the publishing of the Big Book in the Spring of 1939. They call the prior years the "flying blind period." And they treat that period as if it pre-dates Alcoholics Anonymous. Clarence Snyder claimed he was the founder, and that the first meeting of Alcoholics Anonymous was held in Cleveland on May 11, 1939. One would-be expert has now asserted that the "original" program occurred some time after that in the 1940's. And, Bill Wilson made the statement that the first A.A. group began when A.A. Number Three was cured of alcoholism, was visited by Bill Wilson and Dr. Bob in the hospital, and walked from there a "free man" – never to drink again. That happened very shortly after Dr. Bob himself got sober.

So you will have to make up your own mind. FDR changed Thanksgiving. We call Armistice Day Veterans Day. And on and on. Which leads to the conclusion that "founding" days are perhaps far less important than the founding itself. Even more, what it produced. Personally, I'm convinced that A.A. began. It is here; so it must have begun. I am convinced it began at Dr. Bob's Home in Akron. I am convinced that Bob and Bill agreed that it began when Dr. Bob took his last drink. I am convinced that fairly soon after AA began, Bill and Bob agreed that the founding date was June 10, 1935. And thereafter, Bill Wilson attended and actually spoke at "Founders Day" in Akron where the "founding of A.A." on June 10, 1935, is celebrated

Do you know when A.A. was founded? I don't for certain. But I'm very sure it was founded because it was in Alcoholics Anonymous that I took my last drink forever and was cured.

Where Did the Original Program Come From?

I know what A.A. was, where it came from, where it began, when it began, and how it was practiced. But you'd have a heck of a time convincing a lot of AAs today. These are people who have never met or even read much about Bill Wilson, Dr. Bob, or the original days in Akron.

In the first place, people have chosen to call the formative days the "flying blind" period. Yet there never was more light shining on the cure for alcoholism. Certainly far more than that in the murky waters of research and treatment today. Real alcoholics who really tried, who were "seemingly hopeless," "medically incurable," and willing to go to any lengths, were cured in astonishing percentages. By 1938, some forty of them—called the "pioneers"—were maintaining sobriety, half or more for two years. Bill Wilson said so. His wife Lois said so. And A.A.'s own "Conference Approved" literature says so. Moreover, Richard K. of Massachusetts has produced three books now detailing who these forty folks were, when they got sober, and what happened to them. Their names can be found on a dozen rosters. The pictures of many are on the walls at Dr. Bob's Home in Akron. Fifty per cent got sober and stayed sober, despite the fact that many a creative A.A. amateur historian, with no documentation to prove the point, insists that the original gang all died drunk. Nonsense!

In the second place, the program came from the Bible. Maybe that's why doubters and unbelievers want to plaster its formative years and successes with the label, "flying blind" period. The Bible was read to Bill and Bob at the Smith Home each day in the summer of 1935 by Dr. Bob's wife Anne Smith. Bob had studied the Bible all his life and had begun refreshing his memory as a youngster. He read the Bible straight through at least three times. Bob and Bill stayed up until the wee hours of the morning every day that Bill stayed at the Smith home in Akron in the summer of 1935. They studied the basic ideas in the Bible.

Later, when asked a question about the program, Dr. Bob usually said: "What does the Good Book say." He often commented that the old timers felt that the answer to their problems could be found in the Good Book. Over and over, Bob emphasized that the Book of James, the sermon on the mount (Matthew 5, 6, 7), and 1 Corinthians 13 were absolutely essential. I've written much about the specifics AAs borrowed from these three sections of the Bible.[640] And Bob and Bill

---

[640] See Dick B., *The Good Book and The Big Book: A.A.'s Roots in the Bible* (http://www.dickb.com/goodbook.shtml); Dick B., *Why Early A.A. Succeeded* (http://www.dickb.com/aabiblestudy.shtml); Dick B., *The Oxford Group and Alcoholics Anonymous* (http://www.dickb.com/oxford.shtml); Dick B., *Turning Point* (http://www.dickb.com/turning.shtml); Dick B., *When Early AAs Were Cured*

both said that Jesus' sermon on the mount contained the underlying philosophy of A.A., that 1 Corinthians 13 was favored reading, and that AAs thought so much of the Book of James that they wanted to call their Society the "James Club." The Bible was read aloud to the group at every A.A. meeting in Akron for years—not Oxford Group books, not Shoemaker books, not popular Christian literature, not even much from devotionals like *The Upper Room*. The Bible was stressed, and AAs said so. You can read it in *DR. BOB and the Good Oldtimers*, the A.A. Conference Approved title published in 1980. In fact, in his last major talk to AAs—which is on tape, which has been edited and reprinted, and which can be found in A.A.'s own literature—Dr. Bob said A.A. basic ideas came from the Bible.

When Was the Original Program Developed and Completed?

There is a very simple set of facts. Yet many don't want to acknowledge them. They busy themselves by saying (1) Dr. Bob could never get sober studying the Bible or being a member of the Oxford Group, (2) There were "six" Oxford Group Steps (which there weren't), (3) There were "six" word-of-mouth A.A. steps (which there weren't and which Wilson characterized in half a dozen varied ways), (4) that Bill's "twelve" steps somehow represented the "steps" that early AAs took. This fabrication has been perpetuated: (a) even though there were no steps to take—no steps at all, not six, not twelve, not any; (b) even though there was no basic text containing any steps until the Spring of 1939 (shortly after Bill had asked Rev. Sam Shoemaker to write the Steps); (c) even though the actual vote authorizing Bill to write a textbook was controversial, was taken in Akron, and occurred in 1937 or 1938 before Bill ever began writing the Big Book; (d) Dr. Bob himself specifically pointed out that in a major address to AAs that, in the development years, "there were no steps" and that "our stories didn't amount to anything." (e) So, by 1938, when Bill and Bob had counted noses, found that some 40 men were maintaining continuous sobriety—some for as long as two years, and concluded that God had shown them how to pass along their program, the real, original, successful, spiritual program could certainly be said to have

---

and Why; and my article on "The James Club and the Book of James" (http://www.dickb.com/AAsJamesClub.shtml)--which was followed by my recent title: Dick B., *The James Club and the Original Program's Absolute Essentials.*

been completed. It was complete. It was in place. It was being practiced.

What Was the Original A.A. Program?

The original, pioneer, A.A. program in Akron had, under the leadership of Dr. Bob, worked so well that Bill managed to persuade John D. Rockefeller, Jr. to take a careful look at it.

Rockefeller dispatched his representative, Frank Amos, to Akron to investigate. And Amos did just that. He interviewed doctors, judges, AAs, family members, and Dr. Bob himself. He concluded that the program bore close resemblance to First Century Christianity as described in the Book of Acts. He was astonished at its success and at the simple elements that comprised "the" program. He submitted two reports to Rockefeller, and Amos was later to become an A.A. trustee—presumably in recognition of his vital role in the founding of the real, original, A.A. program.

Some of the Amos Reports can be found in *DR. BOB and the Good Oldtimers* (NY: Alcoholics Anonymous World Services, Inc., 1980). But I wanted to see the originals. So I went to A.A. General Services in New York and to the archives at the Bill Wilson home called "Stepping Stones" at Bedford Hills in New York. I saw the reports and verified the basic accuracy of the A.A. excerpts of what Frank Amos actually had written describing the early program.

Amos did not discuss the hospitalizations at Akron City Hospital which were "musts" in the early program. Possibly because a newcomer's program did not really begin until he had detoxed, been relieved of some of his fuzzy thinking, and become a real candidate. Nor did Amos discuss the surrender with Dr. Bob at the conclusion of the brief hospitalization. For it was then that the newcomer dealt with three issues: (1) Did he believe in God. (2) Would he get down on his knees with Dr. Bob and pray. (3) Would he "surrender" his life by accepting Jesus Christ as his Lord and Savior. And if he "passed" that surrender test, out of the hospital he went—to begin the real, original program.[641]

A short description of the original program, as Frank Amos described it, would be:

1. Abstinence—the alcoholic shall realize he must never again drink.

2. Absolute surrender of himself to God.

3. He must remove from his life the sins which frequently accompany alcoholism.

4. He must have devotions every morning—a Quiet Time of prayer and Bible reading.

5. He must be willing to help other alcoholics get straightened out.

6. Important, but not vital, he must frequently meet with other "reformed" alcoholics and form both a social and religious comradeship.

7. Important, but not vital, he must attend some religious service at least once weekly.

There are many more details in terms of the activities themselves—Morning quiet time with Anne Smith at the Smith home, individual quiet time, the regular Wednesday meeting at the T. Henry Williams home, daily informal meetings at the Smith Home, Bible study and prayer and the reading of Christian literature being circulated, talks

---

[641] I have described it at specific and substantial length in several of my published titles, such as: Dick B., *The Akron Genesis of Alcoholics Anonymous*; Dick B., *Real Twelve Step Fellowship History*; Dick B., *When Early AAs Were Cured and Why*; and Dick B., *A New Way In: Reaching the Heart of a Child of God in Recovery With His Own, Powerful, Historical Roots*.

You can find an excellent and concise description of the whole process in my title, *God and Alcoholism: Our Growing Opportunity in the 21st Century*, 2-12. (http://www.dickb.com/Godandalcoholism.shtml).

with Dr. Bob and Anne and Henrietta Seiberling, and visits to newcomers at the hospital. But the "cure"—the permanent solution to their problems--was described as above in the Frank Amos report.

No drunkalogs. No steps. No Big Book. No Traditions. No service structure. No "trusted servants." No "trustees." No "delegates." No GSO, GSR, DCM. No assembly. No conference. No offices. No corporation. No publishing enterprise. And no money! Just the Creator, Jesus Christ, obedience to God's will, the Bible, prayer, fellowship, and witness.

It worked! Note that there was a seventy-five percent documented success rate in those days; and, shortly thereafter, at the beginning of the 1940's, a ninety-three percent documented success rate. Documented by carefully kept rosters, names, dates, addresses, and phone numbers.

The Dick B. 16 Major Recovery Well-Springs Volumes

All A.A.'s Ideas Were Borrowed, said Bill W.; The Basic Ideas Came from Their Study of the Good Book, said Dr. Bob

Early in its founding years, A.A.'s cofounder Bill Wilson put the torch to the idea that A.A. sprang from just one source. He said frankly that nobody invented A.A. He said all its ideas were borrowed. And Dr. Bob broadened the source picture by pointing out that all the basic ideas came from the Pioneers' study of the Bible. Bill never overtly acceded to Dr. Bob's assertion, primarily, it would seem, because he had deliberately dumped mention of the Bible and Jesus Christ, attempted to "universalize" A.A., and re-written the program using primarily an Oxford Group format. Unfortunately, neither cofounder put in writing in one place all the well-springs that produced the streams in A.A. Consequently commentators, both favorable to and critical of A.A., have had a field day with discussions of our roots. And we in A.A. have completely lost track of where our program really came from, how many component parts there were to that program, and how its varied roots came from different activities and produced diverse offshoots at various different times. Most of our fellowship and those in 12 Step programs have a number of erroneous concepts so embedded in their historical approaches that they just never hear, read, or tell it like it is, or like it was.

Some, who don't want to hear the word Bible, may at times acknowledge that the Good Book was somehow involved, but have frequently dismissed this root by saying we left God's Word behind in Akron. One bleeding deacon told a sponsee of mine that the Bible was abandoned because "It didn't work." Some, who have developed a distaste for the words Buchman and Oxford Group, are inclined to adopt Bill Wilson's belated and erroneous statement that the Oxford Group "taught us more about what *not* to do than what to do." This despite the fact that Bill's Big Book virtually codifies the Oxford Group life-changing ideas in its Twelve Steps. And some, who neither understand nor favor either the Bible or the Oxford Group, have tried to quiet the waters by diverting the stream. These folks often say A.A. is "spiritual, but not religious" even though any well-informed historian, scholar, clergyman, and semanticist would probably ask: "What does that mean?" "And what's the difference?" In fact, nobody really knows what the alleged difference might be, but the distinction without a difference leaves many a bewildered newcomer in today's illusory, "peaceful," atheistic no man's land.

The real difference in how we characterize A.A. is that, without a knowledge of A.A.'s various sources—mostly religious—people all too often fabricate their own supposed history and sources. That can rightly be called "self-made religion." And A.A.'s "cofounder" Rev. Sam Shoemaker pointed out that this self-fabricated stuff leads to all kinds of nonsense—including "absurd names for God" and "half-baked prayers" as Sam described them to the AAs themselves.

So it is. Those who do not know or even seem to have an interest in our historical roots, can often be heard to say that the Creator is some kind of strange "higher power" which can be a tree or a pumpkin. Or they may be heard to proclaim that neither the Creator, the tree, or the pumpkin stands the test of being "Conference Approved." Some capitalize the frequently heard words "Higher Power" as if to make "it," "them," of "Something" both sacred and powerful. Others write "higher power" in lower case—timidly offering this idol as "something" greater than yourself. Today, A.A. World headquarters often goes go on to reassure the unwary newcomer that you really don't have to believe in anything at all—leaving the question just what is A.A. if it requires nothing at all but not drinking and sitting in meetings. See *A Newcomer Asks* . . . (York, England, A.A. Sterling Area Services, n.d.); *This is AA. . . . an introduction to the AA recovery program* (NY: Alcoholics Anonymous World Services, Inc., 1984), p. 15. Then, if someone tries to unravel such nonsensical assertions, many will tender such A.A. jabber as, "Don't analyze, utilize" or "Don't think and don't drink," "Take what you want, and leave the rest," or "Look for the similarities and discard the differences." Fortunately, some may add that the Big Book is A.A.'s basic text, but then ignore that text and let it go at that. "The Big Book says it, and that settles it" is a common A.A. expression. And that frequently leaves all of us with what the Big Book says, but mostly what it doesn't say. Moreover, the root difficulty is that our "basic text" doesn't say much about history, roots, diversity, development, splits, or offshoots.

AAs today have been subjected to the fiat that all "official" mention of the Bible has been deleted from their basic text. The same has become true in many other, derivative "anonymous" groups. AAs have seen Jesus Christ mentioned only once in their basic text, and then as a man whose ideas are seldom followed. They've seen the Creator turned into a higher power which has been turned into a radiator. At the same time, they hear about prayer and meditation and haven't the slightest bit of information as to what those ideas meant either in earliest A.A. or even in the Big Book and Steps. Worse, all mention of *cure* has been obliterated and the following substituted: "We in AA believe there is no such thing as a *cure* for alcoholism" (See *A Newcomer Asks*, p. 2).

Such statements flatly contradict the fact that Bill Wilson did believe there was a cure (Big Book, p.191). Dr. Bob did believe there was a cure for alcoholism (Big Book, p. 180). A.A. Number Three (Bill Dotson) did believe there was a cure (Big Book, p. 191). That being the case, what has happened to God—the "God of our fathers," as Bill Wilson called Him? How did the "cure" to which early AAs referred for almost a decade become "no cure" and "recovery" merely a "daily reprieve"—leaving the lurking shadow of relapse as a controlling fear factor supposed to produce adherence to program ideas. What happened to cure?

Today, A.A. newcomers are befuddled and confronted with nonsense. Prayer to a rock? Prayer to a chair or a tree? Meditation with a radiator? Meditation as listening to Something? Praying to what! Chanting to what! Listening to what—a light bulb? For assistance, they are told in their basic text that there are "helpful books," but there is no mention of the Good Book which was the major source for their basic ideas. In fact, most don't dare mention any of the hundreds of religious books the pioneers read. If they do, they may get a letter telling them A.A. is not religious; or they hear from a "bleeding deacon" that religious matters are not appropriate for discussion. All this diversionary fluff is not Alcoholics Anonymous. It just describes what many in Alcoholics Anonymous and in its service structure abhor any mention of religious matters,

But that hasn't driven me from A.A. Nor should it drive you or anyone else to accept nonsense. Early A.A. relied on our Creator. So did I. So can you. A.A.'s Big Book urges you to "find" God and then trust Him. Whether you "find" Him or not, He's there; and you can trust Him. In other words, all the verbiage and literature and meeting talk can't change history, nor eradicate the Bible, nor deprive you or anyone else of the privilege of relying on the power of God IN A.A., and of being a member OF A.A., and of being cured of alcoholism AS an AA. It merely requires that you learn the facts. "Just the facts, ma'am!"

Now let's look at the real record and the facts.

The real purpose of my 18 years of historical research, travel, interviews, writing, and talks has been to gather together as many of the well-springs of A.A. as I could find. It didn't and doesn't matter to me how diverse or conflicting they may be. And to gather them from evidence—however disparate they might seem or be. Not to attempt making them congruous or compatible or even authoritative, but rather to report them so that all could learn the truth about our sources, our roots, our history, our original program, and how the situation has changed today—ignoring the single most important fact about early A.A.

The pioneer early A.A. fellowships of Akron and Cleveland, Ohio, respectively, had documented 75% and 93% success rates among the seemingly hopeless, "medically incurable," real alcoholics who thoroughly followed the A.A. path to a relationship with God. And the alcoholic was cured. In the pioneer program, one didn't try to "find" God; nor did one concern oneself with "coming to believe," nor was one merely looking for a tentative, wobbly "daily reprieve."

The alcoholic was encouraged to believe that God is and that He rewards those who diligently seek him.[642]

Accordingly, one sought a relationship with Him.[643] One sought to become His child by being born again of His spirit.[644]

The way to the new birth, to being born again of God's spirit, was through conversion—salvation—acceptance of Jesus Christ as Lord and Savior.[645] And the Akron pioneers did just that, as independently attested by four pioneers who really did exactly that, as they were directed to do. These men, as shown before, were J.D. Holmes, Ed Andy, Clarence Snyder, and Larry Bauer.

The core library covered by our binders lists the books and materials that present the various elements of the program—however much they may differ, how much they may have changed, and how much they offer to recovery today.

At the core of the library collection is my 28 volume reference set containing the published titles I have written on our history. It is supplemented by more than 170 articles which are now posted on the internet and may soon be compiled and published. Also, by a number of available audio presentations in the form of audio blogs, podcasts, and radio shows.

---

[642] Hebrews 11:6; *DR. BOB and the Good Oldtimers*, 144; *Alcoholics Anonymous*, 4th ed., 53.
[643] *Alcoholics Anonymous,* 4th ed., 29, 100.
[644] 1 John 3:1-2, 4:13, 5:1, 4; John 3:1-8; *Alcoholics Anonymous*, 4th ed., 63
[645] John 14:6, Acts 4:12, Acts 16:30-31, Romans 10:9-10; Dick B., *The Conversion of Bill W.*, 49-50, 52-54, 60-63, 93-96, 100-02; and Dick B., *Real Twelve Step Fellowship History: The Old School A.A. You May Not Know* (Kihei, HI: Paradise Research Publications, Inc., 2006), 9.

The 16 Major A.A. Well-Springs Are Not A.A.'s Basic Ideas—Just Its Sources

I've spent 18 years gathering the sources of our basic ideas. I've published at least one book and many articles on each of those sources. And this description will not repeat the materials in my published titles. I will point out here though that you can find the discussion of the basics in the following of my titles: (1) **The Bible**: *The Good Book and The Big Book; Why Early A.A. Succeeded (a Bible Study Primer); The James Club and the Original A.A. Program's Absolute Essentials; Twelve Steps for You; The Good Book-Big Book Guidebook;* (2) **The contents of Anne Smith's Journal, 1933-1939**: *Anne Smith's Journal, 1933-1939*; (3) **Quiet Time**: *Good Morning: Quiet Time, Morning Watch, Meditation, and Early A.A.*; (4) **The Oxford Group's Life Changing Twenty-Eight Ideas**: *The Oxford Group and Alcoholics Anonymous*; *Henrietta B. Seiberling: Ohio's Lady with a Cause*; (5) **The teachings of Rev. Sam Shoemaker**: *New Light on Alcoholism; By the Power of God; Twelve Steps for You;* (6) **The Christian literature they studied and circulated:** *Dr. Bob and His Library; The Books Early AAs Read for Spiritual Growth; The Akron Genesis of Alcoholics Anonymous; That Amazing Grace; Making Known the Biblical History and Roots of Early A.A.* (7) **The Akron Elements from United Christian Endeavor Society**: *When Early AAs Were Cured and Why; The James Club; Making Known the Biblical History and Roots of A.A.; God and Alcoholism; Cured; The First Nationwide A.A. History Conference;* (8) **The other elements of our history**, including William James, Carl Jung, William D. Silkworth, Rowland Hazard, Ebby Thacher, the Salvation Army, Rescue Missions, the YMCA, conversions, Richard Peabody, New Thought writers like Emmet Fox.: *Introduction to the Sources and Founding of Alcoholics Anonymous; Real Twelve Step Fellowship History; The Conversion of Bill W..*

Other basic ideas came from sources I have researched and which are covered in numerous articles I have published on my websites. They are mentioned below in connection with their sources. And they had a particularly great influence on some of the language Bill used in the Big Book and in his other writings. So much so that one of the very few early New York AAs to get sober (John Henry Fitzhugh Mayo) was defeated in his effort to include the early Christian and Biblical materials in the Big Book. The so-called "dogma and doctrines" of the rescue missions were taken out of the basic text manuscript. At least 400 pages of manuscript were simply tossed out, never to be found—even today. Bill's secretary Ruth Hock said they were mostly Christian and Biblical materials.

But that's not what's at issue. Here we'll take a cursory look at Sixteen Major Well-Springs of A.A. They don't fit in a nice timeline. They are not particularly consistent in belief, nor are they congruous as far as each of A.A.'s historical epochs is concerned. None of them can be found to be present in each and every one of the various streams of A.A. from Switzerland, Harvard, Akron, Cleveland, New York, Gospel Rescue Missions, the Salvation Army, United Christian Endeavor, New Thought writers, Christian devotionals, Christian literature, Quiet Time, Anne Smith, Henrietta Seiberling, Sister Ignatia, Father Ralph Pfau, Ed Webster, Richmond Walker, Father Ed Dowling, Father John C. Ford, or Rev. Sam Shoemaker. They simply ought to be known as part of our history, but not be expected to fit together into a successful program of recovery. They involve evolution, not doctrine; history, not theory; opinions, but not necessarily fact. What's really important, I suppose, is to see what didn't work, as well as what did.

To be brief, our history ought to be known so that recovering people can make intelligent choices and appropriate decisions. Following, then, are the well-springs—some of great importance, some virtually unknown, and many conflicting in direction, meaning, and emphasis. They are presented here with a brief annotated bibliography of each to enable further study, and—subsequently—with a specific description of the books and articles and memorabilia that will be part of each category in the Dick B. Well-springs Library.

The 16 Well-Springs as Sources of Our Basic Ideas

Number One: The United Christian Endeavor Society. Organized in 1881, about the time of Dr. Bob's birth. Initially focused on the young people in a local Protestant Church in Maine. Then on the St. Johnsbury church attended by Dr. Bob and his family in Vermont—a supportive Christian Endeavor Group of young people connected with that church. It produced almost all of the major ideas that were carried

over into early Akron A.A.'s Christian Fellowship led by Dr. Bob. The ideas? Confession of Christ. Bible study. Prayer meetings. Conversion meetings. Quiet Hours, topical discussions, reading of religious literature, witness, and fellowship—all under the banner of "love and service."[646]

For the specific relative historical literature, see the chapter of this book covering Christian Endeavor, and the following two books as major sources for information:

Francis E. Clark. *Christian Endeavor in All Lands* (Np: The United Society of Christian Endeavor, 1906);
Amos R. Wells. *Expert Endeavor: A Textbook of Christian Endeavor Methods and Principles* (Boston: United Society of Christian Endeavor, 1911).

Number Two: The Salvation Army. Organized under General William Booth not long after Christian Endeavor and introducing ideas about working with drunks and street criminals. Its ideas used in missions, observed by Ebby Thacher and Bill Wilson, and exemplified by the practical program of early Akron A.A. The ideas? Abstinence. Resisting Temptation. Confessing Jesus Christ. Relying on the Creator. Elimination of sin. Employing the power of one saved and recovered drunk to bring effectively to another still-suffering drunk the message of salvation, love, and service. Carrying the message of salvation and questing for truth. Perpetuating the fellowship and witnessing among the ranks of those already saved, recovered soldiers.[647]

For specific relative historical literature:

Harold Begbie. *The Gospel Truth: Life of William Booth, Founder and First General of the Salvation Army.* 2 vols. (New York: Macmillan, 1920); William Booth, Vols. I and II;
Harold Begbie. *Twice Born Men* (NY: Fleming H. Revell, 1909);

---

[646] See Dick B., *The James Club and The Early A.A. Program's Absolute Essentials*; *The Good Book-Big Book Guidebook*; *Making Known the Biblical History and Roots of Early A.A.*; and *A New Way Out*.
[647] See Dick B., *When Early AAs Were Cured and Why*; *The First Nationwide A.A. History Conference*; and *A New Way Out*.

Howard Clinebell, *Understanding and Counseling Persons with Alcohol, Drug, and Behavioral Addictions.* Rev. and enl. ed. (Nashville: Abingdon Press, 1998).
Yale Journal of Alcohol Studies Lectures, 1945

Number Three: The Gospel Rescue Missions. Said to have gained ascendancy because of the testimony of Jerry McAuley, they carried into residential and meeting place centers ideas similar to those of the Salvation Army for physical places of rehabilitation and salvation. Bible study and teaching; hymns; testimonies; "soup, soap, and salvation," altar calls and conversion; shelter, with educational and vocational training as well. Their declarations that "Jesus saves" set the stage for religious services involving testimony, music, Bible, prayer, and then the altar call where the afflicted went to the altar where a brother prayed for and with them and they made their decisions for Christ.[648]

For specific historical materials:

Mel B. *New Wine: The Spiritual Roots of the Twelve Step Miracle* (Center City, MN: Hazelden, 1991);
Howard Clinebell, *Understanding and Counseling the Alcoholic*, rev. & enl. ed. (TN: Abingdon Press, 1982)
Bill Pittman. *AA The Way It Began* (Seattle, WA: Glen Abbey Books, 1988)
Historical materials of the Association of Gospel and Rescue Missions.

Number Four: Professor William James and the conversions which later came to be called "spiritual experiences." Just who is the author of Bill's "spiritual experience" expression is not all that clear. The term was used in the Oxford Group. But the source idea is and was always religious *conversion*. Carl Jung told Rowland Hazard that Rowland needed a "conversion" experience. William James wrote *The Varieties of Religious Experience*, which Wilson studied and then believed validated his "hot flash" experience at Towns Hospital. Finally, as he looked back on his life, Bill Wilson concluded he had had five spiritual experiences.[649]

---

[648] See Dick B., *Real Twelve Step Fellowship History*.
[649] See Dick B., *The Conversion of Bill W.*; *Turning Point*. Sam Shoemaker wrote in his first significant book that people needed a "vital religious experience."

For specific historical materials:

William James. *The Varieties of Religious Experience* (NY: First Vintage Press/The Library of America Edition, 1990)
Edwin Diller Starbuck, *The Psychology of Religion: An Empirical Study of the Growth of the Religious Consciousness, with a Preface by William James* (London: Walter Scott, 1899)
James H. Leuba, "A Study in the Psychology of Religious Phenomena." In *The American Journal of Psychology* (Vol. VII. April 1986, No. 3), 309-85.
Books by or about George A. Coe, Carl Jung, Billy Sunday, Charles G. Finney, Dwight L. Moody, T.S. Arthur, John Gough, and Jared Lobdell (full citations in Bibliography)
Samuel M. Shoemaker, Jr. *Realizing Religion* (NY: Association Press, 1923).

Number Five: The conversion ideas of Dr. Carl Gustav Jung. Two or three historians who had not really done their homework claimed several years ago that Jung had no connection with A.A.'s beginnings. They assert that Jung never saw Rowland Hazard as a patient and therefore the "conversion" solution so dominant in Bill Wilson's Big Book program did not come from Jung. But their skimpy research does not support the absurd conclusion that Carl Jung, Rowland Hazard, Ebby Thacher, Bill Wilson, and Sam Shoemaker all lied in order to conjure up a story about the real and original solution for alcoholism. The problem, however, concerns how badly Wilson missed the point of Jung's idea of conversion. Conversion, Jung said, was the solution for Rowland's chronic alcoholism. But conversion, in the mind and words of Carl Jung, did not seem to mean what the Bible describes as a new birth and which Shoemaker and the Akronites were later espousing. Nor was Bill Wilson's response to the altar call at Shoemaker's Calvary Mission a conversion of the kind Jung had in mind, although Wilson apparently thought so.[650]

---

[650] See Dick B., *New Light on Alcoholism: God, Sam Shoemaker, and A.A.; Twelve Steps for You; The Good Book-Big Book Guidebook; The Conversion of Bill W.;* and *Real Twelve Step Fellowship History.*

For specific historical literature:

C.G. Jung. *Modern Man in Search of a Soul* (NY: Harcourt Brace Jovanovich, Publishers, 1933). Among the books owned and studied by Dr. Bob, I found the foregoing Jung book inscribed to Dr. Bob by Bill Wilson. Though reading it is tough sledding, I believe the translator's preface emphasizes Jung's view of rebirth. First, the translator talks about those who reach to attain to more knowledge of the inner workings of their own minds, more information about the subtle but none the less perfectly definite laws that govern the psyche. They believe, he said, they can achieve the new attitude without having on the one hand to "regress to what is but a thinly veiled mediaeval theology, or on the other, to fall victims to the illusions of nineteenth-century ideology." That sounds very little to me like "Christ in you, the hope of glory."

Leslie D. Weatherhead. *Psychology, Religion and Healing.* NY: Abingdon-Cokesbury Press, 1951. Weatherhead examines Jung's ideas in substantial detail. Jung's idea of "conversion" is "individuation," he writes. "Individuation in Jung's sense, is the wise setting of the house of one's personality in order, but it is a task at which one is wise to work for the rest of one's life" (p. 287). Weatherhead states later: "But one wonders where Jung got the idea that the heart of Christianity was 'imitating Christ' . . . To advise people to 'imitate Christ' is no gospel at all. It puts all the strain on the Christian's will-power. The Christian Way becomes something the Christian must achieve. But the heart of the Gospel is something God does in Christ through the Holy Spirit; something He has done and is doing and will do for anyone who trusts Him. The power in Christianity is not in man's effort to imitate Christ, but in Christ's love for man, forgiveness of man and power to change man. . . . St. Paul would not recognize Jung's brand of Christianity at all" (pp. 392-393).

Number Six: The medical ideas and Great Physician prescription of Dr. William D. Silkworth. Once again, historians who have not really done their homework now sometimes claim that Dr. Silkworth did not originate the ideas about alcoholism as a disease. And there is evidence that the disease concept may actually not have originated with Silkworth. But there is equally strong evidence that it was Silkworth who spelled out for Bill Wilson the idea that Wilson was suffering from a mental obsession and a physical allergy—however the details were or would be characterized in the disease arena. Virtually unmentioned by historians, however, is Silkworth's belief—explained to Bill Wilson and other patients—that Jesus Christ, the "Great Physician," could cure them of alcoholism.[651]

For specific historical literature, see:

Norman Vincent Peale. *The Positive Power of Jesus Christ* (NY: Foundation for Christian Living, 1980);
Dale Mitchel. *Silkworth: The Little Doctor Who Loved Drunks* (Center City, MN: Hazelden, 2002);
Bill W: My First 40 Years (Hazelden, 2000).

Number Seven: The Oxford Group—A First Century Christian Fellowship. Not really "organized" until about 1919 when the book *Soul Surgery* was first published. Primarily, a movement which drew its ideas from the eclectic life-changing Biblical concepts of Lutheran Minister Frank N. D. Buchman. Each one of the aforementioned well-springs influenced the ideas that were borrowed and adapted by the Akron program. And to these were added catch-words and ideas that Buchman picked up along the way toward the Oxford Group's actual founding. There were **twenty-eight ideas** in all that impacted upon A.A.'s Big Book and Twelve Steps and existed in greater or lesser degree in some of the practices in the earlier Akron Fellowship. The 28 ideas can be summarized in **eight groupings** of the ideas Buchman put together: (1) **God**—descriptions of Him, His plan, man's duty, believing. (2) **Sin**—that which blocks man from God and others. (3) **Surrenders**—the decision to surrender self and self-will to God's will. (4) **Life-changing art**—the Five C's of the process moving from Confidence to Confession to Conviction to Conversion to Continuance. (5) **Jesus Christ**—His power and the Four Absolute Standards. Sin was the problem. Jesus Christ was the cure. And the result was a miracle, they said. (6) **Growth in fellowship** through Quiet Time, Bible study, prayer, and seeking Guidance. (7) **Restitution—for the harms caused by sin.** (8) **Fellowship and**

---

[651] See Dick B. *Cured: Proven Help for Alcoholics and Addicts; The Conversion of Bill W.; The Good Book-Big Book Guidebook; When Early AAs Were Cured and Why; The First Nationwide A.A. History Conference.*

witness—working in teams loyal to Jesus Christ to change the lives of others.[652]

For specific historical literature:

Garth Lean. *Frank Buchman: A Life*. (London: Constable, 1985);
Frank Buchman. *Remaking the World*, 1961;
Howard A, Walter. *Soul Surgery* (NY: The Oxford Group, 1928);
Harold Begbie. *Life Changers* (NY: G.P. Putnam's Sons, 1926);
A.J. Russell. *For Sinners Only* (London: Hodder & Stoughton, 1932).
Strong. *Preview of a New World*
Tournier, 2 books on healing and Oxford Group Ideas
Oxford Group pamphlets: *How Do I Begin, The Principles of the Group*
Eleanor Forde. *The Guidance of God*
Article by Dick B. on all relevant Oxford Group literature.

Number Eight: The teachings of Episcopalian priest Rev. Samuel M. Shoemaker, Jr. Sam teamed up with Frank Buchman about 1919, then began writing an incredibly large series of many books on the OG ideas and Sam's Bible concepts. He headquartered his efforts at Calvary Church in New York, of which he became Rector in 1925. It is fair to say that the most quoted, the most copied, and the most persuasive influence on Bill Wilson and his Big Book approach came directly from Shoemaker. To the point where Wilson actually asked Sam to write the Twelve Steps, as to which Sam declined in favor of their being written by an alcoholic, namely, Bill. Shoemaker language can be seen throughout the Big Book and in the language of Wilson's famous Twelve Steps.[653]

---

[652] See Dick B., *The Oxford Group and Alcoholics Anonymous: A Design for Living That Works*; *The Akron Genesis of Alcoholics Anonymous*; *Turning Point: A History of the Spiritual Roots and Successes of Alcoholics Anonymous*; *A New Way Out*; *A New Way In*, and *Making Known the Biblical History and Roots of A.A.*.

[653] See the following titles by Dick B.: (1) *New Light on Alcoholism: God, Sam Shoemaker, and A.A.*; (2) *The First Nationwide History Conference*; (3) *When Early AAs Were Cured and Why*; (4) *By the Power of God*; (5) *Twelve Steps for You*; and (6) *Good Morning*.

For specific historical literature:

Samuel M. Shoemaker, *Realizing Religion*;
Three Clarence Snyder Old-timers. *Our A.A. Legacy*.

Number Nine: The lay therapy ideas of Richard Peabody. Dr. Bob and Bill Wilson both owned and studied *The Common Sense of Drinking*—a book by lay therapist Richard Peabody. And though Peabody died drunk, Wilson somehow saw fit to adopt almost verbatim certain words and phrases from the Peabody book. Among the two most unfortunate derivates were: (1) There is no cure for alcoholism. (2) Once an alcoholic always an alcoholic. Both concepts flew in the face of a decade of clear and outspoken declarations by the early AAs and their observers that they had found a cure for alcoholism that rested on the power of Jesus Christ. This was not something Peabody embraced. And how Wilson got switched from God to incurable illness on the basis of the writings of a lay therapist who died drunk is currently a mystery to me.[654]

For specific historical literature:

Richard Peabody. *The Common Sense of Drinking* (Atlantic Monthly Press Book, 1939);
Mel B., *New Wine*, pp. 117-20.
Pittman, *AA The Way It Began*.
Bound Materials on the Emmanuel Movement, Courtney Baylor, and Peabody.

Number Ten: The Bible (which early AAs called the "Good Book"). A.A. cofounder Dr. Bob Smith stated emphatically in a major speech in Detroit in 1948 that he didn't write the Twelve Steps; that he had nothing to do with the writing of them; that A.A.'s basic ideas came from the Bible; that there were no stories (drunkalogs), no Steps, and no basic texts (such as the Big Book). Dr. Bob pointed to the Book of James, 1 Corinthians 13, and Jesus' Sermon on the Mount as absolutely essential to their program. They felt, he said, that the Good Book contained all the answers to their problems. For example, early AAs actually wanted to call their Society the James Club because that

---

[654] See Dick B., *Cured: Proven Help for Alcoholics and Addicts*; *When Early AAs Were Cured and Why*; and *A New Way Out*.

book was their favorite. Bill Wilson confirmed this fact and also favored Corinthians. Bob was insistent that Henry Drummond's *The Greatest Thing in the World* was a "must' in reading; and it was a study of 1 Corinthians 13. Wilson and Smith both said that the Sermon on the Mount contained the underlying philosophy of A.A. There are many Biblical ideas and phrases in A.A.'s later Big Book; and certainly the emphasis on Bible study in United Christian Endeavor, in Dr. Bob's youth, in the Akron fellowship, and in the Christian literature A.A. pioneers studied, was proof enough of the Bible's importance to recovery, cure, and the fellowship long before Wilson took Oxford Group ideas, fashioned his Big Book and Steps, and published Alcoholics Anonymous in the Spring of 1939—four years after A.A. was founded.[655]

For further specific historical materials:

DR. BOB and the Good Oldtimers;
RHS. Memorial on Dr. Bob's Death;
The Co-founders of Alcoholics Anonymous: Biographical sketches Their last major talks (NY: Alcoholics Anonymous World Services, Inc., 1972, 1975);
Four pamphlets published by AA of Akron: *A Guide to the Twelve Steps of Alcoholics Anonymous; A Manual for Alcoholics Anonymous; Second Reader for Alcoholics Anonymous; Spiritual Milestones in Alcoholics Anonymous.*
Three Clarence Snyder Sponsees. *Our A.A. Legacy.*
Harnack. History and Expansion of the Christian Church, 2 volumes (owned by Dr. Bob)
Schaaf. T*he History of the Christian Church,* 8 volumes.

Number Eleven: The Biblical Emphasis from Dr. Bob's youth and Christian Endeavor—the heart of the Akron Christian Fellowship's spiritual program of recovery. A.A. detractors and doctrinaire Christians who dislike the Oxford Group seem impelled to claim that A.A. came from the Oxford Group, that the Oxford Group

---

[655] See Dick B. *The Good Book and The Big Book*; *Turning Point*; *Why Early A.A. Succeeded*; *The Books Early AAs Read for Spiritual Growth*; *That Amazing Grace*; *The Good Book-Big Book Guidebook*; *The James Club and the Original A.A. Program's Absolute Essentials*; *The Akron Genesis of Alcoholics Anonymous*; *Good Morning*; and *Real Twelve Step Fellowship History.*

was an heretical cult, and that its very existence was an example of what A.A. wasn't, rather than what it was. And these erroneous ideas are so heavily entrenched in religious and recovery thinking and writing they may never be dispelled. But they are fallacious and utterly misleading. If you are a student of Oxford Group writings, you simply can't escape the obvious: Bill Wilson's Big Book and Twelve Step program embraced almost every Oxford Group idea—even though Bill Wilson used several ruses which were meant to deny the fact. By contrast, the early Akron program, which produced the documented 75 to 93% success rates among seemingly hopeless "medically incurable" real alcoholics, had very little to do with Oxford Group teams, principles, and practices. The Akron focus was on abstinence—not an Oxford Group principle or practice; hospitalization—not an Oxford Group idea or practice; resisting temptation—not an Oxford Group idea as far as the discussion is Chapter One of the Book of James is concerned; accepting Jesus Christ as Lord and Saviour—not an Oxford Group requirement; relying on the Creator for strength and guidance—a universal idea undoubtedly embraced by the Oxford Group; Bible study meetings—not an Oxford Group emphasis; old-fashioned prayer meetings—not an Oxford Group idea; Quiet Time—a universal idea which pre-dated the Oxford Group and was a big item in Christian Endeavor, the YMCA, and the Oxford Group; religious comradeship—not an Oxford Group idea; favored church attendance—not an Oxford Group idea; love and service as a banner—not an Oxford Group expression, but a Christian Endeavor word of art; working with others—not an Oxford Group emphasis when it came to working with other alcoholics, nor was it particularly a Christian Endeavor idea except as to witnessing and conversion. By contrast, the simple Christian Endeavor program appears to represent the heart of what Akron did and what it was reported in official A.A. literature to have done. That program was not incorporated in the Big Book, but it is reported fully by Frank Amos reports to John D. Rockefeller, Jr. that are part of A.A.'s conference approved literature.[656]

656
. See Dick B., *The First Nationwide A.A. History Conference; The Good Book and The Big Book: A.A.'s Roots in the Bible; Why Early A.A. Succeeded* (A Bible study primer); *The Good Book-Big Book Guidebook*; and *The James Club and The Early A.A. Program's Absolute Essentials*; and *A New Way Out*.

For specific historical literature:

DR. BOB and the Good Oldtimers;
Co-founders Last Talks
Clark, *Christian Endeavor*;
Mitchell K. *How It Worked: The Story of Clarence H. Snyder and the Early Days of Alcoholics in Cleveland*, Ohio (NY: A Big Book Study Group, 1997).
Wally P. *But for the Grace of God*

Number Twelve: The practical records and teachings of Dr. Bob's Wife. How A.A. could have buried Anne Smith's role, her importance, and her spiritual journal is a complete mystery. The facts about Anne Smith's service to early A.A.—housing, cooking, Bible teaching, conducting quiet times, sharing at meetings, counseling alcoholics and their families, organizing the first women's group, reaching out to newcomers—would stand on their own as vitally important history even if she had never written her journal which spanned nine of A.A.'s formative years. As far as I've been able to discover, Bill never ever mentioned Anne's journal, though Dr. Bob's daughter said that Bill and Lois Wilson picked up the Journal after Dr. Bob's death. And Bill Wilson and many pioneers called Anne the "Mother of A.A." The pioneer AAs were housed in her home from the beginning, and those AAs got well. AAs were fed in her home, and it became the first real "half-way" house after hospitalization. Anne read the Bible to A.A.'s founders and to the many who followed them. Anne conducted a quiet time each morning at the Dr. Bob's Home where she led a group of AAs and their families in Bible study, prayer, listening, and topical discussions. Anne counseled and nursed and taught alcoholics; and her work with newcomers in meetings was legendary. They were her special focus. Her journal records every principle and concept that is part of the A.A. picture—Biblical emphasis, prayer, Quiet Time, Guidance, Literature recommended, Oxford Group principles and practices, and practical guides to working with alcoholics. It seems likely that she not only shared the contents of this journal—written between 1933 and 1939—with Bill Wilson, but also that Bill took many of his Oxford Group and other expressions directly from Anne's Journal. If so, the fact has never been mentioned.[657]

For specific historical materials:

Copy of original manuscript of *Anne Smith's Journal*
Lois Wilson. *Lois Remembers*
Borchert. *When Love is Not Enough*

Number Thirteen: The Devotionals and Christian Literature Read and Circulated. We know that A.A.'s basic ideas came from the Bible. The Book of James, Jesus' Sermon on the Mount, and 1 Corinthians 13 were frequently read aloud and studied and were considered absolutely essential. And AAs studied literature that underlined these roots—books on the Sermon by Oswald Chambers, Glenn Clark, Harry Emerson Fosdick, Emmet Fox, and E. Stanley Jones. Devotionals discussing concepts from the Book of James—*The Runner's Bible*, *The Upper Room*, *My Utmost for His Highest*, *Daily Strength for Daily Needs*. There were commentaries on 1 Corinthians 13 written by Henry Drummond and Toyohiko Kagawa and studied by pioneers. And various other concepts were fleshed out through the literature of Shoemaker on all aspects of the Bible, prayer, guidance, Quiet Time, and so on. So also through the many Oxford Group books on these subjects—*Soul Surgery* (and the Five C's), *Quiet Time*, *The Guidance of God*, *Realizing Religion*, *For Sinners Only*, *When Man Listens*, and so on. In addition, there were prayer guides and Bible study guides and healing guides galore—in Dr. Bob's Library and circulated by him to others. The whole picture can be found in my titles.[658]

For specific, historical literature:

Compilations of Glenn Chesnut of Indiana
Harry Emerson Fosdick, *The Meaning of Prayer*

---

[657] See Dick B., *Anne Smith's Journal, 1933-1939; The Akron Genesis of Alcoholics Anonymous*; and *A New Way Out*.
[658] See Dick B., *The Books Early AAs Read for Spiritual Growth*, 7th edition; *Making Known the Biblical History and Roots of A.A.*; *Anne Smith's Journal*; *The Akron Genesis of Alcoholics Anonymous*; and *Dr. Bob and His Library*.

Howard J. Rose. *The Quiet Time.* NY: Oxford Group at 61 Gramercy Park, North, 1937)
Drummond. *The Greatest Thing in the World.*
E. Stanley Jones. *The Christ of the Mount.*
The Upper Room.
Nora Smith Holm. *The Runner's Bible*
Oswald Chambers. *My Utmost for His Highest.*

Number Fourteen: Quiet Time and the Guidance of God. A British evangelist, scholar, and Christian Endeavor leader named F. B. Meyer wrote *The Secret of Guidance*. And his ideas should be given much credit for spawning the "Morning Watch," as it was called in the YMCA and elsewhere; the "Quiet Hour," as it was called in Christian Endeavor; and "Quiet Time" as it came to be called in the Oxford Group. Essentially, and apparently unrealized by most historians and AAs, the first requisite was to become a child of God—to be born again, to receive the spirit of God through a second birth. With that, believers sought God's guidance at every turn. They prepared themselves through prayer, Bible study, group quiet times, seeking guidance, "listening," "journaling," "checking," and discussion. There has been much criticism of the merits of some of these practices. But it is impossible to escape dealing with the Bible verses they cited and which talk of prayer in the morning, of meditation in the morning, of the importance of quietness, of peace, and of asking God for wisdom. Quiet Time was a "must" in early A.A. Its corrupted remnants can be found in the Big Book's Eleventh Step discussion. And the necessity for seeking God's guidance can even be found in the A.A. Twelve Traditions today.[659]

For further specific historical literature:

Eleanor Napier Forde. *The Guidance of God* (London: The Oxford Group, 1927);
Hallen Viney. *How do I Begin?* (The Oxford Group, n.d.);
Howard Rose. *The Quiet Time.*
The cited references in our chapter in this book on Christian Endeavor.

---

[659] How much did AAs seek God's guidance *for their program;* and how much did He provide? See Dick B. *Good Morning; Quiet Time, Morning Watch, Meditation, and Early A.A.*

Number Fifteen: New Thought. Also beginning to take wing through the impetus of Christian Science and similar movements that started to flower at almost the same period as the first two sources. But the New Thought focus was on a new kind of god—a higher power—that took descriptive words from the Bible but saw God, good, and evil in non-salvation terms. New Thought words and phrases like higher power, cosmic consciousness, fourth dimension, and Universal Mind filtered in to the A.A. stream. The New Thought expositors included Mary Baker Eddy, Waldo Trine, William James, Emmanuel Movement writers, and Emmet Fox.[660]

For further historical materials, see Mel B., see *New Wine*.

Number Sixteen: The Young Men's Christian Association. Based on the contents of this book, our extensive acquisition of YMCA books and materials, and our resource binders, I have added a sixteenth well-spring. Research at St. Johnsbury, Vermont, and research of the Y.M.C.A., Moody, and Congregational Church materials have made it quite clear that the YMCA needs to be considered an A.A. well-spring. It should be remembered from our research on *The Conversion of Bill W.* that Bill Wilson, at Burr and Burton Academy, was president of the YMCA and that his lady-love Bertha Bamford was president of the YWCA. The facts about the YMCA in Vermont and its relationship with Academies and churches needs further exploration. Most of the new facts can be found in this present title; and more work needs to be done.

The Whole Picture

As Father Paul Blaes, Ph.D., the Roman Catholic theologian who endorsed my *Turning Point* book, wrote so well: There was a *lacuna* in A.A. history when I began 18 years ago. A *lacuna* is a gap, a hole. And Father Blaes had observed for himself the gaping vacuum in accounts of our history. He therefore welcomed and endorsed my new comprehensive history.

---

[660] See the following titles by Dick B.: *The Books Early AAs Read for Spiritual Growth*, 7th ed.; When Early AAs Were Cured and Why; Dr. Bob and His Library; Good Morning: Quiet Time, Morning Watch, Meditation, and Early A.A.; God and Alcoholism.

When I began, I thought the only missing elements were descriptions of how the Bible was used and what the Oxford Group program really was. And there were plenty of gaps there. Revisionist writers had reported on A.A. only as they saw it thirty years ago. They had ignored the history of A.A. that has been unearthed in part in the last three decades. But such obstructionism was just the tip of the iceberg. A.A. literature said Dr. Bob's library had been given away. Yet I discovered about half of it in his daughter's attic and tracked down the other half to his son's home in Nocona, Texas. And without these books, you just couldn't know what early AAs *were* reading and concluding. Next, I discovered that Anne Smith's Journal had simply never been mentioned in A.A. history accounts, other than in an Ernest Kurtz footnote and collaterally in a biography of Sister Ignatia. And, thanks to Dr. Bob's daughter and A.A.'s now deceased archivist Frank Mauser, I was permitted to get a complete copy and publish my title, *Anne Smith's Journal, 1933-1939.* Then, I began researching the Oxford Group about 1990, and it was at the suggestion of Frank Mauser, that I later wrote the first edition of my Oxford Group title; and over the years I found hundreds of their books, encountered an intense interest among its leaders in my work, and then realized the whole Big Book program was essentially Oxford Group—something broadly suggested in Joe and Charlie Big Book Seminars. From there I went to the Akron story and realized the importance and differences regarding the early Christian Fellowship there. I tracked down the history and wrote the Akron story. Learning from this research the importance of the Bible to early A.A., I tackled the Biblical roots and am only now getting the entire picture together—the words in A.A. from the Bible, the prayers in A.A. from the Bible, the slogans in A.A. from the Bible, and then the immense study of the Bible that AAs did in the Book of James, Sermon on the Mount, and 1 Corinthians 13. Even that, however, was not the end. I stumbled upon Christian Endeavor and began to realize that the whole Akron program was far more founded on Christian Endeavor principles and practices than on those of the Oxford Group. Piece by piece, other details emerged. There was the whole Shoemaker story and my discovery that the words in the Big Book and even the Steps were largely Shoemaker words and that Sam had been asked to write the Twelve Steps, but declined. More? Yes. Lots more research to be done. More on Carl

Jung. More on William James. More on Richard Peabody. More on William D. Silkworth. More on Henrietta Seiberling. More on Clarence Snyder. More on the Wilson manuscripts. More on the deleted materials. More on John Henry Fitzhugh Mayo who witnessed the shelving of A.A.'s Christian materials. More on the whole story and materials connected with Dr. Bob's youth. More on the YMCA in Vermont and at the Academies. More. More. More.

What we had in 1990 didn't add up to the whole picture, or even part of the picture. And the gap had left alkies to their own devices in fashioning substitutes. This happened: When Bill dumped the Oxford Group in the East, the Oxford Group specifics were omitted. When Bob and Anne died, the Bible in A.A. died with them. When Clarence Snyder got on the wrong side of Bill Wilson, the Snyder legacy disappeared until recently. When Henrietta Seiberling was put on the shelf, her loud reprimands to Bill Wilson about phony spirituality, séances, substitute psychology, and sick thinking were ignored, along with her futile protests. People began denying the date of Dr. Bob's sobriety; and they're doing much more in the trivia realm. People began denying that Jung saw Rowland Hazard; and they're doing it even more—with totally inadequate research and documentation. People just never even seemed to want to know about Anne Smith nor the early books nor the Bible verses nor the Sam Shoemaker story nor the devotionals.

Too much religion seemed to be the cry. That from those studying a program so obviously religious at its beginnings and so obviously religious today that one court after another has ruled that A.A. is religious, is a religion, and not explicable by the deceitfully fashioned "spirituality" implantation.

There's a lot more. But cheer up. I've been able to field 31 published titles, 170 articles, 70 audio talks, seminars at the Wilson House, a talk "near" the Minneapolis convention, several large history conferences and cruises, and three websites where freedom of speech abounds and frequent visits have added up to almost one million six hundred thousand these days. Others interested in history are beginning to "let the cats out of the bags." Plural "bags."

Good stuff has just begun to come out about Dr. Silkworth. Good stuff has already come out about Clarence Snyder. Good stuff has emerged about the YMCA in our research for this present title. Interesting facts are emerging from the Lois Wilson stories. Some have dared to mention Bill Wilson's LSD experiments with his wife, Nell Wing, Father Dowling, and others. Also his spiritualism sessions at Stepping Stones. Also his womanizing and the squabbles over his estate. Also his obsession with psychic phenomena, niacin, and book sales. Also the deadening effect his years of severe depressions had on A.A. ideas and historical accuracy. And more.

For a long time, I felt the foregoing didn't belong in the picture. They had to do with Bill rather than A.A., I thought. In fact, at Stepping Stones, I was asked to bypass their locked files on drugs and psychic matters; and I did. Yet I found that others had trod that route and even published on it in A.A.'s *Pass It On*. Then I discovered that the missing records on Shoemaker at the Episcopal Archives in Texas had apparently been trucked off by two A.A. admirers. And that was a real loss because several historians had tried to research them, couldn't find them, and were astonished at the gap. Some assumed they didn't exist. But they did and do, I believe. And are these things part of the whole picture?

I certainly think so, but not the picture I'm interested in. I was and am focused on helping the newcomer through our great A.A. Fellowship. I was and am focused on discovering every aspect of the recovery program that was used in Akron, and then in Cleveland, and then in the Big Book, and then by the host of writers who emerged during Bill's 1943-1955 depression period. It's what worked that counts. It's accuracy that counts. It's the complete picture that counts. And it's the relevance to our getting sober, getting well, getting delivered from the power of darkness, and loving and serving our Heavenly Father that count.

I think the last 18 years have not only unplugged sixteen well-springs; they've started the streams gushing. And I don't think the flood will stop. More and more history conferences and panels are aimed at obtaining information, rather than perpetuating errors, omissions, and falsehoods. Amen.

Additional Treasures in the Well-Springs Library

Here we will just list a large number of categories for the additional important background materials that will be a part of the library:

1. The Bill Wilson manuscripts and materials I obtained from Stepping Stones.
2. The many biographies of Wilson—Cheever, Robertson, Thomsen, White, Raphael, Hartigan, Bill Wilson himself, *Pass It On, Twelve Steps and Twelve Traditions*.
3. Critiques of Wilson and A.A. by Kurtz (3 volumes), Bufe, Peele, Dubiel, and many others.
4. The major specific healing books owned and studied by Dr. Bob: Ethel Willits, *Healing in Jesus Name*; James Moore Hickson, *Heal the Sick*, and others.
5. Background books on temperance, revivals, camps, conversions, and more.
6. Contemporary studies of healing, psychology, and cures.
7. Contemporary studies of recovery techniques, and alternative programs.
8. The four known thorough studies by Richard K. of Massachusetts on the original 40.
9. Photos of significant people and places in early A.A. history.
10. Audio records of talks on early history, and bibliographies.
11. Richard K's four enormous research titles on the first forty A.A. pioneers, on the hundreds of pioneers who told in hundreds of newspapers and magazine reports of cures in A.A.'s first decade, on "reclaiming A.A.," and on "separating fact from fiction."
12. Manuscript materials from scholars and colleagues.

> "Your Heavenly Father will never let you down!"
> *Alcoholics Anonymous*, 4th ed., p. 181

Conclusion

Many a parent must say, when he sees his child go astray, "Where did I go wrong? What mistakes did I make?" So it may be with parents and family of a younger alcoholic. Blame themselves. Perhaps even excuse the youngster's misdeeds.

But did the parents in fact go wrong? Were any mistakes the mistakes of the family's?

Dr. Bob only once made the comment that he was more or less "forced" to go to church and Christian Endeavor five times a week. Again, there is only one report of this comment. And let's compare the cases of the parent that insists that a child eat his peas and carrots? The child may well comment, "I was more or less forced to eat the peas and carrots on my plate." Consider the church case and the carrots case. In either case, did the parent go wrong? Wrong in insisting on religious upbringing? Wrong in insisting on the odious peas and carrots? Did the parent make a mistake? Should the parent make amends? Did the parental discipline lead the child astray?

In the case of alcoholism, I know we hear talk that it is a "family disease." Certainly there are extensive programs for working with the families who have a family member in a treatment program. We know the family members are sometimes described as enablers, as controllers, as sick co-dependents. And, at first, the newly sober alcoholic may buy into the whole process. He may proceed to make his amends but then have high hopes that his family will "recover" too. Maybe the family resorts to counseling, to therapy, or to some program such as Al-Anon. Maybe the members are told they needed to "detach." Or that they must learn to "let go." Or that they need "work" the Twelve Steps themselves.

In my own case, both my parents had died before I got sober; my ex-wife was already a leading light in local Al-Anon. 21 years later, both my sons seem about as healthy as it's possible to be. Furthermore, they both believe in God; they both are children of God; and they both read the Bible and pray. Neither is an alcoholic. Both are married, but not to an alcoholic. My two grand-daughters appear to me to be drug free, alcohol free, and smoke free--pure as the driven snow. I don't say that this happy state of affairs is due to my sons' being "forced" into compliance on the religious front. But I do know that my mother—a devoted Bible student and church-goer— talked to them plenty about the Bible and about God's healing power. I know that we sent them both to Sunday School. They know that their father and mother both belonged to a church. In all probability, therefore, I conclude, subjectively at least, that Dr. Bob had lots to thank his Heavenly Father for, as he looked back over his days as a youngster and saw how much he had learned about God, Jesus Christ, salvation, and the Bible "as a youngster." He seemed to remember well this training and education and to apply thoroughly what he had learned in his early years. None of this is at all surprising.

Let's consider one more time the Smith family and Dr. Bob's youth. Dr. Bob said he had had excellent training in the Bible as a youngster. He said he felt he should refresh his memory of the Good Book. And what does that say about compulsory Sunday School or compulsory peas and carrots? It reminds me personally of the support my own parents for my zealous and successful efforts in high school, college, and law school. It reminds me of the many miles they traveled from California to Spokane to be at my wedding. It reminds me of how much care they provided to each of my sons during the trying and repeated times of my wife's mental illness. It reminds me of their support for my getting an Eagle Scout badge in the Boy Scouts. It reminds me of my mother's taking me to Sunday school, reading me the Bible frequently, and praying for me when I was ill or in difficult situations. It reminds me of my dad's great support for my attending the University of California at Berkeley both before and after the War, and for my attending Stanford Law School following that. I know for sure that my dad's help, encouragement, and enthusiasm for what I was doing was very much responsible for my Phi Beta Kappa key and my post as an Editor of the Stanford Law School. In fact, both of my parents witnessed my professional work with clients, public boards, and the courts as an attorney.

Yes, I blew it with booze many years later. But I didn't even have to refresh my memory of what I learned from my parents. I've never forgotten. Never.

My parental training and support were still an embedded and very valuable part of my past. I feel sure all this underlies and explains much of the appreciation I have for Dr. Bob's role in A.A.

Let's look for the wisdom in the King James Version of the Bible—the one that Judge and Mrs. Smith read, the one that Dr. Bob and Anne read, the one that my own mother read:

> "Train up a child in the way he should go: and when he is old, he will not depart from it" (Proverbs 22:6).
>
> "Remember now thy Creator in the days of thy youth, while the evil days come not, nor the years draw nigh, when thou shalt say I have no pleasure in them" (Ecclesiastes 12:1).
>
> "And ye fathers, provoke not your children to wrath: but bring them up in the nurture and admonition of the Lord" (Ephesians 6:4).

As I reflect on the long-ignored and long forgotten days of Dr. Bob's youth in St. Johnsbury, Vermont, I see a lot of the parental interest and concern by Mr. and Mrs. Walter P. Smith for rearing their child in God's Word. They took him to church and Sunday school and prayer meetings. They participated in all three themselves. They brought him up in a town where the Town fathers (the Fairbanks people) were everywhere setting examples as devout Christians, honest businessmen, devoted supporters of education, workers for salvation, givers of service, stewards of their wealth, and benevolent givers. And it would appear from what we have learned that the Smiths were not far behind in those realms—however poor or affluent they may have been. They were a lot more than just soccer-moms and PTA members—even though I can hazard a guess that they would have been involved had soccer or PTA been available.

What is important, for the purposes of this book and the resource volumes it describes, is how well they depict the youth of a man whose parents loved their Creator and the Lord Jesus, studied God's Word, kept His commandments, and exemplified Christian love and service wherever they found themselves. And what can we say about Dr. Bob when he finally "remembered." He returned to the nurture and admonition of God, and did his best to obey. That's the point:

> "Let us hear the conclusion of the whole matter: Fear God, and keep his commandments: for this *is* the whole *duty* of man" (Ecclesiastes 12:13)

And here is what the Good Book tells us about the reward for that:

> "But without faith, *it is* impossible to please *him*: for he that cometh to God must believe that he is and *that* he is a rewarder of them that diligently seek him" (Hebrews 11:6).

For those afflicted with alcoholism and addictions, the reward for knowing the Biblical roots of A.A. and learning from the Good Book the nature and extent of God's will that we prosper and be in health, is the assurance that there a cure and an abundant life ahead for those who establish a relationship with the one, true, living God, and rely upon Him for what He says He does:

> "Who forgiveth all thine iniquities; who healeth all thy diseases; Who redeemeth thy life from destruction; who crowneth thee with lovingkindness and tender mercies; Who satisfieth thy mouth with good things; so that thy youth is renewed like the *eagle's* (Psalm 103:3-5).

I can't think of anything more needed, and I hope more desired, by those of us who screwed up our lives with drunkenness and other life-controlling problems. Divine forgiveness. Divine healing. Divine redemption from destruction. Yes, and unmerited Divine lovingkindness and tender mercies. I believe also that this mercy and grace shows the appropriateness of relying on two of Dr. Bob's major assurances—derived, I think—from his training days in Vermont: (1) ". . . we were convinced that the answer to our problems was in the Good Book."[661] (2) "Your Heavenly Father will never let you

---

[661] *The Co-founders*, 13.

down!"[662] In my difficult ascent from the depths of demoralization and despair, I have become certain that the Creator hasn't let me down, nor failed to feed me the truth from His Word, nor do I now believe He ever will.

End

Gloria Deo

---

[662] *Alcoholics Anonymous*, 4th ed., 181.

Selected Bibliography

(The bibliographic references for these and other citations are in footnotes)

Dick B. History Titles

B., Dick., *Anne Smith's Journal, 1933-1939*, 3rd ed. (Kihei, HI: Paradise Research Publications, Inc., 1998)
_____. *A New Way In: Reaching the Heart of a Child of God in Recovery with His Own, Powerful Historical Roots* (Kihei, HI: Paradise Research Publications, Inc., 2006).
_____. *A New Way Out: New Path—Familiar Road Signs—Our Creator's Guidance* (Kihei, HI: Paradise Research Publications, Inc., 2006)
_____. *By the Power of God: A Guide to Early A.A. Groups & Forming Similar Groups Today* (Kihei, HI: Paradise Research Publications, Inc., 2000)
_____. *Cured: Proven Help for Alcoholics and Addicts* (Kihei, HI: Paradise Research Publications, Inc., 2003)
_____. *Dr. Bob and His Library*, 3rd ed. (Kihei, HI: Paradise Research Publications, Inc., 1998)
_____. *God and Alcoholism: Our Growing Opportunity in the 21st Century* (Kihei, HI Paradise Research Publications, Inc., 2002)
_____. *Good Morning: Quiet Time, Morning Watch, Meditation, and Early A.A.*, 2d ed. (Kihei, HI: Paradise Research Publications, Inc., 1998)
_____. *Henrietta B. Seiberling: Ohio's Lady with a Cause*, 4th ed. (Kihei, HI: Paradise Research Publications, Inc., 2006)
_____. *Introduction to the Sources and Founding of Alcoholics Anonymous* (Kihei, HI: Paradise Research Publications, Inc., 2007).
_____. *Making Known the Biblical History and Roots of Alcoholics Anonymous* (Kihei, HI: Paradise Research Publications, Inc., 2006)
_____. *New Light on Alcoholism: God, Sam Shoemaker, and A.A.* The Pittsburgh Edition (Kihei, HI: Paradise Research Publications, 1999)

_____. *Real Twelve Step Fellowship History: The Old School A.A. You May Not Know* (Kihei, HI: Paradise Research Publications, Inc., 2006)

_____. *That Amazing Grace: The Role of Clarence and Grace S. in Alcoholics Anonymous* (San Rafael, CA: Paradise Research Publications, 1996)

_____. *The Akron Genesis of Alcoholics Anonymous*, 2d ed. (Kihei, HI: Paradise Research Publications, Inc., 1998)

_____. *The Books Early AAs Read for Spiritual Growth,* 7th ed. (Kihei, HI: Paradise Research Publications, Inc., 1998)

_____. *The Conversion of Bill W.: More on the Creator's Role in Early A.A.* (Kihei, HI: Paradise Research Publications, Inc., 2006)

_____. *The First Nationwide A.A. History Conference: The Comments of Dick B.*, 2d ed. (Kihei, HI: Paradise Research Publications, Inc., 2006)

_____. *The Good Book-Big Book Guide Book* (Kihei, HI: Paradise Research Publications, Inc., 2006)

_____. *The James Club and the Original A.A. Program's Absolute Essentials*, 4th ed. (Kihei, HI: Paradise Research Publications, Inc., 2005)

_____. *The Oxford Group and Alcoholics Anonymous: A Design for Living That Works,* 2d ed. (Kihei, HI: Paradise Research Publications, Inc., 1998)

_____. *Turning Point: A History of Early A.A.'s Spiritual Roots and Successes* (Kihei, HI: Paradise Research Publications, Inc., 1997)

_____. *Twelve Steps for You: Take the Twelve Steps with the Big Book, A.A. History, and the Good Book at Your Side*, 4th ed. (Kihei, HI: Paradise Research Publications, Inc., 2005)

_____. *When Early AAs Were Cured and Why,* 3rd ed. (Kihei, HI: Paradise Research Publications, Inc., 2006)

_____. *Why Early A.A. Succeeded: The Good Book in Alcoholics Anonymous Yesterday and Today (A Bible Study Primer for AAs and other 12-Steppers*) (Kihei, HI: Paradise Research Publications, Inc., 2001)

Alcoholics Anonymous Related Literature

AA of Akron (4 pamphlets) *A Guide to the Twelve Steps of Alcoholics Anonymous; A Manual for Alcoholics Anonymous; Second Reader for Alcoholics Anonymous; Spiritual Milestones in Alcoholics Anonymous*

Alcohol, Science and Society: Twenty-nine Lectures with Discussions as given at the Yale Summer School of Alcohol Studies (New Haven: Quarterly Journal of Studies on Alcohol, 1945)

Alcoholics Anonymous, 4th ed. (NY: Alcoholics Anonymous World Services, Inc., 2001)

Alcoholics Anonymous Comes of Age (NY: Alcoholics Anonymous World Services, 1967)

A Newcomer Asks . . . (York, England A.A. Sterling Area Services, n.d.)

B., Mel. *New Wine: The Spiritual Roots of the Twelve Step Miracle* (Hazelden, 1991)

Begbie, Harold, *Life Changers* (NY: G.P. Putnam's Sons, 1926)

_____.*The Gospel Truth: Life of William Booth, Founder and First General of the Salvation Army.* 2 Volumes (NY: MacMillan, 1920)

_____. *Twice Born Men* (NY: Fleming H. Revell, 1909)

Borchert, William G. *The Lois Wilson Story When Love is Not Enough: A Biography of the Co-founder of Al-Anon* (Center City, MN: Hazelden, 2005).

Chambers, Oswald, *My Utmost for His Highest* (London: Simpkin, Marshall, Ltd., 1927)

_____. *Studies in the Sermon on the Mount* (London: Simpkin, Marshall, Ltd., n.d.)

Cheever, Susan. *My Name is Bill: Bill Wilson—His Life and the Creation of Alcoholics Anonymous* (NY: Washington Square Press, 2004)

Clinebell, Howard, *Understanding and Counseling Persons with Alcohol, Drug, and Behavioral Addictions.* Rev. and enl. ed. (Nashville: Abingdon Press, 1998)

Day, Sherwood Sunderland, *The Principles of the Group* (Oxford University Press, n.d.)

DR. BOB and the Good Old Timers (NY: Alcoholics Anonymous World Services, Inc., 1980)

"Dr. Bob's Last Major Talk: An Excerpt," *AA Grapevine*, November 2003 (online source: AA Grapevine Digital Archive, # 257)

Forde, Eleanor, *The Guidance of God* (London: The Oxford Group, 1927)

Fosdick, Harry Emerson, *The Meaning of Prayer* (NY: Association Press, 1915)

Grensted, L. W., *Psychology and God: Being The Bampton Lectures 1930* (London: Longmans, Green and Co., 1931).

Hartigan, Francis. *Bill W.: A Biography of Alcoholics Anonymous Co-founder Bill Wilson* (NY: Thomas Dunne Books, 2000)

Hickson, James Moore, *Heal the Sick* (London: Methuen & Company, 1925)

Holm, Nora Smith, *The Runner's Bible* (NY: Houghton Mifflin Company, 1915)

James, William, *The Varieties of Religious Experience* (NY: Vintage Books/The Library of America, 1990)

Jones, E. Stanley, *The Christ of the Mount* (NY: Abingdon Press, 1930)

Jung, Carl G., *Modern Man in Search of a Soul* (NY: Harcourt Brace Jovanovich, Publishers, 1933)

K., Mitchell. *How It Worked: The Story of Clarence H. Snyder and the Early Days of Alcoholics Anonymous in Cleveland, Ohio* (NY: Washingtonville, Big Book Study Group, 1991)

K., Richard, *Early A.A.—Separating Fact from Fiction: How Revisionists Have Led OurHistory Astray* (Haverhill, MA: Golden Text Publishing Co., 2003)

_____. *New Freedom: Reclaiming Alcoholics Anonymous* (MA: Golden Text Publishing Company, 2005)

_____. Lean, Garth. *Frank Buchman: A Life* (London: Constable, 1985)

Leuba, James, "A Study in the Psychology of Religious Phenomena" in *The American Journal of Psychology,* Vol. VII., April, 1896, No. 3.

Mitchel, Dale. *Silkworth: The Little Doctor Who Loved Drunks* (Center City, MN: Hazelden, 2002)

Peabody, Richard. *The Common Sense of Drinking* (Atlantic Monthly Press Book, 1939)

Pass It On (NY: Alcoholics Anonymous World Services, Inc., 1984)

Peale, Norman Vincent. *The Positive Power of Jesus Christ: Life-changing Adventures in Faith* (Carmel: NY: Guideposts, 1980)

Pittman, Bill. *AA The Way It Began* (Seattle: Glen Abbey Books, 1988)

Raphael, Matthew J. *Bill W. and Mr. Wilson: The Legend and Life of A.A.'s Co-founder* (Amherst: University of Massachusetts Press, 2000)

RHS (*Grapevine* Memorial Issue on Dr. Bob's death, 1951)

Robertson, Nan. *Getting Better Inside Alcoholics Anonymous* (NY: Fawcett Crest, 1988)

Rose, Cecil, *When Man Listens* (Oxford: Oxford University Press, 1937)

Rose, Howard J., *The Quiet Time* (NY: Oxford Group at 61 Gramercy Park, North, 1937)

Russell, A. J., *For Sinners Only* (London: Hodder & Stoughton, 1932)

Shoemaker, Samuel M., Jr. *Realizing Religion* (NY: Association Press, 1923)

Smith, Bob and Sue Smith Windows. *Children of the Healer: The Story of Dr. Bob's Kids* (Center City, MN: Hazelden, 1992)

Strong, Arthur, *Preview of a New World* (Norway: privately published)

The Co-Founders of Alcoholics Anonymous: Biographical sketches Their last major talks (NY: Alcoholics Anonymous World Services, Inc., 1972, 1975)

The Upper Room (quarterly of the Methodist Church)

This is A.A. . . an introduction to the AA recovery program (NY: Alcoholics Anonymous World Services, Inc., 1984)

Three Clarence Snyder Old Timer Sponsees and Their Wives. comp. and ed. By Dick B.

Our A.A. Legacy (Winter Park, FL: Came to Believe Publications, 2005).

Tileston, Mary W. *Daily Strength for Daily Needs* (Boston: Roberts Brothers, 1893)

Viney, Hallen, *How Do I Begin* (The Oxford Group, n.d.)

Walter, Howard A., *Soul Surgery* (NY: The Oxford Group, 1928)

W., Bill. "Where did the 12 Steps come from?" *AA Grapevine*, July, 1953.

Willitts, Ethel R *Healing in Jesus Name* (Chicago: Ethel R. Willitts Evangelists, 1931)

Wilson, Bill. *Bill W.: My First 40 Years: An Autobiography by the Cofounder of Alcoholics Anonymous* (Center City, MN: Hazelden, 2000)

Wilson, William. *W.G. Wilson Recollections*, manuscript dated
    September 1, 1954

Al-Anon Literature

Wilson, Lois, *Lois Remembers* (NY: Al-Anon Family Group
    Headquarters, Inc., 1987)

Biographies

"Biography of D. L. Moody": http://www.believersweb.org.view.cfm.
Findlay, James F., Jr., *Dwight L. Moody: American Evangelist 1837-
    1899* (Chicago, IL: The University of Chicago Press, 1969).
Folger, Allen. *Twenty-five Years as an Evangelist* (Boston: James H.
    Earle & Company, 1905)
Hopkins, Anson Smith, *Reminiscences of an Octogenarian* (New
Haven, CT: The Tuttle, Morehouse & Taylor Company, 1937).
"Inventory of the Stone family papers, 1849-1998" (The University of
    Vermont: UVM Special Collections)
Jeffrey, William H. *Successful Vermonters* (East Burke, Vermont: The
    Historical Publishing Company, 1904)
Marquis, Albert Nelson. *Who's Who in New England*
Sankey, Ira D., *My Life and the Story of the Gospel Hymns* (NY:
    Harper & Brothers, 1907)
Taylor, Samuel H., *A Memorial of Joseph P. Fairbanks* (___:
    Riverside, 1865)
"The Christian History Timeline: Dwight L. Moody (1873-1899) and
    His World": http://ctlibrart.com
*The National Cyclopaedia of American Biography: Being the History
    of the United States as Illustrated in the Livers of the Founders,
    Builders, and Defenders of the Republic. . . .* Volume VIII
    (NY: James T. White & Company, 1900)
Ullery, Charles G., comp., Hiram A. Huse, ed., *Men of Vermont: An
    Illustrated Biographical History of Vermonters and Sons of
    Vermont* (Brattleboro, VT Transcript Publishing Company,
    1894)

Christian Endeavor Society

Allen, Frank H., *The Quiet Hour* (Boston: United Christian Endeavor Society, n.d.)
Brain, Belle M., *The Morning Watch* (Boston: United Society of Christian Endeavor, n.d.)
Brain, Belle M., *Weapons for Temperance* Warfare (Boston: United Society of Christian Endeavor, n.d.)
Chapman, J. Wilbur, *The Surrendered Life* (Boston: United Society of Christian Endeavor, n.d.)
"Christian Endeavor," *Time Magazine*, July 11, 1927.
"Christian Workers. Convention of the Societies of Christian Endeavor," *The New York Times*, July 6, 1888, page 3.
Clark, Francis E., *Christian Endeavor in All Lands: A Record of Twenty-Five Years of Progress* (Boston, MA: The United Society, 1906)
Clark, Francis E., *Memories of Many Men in Many Lands* (Norwood, MA: The Plimpton Press, 1922)
Clark, Francis Edward, *The Christian Endeavor Manual: A Text-Book on the History, Theory, Principles and Practice of the Society, with complete Bibliography and Several Appendixes* (Boston: United Society of Christian Endeavor, n.d.)
Clark, Francis E. *World Wide Christian Endeavor: The Story of the Young People's Society of Christian Endeavor: From the Beginning and in All Land*s (Philadelphia: Gillespie, Metzger & Kelly, 1895)
Cowan, J. F., *New Life in the Old Prayer Meeting* (NY: Fleming H. Revell Company, 1906)
"How the Christian Endeavor Movement Has Spread" *The New York Times*, July 11, 1892, Page CEE12.
Meyer, F. B., *I Promise* (Boston: United Society of Christian Endeavor, n.d.)
Moody, Dwight L., *Golden Counsels* (Moody: United Society of Christian Endeavor, n.d.)
Murch, James DeForest, *Successful C.E. Prayer-Meetings* (Cincinnati, OH: The Standard Publishing Company, 1930).
"Platform of Principles," *The New York Times*, July 11, 1892.
Sheldon, Charles M., *In His Steps* (NJ: Spire Books Fleming H. Revell Company, 1963)

Wells, Amos R., *Expert Endeavor: A Text-book of Christian Endeavor Methods and Principles For the Use of Classes and of Candidates for the Title of "C.E.E."—"Christian Endeavor Expert"* (Boston: United Society of Christian Endeavor, 1911).

Wells, Amos R., *Prayer-Meeting Methods* (Boston: United Society of Christian Endeavor, n.c.).

Fairbanks Biographical Information

Brown, John Howard, ed., *The Cyclopedia of American Biographies. Comprising the Men and Women of the United States Who Have Been Identified with the Growth of the Nation.* In Seven Volumes, Vol. III: Ericsson-Hempstead (Boston, MA: James H. Lamb, 1900)

Carleton, Hiram, comp. and ed., *Genealogical and Family History of the State of Vermont*, Vol. 1

Crane, Ellery Bicknell, *Historic Homes and Institutions and Genealogical and Personal Memoirs of Worcester County, Massachusetts, with a History of Worcester Society of Antiquity*, Vol. I, illus. (NY: The Lewis Publishing Company, 1907)

Fairbanks, Lorenzo Sayles. *Genealogy of the Fairbanks Family in America, 1633-1897* (Boston: Printed for the Author by the American Printing and Engraving Company, 1897)

"Fairbanks and Keester":
http://www.familyorigins.com/users/k/e/e/Louis-J-Keester/FAM01-0001/d134.htm

Hyde, Charles McEwen, *Historical Celebration of the Town of Brimfield, Hampden County, Mass.; Wednesday, October 11, 1876, with the Historical Address of Rev. Charles M. Hyde. D.D., and Other Addresses, Letters, Documents, etc. ,Relating to the Early History of the Town* (Springfield, MA: The Clark W. Bryan Company, Printers, 1879)

Locke, John Goodwin, *Book of the Lockes: A Genealogical and Historical Record of the Descendents of William Locke, of Woburn, with an Appendix, Containing a History of the Lockes in England, also of the Family of John Locke, of Hampton, N.H., and Kindred Families and Individuals* (Boston: James Monroe and Company, 1853)

The "Fairbanks Papers" 1815-1889, Doc 1-5, Doc 95," Vermont Historical Society Library.
The National Cyclopaedia of American Biography: Being the History of the United States As Illustrated in the Lives of the Founders, Builders, and Defenders of the Republic, . . . Volume VIII (NY: James T. White & Company, 1900)

Genealogies

Carleton, Hiram. Comp. and ed., *Genealogical and Family History of the State of Vermont*, Vol. I.
Crane, Ellery Bicknell, ed., *Historic Homes and Institutions and Genealogical and Personal Memoirs of Worcester County, Massachusetts, with a History of Worcester Society of Antiquity*, Vol. I, illus (NY: The Lewis Publishing Company, 1907)
Fairbanks and Keester. Family origins.com
Fairbanks, Lorenzo Sayles, *Genealogy of the Fairbanks Family in America*, 1633-1897 (Boston: Printed for the Author by the American Printing and Engraving Company, 1897).
Lawrence, John. *The Genealogy of the Family of John Lawrence, of Wisset, in Suffolk, England, and of Watertown and Groton, Massachusetts Continued to the Present Year* (Printed for the Author, 1876—The Riverside Press, Cambridge: Printed by the H. O Houghton and Company)
"Noyes Family," http://noyes.rootsweb.com

Histories

Chadwick, Albert G., *Soldiers' Record of the Town of St. Johnsbury, Vermont, in the War of the Rebellion, 1861-5* (___VT: Civil War Enterprises); HC—reprint of 1883 original.
Fairbanks, Edward T. *The Town of St. Johnsbury, Vt: A Review of One Hundred Twenty-Five Years to the Anniversary Pageant 1912* (St. Johnsbury, VT: Cowles Press, 1924)
Fairbanks, Edward Taylor, *The Wrought Brim: Twelve Discourses Given in the South Church, St. Johnsbury, Vermont* (St. Johnsbury, VT: W.W. Husband, Press of Caledonia Company, 1902)

Giddings, Edward, *American Christian Rulers: Religion and Men of Government* (NY: Broomfield & Company, 1889, 1890)

Johnson, Clare Dunne, *Images of America: St. Johnsbury* (Dover, NH: Arcadia Publishing, 1996)

Johnson, Claire Dunne, *I See by the Paper: An Informal History of St. Johnsbury*, Vols. I & II (Vermont Historical Society, 1987, 1989)

Kendall, John. *History of the St. Johnsbury & Lake Champlain Railroad* (St. Johnsbury, VT: John Kendall, ___), circa 1930's.

Millers for Five Generations: The Story of E.T. and H.K. Ide, Inc., St. Johnsbury, Vermont (St. Johnsbury, VT: _____, 1953)

St. Johnsbury's Past and Present (Illustrated) Sesqui-Centennial Program and Pageant Synopsis. 1937 St. Johnsbury (St. Johnsbury, VT: Cowles Press, 1937).

Stone, Arthur F., comp., *St. Johnsbury Illustrated: A Review of the Town's Business, Social, Literary, and Educational Facilities, with Glimpses of Picturesque Surroundings* (___: Caledonian Press/C.M. Stone & Company, 1891)

Stone, Arthur F., *The Vermont of Today: With Its Historic Background, Attractions and People*, Vols. I-IV (NY: Lewis Historical Publishing Company, 1929).

Streeter, Russell, *The Christian Intelligencer Devoted to Theoretical and Practical Religion*, Vols. I, II (Portland, ME: Argus Office, by Todd & Smith, 1822).

The "Fairbanks Papers: 1815-1990." Vermont Historical Society Library

Towns, Elmer and Douglas Porter. *From Pentecost to the Present: The Ten Greatest Revivals Ever* (Ann Arbor, MI: Servant Publications, 2000)

Williamson, Joseph. *A Bibliography of the State of Maine from the Earliest Period to 1891, in Two Volumes* (Portland, ME: The Thurston Print, 1896).

The Congregational Churches of Vermont

Comstock, John M., *The Congregational Churches of Vermont and Their Ministry, 1762-1942* (St. Johnsbury, VT: The Cowles Press, 1942)

Nutting, John E., *Becoming the United Church of Christ in Vermont 1795-1995* (Burlington, VT: Vermont Conference of the United Church of Christ, 1995)
Smith, C. S., *An Historical Sketch of Home Missionary Work in Vermont, by the Congregational Churches* (Montpelier: Press of the Watchman Publishing Company, 1893)
Minutes of Conferences and Conventions, 1872, 1875, 1878 – citations in footnotes
The American Missionary, Vol. 42, No. 4, April, 1888
The American Missionary, Vol. 43, No. 12, December, 1889
The American Missionary, Vol. 49, No., 3, March, 1895
The Home Missionary: For the Year Ending April, 1889, Vol. 61 (New York: American Home Missionary Society, 1889)

The North Congregational Church of St. Johnsbury

History of North Congregational Church (pamphlet), produced by North Congregational Church, United Church of Christ, St. Johnsbury, Vermont, provided by its archivist to the authors on October 25, 2007.
North Congregational Church Year Book . . . St. Johnsbury, Vt., for 1878
North Congregational Church . . . St. Johnsbury, Vt., Year Book . . . January, 1902 (___: The Caledonian Press, n.d.)
Stone, Arthur Fairbanks, *North Congregational Church, St. Johnsbury, Vermont, 1825-1942* (St. Johnsbury, VT: North Congregational Church, 1942)

The St. Johnsbury Academy

Beck, Richard, *A Proud Tradition A Bright Future: A Sesquicentennial History of St. Johnsbury Academy* (St. Johnsbury, VT: St. Johnsbury Academy, 1976)
Fairbanks, Arthur, Lemuel S. Hastings, James F. Colby, Susan H. Smith, Joseph Fairbanks, Charles H. Merrill and Wendell P. Stafford, *An Historical Sketch of St. Johnsbury Academy 1842-1922* (Trustees of St. Johnsbury Academy, n.d.)
Guide to Student Publications 1875 to present. The Student newspaper. Student Publications. St. Johnsbury Academy Archives.

Guide to the Photograph Collection 1870 to present. St. Johnsbury Academy photographs. St. Johnsbury Academy Archives

Guide to the St. Johnsbury Academy Catalogs 1843 to present. St. Johnsbury Academy Archives.

Russell, Charles Edward, *Bare Hands and Stone Walls: Some Recollections of a Side-Line Reformer* (NY: Charles Scribner's Sons, 1933)

Saint Johnsbury Academy 1897 in 1947 Class Record (50 year reunion), n.d.

St. Johnsbury Academy Catalogs for 1873, 1874, 1875, 1876 (cited in the footnotes)

The Academy Student, 1897, 1898 (issues and contents cited in the footnotes)

The Town of St. Johnsbury

Fairbanks, Edward T., *The Town of St. Johnsbury VT: A Review of One Hundred Twenty-five Years to the Anniversary Pageant, 1912* (St. Johnsbury, VT: The Cowles Press, 1914)

Kingdom Recovery Center Pamphlet: *Bringing People & Recovery Together: Drop-in Center Information, Socialization, Educations, and Referrals* (St. Johnsbury, VT)

St. Johnsbury Vermont: Maple Center of the World—prepared by The St. Johnsbury Chamber of Commerce (St. Johnsbury, VT: Troll Press, 1981)

Stone, Arthur F. *St. Johnsbury Illustrated: A review of the town's business, social, literary, and educational facilities, with glimpses of picturesque surroundings* (St. Johnsbury, VT: C. M. Stone & Company, 1891)

Stone, Arthur F. *The Vermont of Today: With Its Historic Background, Attractions and People.* Vol. II (NY: Lewis Historical Publishing Company, Inc., 1929)

Yale, Allen R., *Ingenious & enterprising mechanics: a case study of industrialization in rural Vermont, 1815-1900* (Ann Arbor, MI: UMI Dissertation Services, 1995)

The Young Men's Christian Association

Adair, Ward, *Memories of George Warburton* (NY: J. J. Little and Ives Co., n.d.)
_____. *The Road to New York* (NY: Association Press, 1936)
Addresses and Papers of John R. Mott, vol. 4 (NY: Association Press, 1946-1947)
Bowman, Louis A., *The Life of Isaac Eddy Brown* (NY: Association Press, 1926)
Braisted, Ruth Wilder. *In This Generation: The Story of Robert P. Wilder* (NY: Association Press, 1941)
Brockman, Fletcher S., *I Discover the Orient* (NY: Harper and Brothers, 1935)
Brown, William Adams, *Morris Ketchum Jessup: A Character Sketch* (NY: Charles Scribner's Sons, 1910)
Chapman, J. Wilbur, *The Life and Work of Dwight L. Moody* (Philadelphia: International Publishing Co., 1900)
Colton, Ethan T., *Forty Years with Russians* (NY: Association Press, 1940)
Doggett, Laurence L., *History of the Young Men's Christian Association* (NY: Association Press, 1922)
_____. *History of Boston Young Men's Christian Association. 1851-1901* (Boston: Young Men's Christian Association, 1925)
Dollar, Robert, *Memoirs of Robert Dollar* (San Francisco: privately printed, 1925)
Eddy, Sherwood, *A Century With Youth: History of the Y.M.C.A. from 1844 to 1944* (NY: Association Press, 1944)
_____. *A Pilgrimmage of Ideas or The Re-education of Sherwood Eddy* (NY: Farrar and Rinehart, 1934)
Ellenwood, James L. *One Hundred Years and Here We Are* (NY: Association Press, 1944)
Folger, Allen, *Twenty-five Years as an Evangelist* (Boston: James H. Earle and Co., 1905)
Gibbons, Herbert Adam, *John Wanamaker*, 2 vols. (NY: Harper and Brothers, 1926)
Hicks, Clarence J., *My Life in Industrial Relations: Fifty Years in the Growth of a Profession* (NY: Harper & Brothers, 1941)
Hopkins, C. Howard, *John R. Mott, 1865-1955: A Biography* (Grand Rapids, MI: William B. Eerdmans Publishing Co., 1979)

Hunton, Addie W. *William Alphaeus Hunton: A Pioneer Prophet of Young Men* (NY: Association Press, 1938)

Knebel, Aaron G., *Four Decades with Men and Boys* (NY: Association Press, 1936)

McCandless, James W., *Association Administration: A Study of the Professional Task of Operating a Young Men's Christian Association* (NY: Association Press, 1927)

McKim, Judson J., *The Operation and Management of the Local Young Men's Christian Association* (NY: Association Press, 1927)

Morse, Richard C., *History of the North American Young Men's Christian Associations* (NY: Association Press, 1919)

_____. *My Life with Young Men: Fifty Years in the Young Men's Christian Association* (NY: Association Press, 1918)

[Mrs. Frederick Morgan Harris], *Frederick Morgan Harris: A Little of His Life and Some of His Letters* (Chicago: privately printed, 1929)

Ninde, H. S., J. T. Bowne, and Erskine Uhl, eds. *A Hand-book of the History, Organization, and Methods of Work of Young Men's Christian Associations* (NY: International Committee of Young Men's Christian Associations, 1891)

Ober, Frank W., ed. *James Stokes: Pioneer of Young Men's Christian Associations* by His Associates in More Than Half a Century of World Service to Young Men (NY: Association Press, 1921)

Personal Memoirs of Lucien Calvin Warner, During Seventy-three Eventful Years, 1841-1914 (NY: Association Press, 1915)

Shedd, Clarence Prouty, and Other Contributors. *History of the World's Alliance of Young Men's Christian Associations* (London: S P C K, 1955)

The Jubilee of Work for Young Men in North America: A Report of the Jubilee Convention of North American Young Men's Christian Associations: Reports of the Commemorative Services of the Montreal and Boston Associations; A World Survey by Countries of the Association Movement (NY: The International Committee of Young Men's Christian Associations, 1901)

Thompson, Robert Ellis, ed. *The Life of George H. Stuart. Written by Himself* (Philadelphia: J. M. Stoddard and Co., 1890)

Williams, Wayne C. *Sweet of Colorado* (NY: Association Press, 1943)

Year Book of the Young Men's Christian Associations of North America, for the year 1896 (Published by the International Committee, 1896)

Index

1 Corinthians 13, xi, 85, 145, 152, 184, 264, 281, 285, 288

A

A. J. Howe, 12, 13, 251

AA Grapevine, 40, 121, 302, 303

Akron, x, xiii, ix, xi, xii, xx, xxi, 16, 17, 38, 39, 40, 41, 45, 46, 47, 49, 54, 66, 72, 73, 75, 76, 81, 83, 84, 85, 87, 94, 96, 97, 98, 99, 100, 104, 105, 106, 109, 120, 133, 134, 139, 140, 143, 145, 148, 149, 150, 152, 162, 163, 164, 165, 176, 177, 179, 180, 183, 239, 261, 262, 263, 264, 265, 266, 269, 271, 272, 273, 274, 275, 279, 282, 284, 285, 288, 290, 300, 301, 319, 321

Alcoholics Anonymous, x, xi, xiii, xiv, xiii, xiv, xv, xvi, xvii, xviii, xix, xxi, 1, 14, 15, 37, 38, 40, 41, 42, 44, 45, 48, 62, 76, 81, 82, 83, 88, 99, 100, 101, 103, 104, 105, 106, 109, 111, 112, 121, 129, 132, 136, 141, 149, 150, 153, 155, 163, 164, 166, 187, 197, 207, 239, 245, 261, 262, 263, 264, 266, 270, 271, 272, 273, 280, 282, 284, 285, 293, 297, 299, 300, 301, 302, 303, 319, 320, 321

Anne Smith, x, xi, 47, 85, 94, 97, 111, 145, 147, 148, 149, 163, 184, 264, 267, 273, 274, 284, 285, 288, 289, 299, 319, 321

Awakening, xvi, 24, 30, 32, 55, 124, 175

B

Bible, x, xi, xiv, xv, xvi, xvii, xviii, xix, xxi, 1, 8, 11, 15, 16, 20, 26, 33, 37, 38, 40, 44, 46, 47, 49, 50, 51, 52, 53, 54, 55, 57, 58, 59, 63, 65, 66, 69, 71, 72, 75, 79, 80, 81, 84, 86, 87, 89, 91, 93, 94, 95, 97, 108, 113, 114, 119, 121, 123, 126, 130, 133, 134, 136, 138, 139, 142, 144, 145, 146, 148, 149, 151, 152, 154, 155, 159, 160, 161, 162, 163, 166, 170, 173, 174, 175, 180, 184, 185, 191, 199, 207, 213, 239, 240, 245, 246, 253, 257, 259, 264, 265, 267, 268, 269, 270, 271, 273, 274, 276, 277, 279, 280, 281, 283, 284, 285, 286, 287,

288, 289, 294, 295, 300, 302, 319, 320, 321

Bible study, xvi, xxi, 52, 53, 57, 69, 71, 95, 135, 152, 154, 163, 185, 240, 282, 283, 284, 285

Big Book, x, 319, 321

Bill Dotson, xiii, 40, 48, 91, 97, 99, 109, 261, 270

Bill W., x, xii, xiv, 14, 39, 40, 46, 48, 73, 75, 76, 78, 79, 81, 97, 98, 99, 100, 101, 102, 103, 104, 109, 153, 154, 162, 183, 268, 272, 273, 276, 277, 279, 287, 300, 302, 303, 321

Bill Wilson, xiii, xiv, xvii, xviii, xxi, 15, 17, 43, 45, 46, 47, 48, 53, 73, 75, 76, 77, 81, 85, 86, 91, 96, 97, 98, 99, 100, 101, 102, 103, 107, 108, 109, 111, 126, 133, 139, 150, 151, 153, 162, 163, 164, 183, 184, 261, 262, 263, 264, 266, 268, 269, 270, 275, 276, 277, 278, 280, 281, 283, 284, 287, 289, 290, 291, 301, 302

Book of James, xi, xx, 42, 85, 145, 152, 179, 184, 264, 281, 283, 285, 288

C

Calvary Rescue Mission, xiv, 73, 75, 76, 81, 99, 100, 101

Christ, 319

Christian, ix, xii, xv, xvi, xvii, xviii, xix, xxi, 1, 2, 3, 5, 7, 8, 12, 13, 14, 15, 17, 19, 21, 22, 23, 25, 27, 31, 32, 33, 34, 35, 37, 38, 39, 40, 42, 43, 44, 49, 50, 51, 52, 53, 54, 55, 56, 57, 61, 63, 65, 66, 67, 68, 69, 71, 72, 74, 76, 77, 81, 83, 84, 85, 86, 88, 89, 90, 91, 92, 93, 94, 95, 97, 98, 100, 104, 107, 112, 114, 115, 117, 118, 119, 121, 122, 124, 125, 130, 132, 133, 134, 135, 137, 139, 141, 142, 143, 144, 146, 148, 149, 150, 151, 152, 153, 154, 155, 156, 157, 158, 159, 160, 161, 162, 163, 164, 165, 166, 167, 168, 169, 170, 172, 173, 174, 175, 176, 177, 178, 179, 180, 181, 182, 183, 184, 185, 189, 190, 191, 193, 194, 195, 200, 208, 210, 222, 223, 226, 229, 239, 240, 241, 243, 244, 245, 246, 247, 248, 249, 250, 251, 252, 253, 254, 255, 256, 258, 259, 260, 265, 267, 273, 274, 275, 278, 279, 282, 284, 285, 286, 287, 288, 293, 296, 304, 305, 306, 307, 308, 310, 311, 312, 320

Christian Endeavor, ix, xii, xv, xviii, xix, xxi, 8, 15, 17, 35, 39, 43, 44, 51, 52, 53, 57, 63, 65, 66, 67, 68, 71, 72, 74, 76, 81, 86, 88, 89, 90, 91, 92, 93, 94, 95, 98, 107, 112, 114, 115, 118, 119, 121, 122, 130, 132, 133, 134, 135, 137, 139, 141, 142, 143, 144, 146, 148, 149, 150, 151, 152, 155, 156, 157, 158, 159, 160, 161, 163, 164, 165, 166, 167, 168, 169, 170, 172, 173, 174, 175, 176, 177, 178, 179, 180, 181, 182, 183, 185, 195, 240, 243, 258, 273, 274, 275, 282, 284, 286, 287, 289, 293, 304, 305, 306

Christianity, 8, 14, 21, 41, 50, 69, 75, 147, 153, 176, 184, 189, 259, 266, 278

Christians, xvii, 8, 11, 20, 21, 22, 28, 43, 52, 65, 84, 122, 158, 161, 175, 185, 194, 282, 295

Church, xv, ix, xii, xiv, xv, xvi, xxi, 1, 2, 3, 4, 6, 7, 9, 16, 23, 24, 25, 31, 32, 34, 35, 37, 39, 40, 45, 47, 49, 50, 51, 52, 53, 54, 55, 57, 60, 61, 62, 63, 64, 65, 66, 67, 68, 69, 70, 71, 72, 73, 79, 86, 87, 88, 90, 91, 92, 93, 94, 95, 103, 112, 114, 115, 116, 118, 119, 121, 122, 123, 124, 126, 127, 128, 129, 130, 131, 132, 134, 135, 136, 137, 139, 141, 142, 143, 144, 145, 150, 151, 152, 156, 157, 163, 164, 165, 166, 167, 168, 169, 173, 175, 181, 193, 195, 197, 205, 206, 207, 208, 209, 210, 211, 213, 214, 215, 217, 218, 220, 221, 225, 227, 228, 237, 239, 240, 241, 243, 256, 258, 259, 274, 280, 282, 287, 303, 307, 308, 309, 319

Clarace Williams, xi, xxi, 145

Clarence Snyder, xiii, 40, 41, 42, 147, 263, 272, 281, 282, 289, 290, 303

Communication, 320

Confession, xxi, 66, 91, 143, 145, 151, 176, 274, 279

Conversions, xix, xxi, 7, 9, 10, 11, 13, 16, 24, 27, 29, 31, 34, 39, 49, 51, 53, 54, 56, 58, 68, 70, 71, 73, 76, 79, 85, 93, 95, 104, 114, 115, 125, 132, 135, 139, 151, 164, 203, 239, 252, 258, 273, 276, 291

Creator, x, xiv, 1, 8, 14, 16, 37, 38, 40, 49, 54, 73, 75, 84, 85, 91, 96, 98, 99, 107, 108, 109, 134, 136, 152, 153, 154, 163, 165, 179, 185, 186, 240, 261, 268, 269, 270, 271, 275, 283, 295, 296, 297, 299, 300

D

Devotion, 15, 47, 88, 134, 144, 168, 174, 189

Dr. Bob, ix, x, xiii, xv, ix, xi, xii, xiii, xiv, xv, xvi, xvii, xviii, xix, xx, xxi, 1, 8, 14, 15, 16, 17, 23, 32, 34, 36, 37, 38, 39, 40, 41, 42, 43, 44, 45, 46, 47, 48, 49, 50, 51, 52, 53, 54, 55, 57, 60, 61, 63, 64, 65, 66, 67, 69, 71, 72, 73, 75, 76, 77, 81, ☐82, 83, 84, 85, 86, 87, 88, 89, 90, 91, 93, 94, 95, 96, 97, 98, 99, 104, 106, 107, 108, 109, 110, 111, 114, 120, 121, 122, 123, 129, 130, 132, 133, 134, 135, 136, 139, 141, 145, 147, 148, 151, 152, 153, 154, 155, 162, 163, 164, 165, 168, 169, 179, 181, 183, 184, 185, 186, 187, 188, 194, 195, 196, 197, 198, 201, 204, 206, 207, 239, 240, 241, 252, 258, 261, 262, 263, 264, 265, 266, 267, 268, 270, 273, 274, 278, 281, 282, 284, 285, 287, 288, 289, 291, 293, 294, 295, 296, 299, 302, 303, 319, 321

Dr. William D. Silkworth, 17, 41, 102, 162, 185, 278

E

Early AAs, x, 319, 321, 322

Edward T. Fairbanks, xv, 3, 4, 25, 26, 71, 129, 192, 195, 196, 217, 251

EVANGELISTS, 70

F

Fellowship, 319

G

God, x, xi, xiii, xv, xvii, 1, 4, 5, 6, 7, 8, 14, 15, 16, 17, 19, 20, 22, 26, 27, 31, 40, 42, 44, 45, 47, 54, 58, 67, 68, 71, 76, 77, 78, 79, 80, 84, 85, 86, 91, 96, 97, 100, 101, 102, 106, 108, 126, 133, 139, 146, 147, 148, 149, 150, 151, 152, 153, 154, 162, ☐163, 164, 166, 168, 170, 171, 172, 174, 176, 177, 178, 179, 180, 181, 184, 185, 245, 261, 262, 265, 266, 267, 268, 269, 270, 271, 272, 273, 277, 278, 279, 280, 281, 284, 285, 286, 287, 294, 295, 296, 299, 302, 319, 321

Good Book, x, xi, xiii, xiv, xi, xii, xiv, xix, xx, xxi, 32, 38, 39, 42, 43, 84, 89, 91, 97, 98, 109, 121, 135, 154, 164, 172, 264, 268, 269, 271, 273, 275, 277, 279, 281, 283, 294, 296, 300, 319, 320, 321, 322

Gospel meetings, xiv, 16, 17, 18, 19, 21, 26, 28, 34, 39, 50, 52, 53, 55, 65, 68, 70, 71, 93, 115, 125, 135, 151, 152, 248, 252

Grace, x, 319, 321

Great Awakening, ix, xv, 1, 2, 3, 7, 8, 9, 18, 23, 25, 27, 31, 32, 34, 39, 49, 51, 55, 69, 70, 72, 74, 81, 93, 121, 123, 124, 132, 135, 151, 164, 169, 200, 203, 250, 252

Guidance, 7, 153, 279, 280, 284, 285, 286, 299, 302

H

Healing, 8, 17, 38, 41, 54, 79, 80, 86, 91, 134, 162, 280, 285, 291, 294, 296

Heavenly Father, xii, xiii, xv, 1, 15, 37, 38, 43, 44, 48, 54, 73, 83, 86, 111, 121, 139, 141, 154, 185, 187, 207, 239, 245, 261, 291, 293, 294, 296

Henrietta Dotson, xiii, 47

Henrietta Seiberling, xi, 53, 83, 107, 133, 162, 263, 267, 274, 289, 319, 321

Holy Spirit, 3, 22, 23, 49, 54, 65, 68, 79, 123, 126, 139, 147, 148, 149, 278

J

John D. Rockefeller, Jr., xi, 183, 266, 283

N

New Testament, 320

O

Oxford Group, x, 17, 41, 44, 85, 103, 107, 109, 133, 134, 139, 150, 151, 152, 154, 155, 163, 183, 184, 263, 264, 265, 268, 269, 273, 276, 279, 280, 282, 284, 285, 286, 288, 289, 300, 302, 303, 319, 321

P

Peter Cartwright, 9
Pioneers, x, xi

Pledge, 74, 134, 143, 144, 159, 160, 161, 166, 173, 174, 177, 180, 182

Prayer, xv, xvii, xix, xxi, 8, 9, 11, 15, 16, 17, 19, 20, 22, 24, 25, 28, 32, 34, 35, 38, 40, 41, 44, 46, 49, 50, 52, 53, 54, 55, 57, 58, 59, 63, 64, 69, 71, 72,

74, 85, 86, 89, 93, 94, 95, 108, 112, 114, 117, 123, 124, 126, 129, 132, 133, 134, 137, 139, 142, 143, 144, 145, 146, 147, 148, 149, 151, 152, 154, 160, 161, 163, 166, 167, 168, 171, 173, 174, 175, 180, 181, 182, 184, 185, 192, 194, 205, 207, 239, 240, 245, 246, 252, 259, 267, 268, 270, 276, 279, 283, 284, 285, 286, 295

Q

Quiet Time, x, 16, 38, 44, 49, 91, 134, 148, 151, 267, 273, 274, 279, 283, 284, 285, 286, 287, 299, 303, 319, 321

R

Recovery, xiv, xi, xii, xiv, xxii, 15, 38, 39, 41, 46, 54, 84, 87, 94, 96, 97, 100, 107, 150, 153, 159, 162, 163, 164, 185, 241, 261, 263, 270, 272, 274, 282, 290, 291, 303, 319, 320

Religion, 319

Rev. Samuel M. Shoemaker, Jr., 15, 280

Revivals, 8, 9, 68, 121, 164, 260, 308

Richard C. Morse, 12, 246, 247, 260

S

Salvation Army, 17, 107, 152, 184, 185, 273, 274, 275, 276, 301

Sermon on the Mount, xi, xx, 42, 85, 145, 152, 184, 281, 285, 288, 301

St. Johnsbury, xv, ix, xi, xii, xiv, xv, xvi, xvii, xxi, 1, 2, 3, 4, 5, 7, 8, 9, 13, 15, 16, 17, 18, 19, 20, 23, 24, 26, 27, 31, 32, 33, 34, 36, 37, 38, 39, 40, 46, 49, 50, 51, 52, 53, 54, 55, 56, 57, 58, 60, 61, 62, 63, 64, 67, 68, 69, 70, 71, 72, 74, 76, 81, 83, 84, 85, 86, 87, 88, 89, 90, 91, 92, 93, 94, 95, 98, 110, 111, 112, 113, 114, 115, 116, 117, 118, 119, 120, 121, 122, 123, 124, 125, 126, 127, 128, 129, 130, 131, 132, 133, 135, 136, 138, 139, 141, 142, 143, 151, 155, 162, 163, 164, 166, 169, 187, 188, 189, 190, 193, 194, 195, 196, 197, 198, 199, 200, 201, 202, 203, 204, 205, 206, 207, 208, 210, 211, 212, 213, 214, 215, 216, 217, 218, 219, 220, 221, 222, 223, 224, 225, 226, 227, 228, 229, 230, 231, 232, 233, 234, 235, 236, 237, 238, 239, 240, 241, 242, 243, 245, 248, 250, 251, 252, 253, 254, 255, 258, 259, 274, 287, 295, 307, 308, 309

St. Johnsbury Academy, xii, xv, xxi, 1, 8, 18, 38, 39, 52, 57, 60, 61, 63, 69, 70, 73, 88, 89, 90, 91, 92, 94, 95, 113, 114, 115, 118, 120, 121, 122, 127, 132, 133, 135, 136, 151, 164, 169, 188, 190, 191, 194, 201, 231, 239, 241, 242, 243, 254, 259, 309, 310

Strength, 16, 19, 43, 131, 145, 148, 159, 160, 161, 178, 202, 248, 283

Sunday School, xv, xix, xxi, 9, 12, 35, 44, 47, 61, 62, 64, 65, 71, 81, 86, 88, 91, 92, 93, 114, 115, 117, 118, 119, 121, 123, 126, 130, 131, 132, 133, 135, 137, 138, 142, 151, 173, 193, 194, 195, 197, 207, 208, 211, 214, 215, 225, 240, 256, 294, 319

7, 10, 11, 12, 13, 15, 17, 18, 23, 24, 26, 27, 30, 31, 32, 33, 34, 37, 38, 39, 46, 48, 49, 50, 51, 53, 55, 56, 57, 60, 61, 62, 63, 64, 65, 66, 67, 68, 69, 71, 73, 75, 76, 83, 84, 86, 87, 88, 89, 90, 91, 92, 93, 94, 98, 102, 110, 111, 116, 118, 121, 122, 123, 124, 125, 127, 128, 129, 131, 132, 134, 135, 136, 138, 141, 142, 143, 144, 150, 152, 155, 162, 164, 190, 197, 200, 203, 207, 208, 209, 211, 213, 214, 215, 216, 217, 220, 221, 222, 223, 225, 226, 227, 228, 231, 235, 236, 237, 238, 242, 243, 245, 248, 249, 250, 251, 252, 253, 254, 255, 258, 259, 274, 287, 289, 295, 296, 304, 306, 307, 308, 309, 310

T

T. Henry, xi, xxi, 41, 47, 53, 83, 85, 145, 262, 267

Towns Hospital, xiv, 81, 100, 101, 102, 103, 108, 276

Twelve Steps, x

V

Vermont, xiii, xv, ix, xi, xii, xiv, xv, xvi, xvii, 1, 2, 5, 6,

Y

YMCA, ix, xiv, xv, 4, 5, 7, 11, 12, 13, 15, 16, 17, 18, 31, 34, 35, 39, 51, 52, 53, 55, 56, 57, 60, 61, 65, 67, 68, 70, 71, 73, 74, 81, 84, 86, 88, 90, 92, 93, 95, 107, 114, 115, 117, 121, 122, 132, 135, 138, 139, 144, 150, 151, 152, 163, 165, 195, 197, 207, 214, 216, 217, 231, 241, 245, 246, 247, 248, 249, 250, 251, 252, 253, 254, 255,

256, 258, 259, 273, 283, 286, 287, 289, 290

About the Authors

Dick B. writes books on the spiritual roots of Alcoholics Anonymous. They show how the basic and highly successful biblical ideas used by early AAs can be valuable tools for success in today's A.A. His research can also help the religious and recovery communities work more effectively with alcoholics, addicts, and others involved in Twelve Step programs.

The author is an active, recovered member of A.A.; a retired attorney; and a Bible student. He has sponsored more than one hundred men in their recovery from alcoholism. Consistent with A.A.'s traditions of anonymity, he uses the pseudonym "Dick B."

He has had thirty-one titles published including: *Dr. Bob and His Library*; *Anne Smith's Journal, 1933-1939*; *The Oxford Group & Alcoholics Anonymous*; *The Akron Genesis of Alcoholics Anonymous*; *The Books Early AAs Read for Spiritual Growth*; *New Light on Alcoholism: God, Sam Shoemaker, and A.A.*; *Courage to Change* (with Bill Pittman); *Cured: Proven Help for Alcoholics and Addicts*; *The Good Book and The Big Book: A.A.'s Roots in the Bible*; *That Amazing Grace: The Role of Clarence and Grace S. in Alcoholics Anonymous*; *Good Morning!: Quiet Time, Morning Watch, Meditation, and Early A.A.*; *Turning Point: A History of Early A.A.'s Spiritual Roots and Successes*, *Hope!: The Story of Geraldine D., Alina Lodge & Recovery; Utilizing Early A.A.'s Spiritual Roots for Recovery Today; The Golden Text of A.A.; By the Power of God; God and Alcoholism; Making Known the Biblical History of A.A.; Why Early A.A. Succeeded*; *Comments of Dick B. at The First Nationwide A.A. History Conference; Henrietta Seiberling: Ohio's Lady with a Cause;* and *The James Club*. The books have been the subject of newspaper articles and reviews in *Library Journal, Bookstore Journal, The Living Church, Faith at Work, Sober Times, Episcopal Life, Recovery News, Ohioana Quarterly, The PHOENIX*, and *The Saint Louis University Theology Digest*. They are listed in the biographies of major addiction center, religion, and religious history sites. He has published over 170 articles on his subject, most posted on the internet.

Dick is the father of two sons (Ken and Don) and has two granddaughters. As a young man, he did a stint as a newspaper reporter. He attended the University of California, Berkeley, where he received his A.A. degree with Honorable Mention, majored in economics, and was elected to Phi Beta Kappa in his Junior year. In the United States Army, he was an Information-Education Specialist. He received his A.B. and J.D. degrees from Stanford University, and was Case Editor of the Stanford Law Review. Dick became interested in Bible study in his childhood Sunday School and was much inspired by his mother's almost daily study of Scripture. He joined, and was president of, a Community Church affiliated with the United Church of Christ. By 1972, he was studying the origins of the Bible and began traveling abroad in pursuit of that subject. In 1979, he became much involved in a Biblical research, teaching, and fellowship ministry. In his community life, he was president of a merchants' council, Chamber of Commerce, church retirement center, and homeowners' association. He served on a public district board and has held offices in a service club.

In 1986, he was felled by alcoholism, gave up his law practice, and began recovery as a member of the Fellowship of Alcoholics Anonymous. He has been cured, and never once relapsed. In 1990, his interest in A.A.'s Biblical/Christian roots was sparked by his attendance at A.A.'s International Convention in Seattle. He has traveled widely; researched at archives, and at public and seminary libraries; interviewed scholars, historians, clergy, A.A. "old-timers" and survivors; and participated in programs and conferences on A.A.'s roots.

The author is the owner of Good Book Publishing Company and has several works in progress. Much of his research and writing is done in collaboration with his older son, Ken, an ordained minister, who holds B.A., B.Th., and M.A. degrees. Ken has been a lecturer in New Testament Greek at a Bible college and a lecturer in Fundamentals of Oral Communication at San Francisco State University. Ken is a computer specialist and director of marketing and research in Hawaii ethanol projects.

Dick is a member of the American Historical Association, Research Society on Alcoholism, Alcohol and Drugs History Society, Organization of American Historians, The Association for Medical Education and Research in Substance Abuse, Coalition of Prison Evangelists, Christian Association for Psychological Studies, and International Substance Abuse and Addictions Coalition. He is available for conferences, panels, seminars, and interviews.

Order Form

Catalog & Order Sheet

*** We suggest the entire 27-Volume Reference Set! ***

How to Order the 27-Volume Set and/or Dick B.'s
Individual Historical Titles on Early A.A.

Order Form

Qty.

____	*A New Way In*	$19.95 ea. $_____
____	*A New Way Out*	$19.95 ea. $_____
____	*Anne Smith's Journal, 1933-1939: A.A.'s Principles of Success (3rd ed.)*	$21.95 ea. $_____
____	*By the Power of God: A Guide to Early A.A. Groups and Forming Groups Today*	$16.95 ea. $_____
____	*Cured!: Proven Help for Alcoholics and Addicts*	$21.95 ea. $_____
____	*Dr. Bob and His Library: A Major A.A. Spiritual Source (3rd ed.)*	$15.95 ea. $_____
____	*God and Alcoholism: Our Growing Opportunity in the 21st Century*	$17.95 ea. $_____
____	*Good Morning!: Quiet Time, Morning Watch, Meditation, and Early A.A. (2d ed.)*	$16.95 ea. $_____
____	*Henrietta Seiberling: Ohio's Lady with a Cause*	$19.95 ea. $_____
____	*Introduction to the Sources and Founding of Alcoholics Anonymous*	$22.95 ea. $_____
____	*Making Known the Biblical Roots of A.A.*	$29.95 ea. $_____
____	*New Light on Alcoholism: God, Sam Shoemaker, and A.A. (2d ed.)*	$24.95 ea. $_____
____	*Real Twelve Step Fellowship History*	$21.95 ea. $_____
____	*That Amazing Grace: The Role of Clarence and Grace S. in A. A.*	$19.95 ea. $_____
____	*The Akron Genesis of Alcoholics Anonymous (2d ed.)*	$24.95 ea. $_____
____	*The Books Early AAs Read for Spiritual Growth (7th ed.)*	$15.95 ea. $_____
____	*The Conversion of Bill W.*	$22.95 ea. $_____
____	*The Golden Text of A.A.: Early A.A., God, and Real Spirituality*	$19.95 ea. $_____
____	*The Good Book and The Big Book: A.A.'s Roots in the Bible (2d ed.)*	$17.95 ea. $_____
____	*The Good Book-Big Book Guidebook*	$22.95 ea. $_____
____	*The James Club*	$22.95 ea. $_____
____	*The Oxford Group & Alcoholics Anonymous (2d ed.)*	$24.95 ea. $_____
____	*Turning Point: A History of Early A.A.'s Spiritual Roots and Successes*	$29.95 ea. $_____
____	*Twelve Step's for You*	$21.95 ea. $_____
____	*Utilizing Early A.A.'s Spiritual Roots for Recovery Today*	$19.95 ea. $_____

| ___ *When Early AAs Were Cured and Why* | $22.95 ea. $_____ |
| ___ *Why Early A.A. Succeeded: The Good Book in A.A. Yesterday and Today* | $17.95 ea. $_____ |

Subtotal $ _____

[SPECIAL OFFER: Dick B.'s entire 27-volume set may be purchased for $359.95 plus $30.00 for Shipping & Handling (= $389.95 per set)]   Qty.: _____ $ _____

Total Enclosed $ _____

Name: _____ (as it is on your credit card, if using one)

Address: _____

City: _____ State: _____ Zip: _____

CC Acct. #: _____ Exp.: _____

Tel.: _____

Signature: _____

Email: _____

** *Please contact us for Shipping and Handling charges for orders being shipped outside of the United States.*

No returns accepted. Please mail this Order Form, along with your check or money order (if sending one), to: Dick B., c/o Good Book Publishing Company, P.O. Box 837, Kihei, HI 96753-0837. Please make your check or money order payable to "Dick B." in U.S. dollars drawn on a U.S. bank. If you have any questions, please phone: 1-808-874-4876. Dick B.'s email address is: dickb@dickb.com. Dick B.'s web site on early A.A.'s history http://www.dickb.com/index.shtml

Paradise Research Publications, Inc.
PO Box 837
Kihei, HI 96753-0837
(808) 874-4876
Email: dickb@dickb.com
URL: http://www.dickb.com/index.shtml
http://www.dickb-blog.com

ISBN 978-1-885803-85-6 $24.95